Lived Resistance
against the War on
Palestinian Children

CHILDREN YOUTH + WAR

Lived Resistance against the War on Palestinian Children

Edited by Heidi Morrison

The University of Georgia Press

ATHENS

© 2024 by the University of Georgia Press
Athens, Georgia 30602
www.ugapress.org
All rights reserved
Set in 10/13 Minion 3 by Kaelin Chappell Broaddus

Most University of Georgia Press titles are
available from popular e-book vendors.

Printed digitally

Library of Congress Cataloging-in-Publication Data
Names: Morrison, Heidi, editor.
Title: Lived resistance against the war on Palestinian children / edited by Heidi Morrison.
Description: Athens : The University of Georgia Press, 2024. | Series: Children, youth, and war |
Includes bibliographical references and index.
Identifiers: LCCN 2024000598 | ISBN 9780820366807 (hardback) | ISBN 9780820366814 (paperback)
| ISBN 9780820366821 (epub) | ISBN 9780820366838 (pdf)
Subjects: LCSH: Children, Palestinian Arab—Political activity—West Bank. | Children, Palestinian
Arab—Political activity—Gaza Strip. | Children, Palestinian Arab—Political activity—Israel. |
Children, Palestinian Arab—West Bank—Social conditions. | Children, Palestinian Arab—Gaza
Strip—Social conditions. | Children, Palestinian Arab—Israel—Social conditions.
Classification: LCC HQ792.W43 L584 2024 | DDC 305.23089/92705694—dc23/eng/20240422
LC record available at https://lccn.loc.gov/2024000598

CONTENTS

ILLUSTRATIONS

Give Us Our Childhood, Give Us Our Lives

AHED TAMIMI AND JANA JIHAD AYAD,
WITH LAMA YAHYA

While researchers in this book unpack the many complex forms of Palestinian resistance, it is only fitting to begin the book with the words of the young themselves. Ahed, a leading Palestinian youth activist, and her cousin Jana, who has been called the youngest journalist in Palestine, have written the following opening statement to this volume:

The title of our piece is the chorus of a popular song we used to chant when we were still children as we played together and carried out our innocent rituals. This song opened our minds and evoked pressing questions. It stirred up our emotions and self-awareness, leading to questions that demanded answers: Who will give us our longed-for childhood and life filled with peace, justice, and dignity like the lives of the rest of the children around the world? The United Nations? International law? This cruel world that sees us as mere numbers presented in the reports of its institutions? We are viewed as mere victims of the systematic violence and injustice carried out by the culture of holocaust survivors against our humanity, existence, and legacy, using the guilt felt by the world after the holocaust, that Palestinians had nothing to do with, as the cover for their crimes against humanity.

We the children of Palestine live today, as yesterday, under all sorts of violence, discrimination, and humiliation at the hands of the Zionist colonial project. The first deadly chapter of this organized crime was opened with the Nakba in 1948, when our people were murdered, and dispersed from their homes. This crime is still ongoing with the birth of every child, with the first cry of life. Our lives in all their details are under the control of the brutal forces of the occupation; it is not really a life. Some of us have lost parents due to execution or imprisonment by the occupiers. Some have lost their homes, or have been expelled from their homes. We have faced all kinds of suffering. As soon as we step outside our homes we are faced with settlements, checkpoints, watch towers, the separation wall, and soldiers who have not yet adopted the more noble values of humanity. They know only weapons, destruction, and war, leaving us with no safe space. Even in the comfort of our own homes and in the safety of our mothers' laps we have been persecuted, denying us even the safety of our most intimate spaces.

We the children of Palestine have known for as long as we can remember that occupation is fear. We have had to conquer our fear in order to create a life. The Zionist project to colonize our land was built on a foundation of racism and religious excuses. To that project we are the "others," whose lives are worth less, who can be killed, eliminated, humiliated, and denied dignity. Our land is seen as a land with no people, a land that can be stolen, used to cement the colonial project. According to their religious excuses, they were granted this land by God. As for us, we have the same entrenched, strong belief that this land is ours, and that we are the indigenous population. We see our existence on this land as a right, and as a form of resistance. Regular confrontations with the different expressions of this occupation and the manifestations of the colonial project are duties we owe to this country, and rights owed to us by humanity.

This is why we have decided to confront, and to keep confronting, this challenge. We have decided that we will not shed tears of fear. The only tears we will shed are tears caused by tear gas, fired in the face of our cries, by the oppressive Zionist machines. Our cries embody our refusal of the Zionist project, enforcing our demand for freedom around the world. To our brethren, our partners in the struggle for justice, who stand with us in the demand for humanity, liberty, justice, and equality, we confirm that we are not victims, and we do not seek their pity. We are freedom fighters, and we are the proponents of one of the most just demands in the world.

The symbolic significance and the contents of this book succeed in expressing our message, empowered by the fact that we have partners in the search for justice. This was the desire of everyone involved in crafting this message, to create a bridge that could connect us with collective humanity and hope, that the cry for childhood and life be heard loud and clear.

"أعطونا الطفولة . . . أعطونا الحياة"

هي لازمة لأغنية شهيرة، كنّا نرددها صغاراً، عند لمّتنا وممارسة طقوس براءتنا . . . هذه الأغنية فتَحَت عقولنا على تساؤلات كبيرة بدأت تلِح علينا، فتثور بها دواخلنا، وتنطقها ألسنتنا، ونطرحها على بعضنا: من ذا الذي سيعطينا طفولتنا وحياتنا المشتهاة، التي عبرها ننعم كما أطفال العالم، بالحرية والكرامة والعدالة والسلام؟ هل هي الأمم المتحدة؟ أم القانون الدولي؟ أم هذا العالم الظالم الذي يرانا مجرد أرقام في تقارير مؤسساته، أو عبارة عن ضحايا لمنهجية الظلم والعنف التي ترتكبها ثقافة ضحايا المحرقة بحق انسانيتنا ووجودنا وكينونتنا وديمومة معاناتنا، ليوفروا لأنفسهم مهرباً من عبء الندم على جريمة ألحقها التاريخ بهم، لم نكن يوماً طرفاً وسبباً فيها.

نحن اطفال فلسطين ، نعيش اليوم كما الأمس ، كل أشكال القهر والعنف والتمييز والاضطهاد من قبل دولة الاستعمار الصهيوني (اسرائيل) ، ذلك عبر جريمة منظمة بدأت أولى فصولها الدامية وقت النكبة ، حينما قُتل وشُرّد شعبنا عن أرضه ووطنه ، ومازالت مستمرة مع كل ميلاد طفل جديد ، وأول صرخة للحياة ؛ فحياتنا في كل تفاصيلها تحت مطرقة الاحتلال الثقيلة لا تشبهها حياة ، فمنّا من قتل والديه أو أسروا ، ومنّا من هدّم بيته أو هجر عن أرضه ، ومنّا من مورست بحقه كل أشكال القهر والمعاناة ، فنحن بمجرد خروجنا من بيوتنا لا نكاد نرى أمامنا غير المستعمرة والحواجز والجدار الفاصل ، وأبراج المراقبة وجنود لم يتعرّفوا بعد على الإنسانية بقيمها النبيلة ، فلا يجيدون غير حمل اسلحة القتل والفتك والارهاب ، ولم يتركوا لنا مكاناً آمناً نلوذ إليه ، حتى أنهم يلاحقونا في بيوتنا و أحضان أمهاتنا ممّا أفقدنا الشعور بالطمأنينة والأمان.

نحن اطفال فلسطين ، أدركنا منذ نعومة أظفارنا أن الإحتلال هو الخوف ، فكان لابد لنا من الانتصار على خوفنا لنتمكن من صنع الحياة ؛ فالمشروع الاستعماري الصهيوني على أرضنا أسس وبني على مفاهيم عنصرية ، وأوهام دينية ، وما نحن في رؤية هذا المشروع الّا مجرد أغيار يحق قتلنا وإستعبادنا وامتهان كرامتنا الإنسانية ، وأرضنا عبارة عن أرض بلا شعب ، من حقهم أخذها وإستلابها وإقامة مملكتهم المزعومة عليها ،يهؤلاء وفق خرقاتها مهلدينية وعد الرا بـالمقدس لمهأمّا نحف رنؤمن شديد الإيمان بنأ هذا هلارض لنا ، ونحن أصحابها الاصلانيين ووجودنا عليها مقاومة وحق مشروع والاشّتبابا كلدائم على تعبيرات هذا الاحتلال وإفرازات هذا المشروع الاستعماري العنصري، والنضال المستمر من أجل حريتنا وكرامتنا ، هما حق وواجب ومسؤولية علينا.

لهذا قررنا أن نواجه وأن نستمر في المواجهة، وأن لا تكون دموعنا دموع خوف، إنّما دموع تسيّلها فقط قنابل الغاز التي تطلقها آلة القمع والإرهاب الصهيونية في وجه صرختنا، التي تجسد التعبير عن رفضنا لهذا المشروع، والتي في ذات الوقت تعلي صوتنا الحق أمام كل الاحرار في العالم، شركاؤنا في النضال، الذين يقفون معنا في خندق نضالي واحد من أجل الإنسان وقضاياه وقيم الحرية والعدل والمساواة، مؤكدين لهم، بأننا لسنا ضحايا، وطلاب شفقة، بل نحن مقاتلو حرية وكرامة وأصحاب أعدل قضية في الوجود.

إنّ هذا الكتاب بدلالته ومضمونه ومعانيه جاء ليعبّر عن رسالتنا، ويعطيها الأمل بأن لنا شركاء في النضال من أجل الانسانية وقيمها النبيلة، فهذا ما أراده كل من ساهم في إنجازه وإخراجه للحياة، ليصنع جسراً للعبور نحو فضاءات الأمل الواسعة والانسانية الجامعة، ويكون صرختنا العالية للبشرية قاطبة بأن أعطونا الطفولة . . . أعطونا الحياة.

بدنا ولادنا

Translation from Arabic to English by Lama Yahya,
with special thanks to Melanie Magidow

Translator's Note

I first met Ahed Tamimi in 2016, when I accompanied a delegation of Irish trade unionists who had heard of Ahed and requested to visit her in her home village of Nabi Saleh. Ahed had just turned fifteen at the time. She was around the same age as my younger brother. Hearing Ahed speak for the first time brought tears to my eyes. She spoke about the Israeli occupation and its invasion of the most intimate areas of her life, about the settlers who take over Palestinian land, about the family members she has lost and those she fears losing, about the movement restrictions that sometimes prevent her father from reaching their home and other times prevent her siblings and her from getting to school.

Listening to Ahed speak I felt conflicted. While I felt very proud of how well she was able to articulate and explain her reality to the delegation despite her young age, the more pressing emotion I experienced was sadness and sorrow at the fact that she was not thinking, acting, or speaking like a child. The content of her talk was nowhere close to being the content that you would expect a child her age to be engaged in. However, Ahed's case is no exception. The Israeli colonial control denies Palestinian children not only their most basic rights, but also their childhood, a concept Hebrew University's Lawrence D. Biele Chair in Law, Nadera Shalhoub-Kevorkian, refers to as unchilding. While Palestinian children are never spared the Israeli army's live bullets, they face an equally great threat: "the genocidal nature of unchilding Palestinian children entails—in most cases—not actually killing or maiming a child, but rather killing the possibility of being a child."[1]

While Ahed's life is a perfect demonstration of unchilding, it also demonstrates the unchilded's ability to fight back and resist, which happens in varied ways, from words and actions to tears and silence, as the chapters in this book all illustrate. In 2017 Ahed witnessed Israeli soldiers shoot her cousin with a rubber bullet to the head, and in reaction she slapped two Israeli soldiers who invaded her house later that day. The incident was caught on tape and the video went viral. Despite the fact that it was clear in the video that Ahed posed no serious threat to the fully armed soldiers, Israel arrested her in a subsequent nighttime raid. As per the logic of settler colonialism, "every act of resistance involving even minimal force to the occupying power" is counted as terrorism, justifying the use of military force, arrest, and detention.[2]

With the awareness that being born Palestinian means having a target on one's back from birth to death, Ahed is keen to prove, first to herself and then to the occupying power, that she is not weak and that she is not crippled by fear of death, arrest, injury, or torture. I recently encountered Ahed again in a demonstration near the Ofer prison. She was in the front lines, where an Israeli soldier pointed his machine gun at her from a watchtower. Ahed did not even flinch. She held her ground in a direct challenge to the soldier's authority and power. Ahed's parents raised her to know that true insecurity does not come from resistance, but from obeying the rules of the oppressors. Perhaps Ahed's greatest contribution to Palestinian resistance is her intangible refusal to live subjugated to fear.

NOTES

The title of this section is inspired by the lyrics of the famous song "Give Us a Chance" performed by child singer Remi Bandali in Lebanon in the 1980s.

1. Shalhoub-Kevorkian, "Unchilding and the Killing Boxes," 498.
2. Aoláin, "Incarcerated Childhood and the Politics," 469.

BIBLIOGRAPHY

Aoláin, F. N. "Incarcerated Childhood and the Politics of Unchilding: An International Law Perspective." *Journal of Genocide Research* 23, no. 3 (2020): 466–71.

Ben-Natan, S. "Above and Beyond Denial: Incarcerated Children in Israel/Palestine." *Journal of Genocide Research* 23, no. 3 (2020): 478–85.

Peleg, N. "Victimizing Children and the Manifestations of Childhood." *Journal of Genocide Research* 23, no. 3 (2020): 472–7.

Shalhoub-Kevorkian, N. "Unchilding and the Killing Boxes." *Journal of Genocide Research* 23, no. 3 (2020): 490–500.

Lived Resistance against the War on Palestinian Children

Introduction

What Is Lived Resistance?

HEIDI MORRISON

For a moment, let us imagine that the piece of children's art featured on this book's cover represents an article published in a fictitious academic journal *Resistance Studies* whose mission statement reads: "This international, peer-reviewed, interdisciplinary scientific journal seeks to advance understandings of oppositional ways of thinking and strategizing as well as discourses that undermine injustice and domination." We can imagine that the article title uses heavy academic jargon, such as: "Alternative Communities: Mapping the Terrain of Hope in a Multi-Generational Refugee Camp," "Repression Resized: Contextualizing the Effects of Israeli Violence from the Bottom Up," or "Beyond Autonomous Personhood: Solidarity Tactics in Palestine."

The purpose of this imaginative exercise is to show that although children's artwork may seem simplistic, it embodies significant symbolism and depth, especially when understood in the context of children's lives. The cover picture, and others like it featured in Amahl Bishara's chapter of this book, embodies the scholarly topics of "performance," "transgression," "hegemony," and "intersubjectivity." Palestinian children from the Aida refugee camp in Bethlehem created the picture featured on this book as part of a project at the Lajee Cultural Center during Israel's 2014 Operation Protective Edge in Gaza, a fifty-day assault that directly resulted in the death of 535 Palestinian children, 68 percent of whom were twelve years old or younger. One Israeli child died in Operation Protective Edge.[1] Children's art is a natural and potentially safe medium of self-expression, so much so that therapists use it as a tool. It is important for academics to stop and listen to children through various means. Children can understand and engage in matters that adults conventionally relegate to the domain of "experts." The imaginative esoteric name that I have given to the cover artwork is based on the expressed intentions of the artists themselves, as detailed in Bishara's chapter about them.

The theme that emerges from this book's engagement with Palestinian children is their will to survive Israeli oppression and demand its end. The victimhood of Palestinian children is no doubt captured in each of the chapters of this book, as well as Israel's age-based apparatus of control over Palestinians,[2] but resistance is tantamount. Resistance to violence merits as much attention as violence itself, particularly regarding children whose age, in the eyes of many adults, contradicts their capacity to resist. Children's lack of conventional political, economic, social, cultural, and symbolic capital is not a complete deficit. The experience of being young plays a powerful role in shaping the innovative tactics children use to undermine oppressive power in their daily lives, a phenomenon this book refers to as lived resistance: the embodied (i.e., the bodily grounding of cognition and experience) process by which people purposefully resist, individually and collectively, unjust domination in their everyday lives.[3] Lived resistance is shaped by a person's interlocking positions in the world, that is, gender, class, race, and (as this book clearly signals!) age. Like violence itself, lived resistance takes many forms: visible and invisible, formal and informal, collective and individuated. The chapters in this book explore this topic in the context of children's experiences in Palestine from the outbreak of the second Palestinian intifada (uprising) in 2000, which followed the failure of the 1990s Oslo peace process, to the present moment, a period of relentless Israeli violence against Palestinian children, many of whom date their ages in wars.[4]

Lived resistance refers to a way of life for children under constant dispossession, as well as a research technique. It refers to what children do and refers as well to the nuanced analytical and methodological approaches adult researchers can employ to write about children in situations of violence. Rather than simply hitching children's resistance to standard theories of resistance, this book meets children on their own terms. One of the unique aspects of academic writing on children is that the subjects themselves rarely, if ever, have a byline. This situation places a particularly heavy responsibility on scholars to arrive at research methods and writing styles that foreground young voices, including those behind Israeli prison bars, as Mohammed Alruzzi, Valentina Marconi, and Yousef Aljamal's and Shahrazad Odeh's chapters deal with, and those martyred by Israeli forces, as Nadera Shalhoub-Kevorkian's and Abeer Otman's chapters discuss. The ethical task of the researcher is to amplify the voices of colonized people, rather than give voice or profess to represent them.[5] In terms of the voices of young people, the researcher must also be attentive to age labels themselves, which some people may ultimately reject being put on them by others. Further, an uncritical approach to "children's voice" risks assuming children's views and perspectives are always closer to the "truth" than others and it risks overlooking how they may at times actually parrot adults.[6]

This book explores lived resistance—as a research category and a research method—in the context of Palestinian children, even though it is a concept that can be applied to any person. The introduction unpacks, considering the chapters, how Palestinian children interrupt the violence around them, that is, how they practice lived resistance. While a larger discussion of the various meanings of the words "resistance" and "violence" will follow in this introduction, I want to signal from the start that there are also certain dangers to connecting the words "resistance" and "violence" to Palestinian children. Palestinian children see the Israeli legal system as an unsafe place for them, where Israel uses words like "resistance" to incriminate Palestinian children and add to their punishments for other allegations against the state, as Odeh's chapter illustrates. Israel's recording of the word resistance (or associate words) in Palestinian children's files often comes from "confessions" during interrogations where they are subject to ill treatment and/or from having to sign documents in Hebrew, a language they do not understand. Scholars using the word resistance in relation to Palestinians must be cautious to not endorse and reify Israeli depictions of Palestinians as a national security risk, as well as Israel's use of age distinctions as tools of control.[7] Palestinian resistance to Israel's illegal occupation is a legally protected right.

A Cartography of Lived Resistance and Palestinian Children

The concept of lived resistance is not totally new. For the past few decades, it has been marginally used in various forms.[8] In this book, lived resistance consists of an agglomeration of three existing concepts—everyday resistance, popular resistance, and nonviolent resistance—none of which, on its own, fully accounts for Palestinian children's experiences or takes stock of methodology. Lived resistance recognizes that existing concepts on resistance were conceived primarily with adults in mind, without necessarily accounting for the subject's age. When we account for young age (or any age, for that matter), we open our eyes to the importance of the body in the experience of resistance. Age, as a biological marker, reminds us that our existence is as much physical as mental, a phenomenon researchers of any age group should acknowledge. In the section that follows, I will illustrate how lived resistance recognizes that the body—in flesh and mind—bears on a person's resistance. I will also explain the concept of lived resistance by showing its similarities to and differences from the three aforementioned concepts as well as with the existing known usages of the term, or some variant of it. I will illustrate examples of lived resistance taken from the chapters of this book.

Classical studies of resistance focus on "real resistance," or the palpable effects laypeople have (or lack) on transforming structures of dominance through mass direct actions, such as demonstrations, strikes, or blockades. Within the field of resistance studies, James Scott developed the concept of everyday resistance (also known as infrapolitics) to refer to subtle and less visible forms of resistance in which people engage within their everyday lives. Scott's trailblazing *Weapons of the Weak* (1985) recognizes that oppressed classes reject domination in ways, such as foot-dragging, false compliance, narrative, etc., that are not always organized public events.[9] He argues that just as power is exercised in diffuse modes, so too is resistance. Asef Bayat's work develops everyday resistance to include "quiet encroachment," or the way that individual subalterns come together (without clear leadership or conscious political intent) to form kin-/ethnic-based networks of resistance. Bayat claims that marginalized people are often driven by their own individual survival and pursuit of a dignified life, before their cumulative numbers transform them into a political force. Overall, everyday resistance takes many forms, and there is no clear-cut typology to decide whether an act should be so identified.[10] Anna Johansson and Stellan Vinthagen provide a good general definition of everyday resistance: "a pattern of acts (practice) done by someone subordinated in a power relation and that might (temporary) undermine or destabilize (some aspect of) dominance."[11]

Everyday resistance is widespread among Palestinians because every aspect of their lives is touched by Israeli power and Palestinians (particularly in the territories) lack formal citizenship as a means of fighting for their rights. As non-Jews living in a Jewish state, Palestinian citizens of Israel maintain a second-class status, facing discrimination in everything from schools to neighborhood infrastructure.[12] Within the illegally Occupied Palestinian Territories, Israel dictates everything from Palestinians' movement to their use of airspace and access to water supplies.[13] The mundane spaces of children's everyday life are politically, emotionally, and symbolically charged.[14] That is not to say more formal and high-profile resistance does not occur, such as during the first (1987–93) and second (2000–2005) intifadas, of which the former came to be associated with the term "children of the stones" for the iconic image of unarmed Palestinian children throwing stones at massive Israeli tanks. However, due to the all-pervasive nature of Israeli oppression, resistance for Palestinians is an everyday phenomenon, not limited to periods of intensified violence.[15]

There are multiple terms that Palestinians use to describe the actions they take to try to restore dignity and justice in the face of chronic violence.[16] Palestinians often use the term *muqawama sha'biya* ("popular resistance") to refer to an organic, community-centered resistance that is born out of and against Israeli military acts and oppressive acts. Popular resistance emerged more than a century ago, alongside the Zionist goal of placing a Jewish state in the center of a multiethnic land, and it remains until today a way to refuse Zionist oppression and dispossession and it largely draws its strengths from the people (civilians) and not institutions or militant groups.[17] Popular resistance is largely unarmed, but nonviolence is not its defining feature, since definitions of violence and justifications for its use are themselves highly relative.[18] *Sumud*, a "repertoire of everyday acts of resistance" directed against the occupation, is the most common expression of popular resistance today.[19] Sumud is concrete behavior, ranging from boycotting Israeli products to maintaining a physical presence on the land despite adversity.[20] It is organized and nonorganized tactics of resistance, individually and collectively enacted. Sumud is also an intangible mindset that drives Palestinians, despite all odds, to keep some form of normality and continuity in one's life, envision a future for oneself, maintain dignity, remember historic injustices, be in solidarity with one another, keep up the inner strength to live through the conditions created by the Nakba of 1948, and sustain awareness of political oppression. To be "in sumud" means to be holding steadfast and persevering.

The problem with existing literature on everyday resistance (and resistance, generally speaking) in Palestine is that it remains largely one-sided, not focusing on the specificities of nearly half of the population: children. If scholars genuinely want to tend to the richness of everyday life, they must recognize that children are front and center to the quotidian. Lived resistance, as I define it, operates from the imperative that we consider age, and hence children, a pillar of "real life." The academic use of the word "lived" to qualify a research topic was popularized in the late twentieth century by religious scholars who sought to move beyond formal theological jargon in their studies. The goal of "lived religion" is to better understand what religious people, in various times and places, do and believe in their daily lives, that is, how they emotionally "live out" their relationship to religion in their tasks and rituals, especially in ways that may not be written down.[21] Lived resistance, similar to recent studies of "lived nation" and "lived citizenship,"[22] echo the tradition of lived religion in acknowledging the complexity of human phenomena. Just as religion cannot be understand solely though the clergy and theological texts, resistance cannot be solely understood through adults and formal political systems.

Despite the increasing volume of scholarship that shows children are political actors,[23] a cohesive framework is lacking to express children's relationship with political power. In conventional resistance studies, children's voices alone are often not considered sufficient to be included in the political community, unless they are joined with others as part of inter- or intragenerational struggles or they are considered from the perspective of empowerment in adult-led policies.[24] Or, it is assumed that children do not usually engage in "real resistance" because of the restraints of their age, that is, lacking full citizenship and operating under a power differential with adults. Further, some people could go so far as to argue that children have the right to be totally spared from politics (to be clear, this is not the implication of the United Nations' Convention on the Rights of the Child [CRC]). The concept of everyday resistance, however, allows us to cast wide the net of what counts as resistance. Numerous scholars have shown that children do engage in resistance in their everyday lives, sometimes even at formal levels.[25] Politics should not be considered the proper domain of adults only.[26] Some children even say they forget they are children, thus feeling that their age is irrelevant to their ability to act.[27] Simply put, children's vulnerability does not make them fools. The essential question to ask is not whether or not children's resistance takes place, but how is it occurring?

For this question, we again must orient ourselves from the concept of "lived." In addition to diversifying the spectrum of actors involved in resistance, the concept of lived adds the layer of the body to the discussion of resistance. Resistance does not just happen out of thin air. The vessel (i.e., the body) through which resistance operates (and generates) must be accounted for. Researchers must remember that their subjects have bodies; persons live in their bodies in ways that bear on their reality.[28] So, how do children effectively *do* (i.e., live) their resistance? In large part, they resourcefully rely on what is available to them: their bodies (in flesh and mind).

Palestinian children live in a "gun to body" context,[29] meaning their bodies are always vulnerable to Israeli violence. Children thus must find ways to transform their minds into "shields" and unarmed bodies into "weapons." This does not mean children should be reduced to their mere physicality. Children manifest bodily resistance through a complex dynamic between physicality and adaptability. "The brain is an adaptive system that is constantly reorganizing itself through dynamic interactions with the larger systems in which it is embedded (the body and the social world), to respond to the challenges and opportunities presented by the environment," write Kirmayer, Worthman, and Kitayama.[30] Lived resistance must be understood as intersectional in nature: the body and mind operate at once, but also *in concert* with one another. While the body and mind are often thought to be distinct elements, they form a whole human embodied entity that interacts with the world. (Arguably, if we see human existence as an embodied experience, we could do away with distinct mental and physical categories altogether, such that reference to the body implies the mind.)

Children's bodies, which include the anatomical entity of the brain and the mind, calls attention to their status as thinking, feeling, and acting beings.[31] The mind is not biologically and universally fixed, but is, in large part, a product of context; it is plastic.[32] It is for this reason, after all, that educational and domestic spaces are particularly heated battlegrounds for power holders in a given society.

We cannot presume that children (or adults, for that matter) are already completely under the spells of cultural hegemony; they are living beings who, despite their vulnerability, process what happens around them and deploy their minds in purposeful modes of resistance, suitable to their context. "The body is not simply the medium through which we experience the world, but the way we take hold of it," write Kirmayer, Worthman, and Kitayama.[33] The child's body is socially and biologically "unfinished" because society inscribes ideas on the child's body and children are shaped by their changing biology.[34] The body shapes our felt experiences, and in many ways, our felt experiences can reconfigure the body (because neural activity functions in response to the meaningful environmental stimuli that we experience).[35] This is clearly seen if we look at the relationship between the senses, the emotions, and thought; there is a "two-way traffic between bodily experience and cognition."[36] Smells, sounds, touches, and other sensory experiences generally inform and feed the emotional experiences, and vice versa.[37]

For example, a person's construction of the concept of cruelty—an emotional disposition in which pleasure or satisfaction is derived from commission of pain—is based upon feelings that are framed by suffering, witnessed in the hearing, olfactory, and visual range, but dependent also upon received moral wisdom, or upon ideas of value.[38] Extrapolating upon this, we can say that resistance to cruelty is shaped by experienced and observed injuries to the mind (and to the soul, in some contexts), which include smells designated as disgusting and sounds interpreted as brutal. To designate an act as "cruel" is to register the pain it causes as real, and the object of cruelty as human. To define, express, and decry this pain—to make it visible—is therefore to politicize it.

Another layer of lived resistance's intersectionality is how it operates both within the individual and/or between individuals. We know that emotions, for example, are not self-evident and universal, but occur in a context. "Show us a human outside of culture and we will show you something that is not human at all," explain Boddice and Smith.[39] A person's emotions are highly contingent upon communal belief and value systems as well as other people's emotions, past and present. Referencing again the example of cruelty, because we know that its meanings have changed over time, we must then understand objections to it as such. Thus, the bodily elements of a human operate in dialogue with one another and the world.

A tangible example of the intersectional nature of Palestinian children's lived resistance is found in the photograph that went viral in 2018 of a nine-year-old Gazan boy, Mohamed Ayyash, wearing a homemade onion face mask while at the front of Land Day protests at the Gaza-Israel border.[40] Mohamed made his "gas mask" by sticking the bulb of an onion in a disposable surgical mask; he later explained that he thought sniffing an onion could neutralize Israeli tear gas,

as he had heard stories of his father using such a technique during the first intifada. Mohamed's face mask is thoughtfully conceived, yet at the same time, it is
playful. In the image, long green onion stalks, still attached to the bulb, protrude
from the mask perpendicular to his nose and rise a few inches above his little
head. The overall image of Mohamed is bittersweet: a young person being silly
yet engaged in a serious fight against the Israeli settler-colonial forces. He seeks
to withstand the toxic smell, blurry vision, and stinging touch of tear gas, while
at the same time draw attention to the memory (and continued practice) of Israel's confiscation of Palestinian land. All the while he does so while standing in a
land that other Palestinian children have described as "non-breathing," nonliving
space.[41] To demand justice, he places his body in a highly symbolic location, at
the limit line of the open-air prison that strips him of all rights to citizenship. He
rebuffs Israel's bodily control and containment of Palestinians through his body
itself. He seems to remain silent, refusing engagement with the language of the
Zionist political regime, yet allowing his presence to be a medium of expression
that says the unspeakable. The image of Mohamed captures how he braids his
body and mind together, in a quintessential form of lived resistance.

The mere act of being alive takes up space, which means that the existence of
Palestinian children's bodies subverts settler-colonial forces that seek to erase the
colonized. As they walk, run, and play on the land, the feet of Palestinian children make visible the Palestinian *home*land underneath, which, literally and figuratively, holds them up and propels them forward. Further, as repositories of past
and future generations of Palestinians, children's bodies defy the settler-colonial
logic that deems Palestinian bodies as exterminable and disposable. (Palestinians
refer to children killed by Israeli forces as martyrs, indicating that even in death
the corpse holds power.) The use of the body to fight for the mere existence of
the body is eloquently captured in the words of the twelve-year-old Palestinian
girl named Sumud who, outraged by the unjust murder of her fourteen-year-old
brother by Israeli police officers and the subsequent agonizing withholding of his
corpse in Israel's refrigerators, proclaims "Ana Sumud (I am steadfastness)."[42] Sumud explains that she is stronger than walls, soldiers, and checkpoints; her will
to live, which includes growing up to become a lawyer, is more powerful than the
Israeli occupation itself. Her body *is* her resistance, and *is a tool for* enacting her
resistance. She uses her body as both "the messenger and the message," to borrow
from the work of Jouni Häkli and Kirsi Pauliina Kallio on the embodied experience of refugees seeking to draw attention to inhumane treatment.[43] Further, her
thinking is grounded in the context of her setting, which, as has been discussed,
includes a culture of sumud as resistance. Thus, Sumud quite literally *lives* her
resistance.

This book contains numerous examples of lived resistance as a braided experience between mind and body, where children use them as an effectual source of power. The chapters by Odeh and by Alruzzi, Marconi, and Aljamal show Palestinian children and families tirelessly navigating the Israeli *in*justice system, refusing to let children's bodies be pushed out of sight (i.e., behind bars) by Israel's excessive Palestinian child imprisonment system. Children in East Jerusalem strategically occupy streets shoulder to shoulder in planned sit-ins, as Amneh Badran's chapter illustrates, effectively staging their bodies to be gazed at. Israeli courts consider Palestinian stone throwing as a threat to the security of Israel, as Odeh's chapter illustrates. Nitin Sawhney describes rows of children in Gaza standing on a beach flying kites, using the strength and dexterity of their hands to draw physical attention to their plight and paint in the sky an image of themselves as anything but a faceless mass. Self-harming and suicidal behavior can also be a way of communicating, as my chapter illustrates. Shalhoub-Kevorkian's chapter focuses on the Palestinian children's corpses systematically withheld by Israel; Palestinian parents insist on grieving their lost children and not letting Israel vanish the *already* vanished bodies. While not included in this book, Hedi Viterbo's research shows how Palestinian children sometimes manipulate their physical appearance (as a determinant of age) or misrepresent their physical age to frustrate Israeli rule.[44] Thus, lived resistance means that the body and mind co-construct one another in dialogue with the context in which they exist. Children empower themselves through training/harnessing their senses and through the deliberate maneuvering of their arms, legs, and so forth, all while the mind and body remain the target of Israeli disciplining and control.

Characteristics of Children's Lived Resistance

This book looks at children's resistance as an embodied experience, which offers the following four insights into children's relationship with political power: their relationship to political power operates from an inclusive model of citizenship and it is social justice oriented, symbolically oriented, and contingently based. Before I elaborate on these domains, I want to first make a distinction. What I refer to in this introduction as lived resistance is sometimes referred to by other scholars as agency.[45] While I recognize that the categories overlap and that there are inherent flaws in the concept of agency (see my chapter in this book, for example),[46] which scholars of lived resistance must avoid, the biggest difference between lived resistance and agency is that lived resistance always places the focus on the embodied purposeful political will of children in their everyday life; this is a narrower lens through which to view children's acts than the lens of agency, or the general capacity to act freely. While dissent agency is a concept that resonates well with lived resistance, particularly in its recognition that young people challenge the state and existing power relations, it does not include the embodied component.[47]

Kallio makes an important contribution to understanding children's relationship with power when she argues that children's politics are forms of de Certeau's concept of tactical political agency.[48] In order to survive webs of discipline, children employ counter acts (i.e., tactics, including those that use the body) to push against structures of power (i.e., strategies). A strategy-tactic framework for understanding children's politics places children's political acts in dialogue with adult authority, formal institutions/structures of discipline, such as the school or healthcare systems, and/or informal (including non-age-related) forms of power. As I already mentioned, for Palestinians, there is no aspect of their life that is unaffected by the Zionist colonial project, in large part due to the occupation. This in no way means that Palestinian children can and should only be understood through politics nor that there is one universal experience of children's resistance (childhood is itself not a monolithic category). Instead, it acknowledges the all-pervasive nature of unchilding (structural and political violence aimed at taking away childhood) in Palestine, which "moves between various contexts (local and global) and spaces (educational, welfare, economic); it invades wombs, families, friendships, homes, schools, hospitals; it is flexible, adaptable, predictable, and unpredictable."[49] The system of unchilding engenders in Palestinian children a constant state of discomfort. Thus, from a lived resistance perspective, there are no clear boundaries between children's lives and the Zionist colonial project, much in the same way that for people living in nations, the nation is everywhere in their lives (i.e., scholars of lived nationalism argue that the nation is "an entanglement of the personal, social, and collective, transcending one-way causalities or top-down hierarchies"[50]). Lived resistance is based on the idea that Palestinian children know and express—explicitly and/or implicitly—the meanings of their actions and political orientations; it is not up to the scholar to discover them.[51]

First, in terms of characteristics of children's resistance, as has been noted, one of the greatest obstacles to practicing classical resistance that minors face is their lack of formal citizenship, which precludes the right to vote. Voting is generally considered the most popular form of resistance in so-called democracies, even though it can also be seen as a form of docile political behavior through which people express that they are content enough with the democratic system through which their polities are organized and led to participate in the system's upholding. Children who want to reject the current order must find ways in their everyday activities. This pushes children to operate from an inclusive model of citizenship, which emphasizes the interconnectedness of human experience, rather than the individual, citizen adult.[52] Engin Isin and Greg M. Nielsen's notion of "acts of citizenship" is particularly useful here, as it denotes the moments and deeds (political, cultural, social, etc.) where subjects stake themselves as worthy of rights, irrespective of their formal citizenship status.[53] For Palestinian children in the Occupied Territories and in Israel proper, the monopoly of Israeli state power and violence is an additional impetus for children (and adults for that matter) to act outside conventional citizen-based models of resistance. Palestinian children face the burden of being dispossessed of their rights owing to living under Israeli military rule and also Israel's two-tier legal system. Many Palestinian children in the Occupied Territories do not feel represented by the two parallel civil organizations that operate separately, that is, the Palestinian Authority (PA) and Hamas. For some Palestinians, the United Nations Relief and Works Agency (UNRWA) is a site to articulate political demands, but humanitarian organizations can reduce the people they seek to help to mere victims, as well as prioritize donor agendas.[54] Religious institutions are also not generally venues for resistance, especially among children who dismiss the crude politicization of religion and insist instead upon unity.[55] In Badran's chapter, one young person states that it is in the grassroots activism of the street that young people feel united, not in official government leadership. Salameh's chapter shows how young Palestinians living in the Al-Am'ari refugee camp feel alienated by the neoliberal policies of the PA. Bishara's research takes place at the Lajee Cultural Center, formed by Palestinians concerned that the PA was not listening to the vibrant activism of the masses.

Second, lived resistance for Palestinian children manifests as the pursuit of social justice rather than the pursuit of legal rights within a state system, although it certainly does not preclude the latter. The concept of lived resistance opens the door for taking children's demands seriously, instead of dismissing them as nonpolitical. While the chapters of Odeh, Alruzzi, Marconi, and Aljamal, and Shalhoub-Kevorkian certainly illustrate how Palestinian children and their parents valiantly negotiate Israel's discriminatory legal system, Bishara and Sawhney's chapters illustrate the more general calls for a better life that children demand. These include the desire to play freely and safely in and around their homes, swim in the sea, and not experience power outages. Further, lived resistance opens the door for conceiving resistance as borderless (and not attached only to national legal systems), which encourages international solidarity among everyone concerned about children. Lived resistance has a synergistic relationship with lived citizenship, which acknowledges the profound effect of physical boundaries of nation-states, but recognizes a more expansive notion of citizenship characterized by flexible and multiple notions of identity and connectedness beyond borders.[56] A notable example is the Palestinian Youth Movement (PYM), a contemporary social movement operating across a number of Arab and Western countries that frames its struggle as an issue of justice and interlocking forms of oppression, as opposed to state-framed human rights discourses.[57] In this book, borderless resistance is explored in Otman's chapter, which looks at how fathers seek justice for their children and themselves in the unbounded space of social media. In Sawhney's chapter, Palestinian children garner worldwide attention in their effort to break the record of the most kites flown at once. The ABC alphabet book, discussed in Bishara's chapter, was a collaborative effort among Palestinian children that is read by children worldwide. The closing statement in this book by Natalia Molebatsi reflects the rich transnational solidarity that exists between South Africans and Palestinians. Thus, lived resistance refers to the ways children resist outside the confines of national legal systems.

Third, children's lived resistance often takes symbolic forms, as opposed to outwardly changing the structures it opposes. Symbolic resistance can be imaginary, such as envisaging a different future; it can also be emotional, such as resisting efforts to control one's psyche. It can contain spiritual and/or ritualistic elements, such as prayer. It can be a way of coming to terms with intangible humiliations to past generations. Symbolic resistance often includes undeclared, as opposed to codified, victories. Although symbolic resistance may not have a concrete impact on political and economic structures of domination, it can have ripple effects by impacting lifestyles and behaviors, cultural ideologies, and social institutions.[58] Nearly all the chapters in this book reference the memory of the Nakba as an ongoing inner wound that children grapple with today. In Palestine, memory of the past often serves as a constant reminder of what remains to be accomplished.[59] Reflecting on the world by grounding oneself in a past is a way of countering the disorientation that persecution creates.[60] Some examples of symbolic resistance in this book include young people seeking to raise public awareness (Badran); the mother-child dyad reenvisioning caretaking in light of disturbances to domestic space (Sousa and Bressi); the child receiving self-affirming messages through communal relations (Morrison); families negotiating a legal and political system that demonizes children and frames them as unworthy of protection (Odeh); children of the camps standing up to the stereotype that they are dangerous (Salameh); bereaved fathers finding virtual ways to continue fathering even after their child is martyred (Otman); and constructing a narrative of closure that goes beyond logic after the martyrdom of a loved one (Shalhoub-Kevorkian).

Fourth, lived resistance for children is contingently based, which is more tangible than symbolic resistance, but still not as straightforward as "real resistance." A contingent approach to resistance looks at power in lateral terms, considering resistance's effects on and relationship with various aspects of life (not just top-down power).[61] Despite the enduring misconception that children are simplistic beings, their identities are shaped by multiple realities. Dichotomies between resistance and dominance are not useful because children are part of the web of society; they are more than nonadults. As Häkli and Kallio's research on the everyday lives of children finds, "When focusing on children's experiences and the subjectivities through which they become active agents in their everyday lives, their position as minors is but one contextual factor among others against which to negotiate their agencies."[62] Because children's actions are conditioned by their social settings, political acts can be found in nonpolitical ordinary aspects of life, that is, the political ordinary.[63] Further, mundane political acts in people's daily lived worlds can become highly politicized if they are recognized as important by communities near and far.[64] Thus, we must look at children's lived resistance from several perspectives and spheres of life, including unpredictable spatial and temporal settings.

I distinguish four different (yet sometimes overlapping) characteristics of contingent resistance displayed in this book. First, if we recognize that a person's subjectivity and agency are always in a state of becoming (because they are oriented by the past, present, and future),[65] then we can say that resistance too has temporal dimensions. The present conditions reflect a bundle of evolving situations. For example, resistance can be cumulative and long term, as opposed to producing immediate results. It can be gradually awakened before exploding. In my chapter, I provide an example of a person who reflects back on his childhood to make empowering changes as a young adult. It can be projected onto future life paths. Badran mentions organized political protests that follow in the wake of children's impulsive and spontaneous resistance activities in the street. She also shows that children can be strategic and use long-term thinking. Second, as opposed to just targeting one vertically positioned power, resistance can have repercussions across various spheres of life, having a particular impact on family relationships. Habashi, for example, argues that a child's political orientation can alter his/her family's political orientation. Alruzzi, Marconi, and Aljamal find that children's political engagement can be a welcome "fast track" to adulthood, allowing them to bypass age hierarchies within their families. Third, contingent resistance can be messy, such that people sometimes use their precarities to fuel new actions.[66] Resistance can be produced out of seemingly contradictory forces. Bishara observes how children can carve out spaces for simple pleasures in the midst of horrible violence. Sawhney notes the ways war-torn children fight against accelerated transitions to adulthood. On the other hand, Alruzzi, Marconi, and Aljamal argue that some children find ways to benefit from being perceived as adultlike due to their political activism. In her work elsewhere, Shalhoub-Kevorkian argues that some Palestinian children engage head on with their wounds, refusing, for example, to cleanse themselves of them or put bandages in their place.[67] Lastly, resistance can even end up reproducing structures

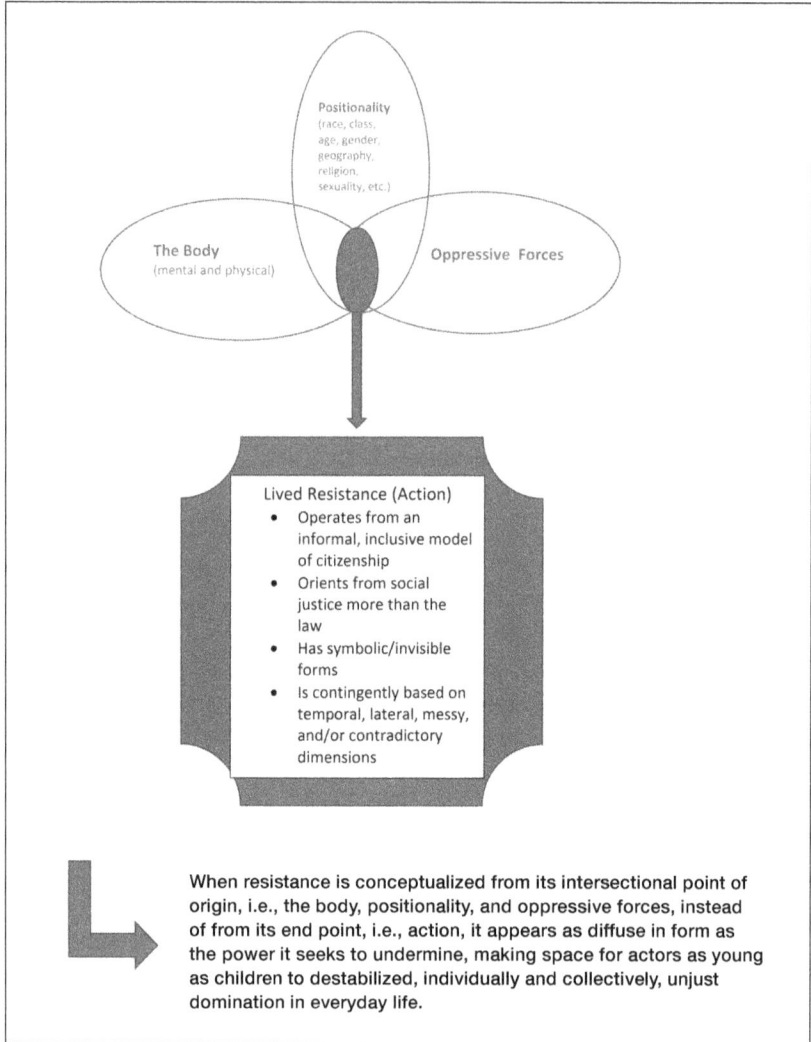

Positionality
(race, class, age, gender, geography, religion, sexuality, etc.)

The Body
(mental and physical)

Oppressive Forces

Lived Resistance (Action)
- Operates from an informal, inclusive model of citizenship
- Orients from social justice more than the law
- Has symbolic/invisible forms
- Is contingently based on temporal, lateral, messy, and/or contradictory dimensions

When resistance is conceptualized from its intersectional point of origin, i.e., the body, positionality, and oppressive forces, instead of from its end point, i.e., action, it appears as diffuse in form as the power it seeks to undermine, making space for actors as young as children to destabilized, individually and collectively, unjust domination in everyday life.

Lived Resistance

of power that push people farther into their own subservience (as opposed to their liberation). Otman notes that in the world of social media, electronic resistance can fortify systems of enemy surveillance. Badran illustrates the ways that children's activism can disrupt their education and even family financial solvency. Alruzzi, Marconi, and Aljamal argue that the tortuous conditions of Israeli prisons can depoliticize politically active Palestinian children. Alruzzi, Marconi, and Aljamal also briefly touch upon the way children's resistance can reproduce exclusionary gender hierarchies in Palestine.[68]

Locating the Researcher in Children's Lived Resistance

Lastly, a critical aspect of lived resistance is not just documenting what children do, but how we as scholars approach the topic of children's resistance. We too have bodies that impact our research. Namely, we are adults.[69] Many of the authors in this book self-reflect on the inherent multiple layers of asymmetrical power involved in being adult researchers of Palestinian children. Habashi encourages scholars to free themselves from the trap that adults know best; children do not think and act as small clones of adults. Badran confides that her initial attempt to distribute questionnaires—so familiar in her world—proved ineffective with some groups of young people that she studied; further, face-to-face focus groups captured an energy and hope that the forms could not. Sawhney uses participatory media and peer-based assessment to allow children to have their own voice and assess their own needs, while speaking about their struggles to a broader audience through media journalism and filmmaking. Shalhoub-Kevorkian attends funerals and hugs the mothers of martyred children, actively participating in the form of emotional solidarity she writes about. Sousa and Bressi argue that the classical, Western theories of motherhood do not do justice to the pragmatics of mother-child relations under occupation.

Another power differential that some researchers account for is their identity as Palestinians. Bishara, for example, acknowledges that as a "[Palestinian-American] mother of two children growing up in a comfortable corner of another settler colony," her work is a modest attempt to create dialogues across power lines. Alruzzi must employ research assistants for interviews in the West Bank since Israel will not allow Palestinians holding Gazan IDs to enter. While not Palestinian myself, I relate to Bishara's observation that research sites can begin to feel like home. As such, I use the deeply intimate method of portraiture to try to recreate life in Palestine, from a holistic mind-body-soul perspective.

In this book, we see new methods of research being deployed in light of the changing world of technology that young people live in today. Young Palestinians are increasingly engaging with information and communication technology (ICT), digital media forms, social media platforms, and the Internet to express their ideas of daily life through various personal and social narratives and engage in popular protests online and offline.[70] The fragmentation of public space in Palestine due to the Israeli occupation means that many young Palestinians connect through translocal virtual spaces, though not without apprehension and obstacles due to Israeli surveillance.[71] To understand father-son relationships under occupation, Otman gets permission to "dig into" Facebook profiles and collect posts. Sawhney distributes digital audio recorders to children, using participatory media, such as audio journaling, as a tool to access the everyday experiences of young Palestinians in Gaza. Bishara utilizes photography created by Palestinian refugees in their own communities to show children what the villages of their grandparents looked like before the Nakba so that they can recreate them in artwork.

As researchers, we must be careful not to reproduce the hegemonic systems that overprivilege the power of some children over others. For this reason, we must think more about what childhood means to some children versus others. Further, there is increasing demand for scholars to heed a theory of youth patiency, which puts the focus on young people's feelings, experiences, endurance, and other responses to institutionalized discriminatory practices to better understand how many marginalized youths might experience resistance.[72] Not all children are like the young Swedish environmental activist Greta Thunberg, who has the ear of some political leaders and the tools to organize multicity protests. My chapter seeks to push beyond agential bias by taking a disenfranchised Palestinian boy's emotional formation, as opposed to formal political participation, as the starting point for understanding his pursuit of dignity. In a place like Palestine, where many families cannot even hold funerals for their martyred children without the approval of Israel, enduring and reappropriating emotional pain can be a form of resistance, as Shalhoub-Kevorkian argues.

Thus the authors in this book take heed of their role as researchers, in addition to the topic of research itself. The bodily implications of resistance have been discussed here in the case of Palestinian children, but this book invites scholars globally to situate lived resistance in the social, historical, political, economic, and cultural contexts of more regions.

Conclusion

As academics, we often find ourselves speaking within silos circumscribed by our regional specialties. This introduction has discussed some of the bodily implications of resistance in the case of Palestinian children and invites scholars globally to situate lived resistance in other social, historical, political, economic, and cultural contexts. Palestinian children have been unchilded for nearly a century by structural forces of violence (namely settler colonialism) that interlink with the global history and current state of imperialism. Further, in our interconnected world, the impact of war on young people, wherever they grow up, shapes our collective future. The University of Georgia Press's Children, Youth, and War book series draws together scholarship from various corners of the world to acknowledge that wars do not belong to regions, but instead to humanity. Further, the multigenerational and multidisciplinary characteristics of the authors included in this book reflect how violence escapes neat categorization. Thus, at the level of an academic press, the book series is, in itself, a manifestation of lived resistance. The scholars in this volume are grateful to take part, on behalf of all the Palestinian young people whose bylines are regrettably missing here. This book includes numerous Palestinian scholars themselves, in an effort to move away from the usual top down, outside-inside external observations of the "natives" or colonized. The book is grouped into three thematic parts, the first focusses on creative forms of lived resistance, the second on the inner workings of unchilding that Palestinians seek to undermine, evade, and resist, and the third on parents' and children's concrete activism.

I want to conclude with a focus on the two young Palestinian women who write the book's opening statement, which has been translated from Arabic and introduced by Lama Yahya.[73] Jana Jihad Ayad (also known as Jana Jihad) has been called the youngest journalist in Palestine, and she is one of the world's youngest press-card-carrying journalists. She began her reporting career at nine years of age by using her mother's iPhone to present the perspective of a child growing up in violence; Jana has more than 600,000 followers on Facebook. Many Palestinian children are increasingly deploying visual images as "weapons" that seek to provide self-defense through documentation and exposure of Israeli violence.[74] Jana's cousin, Ahed Tamimi, is a Palestinian activist who received international media coverage in 2017 when at sixteen years of age she was filmed slapping an Israeli soldier in self-defense after he hit her during a protest. At the same protest, Israeli soldiers also shot with rubber bullets her fourteen-year-old cousin in the face at close range, severely wounding him. Israeli forces forcibly entered Ahed's family home the next night, arresting her.

For their opening remarks in this book, I asked Jana and Ahed, who now fall into the category of youth (which also overlaps with childhood), to comment on the future of children's resistance in Palestine. Interestingly the young women do not write about specific political activities and tactics. Instead, they write about something more fundamental, which is their long-denied right to exist and prosper as Palestinian children. They title their piece with the lyrics from a popular Lebanese song: "Give us childhood! Give us Life!" In equating childhood with life, Jana and Ahed essentially affirm that as long as there are Palestinian children, there will be no end to lived resistance in Palestine. To emphasize that this resistance is in many respects also endless on a global scale, I selected the closing words of this book to be written by Natalia Molebatsi, an activist and writer who grew up in apartheid South Africa and stands in solidarity with the young people of Palestine.

NOTES

I would like to thank the following people for their feedback on the introduction: Hedi Viterbo, Stephanie Olsen, Kirsi Pauliina Kallio, Nadera Shalhoub-Kevorkian, Antti Malinen, Rob Boddice, the three anonymous outside reviewers, James Marten, Mick Gusinde-Duffy, Mary Miller, Connie Caulkins, Jon Davies, and all the contributors to this book. This introduction (and, more generally, my work on this edited volume) received support from the National Endowment for the Humanities (NEH), the Palestinian American Research Center (PARC), the Fulbright Scholar Program, the University of Wisconsin–La Crosse, UCLA's Center of Near Eastern Studies, and Tampere University's Center of Excellence in the History of Experiences.

1. Defense for Children International Palestine, "Operation Protective Edge."

2. For detailed work on this, see Viterbo, *Problematizing Law, Rights, and Childhood*; and Shalhoub-Kevorkian, *Incarcerated Childhood*.

3. Kirmayer, Worthman, and Kitayama, "Co-constructing Culture, Mind, and Body," 11.

4. Khoudary, "Gaza Child: Three Wars Old."

5. Joronen, "Negotiating Colonial Violence."

6. For a discussion of how to engage frankly with children about their advocacy, see Taft, "Is it Okay to Critique?"

7. Viterbo, *Problematizing Law, Rights, and Childhood*, 4.

8. See, for example, Saukko, "Studying Lived Resistance"; Kallio, Wood, and Häkli, "Lived Citizenship."

9. Lilja et al., "How Resistance Encourages Resistance."

10. Johansson and Vinthagen, introduction to *Conceptualizing Everyday Resistance*.

11. Johansson and Vinthagen, 9.

12. See Adalah's Discriminatory Laws Database (DLD), an online resource (https://www.adalah.org/en/content/view/7771) comprising a list of more than sixty-five Israeli laws that discriminate directly or indirectly against Palestinian citizens in Israel and/or Palestinian residents of the Occupied Palestinian Territory (OPT) on the basis of their national belonging. For more information on the experiences of Palestinians in Israel, see Makhoul's "The Palestinian Citizens in Israel." See also Lana Tarour's "Citizenship as Domination."

13. Matar, *What it Means to be Palestinian*.

14. Marshall, "The State of Palestinian Youth."

15. Lori Allen provides a detailed look at how the everydayness of Israeli control shapes how Palestinians respond to the occupation's violence. Lori Allen, "Getting by the Occupation."

16. Rita Giacaman, "Reflections on the Meaning of 'Resilience.'"

17. Qumsiyeh, *Popular Resistance in Palestine*; Julie Norman, *The Second Palestinian Intifada*.

18. Hedi develops this concept in depth in regard to Palestine in his chapter "Violence" in Ben-Naftali, Sfard, and Viterbo, *The ABC of the OPT*.

19. Johansson and Vinthagen, "Dimensions of Everyday Resistance."

20. For information on how sumud has been practiced by political prisoners see Meari, "*Sumud*: A Palestinian Philosophy."

21. Toivo, *Faith and Magic in Early Modern Finland*.

22. Kivimäki, Suodenjoki, and Vahtikari, eds. *Lived Nation as the History*. All of these studies of "lived" experiences interweave with de Certeau's *The Practice of Everyday Life* (1984), which examines the ways people individualize mass culture, as well as second-wave feminism that raised the claim "the personal is the political." Kallio, Wood, Häkli, "Lived Citizenship."

23. For a comprehensive bibliography see Nigel Thomas's "Children and Politics."

24. Baraldi and Cockburn, *Theorising Childhood*.

25. Baraldi and Cockburn; Shalhoub-Kevorkian, "Speaking Life, Speaking Death"; Marshall, "Existence as Resistances"; Maksudyan, *Ottoman Children and Youth*; Prout and Campling, *The Body, Childhood, and Society*.

26. Häkli and Kallio, "Subject, Action and Polis," 182.

27. Collins, *Occupied by Memory*, 162.

28. Häkli and Kallio, "Bodies and Persons," 1–22.

29. Shalhoub-Kevorkian, "Gun to Body."

30. Kirmayer, Worthman, and Kitayama, "Co-constructing Culture, Mind, and Body," 1.

31. Kirmayer, Worthman, and Kitayama, 3.

32. Boddice and Smith, *Emotion, Sense, Experience*, 4.

33. Kirmayer, Worthman, and Kitayama "Co-constructing Culture, Mind, and Body," 11.

34. James, "Embodied Being(s)," 25–26.

35. Kirmayer, Worthman, and Kitayama, "Co-constructing Culture, Mind, and Body," 7.

36. Kirmayer, Worthman, and Kitayama, 11.

37. Boddice and Smith, *Emotion, Sense, Experience*, 6.

38. Boddice and Smith, 10–15.

39. Boddice and Smith, 31.

40. The 2018–19 Gaza border protests were held each Friday, involved thousands of protesters, and demanded that the Palestinian refugees be allowed to return to the lands they were displaced from in what is now Israel. They also sought to draw attention to Israel's Gaza blockade and the United States' recognition of Jerusalem as the capital of Israel. Palestinian Land Day, March 30, is an annual commemoration of the unarmed Palestinian-Israeli citizens killed, wounded, and arrested by Israel in the 1976 general strikes and marches.

41. Shalhoub-Kevorkian, "Gun to Body" 128.

42. Shalhoub-Kevorkian, "Ana Sumud: I Am Steadfastness."

43. Häkli and Kallio, "Bodies and Persons."

44. Viterbo, *Problematizing Law, Rights, and Childhood*, 127–30.

45. Veronese, Cavazzoni, and Antenucci, "Narrating Hope and Resistance."

46. Additionally, see Gleason, "Avoiding the Agency Trap." The new work on childism can also be helpful for understanding children's empowerment from multiple children's perspectives (see, for example, Wall's "From Childhood Studies to Childism," and Spyrou, Rosen, and Cook, *Reimagining Childhood Studies*).

47. See Horschelmann's "Dissent and Youth Citizenship."

48. Kallio, "The Body as a Battlefield"; Kallio, "Performative Bodies."

49. Shalhoub-Kevorkian, "Unchilding and the Killing Boxes," 1.

50. Kivimäki, Suodenjoki, Vahtikari, *Lived Nation as the History*, 1.

51. Some examples of Palestinian young people thinking deeply about their political situation, narrating about it, and shaping politics include Maira, *Jil Oslo: Palestinian Hip Hop*; Asthana, "Youth, Self, Other"; Zelkovitz, *Students and Resistance in Palestine*.

52. Baraldi and Cockburn, *Theorising Childhood*.

53. Isin and Nielsen, eds., *Acts of Citizenship*.

54. Feldman, "The Humanitarian Condition: Palestinian refugees," 155–72.

55. Marshall, "The State of Palestinian Youth," 151–54.

56. Kallio, Wood, and Häkli, "Lived Citizenship," 714.

57. Welchman, Zambelli, and Salih, "Rethinking Social Justice." For a look at the historical background behind PYM, see Qutami, "Transnational Histories of Palestinian Youth."

58. Saukko, "Studying Lived Resistance," 53.

59. Collins, *Occupied by Memory*.

60. Sigvardsdotter, "Presenting the Absent," 134.

61. Saukko, "Studying Lived Resistance," 38.

62. Häkli and Kallio, "On Becoming Political," 59.

63. Häkli and Kallio, 64–66.

64. Kallio and Häkli, "Geopolitical Lives in Topological Polis," 98.

65. Häkli and Kallio, "On Becoming Political," 66–68.

66. See, for example, the work of Joronen, "Negotiating Colonial Violence." Additionally, Warshel's book *Experiencing the Israeli-Palestinian Conflict* shows that Palestinians and Israelis sometimes appropriate outside peace interventions in ways that do not always line up with the intervener's expected outcome.

67. Shalhoub-Kevorkian, "Gun to Body."

68. For more on this topic, see Marshall's "Existence as Resistances."

69. For a rich discussion of the implications of power differentials between adults and children in research, see Bolgrien, Levison, and Vavrus, "Generational Power in Research with Children."

70. Asthana and Havandjian, *Palestinian Youth Media*; Dwonch, *Palestinian Youth Activism in the Internet Age*.

71. Asthana, "Youth, Self, Other."

72. George, "Authority and Agency," 157–58.

73. We are privileged to hear their voices, and encourage future academic work to further break down institutional barriers and preconceived notions that might otherwise block children from contributing actual full-fledged chapters.

74. For a discussion of the ways that visual images have become a battlefield between Palestinian children and Israeli soldiers see Viterbo, *Problematizing Law, Rights, and Childhood*, 221.

BIBLIOGRAPHY

Allen, L. "Getting by the Occupation: How Violence Became Normal in the Second Palestinian Intifada." *Cultural Anthropology* 23, no. 3 (2008): 453–87.

Asthana, S. "Youth, Self, Other: A Study of Ibdaa's Digital Media Practices in the West Bank, Palestine." *International Journal of Cultural Studies* 20, no. 1 (2017): 100–117.

Asthana, S., and N. Havandjian. *Palestinian Youth Media and the Pedagogies of Estrangement.* New York: Palgrave MacMillan, 2016.

Baraldi, C., and T. Cockburn, eds. *Theorising Childhood: Citizenship, Rights, and Participation.* Cham: Palgrave Macmillan, 2018.

Boddice, R., and M. Smith. *Emotion, Sense, Experience.* Cambridge, UK: Cambridge University Press, 2020.

Bolgrien, A., D. Levison, and F. Vavrus. "Generational Power in Research with Children." In *Children and Youth as Subjects, Objects, and Agents,* edited by Deborah Levison, Mary Jo Maynes, Frances Vavrus, 227–43. New York: Palgrave Macmillan, 2021.

Collins, J. *Occupied by Memory: The Intifada Generation and the Palestinian State of Emergency.* New York: NYU Press, 2004.

De Certeau, M. *The Practice of Everyday Life.* Berkeley: University of California Press, 1984.

Defense for Children International Palestine. "Operation Protective Edge: A War Waged on Gaza's Children." April 16, 2015. http://www.dci-palestine.org/operation _protective_edge_a_war_waged_on_gaza_s_children.

Dwonch, A. *Palestinian Youth Activism in the Internet Age.* London: Bloomsbury, 2019.

Feldman, I. "The Humanitarian Condition: Palestinian Refugees and the Politics of Living." *Humanity: An International Journal of Human Rights, Humanitarianism, and Development* 3, no. 2 (2012): 155–72.

George, A. "Authority and Agency." In *A Cultural History of Youth,* edited by Stephanie Olsen and Heidi Morrison, 5:155–72. London: Bloomsbury, 2023.

Giacaman, R. "Reflections on the Meaning of 'Resilience' in the Palestinian Context." *Journal of Public Health* 42, no. 3 (2020): 369–400.

Gleason, M. "Avoiding the Agency Trap: Caveats for Historians of Children, Youth, and Education." *History of Education* 45, no. 4 (2016): 446–59.

Häkli, J., and K. P. Kallio. "Subject, Action and Polis: Theorizing Political Agency." *Progress in Human Geography* 38, no. 2 (2014): 181–200.

———. "On Becoming Political: The Political in Subjectivity." *Subjectivity* 11, no. 1 (2018): 57–73.

———. "Bodies and Persons: The Politics of Embodied Encounters in Asylum Seeking." *Progress in Human Geography* 45, no. 4 (2020): 682–703.

Horschelmann, K. "Dissent and Youth Citizenship." In *Politics, Citizenship and Rights,* edited by Kirsi Pauliina Kallio, Sarah Mills, and Tracey Skelton. Singapore: Springer, 2016.

Isin, E. F., and G. M. Nielsen, eds. *Acts of Citizenship.* New York: Zed Books, 2008.

James, A. "Embodied Being(s)." In *The Body, Childhood, and Society,* edited by A. Prout and J. Campling. London: Palgrave, 2000.

Johansson, A., and S. Vinthagen, eds. *Introduction to Conceptualizing Everyday Resistance: A Transdisciplinary Approach.* New York: Taylor and Francis, 2019.

———. "Dimensions of Everyday Resistance: The Case of Palestinian Sumud." *Journal of Political Power* 8, no. 1 (2015): 109–39.

Joronen, M. "Negotiating Colonial Violence: Spaces of Precarisation in Palestine." *Antipode* 51, no. 3 (2019): 838–57.

Kallio, K. P. "Performative Bodies, Critical Agents and Political Selves: Rethinking the Political Geographies of Childhood." *Space and Polity* 11, no. 2 (2007): 121–36.

———. "The Body as a Battlefield: Approaching Children's Politics." *Geografiska Annaler: Series B, Human Geography* 90, no. 3 (2008): 285–97.

Kallio, K. P., B. E. Wood, and J. Häkli. "Lived Citizenship: Conceptualising an Emerging Field." *Citizenship Studies* 24, no. 6 (2020): 713–29.

Kallio, K. P., and J. Häkli. "Geosocial Lives in Topological Polis: Mohamed Bouazizi as a Political Agent." *Geopolitics* 22, no.1 (2017): 91–109.

Khoudary, Y. E. "Gaza Child: Three Wars Old." *Aljazeera*, July 16, 2014. http://www.aljazeera.com/indepth/opinion/2014/07/gaza-child-three-wars-old-2014716505446437.html.

Kirmayer, L. J., C. M. Worthman, and S. Kitayama. "Co-constructing Culture, Mind, and Body." In *Culture, Mind and Brain: Emerging Models, Concepts and Applications.* Cambridge, UK: Cambridge University Press, 2020.

Kivimäki, V., S. Suodenjoki, T. Vahtikari, eds. *Lived Nation as the History of Experience and Emotions in Finland, 1800–2000.* Cham: Palgrave Macmillan, 2021.

Lilja, M., M. Baaz, M. Schulz, and S. Vinthagen. "How Resistance Encourages Resistance: Theorizing the Nexus between Power, 'Organised Resistance' and 'Everyday Resistance.'" *Journal of Political Power* 10, no. 1 (2017): 40–54.

Maira, S. *Jil Oslo: Palestinian Hip Hop, Youth Culture, and the Youth Movement.* Fairfax, Va.: Tadween Publishing, 2013.

Makhoul, M. H. "The Palestinian Citizens in Israel: A History Through Fiction, 1948–2010." In *Journal of Holy Land and Palestine Studies* 19, no. 2 (2020): 229–31.

Maksudyan, N. *Ottoman Children and Youth during World War I.* New York: Syracuse University Press, 2019.

Marshall, D. J. "Existence as Resistances: Children and Politics of Play in Palestine." In *Politics, Citizenship and Rights: Geographies of Children and Young People*, edited by Kirsi Pauliina Kallio, Sarah Mills, and Tracey Skelton. Singapore: Springer, 2016.

———. "The State of Palestinian Youth—Commentary to Habashi." *Fennia* 197, no. 1 (2019): 151–54.

Matar, D. *What it Means to be Palestinian.* London and New York: I. B. Tauris, 2011.

Meari, L. "Sumud: A Palestinian Philosophy of Confrontation in Colonial Prisons." *The South Atlantic Quarterly* 113, no. 3 (2014): 547–78.

Norman, J. *The Second Palestinian Intifada: Civil Resistance.* London: Routledge, 2010.

Prout, A., and J. Campling, eds. *The Body, Childhood, and Society.* London: Palgrave Macmillan, 2000.

Qumsiyeh, M. B. *Popular Resistance in Palestine: A History of Hope and Empowerment.* London: Pluto Press, 2011.

Qutami, L. "Transnational Histories of Palestinian Youth Organizing in the United States." *Journal of Palestine Studies* 50, no. 2 (2021): 22–42.

Saukko, P. "Studying Lived Resistance." In *Doing Research in Cultural Studies.* London: Sage Publications, 2020.

Shalhoub-Kevorkian, N. "Gun to Body: Mental Health Against Unchilding." *International Journal of Applied Psychoanalytical Studies* 17, no. 2 (2020): 126–45.

———. "Ana Sumud: I Am Steadfastness." 2019. https://book.stopthewall.org/ana-sumud-i-am-steadfastness/.

———. *Incarcerated Childhood*. Cambridge, UK: Cambridge University Press, 2019.

———. "Speaking Life, Speaking Death: Jerusalemite Children Confronting Israel's Technologies of Violence." In *Emerald Handbook of Feminism, Criminology, and Social Change*, edited by Sandra Walklate, Kate Fitz-Gibbon, Jude McCulloch, and Jane Maree Maher. Bingley, UK: Emerald Publishing, 2020.

———. "Unchilding and the Killing Boxes." *Journal of Genocide Research* 23, no. 3 (2020): 490–500.

Sigvardsdotter, E. "Presenting the Absent: An Account of Undocumentedness in Sweden." PhD diss., Uppsala Universitat, 2012.

Spyrou, S., R. Rosen, and D. T. Cook, eds. *Reimagining Childhood Studies*. London: Bloomsbury, 2018.

Taft, J. K. "Is it Okay to Critique Youth Activists? Notes on the Power and Danger of Complexity." In *Children and Youth as Subjects, Objects, Agents*, edited by D. Levison, M. J. Maynes, and F. Vavrus. Cham: Palgrave Macmillan, 2021.

Tarour, L. "Citizenship as Domination: Settler Colonialism and the Making of Palestinian Citizenship in Israel." *Arab Studies Journal* 27, no. 2 (2019): 8–39.

Thomas, N. *Children and Politics*. Oxford Bibliographies in Childhood Studies, ed. Heather Montgomery. https://www.oxfordbibliographies.com/display/document/obo-9780199791231/obo-9780199791231-0067.xml.

Toivo, R. *Faith and Magic in Early Modern Finland*. New York: Palgrave, 2016.

Veronese, G., F. Cavazzoni, and S. Antenucci. "Narrating Hope and Resistance: A Critical Analysis of Sources of Agency Among Palestinian Children Living Under Military Violence." *Child Care, Health, and Development* 44, no. 6 (2018): 863–70.

Viterbo, H. "Violence." In *The ABC of the OPT: A Legal Lexicon of the Israeli Control over the Occupied Palestinian Territory*, edited by Orna Ben-Naftali, Michael Sfard, and Hedi Viterbo. Cambridge, UK: Cambridge University Press, 2018.

———. *Problematizing Law, Rights, and Childhood in Israel/Palestine*. Cambridge, UK: Cambridge University Press, 2021.

Wale, K. *South Africa's Struggle to Remember: Contested Memories of Squatter Resistance in the Western Cape*. London: Routledge, 2016.

Wall, J. "From Childhood Studies to Childism: Reconstructing the Scholarly and Social Imaginations." *Children's Geographies* 20, no. 3 (2018): 257–70.

Warshel, Y. *Experiencing the Israeli-Palestinian Conflict: Children, Peace, Communication*. Cambridge, UK: Cambridge University Press, 2021.

Welchman, L., E. Zambelli, and R. Salih. "Rethinking Social Justice Beyond Human Rights. Anti-colonialism and Intersectionality in the Politics of the Palestinian Youth Movement." *Mediterranean Politics* 26, no. 3 (2020): 349–69.

Zelkovitz, I. *Students and Resistance in Palestine: Books, Guns, and Politics*. New York: Routledge, 2015.

Historical Backdrop
The Right to Resist

HEIDI MORRISON

This book takes Palestinian children's resistance seriously, seeking not only to provide a theoretical framework for it but also to illustrate novel methodological approaches to research with young people. Before this book goes any further in that task, it is essential to explain why Palestinian children are resisting in the first place. As the following overview shows, Palestinians have a right to resist by international law due to a near century of oppression under settler colonialism.

Palestinian Children and the Unfolding of the Zionist Settler-Colonial Project

Settler colonialism is hallmarked by a "logic of elimination"—namely, the attempt to establish and perpetually sustain a colonial society in the expropriated territory by culturally, socially, or physically destroying the indigenous population, as happened in countries like the United States.[1] Settler colonialism works hand in hand with the structural violence of racism, securitization, criminalization, religious exclusivism, proselytizing, sexism, ethnocentrism, and capitalism. The central ideology that drives Israeli settler colonialism is political Zionism, or the movement to establish a Jewish homeland that emerged among the brutally persecuted Eastern European Jewry at the end of the nineteenth century. Palestinian children were (and still are) critical to the unfolding of this movement, which eventually created the state of Israel.

The process by which political Zionism uses young Palestinian bodies as political capital to create, build, and maintain the state of Israel is called "unchilding" (Shalhoub-Kevorkian 2019).[2] Unchilding refers to the stress that Palestinian children face under Israeli settler colonialism, which uses Palestinian children's bodies as legalized instruments to enact state violence against them, their families, and their communities. Unchilding aims to strip Palestinians of their childhood, which this book loosely defines along the lines of the Convention of the Rights of the Child (CRC) as a specific biological, psychological, and social life stage marked by increased vulnerability, educational and physical development, and potentiality. Children in this book are generally defined as being under eighteen years of age; however, the book does not shy away from the overlapping categories of youth (i.e., fifteen to twenty-four) and adolescence (i.e., teenage years).[3] I emphasize the word "loose" in my definition of childhood because valid debates on the definition of childhood abound, particularly as it relates to "unchilding".[4] Children experience childhood in various ways, including ways that may not conform to the CRC's framework but still may be viewed by children themselves as legitimate childhoods. Various actors' deployment of the mainstream children's rights framework also sometimes harms the very children it seeks to protect.[5] Nonetheless, I employ the term "unchilding" in this book because it was developed by a reputable Palestinian scholar who proposed it based on decades of engagement with Palestinian children. Further, I operate from the premise that there is no collective group of people anywhere who would willingly sanction for their young people the kind of political and structural violence described by unchilding. Until a "better" term emerges to refer to the multiplicity of meanings of being young, the benefits of using the term "unchilding" outweigh the drawbacks of not using it for young people in Palestine, in my opinion. While there are many interpretive frameworks for understanding violence against Palestinians, the value of using the term unchilding is the central focus it places on young people, demonstrating that politics cannot be separated from issues relating to childhood. Also, in their own ways, many Palestinian children themselves express ideas like the term unchilding.[6] Unchilding functions by way of the law, theological discourse, spatial reordering, and economic profiteering, and emerged hand in hand with the founding ideologies of political Zionism.[7] Palestinian children are not unwitting innocent bystanders or accidental victims of Israeli settler colonialism, but intentionally used and targeted due to ideological Zionist imperatives and the demographic threat that social reproduction of Palestinian life and families pose—as suggested by Israeli politicians and demographers.[8] Israel's effort to dehumanize Palestinian children and unchild them, framing them using the terms "dangerous," "terrorist," and others, justifies this violence. A brief overview of the intertwined history of Israeli settler colonialism and unchilding follows.

From the outset, political Zionism faced a challenge in that the indigenous people where they wanted to make a sovereign Jewish state (i.e., Palestine) experienced *their* historic homeland through their own individual and collective identities.[9] Scholars have well documented that the early Zionists, in alliance with

the British who held the mandate over Palestine from 1920 to 1948, disenfranchised the existing majority Arabs, transferred their land to Jewish people, and
ultimately expelled Arabs.[10] In order to advance its goals, the Zionist movement
perpetuated the misconception that Palestine was a "land without a people for a
people without a land," even though Palestine was an integral part of the larger
Ottoman Empire until it was deemed part of the British Mandate after World
War I. In his autobiography, Palestinian Fawaz Turki contends that while he was
growing up in early twentieth-century Palestine, British colonial administrators
and Zionists did not see him (and other Palestinian children) as leading the real
and meaningful lives that they did, which included such activities as going to
school, watching townsfolk play backgammon in the evenings, and dreaming of
the future.[11] For instance, he recollects British soldiers assaulting and running
over Palestinian children, including his cousin, with impunity.[12] Further, British
colonial administrators did not grant Palestinians autonomy over their educational system (as they did with the Jewish community), painting them as incapable of educating themselves, yet a potential threat if left to their own devices.
Statutory regulations that do more harm than good for Palestinian children orig-
inated in British laws of this era.[13] "The Arabs assaulted us" was the phrase the
earliest Jewish settlers used to describe Arab boys who earned money by helping
emigrant boats to shore.[14] Nadera Shalhoub-Kevorkian argues that unchilding
relies on categorizing Palestinians as "unacknowledged but dangerous."[15]

   In 1947, and owing largely to decades of steady resistance by the Palestinians,
the British decided that their mandate was untenable and referred the matter to
the UN, which recommended the partition of Palestine into two separate states,
a decree that Zionists readily accepted. Arabs rejected dividing the land on the
basis that they had the sovereign right to all of Palestine. War immediately ensued, with the establishment of the state of Israel occurring in May 1948. Historian Rashid Khalidi details the era's seismic upheaval, known by Palestinians
as the Nakba, or Catastrophe, with the following facts: some 80 percent of the
Arab population of the territory that at war's end became the new state of Israel had been forced from their homes and lost their lands and property; at least
720,000 of the 1.3 million Palestinians were made refugees; and Israel controlled
78 percent of the territory of former Mandatory Palestine and now ruled over the
160,000 Palestinian Arabs who had been able to remain, barely one-fifth of the
prewar Arab population.[16] The war played a critical step in advancing the Zionists' longstanding settler-colonial project.

   Plan Dalet, created by the Jewish paramilitary under the Mandate, served as
the military blueprint for the acquisition of Palestinian land and expulsion of
Palestinians that accompanied the establishment of the state of Israel. Its objectives were "to take any installation, military or civilian, evacuated by the Brit-

ish ... [and] to cleanse the future Jewish state of as many Palestinians as possible."[17] Zionist village files included everything from aerial photographs to details about the inhabitants' ages, sources of income, and religious affiliation.[18] According to historian Ilan Pappé, the Nakba fits the contemporary definition of ethnic cleansing in international law, since it was an organized "effort to render an ethnically mixed country homogeneous by expelling a particular group of people."[19] The Zionist militias and new Jewish state oversaw the destruction of more than five hundred Palestinian villages and towns, which were razed and/or transformed to construct Israeli societal infrastructure, such as Jewish-only settlements and national forests. In the notorious Deir Yassin massacre of April 9, 1948, Jewish fighters attacked the Palestinian Arab village of roughly six hundred people, killing nearly one hundred people in hours, including thirty infants.[20] Survivors recall bloodied children huddled against walls and boys and girls falling to the floor from bullets sprayed by Jewish soldiers; one survivor says he hid under his bed as an Israeli dragged his dead mother out of the house by her heels "like a sack of wheat."[21] In other massacres, Jewish forces followed orders to systematically execute males between the ages of ten and fifty.[22] In Operation Dani, the four-day Zionist assault on Lydda and Ramla that was the largest instance of deliberate mass expulsion of Palestinians during the 1948 war, Zionists practiced "caging" (physical and metaphysical incarceration as well as simultaneous loss of protection, space, and mobility) of Palestinian children.[23] The subject of the Nakba has been extensively documented by numerous scholars.[24]

The Israeli state's deliberate and methodological destruction and depopulation of Palestinian villages continued in the decades following the Nakba. Some of the best-known massacres include Kafr Qassim in 1956 (including nearly 25 Palestinian children)[25] and Khan Yunis in 1956 (including 274 Palestinian civilians).[26] As a new state, Israel passed legislation that forcibly evicted Palestinians from their homes and re-expelled any refugee who tried to return home. The 1950 Absentees' Property Law and 1953 Land Acquisition Law, for example, allowed the Israeli government to confiscate and claim title to the land of any person deemed an "absentee," including internal refugees who were not allowed to return to their homes owing to Israel's placing all Arabs under military administration.[27] After 1948, the Israeli government allocated greater per-student resources to the Jewish educational system than its Arab counterpart.[28] Even though Arabs represented 20 percent of the Israeli population, by 1966, there were 1,254 Jewish primary schools compared to 181 Arab primary schools; 131 schools for handicapped Jewish children and one for handicapped Arab children; 167 Jewish secondary schools and four Arab.[29] (The statistics today on per-student funding show that Jewish children receive six times the funds allocated to Arab children.[30] Additionally, gross socioeconomic disparities between Jewish and Arab families means that Palestinian children have a harder time concentrating at school because of poverty.[31]) Since 1948, Israel has used discriminatory policies against Palestinians to make the conditions for Palestinian parents to provide for children so difficult that the Israeli state sometimes deems the parents unfit for their roles and, hence, the Palestinian children in need of the Israeli state to "save" them.[32] The chapters by Shalhoub-Kevorkian, Cindy Sousa and Sara Bressi, and Abeer Otman show how Palestinian parents push back against "unmothering" and "unfathering," or the larger Israeli disruption of familial, demographic, social and cultural reproduction of Palestinians. The elaboration of unparenting in Palestine as a form and offshoot of unchilding in Palestine is an innovative contribution of this book.

At the same time that the new Israeli state restricted movement of Palestinians and confiscated Palestinian land internally, it also worked to expand its size and national borders. Israel launched attacks across armistice lines, which the UN Security Council repeatedly rejected as not done in self-defense.[33] In 1950, Israel's parliament adopted the Law of Return, giving Jews anywhere in the world the right to live in Israel and gain Israeli citizenship. A 1970 amendment to the Law of Return extends the right to return to non-Jews with a Jewish grandparent, as well as to spouses of those with a Jewish parent or grandparent. In 2018, the Israeli Basic Law defined Israel as the nation-state of the Jewish people, reaffirming the second-class status of Israel proper's remaining Palestinian minorities. Palestinian Nakba refugees and their descendants have demanded Israel heed their (internationally recognized) right to return to their ancestral homeland as civilians displaced by war. Socioeconomic indicators for Palestinian refugee children living in refugee camps are extremely poor owing to high population density and lack of basic infrastructure.[34] Amahl Bishara and Rami Salameh's chapters explore the trying experience of youngsters who grow up in refugee camps.

Israel's expansionist vision resulted in the 1967 war (also known as the Six-Day War) in which Israel captured and occupied the West Bank (including East Jerusalem) and Gaza (the last two remaining parts of ex-Mandate Palestine), the Golan Heights (Syrian territory), and the Sinai Peninsula (which Israel returned to Egypt in 1979 in exchange for Egypt's recognition of Israel's right to exist). Under heavy international condemnation, Israel officially annexed Occupied East Jerusalem (OEJ) in 1980 and the occupied Golan Heights in 1981, granting the local populations permanent Israeli residency status (but not Israeli citizenship). In 1967, some 300,000 Palestinians, many of them already refugees from villages conquered by Israel in the 1948 war, fled the West Bank and Gaza mostly for Jordan. The Israeli Minister of Defense, Moshe Dayan, said that Palestinian homes were destroyed to "chase away the inhabitants."[35] Ibtisam Barakat writes in her autobiography of childhood, *Tasting the Sky*, that the moment word spread of the war's outbreak, there was "a stream of people from neighboring villages fleeing their homes."[36] In Raja Shehadeh's coming-of-age memoir *Strangers in the House*, he similarly recalls a perpetual sense of danger felt among children during the war: he slept with slippers by his bed, so that he could quickly flee if a bomb fell at night.[37] There is mounting evidence that in the 1967 war, Israeli soldiers committed massacres of innocent villagers in Gaza.[38] After 1967, Israel required Palestinians in the Occupied Territories to register with the Israeli central database in order to obtain ID cards.[39] Even today and depending on the type of ID card a Palestinian receives, a Palestinian can, for extended periods of time, be prevented from living with or visiting family members who reside in other parts of the Occupied Territories, Israel proper, or abroad.

After the 1967 war, Israeli citizens, authorized and backed by the state, began constructing communities in the illegally occupied territories. The total Israeli settler population in the West Bank, Gaza, Golan Heights, and East Jerusalem grew from approximately 10,000 in the early 1970s to over 700,000 (and growing) today. Israeli settlements are linked to the confiscation of land, destruction of farmland, the economic dispossession of families, and the demolition of Palestinian homes, leaving children in poverty, homeless, without schooling and in distress.[40] For most of the last fifty years, Israel has treated the Occupied Territories as closed military zones, which means that Palestinians have also been unable to move freely between the West Bank, Gaza, and Israel. Israeli settlers have access to numerous modern bypass roads that connect settlements and avoid the separation wall. Palestinians must travel on circuitous, unmaintained roads encumbered by permanent Israeli security checkpoints and spontaneous road closures. These impediments to movement disrupt Palestinian children's access to schooling and medical care. For example, according to Defense for Children International, harassment by Israeli settlers of Palestinian children going to school and intimidation, arbitrary arrest, searches, and assault of Palestinian children by Israeli soldiers at checkpoints create fear in the children that impedes education.[41] Amneh Badran's chapter illustrates this situation in the case of children in Silwan village, south of the Old City of Jerusalem. Creating "liminal and anxiety-driven space" facilitates unchilding because children cannot safeguard their bodies, families, loved ones, and land.[42]

To this day, Israel maintains an illegal blockade on the Gaza Strip and an illegal occupation of the West Bank, which consists of noncontiguous Palestinian "Bantustans" partitioned by Israeli-controlled checkpoints and Jewish-only settlements and roads. The separation wall, whose construction began in 2002, runs 440 miles, with most of it cutting deep into the borders of the 1949 West Bank Armistice Demarcation Line. By fragmenting and encircling Palestinian villages and towns, the wall separates Israeli settlements and Israel proper from the West

Bank Palestinian population. Observers, human rights groups, and Palestinians themselves refer to the visual appearance of the wall and its restrictions on mobility as an open-air prison noting, however, that even prisons typically do not have their electricity and water shut off daily.[43] Most of the barrier is made of twenty-five-foot-high concrete slabs and fencing material, combined with barbed wire, observation posts, trenches, cameras, electric sensors, sniper towers, razor wire, and electric fencing. The barrier restricts Palestinian freedom of movement, hindering thousands of Palestinians from accessing their agricultural lands, obtaining crucial medical and educational services, maintaining business ties, and seeing relatives on the other side of the barrier. For instance, after the wall separated the neighboring West Bank towns of Qalqilya and Habla, children and teachers had to pass through gates in the wall to get to school. The erratic opening hours of the gates and harassment by Israeli soldiers means that students miss exams and are absent or late to lessons, and teachers must cancel classes.[44] The wall intensifies local patriarchal systems that seek to overprotect girls, making it more difficult for girls to meet and converse in parks and/or friends' houses, for example.[45] The separation barrier is the ultimate manifestation of Israel's caging of Palestinian children.

Another aspect of the illegal occupation with a severe impact on children is Israel's military courts. Since 1967 Israeli military law has been applied to the whole West Bank Palestinian population; Jewish settlers living in the same territory are rarely subject to it in practice.[46] The military courts lack basic fundamental due-process guarantees, with the majority of Palestinian children denied access to their family or a lawyer until the first appearance in military court.[47] Palestinian children, typically arrested in their homes at night, are subject to physical, psychological, and verbal abuse in detention centers, including to obtain false confessions.[48] Military judges employ evidence collected during interrogations, including forced confessions, which can be false and/or written in a language they do not understand. Most children face charges of stone throwing, although Israel also practices administrative detention, which allows for the arrest of Palestinians on "secret evidence," without trial and for an indefinite period. The international community considers it to be a violation of several articles of the Geneva Conventions that 60 percent of Palestinian child detainees serve their sentences in prisons inside Israel, where their family cannot visit them regularly because of restrictions on movement.[49] In OEJ, the Israeli state frequently puts Palestinian children under house arrest, turning parents into prison guards and disrupting the intimacy of the home.[50] Shahrazad Odeh's chapter explores the different types of rehabilitation that the Israeli juvenile system offers to Palestinian children versus their Jewish Israeli counterparts accused of similar offences.

Over the last two decades, Israel has employed a "mowing the lawn" strategy in the Palestinian territories. This popular metaphor used by Israeli politicians refers to the IDF's periodic offensive strategy in Gaza, involving indiscriminate bombing. Noam Chomsky refers to the disproportionately violent nature of the attacks as "shooting fish in a pond."[51] Since 2000, at least 15,864 Palestinian children have been killed by Israelis, while 179 Israeli children have been killed by Palestinians.[52] The three-week Israeli onslaught on Gaza in 2008–9 (Operation Cast Lead) resulted in the deaths of 344 minors, only 22 of whom were known to have been taking part in the hostilities. Zero Israeli children were killed in the fighting.[53] A similar massacre occurred in 2014, as already discussed in the context of the cover art for this book in the book's introduction. During the 2018–19 Great March of Return protests in Gaza, human rights organizations documented Israel's use of excessive force against child demonstrators.[54] The 2023 Israeli war on Gaza, where nearly half of the residents are under eighteen, reduced entire neighborhoods to rubble. Israel's permissive rules of engagement against Palestinian children mark them as "helpless, born to die."[55] Shalhoub-Kevorkian's chapter details Israel's exploitative use of Palestinian children's bodies even after their murder by Israel.

In sum, from massacres to discriminatory policies, attacks on Palestinian children have been and continue to be a central component to the building of the Israeli state. With or without physical death, unchilding works in a circular manner to frame children as dangerous, a "security threat," and disposable entities. Unchilding dispossess Palestinian children of opportunities to grow up safely, play, move, receive medical care, visit family members, and attend school. It also destabilizes parental roles.[56] Unchilding is a manifestation of the larger process of dehumanization that all Palestinians experience at the hands of the Zionist colonial project. The category of the child, or the ideal of childhood, is an incredibly instrumental tool to facilitate dehumanization. In conflict, attacking the opponent's children has strategic value because of the larger instability it can cause to the family and social structure, which can lead to multigenerational damage.[57] Further, the mere existence of indigenous children in a settler-colonial space haunts the settler and stands in the way of the existence of the settler-colonial state as a fait accompli.[58] For Israeli authorities, age is an indispensable governance tool, as it is on the basis of age that Israel limits movement and thus denies access to work, medical treatment, education, and social relations.[59] Despite this cruel reality, Palestinian children (and their adults) find ways to interrupt unchilding, as this book demonstrates in the context of the contemporary era.

NOTES

1. Wolfe, "Settler Colonialism," 387–89.
2. Before Shalhoub-Kevorkian started using the term "unchilding," it had already been

used by others in other contexts. The term "unparenting" had likewise previously been
in use. For example, the widely quoted poem "The Wreck of the Deutschland" (1875) by
Gerard Manley Hopkins speaks of "the widow-making unchilding unfathering deeps."
The influential preacher Charles Spurgeon wrote, in his 1866 book *His Name the Everlasting Father*, "There is no unfathering Christ, and there is no unchilding us." Similarly, the Argentinian poet Juan Gelman repeatedly used the terms "hijar" and "deshi-
jar" (respectively, "to child" or "to unchild"), and this terminology was later analyzed
by the highly influential French thinker Jacques Derrida in his "Mnemosyne," which
was published in *Memoires for Paul de Man*. Scholars had also used these terms prior to
Shalhoub-Kevorkian's use of them. See, e.g., Glausiusz, "Child Development" (discussing an earlier use of the term "unparenting"). More recently, the Canadian novelist Kyo
Maclear published an academic article lamenting "the unchilding of Black children who
are . . . tried as adults and carted off to adult prisons." See Maclear, "Something So Broken." Some of these uses of the terms "unchilding" and "unparenting," in academic circles
and beyond, differ from those that now refer to Palestine (although Maclear's conception
of "unchilding" is very similar to Shalhoub-Kevorkian's).

3. Standardized meanings of age can miss the interactions of the individual with the
world, or how age is socially constructed (Habashi, *Political Socialization of Youth*). Israeli law, for example, has a history of applying a range of conflicting age thresholds (via
legal exceptions) to noncitizen Palestinians in the West Bank, based on what serves Israeli and not Palestinian children's best interests. (Viterbo, "Youth," 499–515 and Viterbo,
Problematizing Law, Rights, and Childhood in Israel/Palestine, 100–103). Further, standardized definitions of age can reinforce developmentality paradigms which view human
development as a linear path toward adulthood (Viterbo, *Problematizing Law, Rights,
and Childhood*, 8).

4. For a critical discussion of the normative vision of childhood implied by Shalhoub-
Kevorkian's concept of unchilding, see Peleg's "Victimizing Children," and for a discussion of the potential harm caused by the "loss-of-childhood" narrative, i.e., the essential-
ist, universalist, developmentalist critique, see Viterbo, *Problematizing Law, Rights, and
Childhood*, 188–93; 200–211.

5. Viterbo, *Problematizing Law, Rights, and Childhood*.

6. Shalhoub-Kevorkian says in her article "Unchilding and the Killing Boxes" that
children are quite capable of "their own theorizations about their childhood" and "can
decide what childhood is for them and when they are being unchilded," 494.

7. Shalhoub-Kevorkian, *Incarcerated Childhood*, "Unchilding and the Killing Boxes."

8. Shalhoub-Kevorkian, *Incarcerated Childhood*.

9. For an in-depth discussion of how the identity of Palestine evolved throughout time
through the eyes of the indigenous people, see Masalha's *Palestine: A Four Thousand Year
History*.

10. See Abu-Lughod (ed.), *The Transformation of Palestine*; Essaid, *Zionism and Land
Tenure*; Morris, *Righteous Victims*; Zureik, *Israel's Colonial Project in Palestine*; Rodinson, *Israel: A Colonial-Settler State?*; Stein, *The Land Question in Palestine*; Pappé, *A History of Modern Palestine*; Likhovski, *Law and Identity in Mandate Palestine*; Masalha,
Expulsion of the Palestinians; and Huneidi, *A Broken Trust*.

11. Turki, *The Disinherited*, 19.

12. Turki, 12.

13. Viterbo, *Problematizing Law, Rights, and Childhood*.

14. Pappé, *The Idea of Israel*, 30.

15. Shalhoub-Kevorkian, *Incarcerated Childhood*, 103.

16. Khalidi, *The Hundred Years War on Palestine*, 58.

17. Pappé, *A History of Modern Palestine*, 129.

18. Pappé, *The Ethnic Cleansing of Palestine*, 19.

19. Ibid., 3.

20. Ibid., 40.

21. McGowan and Ellis, *Remembering Deir Yassin*, 51.

22. Pappé, *Ethnic Cleansing*, 110.

23. Shalhoub-Kevorkian, *Incarcerated Childhood*, 40. See also Busailah, *In the Land of My Birth* and Khoury's *The Children of the Ghetto*.

24. Masalha, *The Palestine Nakba*; Pappé, *Ethnic Cleansing*; Abu-Lughod, *The Transformation of Palestine*; Khalidi, *From Haven to Conquest*; Saʿdi and Abu-Lughod, *Nakba*; Tannous, *The Palestinians*.

25. In the months following the massacre, there occurred in this region a series of land mine explosions and military shooting exercises that resulted in the deaths of twenty-two children and the injury of eight others. The Israeli state did not investigate the matter, but instead continued to facilitate the settlement of the Jewish residents on local land expropriated from Palestinian families. Robinson, *Citizen Strangers*, 178.

26. Masalha, *A Land without a People*, 40.

27. Quigley, *Palestine and Israel, 108–9*.

28. Ibid., 112.

29. Cochran, *Democracy in the Middle East*, 176.

30. Ibid., 177.

31. For an overview of many of the Israeli laws since the 1950s that have forbidden Arabs from receiving government social services, see Quigley, *Palestine and Israel*, 138–44.

32. For further discussion of Israel's child saving discourse, see Shalhoub-Kevorkian's *Incarcerated Childhood*, 54, 68–71. For a discussion of the removal of children from their parents and communities in similar settler-colonial discourses and settings, see Viterbo, "Ties of Separation."

33. Quigley, *Palestine and Israel*, 154.

34. For more on the dire conditions in Palestinian refugee camps, see Peteet, "Camps and Enclaves"; Feldman, "What Is a Camp?"; Abourahme and Hilal's "Intervention, (Self) Urbanization"; Bishara's "An Ongoing Violence"; Hatoum's "For 'a No-State'"; and Kushner's "'We are Orphans Here.'"

35. Morris, *Righteous Victims*, 326.

36. Barakat, *Tasting the Sky*, 22.

37. Shehadeh, *Strangers in the House*, 41.

38. Their precise nature is difficult to discern owing to Israel's destruction of the USS *Liberty* (which held recordings of communications between Israeli troops) and the Is-

raeli military censors' erasure of Israeli soldiers' testimonies. See Pappé, "New Evidence from 1967 War."

39. Even after the Palestinian Authority was established following the Oslo Accords, Israel retained its hold on the population registry in the Occupied Territories. Lyon, Abu-Laban, and Zureik, *Surveillance and Control in Israel/Palestine.*

40. See United Nations Office for the Coordination of Humanitarian Affairs, "Vulnerability Profile of Palestinian Communities"; B'Tselem, "2016 Sees Israel Demolish Record" and "House Demolitions."

41. Defense for Children International Palestine, "Right to a Childhood."

42. Shalhoub-Kevorkian, *Incarcerated Childhood,* 26–27.

43. Feldman, "Gaza as an Open-Air Prison."

44. Makdisi, *Palestine Inside Out,* 26.

45. Shalhoub-Kevorkian, *Facing the Wall,* 27–30. For details on how Israeli violence impacts girls' education, see Shalhoub-Kevorkian, "The Gendered Nature of Education."

46. Viterbo, "Outside/Inside," 314.

47. For a discussion of the ways in which recent (so-called) Israeli statutory "reforms" fail to meaningfully impact Palestinian children's rights in Israeli military courts, see Viterbo's "Youth," 499–515.

48. Cook, Hanieh, and Kay, *Stolen Youth.*

49. Defense for Children International Palestine, "Military Detention," and Viterbo, "Security Prisoners," 389. For a discussion about generational segregation as a tool of settler colonialism in Palestine see Viterbo, "Ties of Separation."

50. Shalhoub-Kevorkian, *Incarcerated Childhood,* 85.

51. Democracy Now, "'A Hideous Atrocity.'"

52. "If Americans Knew: What Every American Needs to Know about Israel-Palestine." https://ifamericansknew.org/stat/children.html. Accessed March 12, 2024.

53. B'Tselem, "Fatalities During Caste Led."

54. See, for example, Amnesty International, "Israel/OPT," and Adalah, "Adalah and Al Mezan Petition."

55. Shalhoub-Kevorkian, *Incarcerated Childhood,* 103.

56. For additional firsthand accounts of the impact of occupation on Palestinian young people, see Robinson and Young's *Young Palestinians Speak.*

57. For example, Viterbo, in "Rights as a Divide-and-Rule Mechanism," provides a detailed illustration of how Israel's increased separation of Palestinian adults and children in Israeli custody can weaken political ties between generations.

58. Dhillon, "Indigenous Girls."

59. Viterbo, *Problematizing Law, Rights, and Childhood.*

BIBLIOGRAPHY

Abourahme, N., and S. Hilal. "Intervention, (Self) Urbanization, and the Contours of Political Space in Dheisheh Refugee Camp." *Jerusalem Quarterly,* no. 38 (2009): 42–45.

Abu-Lughod, I., ed. *The Transformation of Palestine: Essays on the Origin and Development of the Arab-Israeli Conflict.* Evanston, Ill.: Northwestern University Press, 1972.

Adalah. "Adalah and Al Mezan Petition Supreme Court: Order Israeli Army to Stop Using Snipers, Live Ammunition against Gaza Protests." April 24, 2018. https://www.adalah.org/en/content/view/9488. Amnesty International. "Israel/OPT: Israeli Forces Must End the Use of Excessive Force in Response to 'Great March of Return' Protests." April 13, 2018. https://www.amnesty.org/en/latest/news/2018/04/israelopt-israeli-forces-must-end-the-use-of-excessive-force-in-response-to-great-march-of-return-protests/#.

Barakat, I. *Tasting the Sky: A Palestinian Childhood*. New York: Farrar, Straus, and Giroux, 2007.

Bishara, A. "An Ongoing Violence, a Sustained Resistance: Israel's Racist Separation Wall at Aida Refugee Camp." In *Walling in, Walling Out*, edited by Laura McAtackney and Randall H. McGuire. Santa Fe: University of New Mexico Press and School of Advanced Research Press, 2020.

B'Tselem: The Israeli Information Center for Human Rights in the Occupied Territories. "2016 Sees Israel Demolish Record Number of West Bank Homes." February 14, 2017. http://www.btselem.org/planning_and_building/20170213_2016_demolitions.

———. "Fatalities during Operation Cast Lead." April 24, 2018. http://www.btselem.org/statistics/fatalities/during-cast-lead/by-date-of-event.

———. "House Demolitions: Demolition of houses as punishment." [2023] https://statistics.btselem.org/en/demolitions/demolition-as-punishment?tab=overview.

Busailah, R. *In the Land of My Birth: A Palestinian Boyhood*. Washington, D.C.: Institute for Palestine Studies, 2017.

Cochran, J. *Democracy in the Middle East: The Impact of Religion and Education*. Lanham, Md.: Lexington Books, 2013.

Cook, C., A. Hanieh, and A. Kay. *Stolen Youth: The Politics of Israel's Detention of Palestinian Children*. London: Pluto Press, 2004.

Defense for Children International Palestine. "Military Detention." http://www.dci-palestine.org/issues_military_detention.

———. "Right to a Childhood." http://www.dci-palestine.org/issues_right_to_a_childhood.

Democracy Now. "'A Hideous Atrocity': Noam Chomsky on Israel's Assault on Gaza and U.S. Support for the Occupation." August 7, 2014. https://www.democracynow.org/2014/8/7/a_hideous_atrocity_noam_chomsky_on.

Derrida, J. "Mnemosyne." In *Memoires for Paul de Man*. Translated by Cecile Lindsay, Jonathan Culler, Eduardo Cadava, and Peggy Kamuf. New York: Columbia University Press, 1986.

Dhillon, J. K. "Indigenous Girls and the Violence of Settler Colonial Policing." *Decolonization: Indigeneity, Education & Society* 4, no. 2: (2015): 1–31.

Essaid, A. A. *Zionism and Land Tenure in Mandate Palestine*. New York: Routledge, 2014.

Feldman, I. "Gaza as an Open-Air Prison." *Middle East Research Information Project* 275 (Summer 2015). https://merip.org/2015/06/gaza-as-an-open-air-prison/.

———. "What Is a Camp? Legitimate Refugee Lives in Spaces of Long-Term Displacement." *Geoforum* 66 (2015): 244–52.

Glausiusz, J. "Child Development: A Cognitive Case for Un-Parenting." *Nature* 536 (2016): 27–28.

Habashi, J. *Political Socialization of Youth: A Palestinian Case Study*. New York: Palgrave, 2017.

Hatoum, N. A. "For 'a No-State Yet to Come': Palestinian Urban Place-Making in Kufr Aqab, Jerusalem." *Environment and Planning E: Nature and Space* 4, no. 1 (2020): 85–108.

Hopkins, G. M. "The Wreck of the Deutschland." 1875. https://www.poetryfoundation .org/poems/44403/the-wreck-of-the-deutschland.

Huneidi, S. *A Broken Trust: Sir Herbert Samuel, Zionism, and the Palestinians*. London and New York: I. B. Tauris, 2001.

"If Americans Knew: What Every American Needs to Know about Israel-Palestine." https://ifamericansknew.org/stat/children.html. Accessed March 12, 2024.

Khalidi, R. *The Hundred Years War on Palestine: A History of Settler Colonialism and Resistance, 1917–2017*. New York: Metropolitan Books, Henry Holt, 2020.

Khalidi, W. *From Haven to Conquest: Readings in Zionism and the Palestine Problem Until 1948*. Washington, D.C.: Institute for Palestine Studies, 1971.

Khoury, E. *The Children of the Ghetto: My Name is Adam*. Translated by Humphrey Davies. Brooklyn: Archipelago, 2019.

Kushner, R. "'We Are Orphans Here': Life and Death in East Jerusalem's Palestinian Refugee Camp." *New York Times Magazine*. December 1, 2016. https://www.nytimes .com/2016/12/01/magazine/we-are-orphans-here.html?_r=0.

Likhovski, A. *Law and Identity in Mandate Palestine*. Chapel Hill: The University of North Carolina Press, 2006.

Lyon, D., Y. Abu-Laban, and E. Zureik, eds. *Surveillance and Control in Israel/Palestine: Population, Territory, and Power*. London: Routledge, 2013.

Maclear, K. "Something So Broken: Black Care in the Wake of Beasts of the Southern Wild." *Interdisciplinary Studies in Literature and Environment* 25, no. 3 (2018): 603–29.

Makdisi, S. *Palestine Inside Out: An Everyday Occupation*. New York: W. W. Norton, 2008.

Masalha, N. *Expulsion of the Palestinians: The Concept of "Transfer" in Zionist Political Thought 1882–1948*. Beirut: Institute of Palestine Studies, 1992.

———. *A Land without a People: Israel, Transfer, and the Palestinians 1949–96*. London: Farber and Farber, 1997.

———. *Palestine: A Four Thousand Year History*. London: Zed Books, 2018.

———. *The Palestine Nakba: Decolonising History, Narrating the Subaltern, Reclaiming Memory*. London: Zed Books, 2012.

McGowan, D., and M. H. Ellis. *Remembering Deir Yassin: The Future of Israel and Palestine*. New York: Olive Branch Press, 1998.

Morris, B. *Righteous Victims: A History of the Zionist-Arab Conflict, 1881–2001*. New York: Vintage Books, 2001.

Pappé, I. *The Ethnic Cleansing of Palestine*. Oxford: Oneworld, 2006.

———. *The Idea of Israel: A History of Power and Knowledge*. London and New York: Verso, 2014.

———. "New Evidence from 1967 War Reveals Israeli Atrocities." *The Elec-

tronic Intifada. June 23, 2015. https://electronicintifada.net/content/
new-evidence-1967-war-reveals-israeli-atrocities/14635.

———. *A History of Modern Palestine: One Land, Two Peoples.* 3rd edition. Cambridge: Cambridge University Press, 2022.

Peleg, N. "Victimizing Children and the Manifestations of Childhood." *Journal of Genocide Research* 23, no. 3 (2021): 472–77.

Peteet, J. "Camps and Enclaves: Palestine in the Time of Closure." *Journal of Refugee Studies* 28, no. 2 (2016): 208–28.

Quigley, J. *Palestine and Israel: A Challenge to Justice.* Durham and London: Duke University Press, 1990.

Robinson, A., and A. Young. *Young Palestinians Speak: Living Under Occupation.* Northampton, Mass.: Interlink Books, 2017.

Robinson, S. *Citizen Strangers: Palestinians and the Birth of Israel's Liberal Settler State.* Stanford, Calif.: Stanford University Press, 2013.

Rodinson, M. *Israel: A Colonial-Settler State?* New York: Monad Press, 1972.

Sa'di, A. H., and L. Abu-Lughod, eds. *Nakba: Palestine, 1948 and the Claims of Memory.* New York: Columbia University Press, 2007.

Shalhoub-Kevorkian, N. *Facing the Wall: Palestinian Children and Adolescents Speak about the Israeli Separation Wall.* Jerusalem: World Vision, 2007.

———. "The Gendered Nature of Education Under Siege: a Palestinian Feminist Perspective." *International Journal of Lifelong Education* 27, no. 2: (2008): 179–200.

———. *Incarcerated Childhood and the Politics of Unchilding.* Cambridge: Cambridge University Press, 2019.

———. "Unchilding and the Killing Boxes." In *Journal of Genocide Research* 23, no. 3 (2020): 490–500.

Shehadeh, R. *Strangers in the House: Coming of Age in Occupied Palestine.* New York: Penguin Books, 2003.

Spurgeon, C. *His Name—the Everlasting Father.* 1866. https://www.spurgeon.org /resource-library/sermons/his-name-the-everlasting-father/#flipbook/.

Stein, K. W. *The Land Question in Palestine, 1917–1939.* Chapel Hill: The University of North Carolina Press, 1984.

Tannous, I. *The Palestinians: A Detailed Documented Eyewitness History of Palestine Under British Mandate.* New York: I.G.T. Company, 1988.

Turki, F. *The Disinherited: Journal of a Palestinian Exile.* New York and London: Monthly Review Press, 1972.

The United Nations Office for the Coordination of Humanitarian Affairs (OCHA). "Vulnerability Profile of Palestinian Communities in Area C." https://ochaopt.org/page /vpp.

Viterbo, H. "Outside/Inside." In *The ABC of the OPT: A Legal Lexicon of the Israeli Control over the Occupied Palestinian Territory*, edited by Orna Ben-Naftali, Michael Sfard, and Hedi Viterbo. Cambridge, UK: Cambridge University Press, 2018.

———. *Problematizing Law, Rights, and Childhood in Israel/Palestine.* Cambridge, UK: Cambridge University Press, 2021

———. "Rights as a Divide-and-Rule Mechanism: Lessons from the Case of Palestinians in Israeli Custody." *Law and Social Inquiry* 43, no. 3 (2018): 746–95.

———. "Security Prisoners." In *The ABC of the OPT: A Legal Lexicon of the Israeli Control over the Occupied Palestinian Territory*, edited by Orna Ben-Naftali, Michael Sfard, and Hedi Viterbo. Cambridge, UK: Cambridge University Press, 2018.

———. "Ties of Separation: Analogy and Generational Segregation in North America, Australia, and Israel/Palestine." *Brooklyn Journal of International Law* 42, no. 2 (2017): 686–749.

———. "Youth." In *The ABC of the OPT: A Legal Lexicon of the Israeli Control over the Occupied Palestinian Territory*, edited by Orna Ben-Naftali, Michael Sfard, and Hedi Viterbo. Cambridge, UK: Cambridge University Press, 2018.

Wolfe, P. "Settler Colonialism and the Elimination of the Native." *Journal of Genocide Research* 8, no.4 (2006): 387–409.

Zureik, E. *Israel's Colonial Project in Palestine*. London and New York: Routledge, 2016.

PART 1

Agency, Creativity, and Resilience

A Refugee ABC

Creativity and Collage in the Face of War

AMAHL BISHARA

On the afternoon of Sunday, February 5, 2017, a staff member at Lajee Center, a youth organization in Aida refugee camp in the Israeli-occupied West Bank, broadcast live on Facebook as Israeli soldiers entered the building. In the staff member's video, later watched by people on at least three continents, Israeli soldiers wear helmets with face shields and brandish their standard issue M-16s amid the Palestinian twentysomethings in street clothes. The Palestinians wield only their smartphones. The soldiers say something about *yeladim* (Hebrew: children), and the Palestinians respond talking about *awlād* (Arabic: children). Then they settle into English: A soldier inquires after the "Boy? Little boy with, ehh . . ." One of the staff members replies crisply, "There is no little boy here." The Palestinian staff was not in the business of locating children for the Israeli army.

After two decades of Israeli military occupation of the West Bank and Gaza Strip, Palestinian writer Anton Shammas observed, "For twenty years now officially there has been no childhood in the West Bank and the Gaza Strip . . . A ten-year-old boy shot by the military forces is reported to be a 'young man of ten.'"[1] Now these children who were never children have grown up and have children who themselves are not children—or at least not in the eyes of the Israeli government that rules over them. Nadera Shalhoub-Kevorkian writes about this systematic theft of childhood under Israeli settler colonialism as unchilding.[2]

In the summer of 2014, I set out with youth and volunteers at a community center in Aida to defy this violation of childhood. We made a book that would recover a child's perspective on and symbolic presence in Aida, *The Aida Camp Alphabet*.[3] For a few hours each afternoon, we created a space with a diligent kind of whimsy, a colorful and layered sensibility—a space for being a Palestinian child. The book was the product of many hands, large and small. It was the product of a group of children's determination, their joy, their suffering, their creativity, and their wisdom, all cut out carefully and pasted back together in new shapes and arrangements.

Aida refugee camp, on the northern edge of Bethlehem, was established by the United Nations Relief and Works Agency (UNRWA) in 1951 to serve refugees whose families were dispossessed of their land in 1948 with the establishment of Israel. The 7,100 registered refugees of Aida are among the approximately 871,000 registered refugees living in the West Bank who were dispossessed of their family homes over seven decades ago and whose families have lived under military occupation since 1967.[4] Today, the area is overcrowded, with an estimated density of 77,464 per square kilometer in this quite small place, and the housing stock varies widely in quality; residents also suffer from an inadequate supply of water, especially in the summer.[5] Children are a vital part of this community. UNRWA has estimated that 60 percent of the population of Aida is under the age of twenty-five.[6] Similarly in 2022, the percentage of Palestinians in the West Bank and Gaza that was fourteen or under was 38 percent.[7]

In 2002, Israeli authorities announced the construction of a structure of separation in the West Bank. The separation wall's path surrounded Aida on two sides. The construction site and then the wall itself have been the target of waves of Palestinian resistance.[8] Today, the wall cuts off Aida from neighboring Palestinian areas as well as treasured open space, and it intensifies the Israeli military presence in Aida. The year 2014 was a time of renewed resistance and a corresponding resurgence in violent Israeli repression. While in 2012, 23 people in Aida were reported injured by the Israeli army, including 2 children under the age of 18, in 2013, 215 people were reported injured, including 49 children, and in 2014, 282 people were reported injured, including 33 children. Israeli arrest raids also increased from 31 in 2012 to 101 in 2013 and 186 in 2014. Aida Camp had suddenly become the focal point of protests in the West Bank.[9] Children have been targets of Israeli violence, and they bear witness to it as well.

I have been visiting and sometimes living in Aida refugee camp since 2003. It was not the primary location of my first major research project on journalism, nor was it the center of analysis for my second research project on the relationship between Palestinian citizens of Israel and Palestinians in the West Bank. Nor is it the place from which my natal family comes. Yet it became an important home for me in Palestine. What responsibilities do anthropologists have to these places that become like home? What responsibilities do Palestinians in diaspora like myself have to Palestinians living under Israeli rule or living in poverty and with few rights as refugees? And what responsibilities does the mother of two children growing up in a comfortable corner of one settler colony have toward children in another much less comfortable place that she loves in another settler colony, where she takes her children for summer vacation?

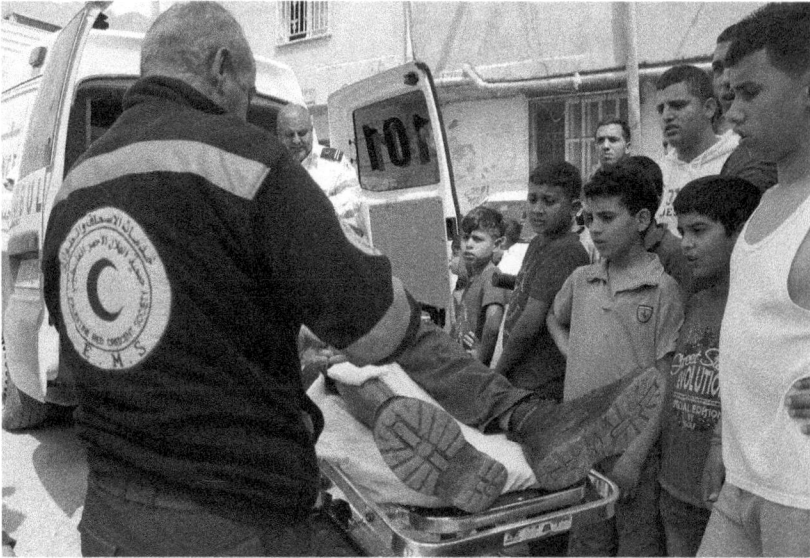

Children look on as a neighbor who has been injured by Israeli fire during a demonstration is wheeled into an ambulance on March 24, 2014.
Photo: Mohammad Al-Azza, used with permission.

My time in Aida is part of a long series of exchanges that only increases my connections—and surely also my obligations—to people there. I do not expect these obligations to ever be fulfilled, not even at the time of Palestinians' liberation. A children's book was a modest attempt that summer to contribute something to the days of Aida's children. It was also an experimental way of carrying out ethnography in a new form, and partially through the wise eyes of Aida's youngest residents. In this article, I continue that experiment, offering parts of this children's book—as well as the story of how it was made—in the less charming form of an academic chapter. I reflect on Palestinian childhood in a refugee camp under military occupation.

Aida Camp is a small location in a larger settler-colonial project, one that operates according to slightly different logics for different Palestinian groups.[10] Israel's settler-colonial project has dispossessed refugees outside of historic Palestine of their land and of their right to return, as established in international law.[11] It systematically discriminates against Palestinians inside Israel—who make up about 20 percent of the population—across all fields of life, including access to land, education, and cultural and political expression.[12] It rules Palestinians in the Occupied Territories with a combination of neglect and force in what Achille Mbembe has called a "late modern colonial occupation."[13] This military occupation has in recent decades operated with the complicity of the Palestinian Authority.[14]

Across these areas, there are differences in how the project of Israeli settler colonialism operates, and yet there is an overarching logic, too. As Patrick Wolfe wrote, "settler colonialism is inherently eliminatory but not invariably genocidal."[15] That is, settler colonialism sometimes operates by killing people and groups, but it also operates by pushing them off lands or by restricting their ability to constitute themselves as a group. The idea that settler colonialism seeks to eliminate groups presses us to attend to the experiences and perspectives of children, since they carry each society through to the next generation. Children not only signify but also embody the future.[16] Indeed, children have been targeted across settler-colonial projects, as by residential schools in the United States, Canada, and Australia that severed connections between children and their communities, and by legal structures and environmental threats. For Palestinian children living under military occupation, threats likewise come in a variety of forms, including high rates of youth imprisonment, Israeli army violence, and the structural violence of poverty that undermines their sense that a vibrant future awaits them. This poverty is a result of dispossession from lands and other Israeli occupation policies.

We made the children's book at Lajee Center, a home for politically engaged creativity in Aida Camp. One of at least three youth-oriented community-based organizations in Aida, Lajee Center was founded in 2000 by former political prisoners who had concerns that the Palestinian Authority's establishment in 1994 meant the end of the kind of vibrant grassroots politics that had yielded the first intifada, a society-wide uprising against Israeli occupation from 1987 to 1993. Lajee Center houses a library, a dance troupe, a musical ensemble, a media unit, and an environmental unit, each led by Palestinian staff, in almost all cases from Aida Camp. Nonpartisan and nonprofit, Lajee Center has given me and many other visiting internationals a space to meet people and learn about the community. As time went on, it also gave me a space for deep collaboration with people from whom I had learned a great deal. In 2004, I worked with children and adult volunteers at Lajee Center to make a bilingual children's book entitled *The Boy and the Wall*.[17] Modeled on the classic American children's book *The Runaway Bunny*, it was a dialogue between a mother and son that was meant to speak to readers about Palestinian traditions and ingenuities of resistance, as well as our maternal love.[18] For that book, I wrote the words and worked with children to create collage illustrations. A decade later, having been thinking ethnographically about Aida refugee camp for years and impressed by the burgeoning activities with young children led by the Lajee Center librarian, I wanted to help make something even more collaborative.

I wanted to work with children to make a children's book for other reasons, too. Working in conditions of harshly militarized settler colonialism, I felt the urge to contribute to something concrete. For years, I had been buoyed by news that *The Boy in the Wall* was still in demand. Visitors to Lajee Center often bought it, and it had won an award. A new book, I thought, would be a modest income generator for Lajee Center. It would help for children in Aida to see their community dignified through a representation that they helped to make, one that neither had a single-minded focus on Israeli occupation nor sugarcoated life in Aida—one that was, like they often were, matter-of-fact about the violence they faced every day but that also recognized the vitality of their community. On a personal level, managing the violence and racism of Israeli rule—both while doing fieldwork and while reflecting on it while in the United States—was also challenging. Creative work seemed to be a way of processing this ugliness and expanding my intellectual and creative horizons. Additionally, I wanted my daughter to have a window into life in Aida even when we left loved ones behind to return to our home in the United States. A bilingual Arabic alphabet book—a compendium of things you might find in Aida if you visited—seemed a perfect way to juxtapose the camp's strange co-presence of small daily pleasures and truly horrible forms of violence. An alphabet book was a way of centering the Arabic language, while also making the book welcoming and accessible to outsiders.[19]

The children's book and this chapter attempt a decolonizing anthropology in several ways.[20] Creating this children's book made space for collaboration among children, and between children and community members. The book centers their experiences and their language and is rooted in their everyday lives. It builds power by connecting people and building voice and trust, like other successful processes of media production in such youth centers.[21] This chapter, for its part, aims to disrupt dominant ways of knowing Palestinian refugee camps. Too often, when news articles report on Israeli violence, they do so by citing official Israeli press releases alongside those of Palestinian officials or NGOs. We can produce other forms of knowledge that attend to the local lived realities of dispossession. As we realize that states are not going to listen to our policy advice, because they simply do not have the best interests of communities in mind, scholars committed to justice can work to build community resources and to educate others who might work in solidarity to stand up to power. Both the book and this chapter also seek to recognize ways in which we can produce cultural representations that act in the world. We inherit and treasure traditions, and we also can reinterpret them on our own terms to strive toward multiple liberations.

During the summer of 2014, Israel's ferocious war on Gaza raged. In 51 days, Israeli attacks killed 2,251 Palestinians. Of the 1,462 Palestinian civilians killed, 299 were women and 551 were children; Palestinian fighting and rockets killed 67

Israeli soldiers and 6 Israeli civilians.[22] The war devastated Palestinian schools, hospitals, homes, and infrastructure in Gaza. In the West Bank, many people watched the horrific videos on television, and then took to the streets to protest. The Israeli army was right outside Lajee Center's door to repress protests, as youth and children gathered to make our book.

We had started our work right after the children's school exams finished in midsummer—late because of the winter UNRWA teachers' strike. First, led by Lajee Center's librarian, Kifah Al-Ajarma, we brainstormed by letter a list of objects and ideas relevant to the camp. The children came up with the great variety of words. Some were a source of pride and some of pain, some mundane and others related to Palestinian heritage, some abstractly political and some quite concretely so. We also asked grownups from Aida for their ideas for each letter. In the end, I curated the final list of words and wrote their descriptions for the book in Arabic and English. Putting all of these suggestions together to create a portrait of the camp to which the children could relate was a puzzle that I could only approach because of my years of experience in and following news of Aida refugee camp.

Then we started planning the collages. On the first day, we learned how to cut and paste to make paper people, with the help of my mother, a retired kindergarten teacher, and two American volunteers, high school students with a background in art. Then, throughout our month of workshops, the children took that simple template and made paper people who were tall and small, serious and funny, traditional and downright funky. Some of the children excelled in the close work of cutting out letters for the people's T-shirts, mirroring the political T-shirts commonly worn around Aida. Children stayed late to cut out dozens of tiny leaves for an olive tree, or to glue their work onto the pages. Everyone enjoyed making the colorful Palestinian *thawb* embroidered dresses, the laughing balloons, and their own versions of the famous Palestinian child political cartoon figure, Handala. A ten-year-old girl learned to cut out hearts and then did not want to stop.

Because Lajee Center has a thriving media center in which teenagers and children had been learning photography for a decade, we relied on Lajee Center's photography archive for reference. When we wanted to make a traditional Palestinian house, for example, we looked to a photograph of a house from a pre-1948 village, taken the one time in the mid-2000s when Lajee Center applied for and received permits from Israel for children to visit their families' ancestral villages. The children seemed to not need a visual prompt for the strikingly realistic soldiers whom they see, all too often, on their afternoon walks home from school.

We worked without food or drink during Ramadan on hot afternoons, and we worked after Ramadan over juice and pretzels. We saved scraps of paper not just to be economical but also because, well, who knew what they might inspire? We turned off the fan so that it wouldn't blow away our fine works in progress. We posted pictures of our fun on Facebook. Here, I present a slightly more grownup version of parts of our alphabetical ethnography, mostly in Arabic alphabetical order. The sentences in block quotes are taken directly from the book, while the accompanying paragraphs are my elaboration. Our story time for grownups seeks to teach you a bit more about Aida refugee camp and also to invite you into a child's perspective on life there. You can see how children are at the center of a Palestinian politics of insisting on survival.

Nūn Is for *Nakba*, Catastrophe

> Nūn is for *Nakba*, the big *catastrophe* of 1948 that displaced our grandparents and brought us to Aida, and the smaller catastrophes of violence and dispossession that we live every day. And nūn is for *niḍāl*, our *struggles* big and small for justice.

The letter nūn comes near the end of the alphabet, but the Nakba is what created the refugee crisis, and so in this chapter it comes first. Palestinian children in Aida refugee camp come from thirty-five different ancestral villages, some of which are just a twenty-minute drive away but are utterly inaccessible due to Israel's system of closure. Still in many of those villages are the houses—or remains of houses—where the children's grandparents and great-grandparents lived before they were forced to flee upon the establishment of the state of Israel in 1948. This is the Nakba, one of the foundational moments in modern Palestinian history and a pivotal event advancing Israeli settler colonialism. During this time, approximately 750,000 Palestinians became refugees and over four hundred Palestinian villages were depopulated.[23] This is what eventually brought these children's grandparents and great-grandparents to Aida as refugees.

Yet the Nakba is not a thing of history. Patrick Wolfe reminds us, "settler colonizers come to stay: invasion is a structure not an event."[24] Palestinians have an expression to make the same point: "*al-nakba mustamirra,*" or the Nakba is ongoing. Children in Aida of a certain age are likely to have heard this phrase. But even if they do not know the phrase, they know what it means: that their lives and safety are continuously under threat, that everyday comforts are fleeting, that they can expect less from life, in virtually every domain, than the Jewish Israelis who live in sight of some of their homes in the settlement of Gilo just a few kilometers away. They will have less water, less clean air, less space, poorer schools, much less security.[25]

Still, the children's familiarity with the term *Nakba* itself represents a kind of victory. One of the things of which Palestinians have been largely dispossessed has been the usual national institutions of collective history, such as archives and museums.[26] So children learn the history of the term *Nakba* through the annual Nakba Day, commemorated on May 15 of each year. Each spring, new T-shirts appear in adult and children's sizes, calling attention to the history of dispossession in 1948 and the as yet unfulfilled right of Palestinian refugees to return home, as established in UN Resolution 194. These T-shirts are immediate visual markers of history that even the youngest can grasp, as people around them all start wearing the same shirt. In Aida Camp, public commemorations often involve youth, as in Lajee Center's annual kite-flying contest that sees dozens of kites flying high above the camp and even above the separation wall. Recently, a "train of return" has also become an important part of the commemorations. These popular activities make history tangible for children, and they make it possible for children to participate in ways that are engaging and rewarding. So it is that the catastrophe, Nakba, is nevertheless connected to struggle, *niḍāl*, for these Palestinians. These commemorations are only one face of Palestinians' ongoing, active struggle for justice and for a better life. This is why the illustration for this page highlighted Palestinians' resistance to erasure as they participated in a demonstration waving the Palestinian flag.

Jīm Is for *Jidār*, Wall

Jīm is for *jidār*, the *wall* that looms over our homes, and *jaysh*,
the *army* that comes in *jeyāb*, *jeeps*, to terrorize and arrest.

The illustration for this page is of Israeli soldiers standing next to their jeeps, guns pointed in the direction of the houses of the camp against a backdrop of tear gas. One of the most conspicuous instruments of Palestinians' ongoing dispossession in Aida is the separation wall, which, in this area, is eight meters tall and made of concrete. The wall in Aida is part of a barrier that stretches more than seven hundred kilometers within the West Bank and on the Green Line that delineates the West Bank. Here, the Nakba is ongoing also in terms of limiting the space in which Palestinians live and the quality of that space. Those most directly affected by the path of the wall in this area were never consulted. Instead, youth protested throughout the period of construction, delaying completion of the wall until 2005 with their determined resistance.

Then, the wall cut Aida Camp off from a field of olive trees that leads to Jerusalem. Unlike in villages where Palestinians lost vitally important agricultural land, residents did not own this land. Instead, it is owned by a church. This meant that residents could not raise a case against the Israeli government. However, they had strong connections to this place. It is said that in the years after the camp was established, a woman had a café located in the olive grove. Her name had been Aida—a name that means "one who is returning." The camp, people say, was named after her and her café, with the powerful resonance of the right to return. In the years before the wall was built, residents had been paid by the church to tend the olive grove. Residents had also used this land as a soccer field or even to do homework when their houses were too crowded, or they did not have electricity. This sense of space and even of local history was lost with the building of the wall. As one adult put it early in the years of the wall's construction, "The wall will be a project of forgetting."[27] The wall also cut Aida off from other neighborhoods in Bethlehem, making it feel more isolated from the rest of the town.

Another major consequence of the wall has been to militarize space in Aida Camp, bringing the Israeli army into much more regular contact with Palestinians there. The wall is no neutral infrastructure; it is offensive, endangering. This is why the combination of words for the letter "jīm" (jidār, wall; jaysh, army; jeyāb, jeeps) goes beyond an alliterative logic. Embedded in the wall's structure are five watchtowers and a military base, from which soldiers regularly enter Aida to conduct raids. Soon after the wall was completed, in 2006, Meras, aged twelve, was playing on his uncle's veranda with his siblings and cousins when an Israeli soldier shot him with live ammunition in the stomach.[28] The soldiers involved were never held accountable; instead, just days after he returned from the hospital, they raided his house in the middle of the night, bringing the terror of military occupation inside the home once more. Stories like these were one reason that residents in the camp came to develop a new sense. They are able to tell you, without looking, when they are in the line of fire of an army watchtower.

Salah Ajarma, then executive director of Lajee Center and a lifelong resident of Aida, explained the Israeli army presence in the camp as follows: "The presence of Rachel's Tomb military base and the watchtower close to a population center creates a confrontation point at which youth resist the presence of the occupation. The army comes on calm days to incite violence, too. They know this is a neglected area. Their incursions are also sometimes training for the army."[29] In Aida, the streets can seem to belong to children, who make up such a large proportion of the population. Children while away hours chatting or playing street soccer after school; they walk to buy a falafel sandwich. All of these ordinary activities become more dangerous because of the wall.

In response to decades of dispossession and militarization, residents of Aida Camp, similar to residents of many other Palestinian refugee camps, have launched waves of resistance, even after the Israeli army completed the wall. During fall 2012 protests of an Israeli attack on Gaza, Aida teenagers realized that the fires they lit next to the wall as cover against the army were degrading the concrete of the wall. It was an improvisatory revolt of necessity. They became determined to break the wall down. In January 2013, they succeeded in punctur-ing the wall, making an opening wide enough for a child to pass through. This boy was, momentarily, an honorary emissary to Jerusalem. Though he turned back quickly, and though the Israeli army swiftly closed the hole in the wall, this story is remembered by some youth as one of momentary liberation, alongside the time when, just after the wall was completed, a sixteen-year-old built a ladder and used it to hoist a flag above the wall,[30] or when another teenager hoisted the Palestinian flag atop the structure during the 2012 protests.

But the protest movement of 2012 had a high cost, and this, too, fell heav-ily on children. Days after protesters successfully breached the wall, on January 18, 2013, an Israeli soldier shot fifteen-year-old Saleh Al-Amareen in the head with live ammunition. There had been protests that day, but Saleh, who was un-armed, was killed in a quiet moment. He surely posed no threat to the soldiers. He died a week later. Instead of holding the shooter accountable, Israel rescinded the work permit upon which his father had relied to reach construction jobs in Israel. Saleh is remembered in dozens of stencils on the walls of both Aida Camp and Al-Azza Camp, the nearby refugee camp where Saleh lived. Two years af-ter he died, youth continued their memorializations of Saleh, as two teenagers, friends of Al-Amareen, painted a mural on his home.[31]

Two and a half years later, another child would be shot just a few meters away, from the same military base embedded in the same cruel wall. On October 5, 2015, an Israeli soldier shot Abed Ar-Rahman Shadi Obeidallah, thirteen, in the chest. The Israeli soldier had been standing in the gate of the military base em-bedded in the separation wall at Aida. Abed Ar-Rahman, or Abed, was standing about 70 meters away, not participating in protests, his backpack still on his back from school.[32] The detail of the backpack came up often in accounts of his death. It indicated his lack of involvement in protests: Who can throw a stone well with a backpack strapped to his back? But it was also a symbol of his youth, of his fam-ily's hopes for his future.

When he was shot, Abed had been standing next to a United Nations flag that hangs from the UNRWA services building in Aida. He was also underneath a gi-ant key that symbolizes Palestinian refugees' right to return to the villages from which they were displaced in 1948. For residents of Aida, the symbolism was un-mistakable: The international system of human rights had not protected Abed. Only return—a restoration of rights—would secure the safety of these refugees.

A soldier standing in the gate of the wall had shot Abed with a .22-caliber Ruger rifle designed for "riot dispersal." This is a model that is supposed to be less lethal. A senior IDF officer described the shooting as "unintentional."[33] Shadi Obeidallah, Abed's father, responded to the officer's comment with incredulity in a phone interview with me just days after his son had been killed: "How can they kill an innocent child and say it was unintentional? The sniper aimed at him. He was assassinated."[34] What threat could he have posed in any case? The soldiers could have just closed their heavy metal gate, or left the outpost altogether.

Abed's family set up the mourning tent at the site where he was shot. Thousands of people came to mourn Abed, said the director of Lajee Center, Salah Al-Ajarma. He himself had helped carry young Abed's body during the funeral procession. But, he said, some international NGO representatives had waited for permission from their offices to come to Aida. Aida was considered too dangerous to visit. This exasperated him. "Our families and our children live in danger," said Al-Ajarma, "though we strive to live a normal life."[35]

At times like this, though, that all seems to be at risk. Amani Asad, then the director of a human rights education program at Lajee Center, witnessed Abed's shooting from Lajee Center's balcony. She reflected, "We teach children about human rights, and they are aware, but they know these rights have been robbed from them. No right to security, to life, even to education."[36] The schools in Aida refugee camp were closed for a few days after Abed's death. UNRWA officials gave the explanation that they could not guarantee children's safety. Lajee Center, too, cancelled its activities for a week. Nevertheless, they took over seventy children to the mourning tent to pay their condolences to Abed's family. This cohesiveness carries them all through unbearable times. But coming home from the last day of mourning, Shadi, Abed's father, recognized the grief that would stay with him. The atmosphere had been supportive, but now the family was home on their own. "It is extremely painful," he said. "It's a disaster."[37]

Ḥā Is for *Hisān*, Horse

Ḥā is for *ḥurriya*, the *freedom* for which we struggle, and for
ḥiṣān, a *horse*, racing through our *ḥāra*, *neighborhood*!

We based our illustration for this page on a photograph taken a few years earlier by a young man who learned photography at Lajee Center. Only a local photographer would have caught the moment: a boy riding a horse on a main street of the camp, just in front of the separation wall. The boy is blurred with speed, the wall is solid, gray. A horse in a refugee camp? When he was thirteen, a resident of Aida Camp, Anan, had pleaded with his father to buy him a horse. His father had obliged, even though space was tight. Anan raced down the street between the houses and the wall. He charged kids a few shekels for a ride. The ḥāra, or neighborhood, is, after all, the space of so many escapades. The excitement hardly lasted a few weeks before the impracticality of the arrangement set in, and they gave the horse back. For me, the photo, taken by Mohammad Al-Azza of the Lajee Center Media Unit (and now the director of Lajee Center), has always been

This image of a boy riding a horse near the separation wall is from the series "Behind the Screen," which explored the politics of representation of Aida Camp. Photo: Mohammad Al-Azza, used with permission.

"Ḥā is for *Hisān*, horse," from *The Aida Camp Alphabet*. Courtesy of Lajee Center.

about the whimsy of youth, about how swiftly it passes, about how elusive freedom can feel in places like Aida, and about the neighborhood, a site of possibility despite it all. Our alphabet page was inspired by the photograph, a reminder of the gifts a community center bequeaths year after year.

Dāl Is for *Dālia*, Grapevine

Dāl is for *dālia* the *grapevine* over the patio where my family celebrates
graduations and engagements, where we greet you when you
come to visit and where we will say goodbye to you at the end of
your trip. And dāl is for *dardasha*, *chatting* for hours on end.

Our children's book featured a lot of fruits. Tā was for *tīn, tūt,* and *tufāḥ*—figs, mulberries, and apples, because some of the most spacious gardens in the camp do manage to have a fruit tree or two. As a serendipitous effect of the overcrowding, the edges of the trees become communal. A giant fig tree overhangs a garden wall, so that everyone may enjoy its great fuzzy leaves and then, if they are lucky, in July or August they might reach a ripe fig.

But perhaps no plant in Palestine signifies communality like a grapevine—a verdant, living hearth that nourishes in more ways than one. Our illustration for this page showed a grapevine like this, with two children sitting under it, arms around each other's shoulders. While social problems are on the rise in Aida as in many Palestinian communities, intergenerational family cohesion continues to play a positive role in promoting resilience in the face of trauma after trauma.[38] Often, three or even four generations live around a shared patio, and if a family is lucky, a grapevine will provide this veranda with shade. Large extended families are a social focus for children growing up with many cousins, and the veranda is where the bulk of summer socializing occurs, whether in the rhythm of the everyday rounds of fruit and tea or for special occasions when long tables are extended for a shared meal. Sometimes, family members sit under the grapevine to stuff its leaves with rice and spices, making the traditional Palestinian dish of *waraq diwāli.* The vines can live for generations, and people even graft vines from their pre-1948 villages onto vines in the camp. In this sense, the grapevines themselves are an element of continuity. Our image celebrated that communal family space, and it also celebrated cousins who are like best friends and best friends who are like cousins—like the two boys who worked on this page, who once had me snap a photo of them, with their arms slung happily around each other's shoulders, that looked strikingly like the cut paper image they had made.

"Dāl is for *dālia*, grapevine," from *The Aida Camp Alphabet*. Courtesy of Lajee Center.

Children pose with their artwork. Photo: Amahl Bishara.

Dhāl Is for *Dhaki*, Smart

Dhāl is for *dhaki, smart*. My father says we are smart because
we study, we watch the world around us, and we listen to
the *dhikrayāt, memories*, of our grandparents.

How to capture the specific cleverness of children in Aida? Many, like other Palestinian children, clamber for good grades in school, where a rigid grading system begins in elementary school and continues through the national *tawjīhī* high
school exams that determine young adults' educational pathways. While these
exams can be stultifying, education has long been a strength of Palestinian refugees, as for other Palestinians. UNRWA has run primary education for children
for decades, and Palestinians in the West Bank and Gaza have a high literacy rate
relative to the region, with refugees having an even higher rate than other Palestinians.[39] Palestinian refugees have long hoped that education of various kinds
will help them overcome the great national losses they have endured.[40]

But the cleverness of children in Aida goes beyond schooling. In Aida, childhood is not—cannot be—apolitical. Families prize a child's ability to confront the
army—with a word, a look, or a stone—alongside success at school and being a
kind and helpful sibling, child, and grandchild. Children learn by watching what
happens around them and learn—all too early, it is certain—the blunt logic of Israeli occupation, which relies entirely on force. They, too, help narrate the story
of the only home they have known. In a video produced through Lajee Center, a young girl introduces herself as she provides the voiceover for the video:
"My name is Shahd Awais and I live in Aida refugee camp. My family is originally from the village of Allar. What I love most about the camp is that here I am
holding onto my land. I am always defending it in my own way."[41] Shahd plays
the *qānūn*, akin to a zither, in the Lajee Center music troupe, and her generation
conceives of their musical practice as a kind of cultural resistance. They perform
at Mother's Day celebrations and memorials, and they make music videos honoring political prisoners. The more experienced musicians teach the younger ones.
Musical cohesion and social cohesion amplify each other.

Children also learn about their own histories through community resources.
They listen to elders in their community who tell stories of pre-1948 villages and
the crops their families used to grow. Or parents tell of earlier times of resistance
like the first intifada. Historical knowledge comes not only from home but also
from the streets themselves. On one wall on the edge of the camp stretches a series of murals, one from each of the pre-1948 villages from which camp residents
come. Another mural tells the story of refugees' dispossession and resistance,
with panels on life before 1948, becoming refugees, building the camp, and engaging in protests. The last panel quotes a poem by the beloved Palestinian poet

Mahmoud Darwish: "If the olive trees knew the hands that planted them, their oil would become tears." From all of these sources, children gain not only an understanding of their pasts, but also a sense that another world is possible.

Sīn Is for *Sijn*, Prison

Sīn is for *sijn*, *prison*, but it is also for *sillam*,
ladder, and for the *samā'*, *sky*, above.

Bullets are not the only thieves of childhood in Aida refugee camp. Imprisonment steals youth, and steals loved ones from children, too.[42] Over the last ten years, the number of Palestinian children incarcerated by Israel has ranged from a high of over 470 in 2015 to a low of 126 in 2021.[43] In 2017, Lajee Center staff counted seventy-six people from Aida Camp in Israeli prisons, including many teenagers. These numbers belie the specific kinds of pain entailed in each story of arrest. At about nine at night after a series of protests on September 2, 2015, Fares, who sells vegetables in the camp, heard a single gunshot. Neighbors rushed to tell him the Israelis had taken his fourteen-year-old son, Anan, just after they had shot him. This was the boy who had once insisted on a horse. Alarmed, he and his wife hurried out. A crowd had gathered near the giant key, but their son was gone.

The next day, he told me, his wife and he applied for and received military permits to visit Anan in Hadassah hospital, in Israel. Yet when they arrived, they were not permitted into his room. Only three days later were they allowed to see him for a few minutes. In the coming months, they saw him only from a few meters away at a series of court sessions. His mother admits to being tearful during these brief encounters, and she felt guilty about it. "Mother, you're killing me with your tears," he told her. "I stay awake weeping as I think of your tears."[44] He marked his fifteenth birthday in the prison hospital, alone.

Anan is one of dozens of children from Aida who have been imprisoned in recent years. Most often they are taken from their homes in the middle of the night, but sometimes they are arrested from the street, as was Anan. In any case, Israel almost always holds them in prison while their case is being processed. In general, over 99 percent of Palestinians are found guilty in Israeli military courts.[45]

In one of those brief encounters with his parents while he was under arrest, Anan directed his father to a stash of money in his room. He had saved 500 shekels—about $130—toward buying another horse. Now, he told his father, this should go toward the fine his family would inevitably pay Israel in order to lighten his sentence. After their long pretrial detentions, Palestinians often buy out some prison time by paying around 1,000 shekels per month.[46] How much would you pay for a month of childhood for a young person dear to you?

Shīn Is for *Sha'b*, the People

Shīn is for *sha'b*, the *people*, and *shi'ārāt*, *graffiti*.

Yes, and shīn is also, as it turns out, for *shi'ba*, or slingshot. On this page of our book and one other, there are protesters holding slingshots of one kind or another against a backdrop of graffiti written on the separation wall. In so many "calls for proposals" from European and American grant-making organizations, Palestinian NGO workers read language asking for projects for Palestinians that will support women and children and promote peace and nonviolence.[47] In Aida, where the violence of the occupation presses down on everyone, every day, the value of nonviolence is abstract. Palestinians often speak of their right under international law to resist a foreign occupation. Rather than reifying nonviolence,[48] many residents of the camp instead focused on the key term *muqawama sha'biya*, or popular resistance. The word popular, sha'biya, is related to the word for "the people," al-sha'b. Popular resistance is part of a Palestinian heritage of resistance that goes back to the British Mandate and earlier.[49] In current iterations, it involves confronting soldiers—with their armored jeeps and automatic rifles—with stones and fireworks. For many Palestinians in Aida, the morality of this resistance is clear, even if community members worry about how these protests could escalate due to the grossly disproportionate use of violence by Israeli soldiers in response.

"Shīn is for *sha'b*, the people," from *The Aida Camp Alphabet*. Courtesy of Lajee Center.

So it was that our book would not bracket out these forms of resistance. While youth activities at community centers can sometimes seem to be part of a counterrevolutionary strategy for keeping youth busy and quiet, this page presented a different opportunity for children to present their community to outsiders in a way that recognized the complexity of their situation and their place in long-standing Palestinian traditions. Demonstrations are as Palestinian as *kufiyyas* (see kāf) or Palestinian embroidery (see thā, *thawb*).

Ṭā Is for *Ṭabla*

Ṭā is for *ṭabla*, a *drum* that helps us sing old songs and make up new ones. We gather, we sing, we stomp, we dance! We giggle, we clap, we wink, we chant!

For this simple illustration, hands moved over a *doumbek* goblet drum. Whether on a daytrip to a nearby spring or on a bus ride to or from the destination, after a long lunch during a summer camp or even passed around at home, the age-old combination of a drum and a group of children will, in so many circumstances, instantly constitute a party. Drums suit these impromptu gatherings: inexpensive, durable, portable, loud. The repertoire of songs is familiar for the children: "Wayn 'A Ramallah" or "'Ala Dal'una," Palestinian songs that celebrate place, love, and rhythm itself. But just as often, a drummer will start with a simple rhyme that veers somewhere new.

Ghayn Is for *Ghāz*, Tear Gas

Ghayn is for *ghasīl*, *ghuyūm*, and *ghāz*—laundry, the *clouds*, and *tear gas*. And ghayn is for *ghaza*, Gaza.

Our illustration for this page showed laundry strung out to dry on a clothesline. A T-shirt had the word "Gaza" painstakingly cut out from construction paper and pasted onto it; another read "1948." Above the clothesline were spirals of tear gas in a stark black and white stripe against gray clouds. Israel's attack on Gaza darkened everything during the summer of 2014. It was a dreadful season in Aida, as too many children watched so much death rain down on a Palestinian community just an hour away. Meanwhile, outside their own doorsteps was a near constant, active, boots-on-the-ground Israeli military presence. If watchtowers and the threat of an Israeli arrest raid or training excursion always loomed, now the soldiers were in the streets every day. A coalition of local community organizations prepared ways for children to support Palestinians in Gaza and express their solidarity. On the first day of Eid al-Fitr, which should be one of the most festive days of the year, children showed up early in the morning to paint on a wall in the camp the names of children in Gaza who had perished in

"Ghayn is for *ghāz*, tear gas," from *The Aida Camp Alphabet.* Courtesy of Lajee Center.

the war. On another afternoon, children participated in a drive for donations of money and water to be sent to Gaza.

Lajee Center's summer camp was also scheduled to occur during the war. Parents and children rely on the camp as an annual activity that breaks up the long summer vacation. But this summer, how could children enjoy themselves while they knew that other children so close to them were losing their homes, their schools, their families, and even their lives? The Lajee Center T-shirt usually bears its logo, but in 2014, Lajee Center printed T-shirts that declared in calligraphy a line from Mahmoud Darwish's poetry: "On this earth is what makes life worth living." It was a bold and optimistic declaration.

One day during the camp, a girl came to me complaining that her face was burning. I immediately thought of the tear gas that the soldiers catapulted toward the camp almost daily, sometimes to repress protests and sometimes for no apparent reason. But I was perplexed: Soldiers had shot no tear gas that day. Perhaps, I suggested, it was a particularly strong sunscreen? Or, I inquired, had she eaten something spicy and rubbed her eyes? No on both accounts, she said with some confusion. She said she had been playing in the dirt in Lajee's treasured playground. The amount of tear gas in the environment was so great that it had soaked into the ground around us. Recent research finds that Aida is one of the most intensively tear-gassed places in the world.[50] Israel uses tear gas in such quantities that it sometimes hangs above the houses, mingling with the drying laundry (ghasīl) in what could be mistaken for a cloud (*ghayma*). The horrific intensity of hot war, as was happening in Gaza, is one face of Israel's rule, described by human rights monitors as disproportionate warfare in violation of international laws of war. Tear gas is a metonym for another face of the violence of the ongoing occupation: relentless and pervasive, damaging to physical and psychological health, a kind of violence that both hits you all at once and accumulates over time, settling into every outdoor surface.[51]

Kāf Is for *Kufiyya*

Kāf is for *ka'k*, yummy *sesame bread* that reminds us of
Jerusalem, and it is for *kufiyya*, the world-famous Palestinian
scarf that you can see in Aida every single day.

How were we to manage evoking both pride in tradition and sadness over the ongoing threats to tradition, two sentiments that coexist for so many Palestinians? Most of the children who made the book had never been to Jerusalem's Old City, though it is only a twenty-minute drive away. Because their parents required difficult-to-obtain permits to go to Jerusalem, most children had never seen holy sites like the Al-Aqsa Mosque, nor had they eaten the famous Jerusalem ka'k.[52] Kufiyyas, on the other hand, they draped around their necks. Kufiyyas were iconic—in posters and on television—and everyday, often worn for warmth or wrapped carefully around a demonstrator's face as cover. Our picture showed the rounds of ka'k and the distinct black and white pattern of a kufiyya in a pairing of an element of Palestinian tradition that was inaccessible and another that they often saw in their own neighborhood.

Lām Is for *Lajee*, Refugee

Lām is for *lajee*. Being *refugees* means we lost our homes long
ago, but also that we have the right to go back to them. We carry
old keys and make new ones to express our right to return.

For this page, we assembled a collage of keys, a Palestinian symbol of the right of Palestinian refugees to return to their villages. In Palestinian society, there can be a subtle hierarchy of city and village people over those living in refugee camps.[53] But Palestinian activists work hard to ease the stigma associated with the term "refugee." Through such commemorations as Nakba Day, Palestinians reappropriate the term to stand for an assertion of rights, including the right to return. The sense that young and old Palestinians are equally committed to return comes through in the Lajee-produced video "What Will You Do When You Go Back to

Your Village?"[54] The giant key hanging over the entrance to Aida has also become an icon for Palestinian refugees in Aida and beyond. One of the subtle goals of the children's book, from my perspective as an anthropologist and activist who is committed to recognizing and communicating to children that we should not let tradition be a hegemonic force, but rather an inspiration for each generation, was to let children use these nationalist symbols and tropes in their own ways. So for our book, we asked children to make their own keys to symbolize the right of return. Every child could make a key, just as each child held onto that right of return. For another page, children made their own versions of Handala, and imagined them walking over the hills to cities and villages in an act of return.

Mīm Is for *Markaz Lajee*, Lajee Center

Mīm is for *Markaz Lajee, Lajee Center*, and many things we have at Lajee: *maktaba, library, mal'ab*, a *soccer field, murjeha*, a *swing set*, and *muṣawirīn, photographers*. We even have the poet Mahmoud Darwish!

The letter mīm comes near the end of the alphabet, and this offered a chance for us to reflect on the place at the center of our book, Markaz Lajee. NGOs have been regarded as depoliticizing forces that can mask structural problems, and this certainly can be the case for Palestinian NGOs, too.[55] Still, I have found that savvy and small Palestinian organizations can create spaces for civil society to thrive. Palestinians in the West Bank can build and strengthen local institutions to counter Israeli settler-colonial violence and even to challenge the related repression of the Palestinian Authority.[56] Community-based organizations play an especially important role for children in refugee camps, whose UNRWA schools are financially and often politically constrained in their ability to address issues regarded as controversial by the donor community.[57] Parents can also be stretched thin by poverty, imprisonment, and long work hours. With Palestinian children—and even the possibility of Palestinian childhood itself—under attack in so many ways, Lajee Center and youth organizations like it throughout the Occupied Territories insist on preserving a public space for Palestinian childhood.[58] In our collage for the letter mīm page, it was impossible to fit in elements that pointed to all of the facets of Lajee Center's work. But we made sure to put Mahmoud Darwish, the famous poet, on a swing. Palestinian icons should feel accessible to refugee youth—and everyone should have the chance to play.

As we made our book during the terrifying summer of 2014, the shadow of the deaths in Gaza hung over us. The Israeli army loomed too close to the building where we worked. On many afternoons, we closed our windows so that the tear gas would not come into the library where we snipped and glued. We tried to muffle the bursts of sound grenades and bullets shot by the Israeli army. Some-

One of the artists holding the swing set with the poet Mahmoud
Darwish perched on a swing. Photo: Amahl Bishara.

times we had to wait to send the children home until the soldiers returned to
their military base or the situation calmed. Sometimes we had to convince the
children to stay with us to finish the page we were working on rather than joining
the protests. But more often, the children were happy to work together for those
few hours, making slingshots, or fruit, or cats, or friends sitting arm in arm, just
like they did. This, too, we all hoped, would contribute to our community and
reclaim a distinctly Palestinian childhood.

NOTES

1. Shammas, "Stone's Throw."
2. Shalhoub-Kevorkian, *Incarcerated Childhood*.
3. Lajee Center, *The Aida Camp Alphabet*.
4. United Nations Relief and Works Agency (UNRWA), "Aida Camp," https://www
.unrwa.org/where-we-work/west-bank/aida-camp; "Where We Work: West Bank,"
https://www.unrwa.org/where-we-work/west-bank.
5. United Nations Relief and Works Agency (UNRWA), "Aida Camp," https://www
.unrwa.org/where-we-work/west-bank/aida-camp; Al-Azza, *Everyday Nakba*; and Bishara et al., "Multifaceted Outcomes."
6. UNRWA, "Aida Refugee Camp," n.d.
7. Palestinian Central Bureau of Statistics, "PCBS Presents the Conditions of Palestin-

ian Populations on the Occasion of the International Population Day," https://www
.pcbs.gov.ps/portals/_pcbs/PressRelease/Press_En_InterPopDay2022E.pdf.

8. Bishara, "An Ongoing Violence, a Sustained Resistance."

9. UNRWA, "Profile: Aida Camp, Bethlehem Governorate," https://www.unrwa.org
/sites/default/files/aida_refugee_camp.pdf.

10. Bishara, *Crossing a Line;* Lloyd, "Settler Colonialism and the State"; Lustick, *Unsettled States, Disputed Lands*; Rouhana and Sabbagh-Khoury, "Settler-Colonial Citizenship"; Salamanca et al., "Past Is Present"; and Zureik, *The Palestinians in Israel.*

11. Sa'di and Abu-Lughod, *Nakba*; and Akram, "Palestinian Refugees."

12. Rouhana and Sabbagh-Khoury, "Settler-Colonial Citizenship"; Robinson, *Citizen Strangers*; Zureik, *The Palestinians in Israel*; and Shihade, "Settler Colonialism and Conflict."

13. Mbembe, "Necropolitics."

14. Mustafa, "Damming the Palestinian Spring"; Sayigh, "Policing the People, Building the State."

15. Wolfe, "Settler Colonialism," 387.

16. Razack, "Race and Unchilding."

17. Lajee Center, *The Boy and the Wall.*

18. Brown, *The Runaway Bunny.*

19. Young and old should also read Bashi and Nafisi's *P is for Palestine* for another beautiful Palestinian alphabet book.

20. Bishara, "Decolonizing Middle East Anthropology"; Harrison, *Decolonizing Anthropology.*

21. Norman, "Creative Activism."

22. Human Rights Council, "Report of the Independent Commission."

23. Sa'di and Abu-Lughod, *Nakba*; Khalidi, *All That Remains.*

24. Wolfe, "Settler Colonialism and the Elimination of the Native," 388.

25. Bishara et al., "Multifaceted Outcomes"; Bishara, "An Ongoing Violence, a Sustained Resistance"; Haar and Ghannam, "No Safe Space"; UNRWA, "Profile: Aida Camp, Bethlehem Governorate."

26. See Abu-Lughod, "Imagining Palestine's Alter-Natives."

27. Bishara and Al-Azraq, *Degrees of Incarceration.*

28. For more details on this case, see Saed Bannoura, "Child Seriously Injured in Aida Refugee Camp," International Middle East Media Center, December 8, 2006, https://imemc.org/article/23114/.

29. Interview conducted October 8, 2015, by phone. For more on the history of Rachel's Tomb, see Bowman, "Weeping on the Road."

30. His story was featured in a video called *Ali Wall*, which can be viewed at: https://www.youtube.com/watch?v=xk2CoYREDIU&t=182s.

31. Shams, "2 Years after Youth Shot."

32. DCI Palestine, "Palestinian Boy Shot Dead."

33. Harel, "Killing of Palestinian Youth."

34. Interview conducted October 10, 2015, by phone.

35. Interview conducted October 8, 2015, by phone.

36. Interview conducted October 8, 2015, by phone.

37. Interview conducted October 10, 2015, by phone.

38. Atallah, "A Community-Based Qualitative Study."

39. Alghoul, "Defying Odds."

40. Fasheh, "Community Education"; and Hallaj, "Mission of Palestinian Higher Education."

41. Al-Azza, *We Have a Dream to Live Safe.*

42. Ben-Natan, "Above and Beyond Denial"; Cook, Hanieh, and Kay, *Stolen Youth*; Shalhoub-Kevorkian, *Incarcerated Childhood.*

43. B'Tselem, "Statistics on Palestinian Minors."

44. Interview conducted October 12, 2015, by phone.

45. Addameer, "Eyes on Israeli Military Court"; Levinson, "Nearly 100% of All Military."

46. Addameer, "Economic Exploitation," 42.

47. See Marshall, "Save (Us From) the Children," for more on how Palestinian childhood is governed by international NGOs.

48. See Salameh, this volume, for more on how Palestinian children define violence.

49. Anderson, "State Formation from Below"; Banko, "Citizenship Rights"; Farraj, "The First Intifada"; Lockman and Beinin, *Intifada*; and Swedenburg, *Memories of Revolt.*

50. Haar and Ghannam, "No Safe Space."

51. Bishara, "Killing Space, Stealing Time"; Cahill and Pain, "Representing Slow Violence and Resistance."

52. For more on closure, see Berda, *Living Emergency*; Hass, "Israel's Closure Policy"; Hammami, "Qalandiya"; and Peteet, *Space and Mobility in Palestine.*

53. Feldman, "Difficult Distinctions."

54. Al-Azza, *Everyday Nakba.*

55. Ferguson, *The Anti-Politics Machine*; Allen, *Rise and Fall of Human Rights*; Feldman, *Life Lived in Relief*; and Hanafi and Tabar, *Emergence of Palestinian Globalized Elite.*

56. Mustafa, "Damming the Palestinian Spring"; Sayigh, "Policing the People, Building the State"; and Zureik, Lyon, and Abu-Laban, *Surveillance and Control in Israel/ Palestine.*

57. Al Husseini, "UNRWA and the Refugees"; and Schiff, "Between Occupier and Occupied."

58. Shalhoub-Kevorkian, *Incarcerated Childhood.*

BIBLIOGRAPHY

Abu-Lughod, L. "Imagining Palestine's Alter-Natives: Settler Colonialism and Museum Politics." *Critical Inquiry* 47, no. 1 (2020): 1–27.

Addameer Prisoner Support and Human Rights. "The Economic Exploitation of Palestinian Political Prisoners." Ramallah: Addameer, 2016. http://www.addameer.org /sites/default/files/publications/final_report_red_2_0.pdf.

———. "Eyes on Israeli Military Court." Ramallah: Addameer, 2012. http://www
.addameer.org/sites/default/files/publications/eyes_on_israeli_military_court-_a
_collection_of_impressions.pdf.

Akram, S. "Palestinian Refugees and Their Legal Status: Rights, Politics, and Implications for a Just Solution." *Journal of Palestine Studies* 31, no. 3 (2002): 36–51.

Al-Azza, M. *Everyday Nakba.* September 12, 2011. https://vimeo.com/28922804.

———. *We Have a Dream to Live Safe.* Lajee Center. November 28, 2016. https://www
.youtube.com/watch?v=mUi3bxsCwUE.

———. *What Will You Do When You Go Back to Your Village?* Lajee Center, 2017. https://
www.youtube.com/watch?v=2qvFZllKH7s.

Al Husseini, J. "UNRWA and the Refugees: A Difficult but Lasting Marriage." *Journal of
Palestine Studies* 40, no. 1 (2010): 6–26.

Alghoul, D. "Defying Odds: Palestine has one of the Highest Literacy Rates in the
World." *The New Arab*, September 6, 2018. https://www.newarab.com/news/palestine
-has-one-highest-literacy-rates-globally.

Allen, L. *The Rise and Fall of Human Rights: Cynicism and Politics in Occupied Palestine.*
Stanford: Stanford University Press, 2013.

Anderson, C. "State Formation from Below and the Great Revolt in Palestine." *Journal of
Palestine Studies* 47, no. 1 (2017): 39–55.

Atallah, D. "A Community-Based Qualitative Study of Intergenerational Resilience with
Palestinian Refugee Families Facing Structural Violence and Historical Trauma."
Transcultural Psychiatry 54, no. 3 (2017): 357–83.

Banko, L. "Citizenship Rights and the Semantics of Colonial Power and Resistance:
Haifa, Jaffa, and Nablus, 1931–1933." In *Violence and the City in the Modern Middle
East*, edited by Nelida Fuccaro. Stanford: Stanford University Press, 2016.

Bannoura, S. "Child Seriously Injured in Aida Refugee Camp." International Middle East
Media Center, December 8, 2006. https://imemc.org/article/23114/.

Bashi, G., and G. Nafisi. *P Is for Palestine: A Palestine Alphabet Book.* N.p.: Dr. Golbarg
Bashi, 2017.

Ben-Natan, S. "Above and Beyond Denial: Incarcerated Children in Israel/Palestine."
Journal of Genocide Research 23, no. 3 (2020): 478–85.

Berda, Y. *Living Emergency: Israel's Permit Regime in the Occupied West Bank.* Stanford:
Stanford University Press, 2017.

Bishara, A. *Crossing a Line: Laws, Violence, and Roadblocks to Palestinian Political Expression.* Stanford: Stanford University Press, 2022.

———. "Decolonizing Middle East Anthropology: Toward Liberations in SWANA Societies." *American Ethnologist 50, no. 3 (2023): 396–408.*

———. "Killing Space, Stealing Time: The Stink and Burn of Occupation." Fieldsites,
"Ecologies of War," Society for Cultural Anthropology, 2022. https://culanth.org
/fieldsights/killing-space-stealing-time-the-stink-and-burn-of-occupation.

———. "An Ongoing Violence, a Sustained Resistance: Israel's Racist Separation Wall at
Aida Refugee Camp." In *Walling In and Walling Out: Why Are We Building New Barri-
ers to Divide Us?* edited by Laura McAtackney and Randall H. McGuire. Albuquerque:
University of New Mexico Press, 2020.

Bishara, A., and N. Al-Azraq, dirs. *Degrees of Incarceration.* [Palestine and U.S.]. 2010. https://vimeo.com/514413925/98db303bbf.

Bishara, A., N. Al-Azraq, Shatha Alazzeh, and John Durant. "The Multifaceted Outcomes of Community-Engaged Water Quality Management in a Palestinian Refugee Camp." *Environment and Planning E: Nature and Space* 4, no. 1 (2021): 65–84.

Bowman, G. "A Weeping on the Road to Bethlehem: Contestation over the Uses of Rachel's Tomb." *Religion Compass* 7, no. 3 (2013): 79–92.

Brown, M. W. *The Runaway Bunny.* New York: HarperCollins, 1942.

B'Tselem: The Israeli Information Center for Human Rights in Occupied Territories. "Statistics on Palestinian Minors in the Custody of Israeli Security Forces." September 7, 2023. https://www.btselem.org/statistics/minors_in_custody.

Cahill, C., and R. Pain. "Representing Slow Violence and Resistance: On Hiding and Seeing." *ACME: An International Journal for Critical Geographies* 18, no. 5 (2019): 1054–65.

Cook, C., A. Hanieh, and A. Kay. *Stolen Youth: The Politics of Israel's Detention of Palestinian Children.* London: Sterling Press, 2004.

DCI Palestine. "Palestinian Boy Shot Dead Near Bethlehem Amid Rising Tensions." October 5, 2015. http://www.dci-palestine.org/palestinian_boy_shot_dead_near _bethlehem_amid_rising_tensions.

Farraj, K. "The First Intifada: Hope and the Loss of Hope." *Journal of Palestine Studies* 47, no. 1 (2017): 86–97.

Fasheh, M. "Community Education: To Reclaim and Transform What Has Been Made Invisible." *Harvard Educational Review* 60, no. 1 (1990): 19–36.

Feldman, I. "Difficult Distinctions: Refugee Law, Humanitarian Practice, and Political Identification in Gaza." *Cultural Anthropology* 22, no. 1 (2007): 129–69.

———. *Life Lived in Relief: Humanitarian Predicaments and Palestinian Refugee Politics.* Berkeley: University of California, 2018.

Ferguson, J. *The Anti-Politics Machine: "Development," Depoliticization, and Bureaucratic Power in Lesotho.* Minneapolis: University of Minnesota Press, 1994.

Haar, R., and J. Ghannam. *No Safe Space: Health Consequences of Tear Gas Exposure Among Palestine Refugees.* University of California Berkeley: Human Rights Center, School of Law, 2018.

Hallaj, M. "The Mission of Palestinian Higher Education." *Journal of Palestine Studies* 9, no. 4 (1980): 75–95.

Hammami, R. "Qalandiya: Jerusalem's Tora Bora and the Frontiers of Global Inequality." *Jerusalem Quarterly* 41 (2010): 29–51.

Hanafi, S., and L. Tabar. *The Emergence of Palestinian Globalized Elite: Donors, International Organizations, and Local NGOs.* Jerusalem: Institute of Jerusalem Studies, 2005.

Harel, A. "Killing of Palestinian Youth in Bethlehem Was 'Unintentional,' Preliminary IDF Inquiry Finds." *Haaretz*, October 6, 2015. http://www.haaretz.com/news /diplomacy-defense/.premium-1.679057?utm_campaign=Echobox&utm_medium =Social&utm_source=Facebook.

Harrison, F. V. *Decolonizing Anthropology: Moving Further Toward an Anthropology for Liberation.* Arlington, Va.: Association of Black Anthropologists, American Anthropological Association, 1997.

Hass, A. 2002. "Israel's Closure Policy: An Ineffective Strategy of Containment and Repression." *Journal of Palestine Studies* 31, no. 3 (2002): 5–20.

Human Rights Council. "Report of the Independent Commission of Inquiry Established Pursuant to Human Rights Council Resolution s-21/1." United Nations, 2015.

Khalidi, W. *All That Remains: The Palestinian Villages Occupied and Depopulated by Israel in 1948*. Washington, D.C.: Institute of Palestine Studies,1992.

Lajee Center. *The Aida Camp Alphabet*. Palestine: Lajee Center, 2015.

——. *The Boy and the Wall*. Palestine: Lajee Center, 2005.

Levinson, C. "Nearly 100% of All Military Court Cases in West Bank End in Conviction, Haaretz Learns." *Haaretz*, November 29, 2011. https://www.haaretz.com/1.5214377.

Lloyd, D. "Settler Colonialism and the State of Exception: The Example of Palestine/Israel." *Settler Colonial Studies* 2, no. 1 (2012): 59–80.

Lockman, Z., and J. Beinin, eds. *Intifada: The Palestinian Uprising Against Israeli Occupation*. Boston: South End Press, 1989.

Lustick, I. S. *Unsettled States, Disputed Lands: Britain and Ireland, France and Algeria, Israel and the West Bank-Gaza*. Ithaca and London: Cornell University Press, 1993.

Marshall, D. J. "Save (Us From) the Children: Trauma, Palestinian Childhood, and the Production of Governable Subjects." *Children's Geographies* 12, no. 3 (2014): 281–96.

Mbembe, A. "Necropolitics." *Public Culture* 15, no. 1 (2003): 11–40.

Mustafa, T. "Damming the Palestinian Spring: Security Sector Reform and Entrenched Repression." *Journal of Intervention and Statebuilding* 9, no. 2 (2015): 212–30.

Norman, J. "Creative Activism: Youth Media in Palestine." *Middle East Journal of Culture and Communication* 2, no. 2 (2009): 251–74.

Palestinian Central Bureau of Statistics. "PCBS Presents the Conditions of Palestinian Populations on the Occasion of the International Population Day," 2022. https://www.pcbs.gov.ps/portals/_pcbs/PressRelease/Press_En_InterPopDay2022E.pdf.

Peteet, J. *Space and Mobility in Palestine*. Bloomington: Indiana University Press, 2017.

Razack, S. H. "Race and Unchilding." *Journal of Genocide Research 23, no. 3 (2021): 486–89*. https://doi.org/10.1080/14623528.2020.1829839.

Robinson, S. *Citizen Strangers: Palestinians and the Birth of Israel's Liberal Settler State*. Stanford: Stanford University Press, 2013.

Rouhana, N. N., and A. Sabbagh-Khoury. "Settler-Colonial Citizenship: Conceptualizing the Relationship Between Israel and Its Palestinian Citizens." *Settler Colonial Studies* 5, no. 3 (2015): 205–25.

Sa'di, A. H., and L. Abu-Lughod, eds. *Nakba: Palestine, 1948, and the Claims of Memory*. New York: Columbia University Press, 2007.

Salamanca, O. J., M. Qato, K. Rabie, and S. Samour. "Past Is Present: Settler Colonialism in Palestine." *Settler Colonial Studies* 2, no. 1 (2012): 1–8.

Sayigh, Y. "Policing the People, Building the State: Authoritarian Transformation in the West Bank and Gaza." Washington, D.C.: The Carnegie Endowment for International Peace, 2011.

Schiff, B. "Between Occupier and Occupied: UNRWA in the West Bank and the Gaza Strip." *Journal of Palestine Studies* 18, no. 3 (1989): 60–75.

Shalhoub-Kevorkian, N. *Incarcerated Childhood and the Politics of Unchilding*. Cambridge: Cambridge University Press, 2019.

Shammas, A. "A Stone's Throw." *The New York Review of Books*, March 31, 1988. http://www.nybooks.com/articles/1988/03/31/a-stones-throw/.

Shams, A. "2 Years after Youth Shot by Soldiers, Friends Honor Him with Mural." Maan News Agency, January 15, 2015. Archived at: https://alexshams.com/2015/01/15/2-years-after-youth-shot-by-soldiers-friends-honor-him-with-mural/.

Shihade, M. "Settler Colonialism and Conflict: The Israeli State and Its Palestinian Subjects." *Settler Colonial Studies* 2, no. 1 (2012): 108–23.

Swedenburg, T. *Memories of Revolt: The 1936–1939 Rebellion and the Palestinian National Past.* Minneapolis: University of Minnesota Press, 1995.

United Nations Relief and Works Agency (UNRWA). "Aida Camp." N.d. Accessed September 28, 2023. https://www.unrwa.org/where-we-work/west-bank/aida-camp.

———. "Profile: Aida Camp, Bethlehem Governorate." Jerusalem: UNRWA, 2015. http://www.unrwa.org/sites/default/files/aida_refugee_camp.pdf.

———. "Where We Work: West Bank." N.d. Accessed September 28, 2023. https://www.unrwa.org/where-we-work/west-bank.

Wolfe, P. "Settler Colonialism and the Elimination of the Native." *Journal of Genocide Research* 8, no. 4 (2006): 387–409.

Zureik, E. *The Palestinians in Israel: A Study in Internal Colonialism.* London: Routledge and Kegan Paul, 1979.

Zureik, E., D. Lyon, and Y. Abu-Laban, eds. *Surveillance and Control in Israel/Palestine: Population, Territory and Power.* London: Routledge, 2013.

Invisible Lives, Visible Determination

Creative Agency as Resilience among
Palestinian Children under Siege in Gaza

NITIN SAWHNEY

Palestinian children in Gaza are often depicted in mainstream media as trau-matized victims of an ongoing Israeli blockade and occupation, with little at-tention paid to their capacity for creative and civic agency amid violence and conflict. Gaza has sustained a devastating blockade since 2006, and children of this generation have experienced several disastrous wars, witnessing cycles of violence, destruction, and dismal efforts at reconstruction. While these events have had devastating effects, what is often missed are the ways in which many children continuously find creative ways not only to cope with ongoing violence and conflict but also to develop new capacities to sustain mental well-being, self-expression, narrative imagination, and agency despite extreme adversity. There is no singular childhood experience, and children living in varying cultural, social, physical, political, and economic situations develop different understandings of their own childhood, including the roles they can plan in their households, fam-ilies, and communities.[1] The question is not if children growing up in conditions of perpetual crisis are proactive agents in making their own choices, but in what ways do they respond to the adversities they experience.

In this chapter, I examine this question of agency despite adversity among Pal-estinian children in Gaza through ethnographic experiences and insights gained in the context of participatory media workshops and trainings, qualitative re-search (interviews, focus groups, and informal everyday interactions), and the production of a feature-length documentary film. I conducted these activities over numerous visits to Gaza from 2010 to 2013, working closely with a team of local and international educators, photographers, artists, and filmmakers, and dozens of young participants (including several cohorts of twenty to twenty-five children). We conducted most of our work in the Jabaliya refugee camp and al-Seifa area near the frontier with Israel.[2] During this time, among the children we met, our team closely followed a proactive young girl, Abeer, from Jabaliya camp and a pair of engaging teenaged siblings, Musa and Widad, from al-Seifa, along with their families. Over the years Abeer, Musa, and Widad inadvertently played a central role in these interactions and activities; my accounts thus highlight their experiences and narratives to a greater extent.

This chapter reveals a complex picture of childhood struggles, vulnerability, and forms of resilience through narrative expression, creative play, and peer-based coproduction in the context of conducting participatory media programs and filmmaking. What emerges is children's remarkable capacity for creative making, self-expression, and civic agency, despite their struggles coping with adolescence, family/social obligations, and traumas induced by the disruptive displacement (loss of home) and violence experienced during recent wars in Gaza.

This chapter also highlights the crucial importance of supporting an ongoing capacity for play, narrative expression, peer-based coproduction, and civic agency among children through the wider ecology of their extended family, teachers, and neighborhood rather than simply focusing on individual educational and mental health interventions.[3] Through illustrative examples of youth media narratives, kite-making activities we filmed, and investigative journalism conducted by youth in the midst of war, I highlight the ways in which creative agency can emerge as a form of resilience for young Palestinians, while recognizing its very real limitations in the face of the unending violence and displacement experienced in their everyday lives. I begin by examining the devastating situation for children in Gaza, through the lens of our filmmaking experiences there, interweaving; humanistic narratives with grim descriptions of how unending cycles of war and violence have shaped their reality.

Flying Kites in a Land Under Siege:
Understanding the Situation of Children in Gaza

> Two six-year-old girls stand on a dusty road holding a handmade kite not far from the shores of the Mediterranean Sea. The girls playfully negotiate who will fly the kite. The more assertive one runs down the road holding the strings of her colorful paper kite as it lifts into the sky, while children around her scream excitedly, "It's flying . . . it's flying!"
>
> —*Flying Paper*, 2013

This is the first scene of a documentary film, *Flying Paper* (2013), that I began filming with my codirector Roger Hill in 2010, as we conducted participatory media workshops and filmmaking with children in Gaza that summer. The film examined the creative culture of kite making and flying under adversity, through the lens of Palestinian children living in Gaza. With our young coproducer Abeer,

A scene from the film *Flying Paper* with a boy holding his kite in al-Seifa, Gaza. Photo: Amber Fares, used with permission.

an enterprising sixteen-year-old girl, the film also captured some of the stories of Palestinian children striving to break the Guinness World Record for the most kites flown at once. Abeer, along with dozens of other Palestinian children, had trained with us in filmmaking techniques, during our participatory media workshops conducted in the Jabaliya refugee camp that summer.

Two of the children featured in our film, the siblings Musa and Widad, lived with their grandfather Abu Ziad, an expert kite maker in al-Seifa. Musa was a charismatic, confident fourteen-year-old who enthusiastically built large kites with great precision using newspaper, sticks, and wheat-paste. His twelve-year-old sister Widad competed with Musa to build her own colorful kites while teasing Musa with witty humor and sarcasm. Musa and Widad's excitement about kite flying emerged in a place deprived of many opportunities for childhood experience afforded elsewhere. Musa and Widad wanted to participate in the record-breaking event so that the world would take notice of the war-torn, besieged coastal strip of land that is their home. In trying to be seen and heard, the children in Gaza also asserted a right to play despite their living conditions, as captured in the film.

The Gaza Strip has over 2 million inhabitants, at least half of whom are children. Years of conflict and embargo have impacted almost every facet of their daily lives, from education and employment to health, housing, and the freedom of play and expression. Children in Gaza grow up in deprivation and extreme

A scene from the film *Flying Paper* with the siblings Musa and Widad
building a kite using newspaper, sticks, and wheat paste in al-Seifa, Gaza.
Photo: Amber Fares, used with permission.

economic and social distress. According to a UNICEF report conducted before
October 7, 2023, youth unemployment in Gaza was 60 percent, one of the highest rates in the world, while over half of all young people's families experienced
poverty.[4] Additionally, nearly 80 percent of the population relied on some form
of humanitarian assistance.[5] According to a UNICEF report, "Coping mechanisms are eroding fast, with some children and families resorting to negative
strategies like school drop-out, child labor, substance abuse and early marriage."[6]

In the initiatives I led with my team from 2010 to 2013, we sensed this urgency
to engage with young people in Gaza through participatory media and documentary film, allowing children to showcase their own narratives of struggle and
resilience. Another scene from our film illustrates the voices of children discussing how even the simple act of kite making and flying is a form of creative political agency.

"I am expressing myself and writing a message to the entire world," one kite-
flying girl declared on the day of the Guinness competition. The message written on her kite? *I have the right to freedom, pride, education, justice, and equality.* When Abeer asked the girl what she would choose most, she said freedom

A scene from the film *Flying Paper* with Musa rescuing his kite
from a shed rooftop near the seaside in al-Seifa, Gaza.
Photo: Amber Fares, used with permission.

(from the Israeli blockade of Gaza) and equality for all men and women. Musa
in his wisdom also felt that kite flying had another crucial role to play among
Palestinian children. "It will help us forget the trauma of war," he told us in another notable scene in the film. (*Flying Paper*, 2013)

When we began filming in 2010, many of the children we met, including Musa
and Widad, had already lived through the devastating 2008–9; Israeli assault in
the Gaza Strip known as "Operation Cast Lead." In its investigation, the human
rights group Amnesty noted that by mid-January 2009, when unilateral ceasefires were announced by both Israel and Hamas, over 1,400 Palestinians had
been killed there, including 300 children and hundreds of other unarmed civilians; Gaza's already dire economy was left in ruins with thousands left homeless
and large areas razed to the ground.[7] In November 2012, Gazans would survive
yet another violent Israeli campaign of aerial bombardment that led to over 165
Palestinians, including more than 30 children and some 70 other unarmed civilians, being killed in just over a week of hostilities.[8] This assault was documented
by our coproducer and associate cinematographer, Anne Paq, an award-winning
photojournalist who happened to be in Gaza at the time capturing additional
footage for our film.

In the summer of 2014, children in Gaza endured a third Israeli war, "Operation Protective Edge," which lasted for fifty days between July 8 and August 26. This assault claimed the lives of 2,220 Palestinians, including at least 1,492 civilians, according to the United Nations Office for the Coordination of Humanitarian Affairs (OCHA).[9] It was traumatic enough during Operation Cast Lead, when Musa and Widad's family huddled together in one room as the children screamed in fear from loud detonations surrounding them. On July 22, 2014, their home was destroyed altogether and the entire family displaced. The following night the International Committee of the Red Cross (ICRC) evacuated the family to Gaza City.

On July 24, 2014, Abeer wrote in her journal from her home in Jabaliya camp: "When we hear the warning missiles or drones, we run outside. We never know if we should stay together or disperse . . . we never know. Everyone is anticipating their own death, not knowing who will go first. I look intently into the faces of my siblings and mother at every moment, fearing I will lose them next. At night one can't sleep from the sound of mortar shelling and bombing. And when I am finally able to sleep for a few hours, the scenes and sounds of war and killing haunt me in my dreams. The children wake up screaming, frightened with terrifying nightmares from their direct encounters with the war in front of them and on TV."

About 40 percent of Gaza's population at the time was under the age of fourteen, so any indiscriminate bombardment there inevitably endangered children disproportionately. Defense for Children International Palestine (DCIP) independently verified the deaths of 547 Palestinian children killed in Gaza, nearly 68 percent of them twelve years old or younger.[10] According to DCIP, children were attacked in their homes, in parks and playgrounds, in hospitals, even in United Nations schools designated as safe areas to shelter displaced civilians. On July 28, 2014, the first day of the Muslim holiday Eid al Fitr, Israel shelled a playground in Beach refugee camp, killing eight children. Widad and Musa's own three-year-old sister Afnan was severely injured a week earlier by an Israeli tank shell fired at their home. According to the United Nations, at least 373,000 children in Gaza needed some form of direct and specialized psychosocial support after the war in 2014.[11]

Gaza's children have endured hardships beyond these repeated assaults, through the effects of the unending siege imposed upon its residents. Israel's crippling blockade of the Gaza Strip over land, air, and sea since 2006 has led to a level of deprivation that human rights organizations have condemned as collective punishment. Lack of economic development, trade, employment, and severe restrictions on opportunities for education and travel have been devastating, as have the frequent shortages in food, medicine, and construction materials, leaving Palestinians in Gaza with an unbearable situation. The UN report "Gaza in

2020: A Liveable Place?" warned in August 2012 that unless action was taken to improve basic services in the territory, Gaza would become uninhabitable by 2020. It estimated the territory would need double the number of schools and hundreds more hospital beds by 2020, while tackling a severe housing shortage. This was all before the obliteration caused by the Israeli attacks after October 7, 2023.

Palestinian children increasingly bear the brunt of the hostilities each time Gaza is devastated by military assaults and violence. The ongoing siege in Gaza, compounded by cycles of war, has left surviving children there grappling with ways to make sense of the violence perpetuated around them, not to mention finding ways to cope with the aftereffects of the devastation caused to their neighborhoods, their family and social fabric, and their everyday lives. In my work over the years, I have tried to make sense of how Palestinian children and adolescents in Gaza develop capacities to sustain their mental well-being, self-expression, and civic agency despite such extreme adversity. In this chapter, I examine how these facets can emerge in the context of participatory media workshops and filmmaking activities with young people in Gaza.

Childhood and Adolescence in Conflict: Understanding Risks and Resilience

We can gain a better perspective on the adverse conditions and responses emerging among young people in Gaza by examining some of the prior theoretical work and research studies conducted in similar conditions of conflict. These studies consider how children and adolescents are affected by the trauma and violence of war, while examining the ways in which they cope or develop forms of resilience in these contexts. Ethnographers have conducted research on children living in crisis situations in the Global North and South to gain insights into their lived experiences of poverty, inequality, displacement, ecological degradation, and war in countries like Haiti, Argentina, and Palestine.[12] Such ethnographic accounts reveal how children's agency operates in these settings. One finding is that while children in crisis face imminent dangers, they are often central to the functioning of families and communities, with many contributing to household livelihoods. We have to critically examine the notion of resilience among young people confronting adversity, and how resilience is potentially affected by their engagement with community, narration, and agency. In this chapter, I particularly focus on how "narrative" construction, peer-based cocreation, and creative agency can be crucial factors affecting resilience among children and adolescents in conflict situations.

It is crucial to see how adolescence is distinct from early childhood, to make sense of the ways in which these factors and conditions change in the course of a child's development, and how such development is in itself affected by a young person's exposure to violence and conflict. Adolescence is often characterized as the phase of a young person's life stretching between childhood and adulthood. However, this definition has posed a conundrum for health and developmental researchers.[13] Adolescence encompasses both aspects of biological growth and key transitions in social roles undertaken by a young person. The timing of many of these role transitions for adolescents have seen changes or delays over the course of the past century, shifting perceptions of when childhood moves into adulthood. Researchers propose more expanded and inclusive definitions of adolescence, from age ten to age twenty-four, corresponding more closely to the nature of developmental growth and popular perceptions of their roles and responsibilities in society.[14] While researchers would argue that adolescence is understood to be delayed in Western societies, I believe that in the context of war and conflict, where life experiences, stressors, and adaptations are amplified among young people, a transition to adolescence may actually be accelerated. This relates to the notion of elasticity during adolescence, pointing to a potential for socio-emotional learning among young people growing up in situations affected by adversity.[15]

To consider how children and adolescents cope with risks and adversity or develop healthy psychosocial functioning in the face of stressful life events, it's useful to examine the concept of resilience. Resilience among adolescents is generally understood as the attainment of desirable social outcomes and emotional adjustment, despite exposure to considerable risk. Here risk is defined as a psychosocial adversity or event considered a stressor that may hinder normal functioning.[16] Understanding of resilience in research has developed along four overlapping waves that have focused on individual traits, protective mechanisms, developmental assets, and social ecological factors.[17] While the initial conceptualization of resilience focused on individual traits based on attachment theory, whereby infants learned to cope with separation and adversity, it was later understood as a dynamic process and interaction between genetic and environmental factors as internal and external protective mechanisms to adapt to situations.[18] Over time a more ecological interpretation of resilience emerged, taking into account interactions between individuals, their community, and their environment as developmental assets,[19] to explain, for example, the progression of children's resilience through their school contexts. However, there remain many limitations to understanding resilience through these factors alone, and many individuals may be more or less resilient in spite of these factors. Cultural and contextual factors can also affect dynamic interactions between the sources of resilience.[20] It has been argued that cultural values play a crucial role in the collective resilience of individuals and communities, particularly in politically violent contexts.[21] In the context of Palestinian culture, the related notion of *sumud* is interwoven with ideas of personal and collective resilience and steadfastness.[22] Sumud is deeply rooted in historical and religious contexts in Palestinian culture as a sociopolitical concept referring to surviving occupation, adversity, displacement, and limited resources, while staying steadfast on one's homeland. Health-related resilience may serve as a prerequisite for sumud though it has a broader sociocultural and political significance. Hence, any comprehensive inquiry of resilience among Palestinians would benefit from engaging with the concept of sumud as an interrelated idea, though it remains underresearched with few empirical studies conducted thus far.[23]

To understand the experience of Palestinian childhood under Israeli occupation, Nadera Shalhoub-Kevorkian has powerfully argued for engaging with the concept of "unchilding," emphasizing the effects of racial violence and colonialism on the intimate lives of children.[24] The concept reveals the multiple layers of state violence and how it manifests across the many spheres of a child's life from their home, school, and neighborhoods to their health and mental well-being, as well as economic, social, and political agency. Unchilding marks Palestinian children as dangerous racialized "others," enabling their eviction from the realm of childhood itself.[25] In this context of oppression and violence, how do young Palestinians cope and develop forms of resilience and sumud over time?

While psychosocial stress and trauma among children has been examined in the context of protracted conflict and violence, some recent studies have also considered the potential positive outcomes of adaptation and resilience. In the context of the Occupied Palestinian Territories, a qualitative study by Viet Nguyen-Gillham and others explored the construct of resilience among adolescents in the West Bank; it examined how Palestinian adolescents living in the city of Ramallah (who attended school in grades tenth to twelfth) interpreted concepts of resilience under abnormal conditions of protracted conflict.[26] Focus group interviews with 321 Palestinian youth revealed the normalization of everyday life despite adversity, and a form of collective and dynamic resilience. Feelings of desperation, emotional distress, boredom, and apathy are intermingled with optimism through the ever-changing rhythms of disruption and normalcy experienced by adolescents living in the West Bank (primarily in the urban centers).

Sociologist Brian Barber and psychosocial researcher Theresa Betancourt have examined the nature of resilience among children and adolescents through longitudinal studies conducted in conflict areas such a Bosnia, the Palestinian Territories, Sierra Leone, and Uganda.[27] Their studies point to culturally appropriate framing and localized mixed methods, as well as positive indicators of resilience and pro-social attitudes, emerging among affected youth under certain conditions of community engagement, narrative, and civic agency. Researchers have examined the prevalence of resilience among Palestinian children and adolescents in Gaza during traumatic events related to the violence of war. A recent study in Gaza investigated the role of commitment, control, and challenge (characteristics of resiliency) in protecting children's mental health from negative trauma impacts;[28] one marginal gender difference observed was that of girls reporting more feelings of control than boys. The overall results revealed that a quarter of children in the study exhibited resilient characteristics while over 22 percent were traumatized, with presence of both high exposure to trauma and occurrence of post-traumatic stress disorder (PTSD). There have also been critiques about the utility of the construct of resilience given the challenges of assessing the functioning of youth (using better defined measures) in such acute and chronic conditions that are part of extended contexts of adversity and conflict in war.[29] Other critiques suggest that resilience is sensitive to complex multidimensional interactions depending on the context.[30] A young person considered to be resilient in one situation may not sustain it in every stage of their life. The protective and risk factors in their environment may manifest differently from time to time, one being converted to the other in some situations. For example, a child's parents can serve both as protective factors to face adversity but may also become risk factors at other times.[31] Hence, the cultural and contextual environment play a crucial role in mediating the dynamics and interactions of risk and resilience.

Taking this ecological and cultural perspective, it is helpful to understand how resilience emerges during children's development from long-term interactions between them and their surroundings, including family, schools, and the community. In retrospective studies conducted with war-affected Bosnian adolescents during the ethnic conflict in the Balkans versus Palestinian youth in the Gaza Strip after the first intifada (the uprising that began in 1987), Barber found stark differences in resilience.[32] This was due to factors including peer/family support, understanding the rationale for violence, and the ability to actively engage in forms of resistance and activism in the case of Palestinian youth. In her work, Betancourt examines resilience outcomes through an ecological approach, as a dynamic phenomenon that is influenced by both protective factors (internal and psychosocial) and subsequent protective processes (family, peers, community). Betancourt suggests developing localized psychosocial assessment instruments and ethnographic methods to examine resilience in such contexts. In studies of recovery among child soldiers and adolescent survivors of armed conflicts in Uganda and Sierra Leone, researchers examined the role of supportive community settings, participation in demobilization interventions, and culturally appropriate approaches that ease the social stigma of violence perpetuated and experienced by youth participating in the war.[33] A recent book examines how children both struggle within and shape conflict zones, illustrating this through examples and case studies of child soldiers from Vietnam, child forced migrants in Australia, young peace builders in postconflict zones, youth in the international justice system, and child advocates across South Asia and the Middle East.[34]

How is resilience in conflict situations constructed through the narratives of young people? The role of narration was examined among adolescents in highly contentious situations after the war in the Balkans, as self-expressions of identity and critical understanding of their sociopolitical environment.[35] Storytelling was used as a cultural probe to understand social relations, emerging ideologies based on societal discourses, situational coherence in crisis, and as opportunities for imagination and transformation of one's circumstances. The study conducted workshops and writing exercises with 108 adolescents across four locations to elicit hypothetical narratives that were subsequently analyzed linguistically. The results revealed the emergence of coherent and moral narratives with a "relatively universal script of inclusive and collective human action to overcome obstacles."[36] Most adolescents used the relative freedom of fiction writing (and fictional characters) to handle challenging issues and intense emotions surrounding war and conflict as experienced by them and their communities, which could not easily be expressed in direct interviews or autobiographical accounts. These findings encouraged my team to consider how we could engage young Palestinians in community-based narrative construction activities through participatory media programs, as one avenue to develop greater agency and resilience in the face of adversity.

Voices beyond Walls:
Conducting and Assessing Participatory Media
Programs with Young Palestinians in Gaza

How do we examine the value of narrative construction and creative agency among youth, and in what ways can they contribute to forms of resilience? In the summer of 2006 I established a nonprofit initiative *Voices Beyond Walls* to conduct digital storytelling and participatory media programs with local teams of artists and educators at community-based centers in Palestinian refugee camps in East Jerusalem, the West Bank, and Gaza.[37] While we have drawn many pedagogical lessons from these experiences,[38] we needed to better understand cultural constructs of resilience among Palestinian adolescents. We wanted to investigate the role of creative narratives and participatory media programs in fostering greater self-expression, pro-social attitudes, and civic agency as locally perceived by the young participants and their communities. We conducted this work with an orientation toward *Participatory Action Research* (PAR), which seeks to facilitate self-reflective inquiry for collective action. PAR is ideally undertaken by researchers and participants through an iterative cycle of collecting, analyzing and acting for change; the reflective process being directly linked to action, and influenced by an awareness of the local context and power relationships.[39] As part of this effort, we began establishing working methods for the study, training for long-term capacity building, and building rapport with local communities and organizations in Gaza since 2010.

We designed and conducted our pilot research study at the UN Women's Health Centre in the Jabaliya refugee camp near Gaza City in June–July 2011 with twenty to twenty-five Palestinian adolescents (aged twelve to sixteen), including their caretakers and teachers. The research protocol was approved by the Institutional Review Board (IRB) at the Massachusetts Institute of Technology, with local oversight and support provided by the Gaza Community Mental Health Programme (GCMHP). The project used a mixed-methods approach drawing insights from questionnaires, creative probes about family and self, focus group discussions, semistructured interviews, and narrative exercises conducted (in Arabic) with participants to learn about their interests, backgrounds, and life experiences. Thereafter, photography-based portraits, neighborhood photo/mapping activities, and video-based storytelling activities were conducted to engage the young participants in creative media-based expression, followed by focus-group debriefings at the end of the week-long workshops.

We used diary-based methods, using audio recording with young participants as a creative probe to elicit reflections from digital images, hand-drawn sketches, and physical artifacts. We found these better suited to our resource-constrained field settings, easily and reliably deployed, and quickly adopted by adolescents, without significantly distracting them from their learning and coproduction activities.[40] In this work we use the term "audio journaling" as a multifaceted practice and participatory research method encompassing audio-based diaries, individual and peer-based practices such as autobiographical, self-reflective and narrative storytelling, and place-based observational and conversational recording, as well as approaches to organize, review, and analyze content. Activities can range from solicited to impromptu journaling activities over time. The key is to facilitate greater agency among participants to adopt audio journaling as a regular practice for self-reflection and narrative inquiry, aspects of which they may choose to share with others as needed. Allowing most participants to take audio recorders home during the workshops, the journaling expanded the space of reflection into their domestic settings. As many participants used the audio record-ers during their soundwalks in urban neighborhoods, their on-site journaling also captured these soundscapes along with their spontaneous commentaries.

A crucial aspect of these projects was the involvement of and capacity-building for the local staff and young researchers based in these communities. We led a comprehensive three-day training workshop with twelve to fifteen young adults (aged eighteen to twenty-five), with backgrounds in youth coun-seling, child development, and clinical psychology. Adopting a PAR-based ori-entation in our work, we developed the research goals, methods, and analytic approaches in conjunction with the young Palestinian researchers, whom we considered domain experts and joint stakeholders in the research. This not only aided in much needed capacity-building in qualitative research methods with the team (who were mostly trained in quantitative and clinical methods), but also leveraged their own childhood experiences growing up in similar sociopolitical conditions and neighborhoods as the adolescents we engaged.

Consequently, the young program educators and researchers were able to use their "sub-cultural capital" to forge meaningful relationships with participants in the workshops during the process.[41] In particular, they were able to better fa-cilitate participants' use of audio recording, photography, and video to capture seemingly authentic and intimate narratives, while jointly reviewing and analyz-ing their meanings. The young team members carefully navigated their "insider status" with the children and adolescents to establish a familiar mentoring rela-tionship as captive listeners, but also better recognized the "performance of self-hood," social and cultural constructs expressed by participants. We subsequently conducted participatory content analysis for reflective peer review of the audio and visual narratives collaboratively produced by youth participants.[42] The par-ticipatory media workshops we conducted offered some insights about the role of narrative construction and civic agency among the participating youth, as we consider in the following sections. These workshops later engaged many of these young participants in the process of capturing kite flying through the documen-tary film *Flying Paper*; both of these interrelated initiatives, conducted concur-rently, reveal facets of creative agency among Palestinian youth.

Participatory Media Workshops:
Youth Experiences from Audio Journaling,
Storytelling, and Peer-Based Coproduction

Before the participatory media workshops, which I described above, began in June–July 2011 my research team conducted two preliminary focus group ses-

sions with a small group of six mothers and eight children who planned to participate in the workshop. We discussed the key issues of critical concern among
mothers about the lives of their children in the camp including psychosocial
trauma from the war, ongoing political conflict, blockade and everyday concerns
regarding the frequent power outages, health, safety, and attitudes/behaviors of
children at home and in the community. We discussed their hopes and expectations, evidence of creative engagement, and media exposure among their children. The mothers were more than willing to talk about a wide range of issues
their children were confronting and appreciated our interest in better understanding these aspects of their lives.

We then probed the youth group (two boys and six girls aged twelve to fifteen) about these issues through an exploratory exercise of having them draw
their hands on a sheet of paper and noting their background information (name,
age, their siblings, etc.) and drawing out a sample daily diary of their everyday
lives. This provided some background information on their routines, media consumption patterns, socialization, family life, and sleep, much of it apparently
shaped by the nature of power cuts experienced on any given day.

Inevitably, socializing with friends and family through face-to-face and online means constituted an important part of their lives, at least during the summer. When asked about a significant moment in their life over the past year, most
discussed effects of the war, personal loss, or challenging events at school. As
for problems they faced nearly all mentioned power cuts and the political situation (particularly factional fighting) as primary issues. Interestingly, children
with greater media usage patterns and socialization seemed more open and optimistic—yet this remains anecdotal evidence at this early stage. The focus groups
helped us develop a more detailed questionnaire and approach, which we hoped
to administer among all children participating in the workshops thereafter.

Audio journaling was incorporated in many key aspects of the participatory
media workshops using several handheld H2 Zoom digital audio recorders. The
five- to seven-hour long workshops began with icebreakers and focus-group debriefings among all participants about the goals, activities, and outcomes expected during the program. Thereafter, the young researchers were assigned to
lead small groups of three to five youth participants in audio-recorded activities,
including hand-drawn representations of the self, family, and neighborhood, illustrations of a day in their life, and creative photo portraits of one another. Researchers also asked participants to lead their own audio interviews in pairs, asking each other to reflect on what the drawings revealed to them, while listening
in and facilitating their discussions. With this warm-up exercise, as participants
became more comfortable using audio recorders, the researchers asked them to
undertake narrative activities whereby participants recited short stories to one

A scene from the film *Flying Paper* with over 7,500 kites being flown by children during the kite festival organized by the United Nations Relief and Works Agency for Palestine Refugees in the Near East (UNRWA) in Gaza, July 2010. Photo: Amber Fares, used with permission.

another about significant events in their lives over the past year, and why they felt they were memorable.

During the course of the three week-long workshops an overwhelming amount of mixed-media content was generated from participatory activities conducted with two dozen Palestinian children and adolescents. These written and audio-recorded materials were carefully archived and organized at the end of each day by our team of researchers, and we regularly discussed them in debriefing sessions held after the workshops. The data was used to draw out individual and collective themes, patterns, and psychosocial constructs that the adolescents perceived, and how it shaped their sense of self, belonging, and agency despite the daily struggles, injustice, and violence they regularly experienced. While only a portion of the data collected has been translated and transcribed from Arabic, I focus here on some findings primarily drawn from a selection of the audio-recorded activities.

When asked to share a significant moment in their lives over the past year, most children mentioned narratives that included adverse effects experienced during the war in January 2009, the personal loss of a family member or challenging events occurring in school. Many brought up the regular electric power cuts experienced in the Gaza Strip each day; discussions between two young participants provides additional nuance about why this may have been disturbing. Below are some quotes from our audio-recorded interviews.

> Boy A: "I am disturbed when the electricity is shut off . . . because this is unacceptable."
>
> Boy B: "What disturbs you?"
>
> Boy A: "When the electricity is shut off, they turn on the generators, and that disturbs me. It hurts my head."

In this segment, their tone of voice becomes more subdued, and less enthusiastic than in the prior discussion. Later on, as the boys appear to discuss an everyday scenario through storytelling, even the mundane reveals something unusual for childhood experience in Gaza.

> Boy B: "Can you tell me a true story from your life?"
>
> Boy A: "Yes, of course, this is possible. One time my friends and I decided to go to the beach. We put together our money and we bought fruit, lunch, and mixed nuts. We went to the beach from 7:00 in the morning until 9:00 in the evening and we did not encounter *any problems*. And we swam and we were happy, and we did not face *any problems*."

A feeling of success and achievement is heard in the boy's voice; a happy day, without problems; that's the day the boy chose to describe after only being asked to tell a true story from his life. While their tone becomes eager in this segment, it's interesting to note the emphasis on not facing any problems, repeated twice. The passage only highlights how a normal day by the sea in Gaza is considered extraordinary for these children.[43]

Several of our young participants discuss ongoing turmoil over the local political situation, which they were highly aware of through the media. Interestingly, the research team found that many children and adolescents with greater media usage and communication patterns (through TV and social media) and socialization with family and friends (inferred from the initial questionnaires and interviews) seemed more open and optimistic about their future, as expressed in the positive themes in their storytelling. These relate to the potential ways in which young people used media consumption as a means for coping and making sense of their own everyday reality; this emerged from focus groups we conducted with the mothers of participants. Many of them also appeared to adopt prosocial attitudes, support networks, and forms of agency and solidarity through their interactions with peers in their neighborhoods and online networks. This may have allowed them to alleviate some of the stressors experienced in daily life and the political injustices that they perceived.

In the peer-based storytelling component of the assessment, participants recorded each other reciting a fictional story (1–3 minutes long), which they had written earlier. One set of stories tended to evoke simplistic and mundane themes recurring across them, including the despair of living in Gaza, a thirst to go to the seaside, and to travel abroad freely; others emerged as metaphors for the political infighting and violence of war in Gaza. The intonation in their voices usually demonstrated an apathy and calm acceptance of the everyday reality surrounding them. They were mostly spoken in a monotonous and unexcited manner using formal Arabic. As we later realized, these most often emerged in readings of prewritten stories to older teachers in a classroom setting.

In another set of stories, that were spoken and recorded primarily among peers, many explored similar concerns but in slightly more imaginative ways using magical themes and comic book characters. More significantly, the peer-based conversational mode allowed the young interviewers to ask probing follow-up questions about the plot and characters, while the storyteller offered more enthusiastic and spontaneous responses. The peer-to-peer dynamic and subcultural access available among young participants likely evoked a more playful and fluid narrative delivery, breaking out of the formal scripts expected and which they may have felt were imposed on them otherwise.

On subsequent days of the workshops, the team asked participants to lead neighborhood walks to share meaningful places and routes traversed in their everyday lives, while photographing them and capturing their own reflections. These narrative audio activities complemented the digital storytelling activities conducted, helping generate characters and scripts for autobiographical stories or fictional scenarios they recreated in their short films. Collectively, their recordings, photography, and digital storytelling provided a rich source of narrative and audiovisual content used to analyze complex issues of adolescent identity, self-esteem, gender norms, domestic life, and sociopolitical struggles of living in the impoverished refugee camp. Later in the workshop these were further developed into short video narratives, combining their photography and spoken narratives with edited video segments.

For one of the neighborhood explorations, I shadowed a group of youth participants who decided to examine experiences of special needs children in the camp. We visited a center that introduced us to a young hearing-impaired girl called Amna. The group managed to conduct an interview with her through a sign translator, and then proceeded to give her a digital camera to take some photos with them to share a part of her world through the language of photography. Amna was quite receptive and the youths took a liking to her right away. The group tried to imagine a silent world as we walked along with Amna in the busy, noisy streets of the camp. Amna's photos were far more engaging than the group had expected; the group incorporated many of these photos into their narrative, with a silent soundtrack to represent Amna's perceptions of the world in their short film. They also playfully photographed shadows of their hands doing sign language to add to their photo montage in the emerging narrative piece.

That afternoon the group continued to work on their first photomontage using video editing software at the youth center, despite many frustrating challenges due to power outages, viruses on laptops, and a steep learning curve to master the technical aspects of the tool without much training. Despite all these struggles, the group produced a touching story that they felt had transformed their experience of the refugee camp while spending time with Amna. While their everyday experience of the camp was one of noise from street vendors and power generators, spending a day with Amna offered a different sensory mode of exploring the place, as captured in their rich audiovisual narrative. Hence, the group decided to make a short film called *I Wish I Were Deaf* that transitioned from an annoying noise-filled day in the life of a child in the camp, to meeting a

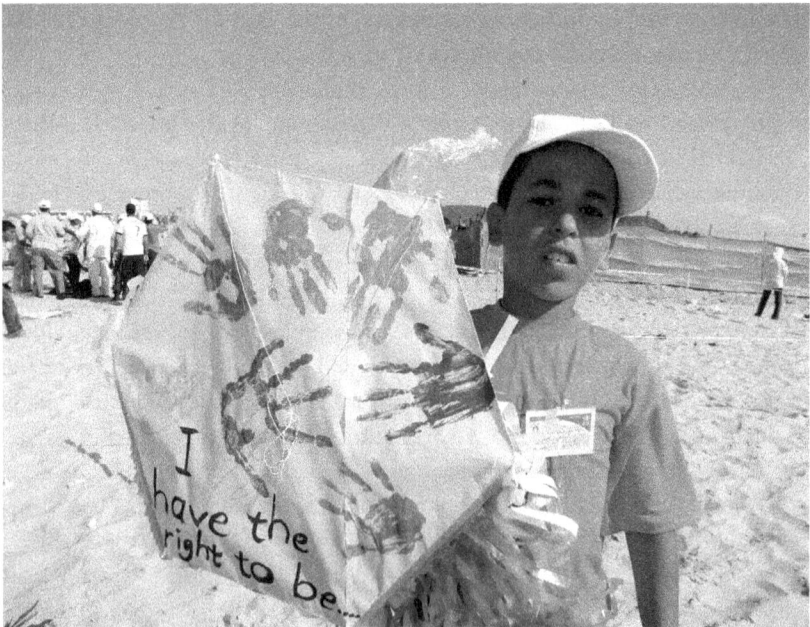

A scene from the film *Flying Paper* with a boy holding his own handmade kite, inscribed with a message "I have the right to be . . . ," during the kite festival in Gaza, July 2010. Photo: Amber Fares, used with permission.

hearing-impaired girl and learning to appreciate the richness of her world as she experienced it.

I shadowed another youth group who decided to examine the human rights situation in their camp through neighborhood narratives. They began by meeting with two different human rights offices in the camp and interviewed their staff. I was impressed with their interview skills and team coordination while some wrote summaries and others photographed. One of the staff members took the group to meet a family whose home had been bombed during the siege in January 2008. We met the father who had lost his right hand in the tragic incident, and one of his children who suffered shrapnel wounds. I only learned about all this as the interview progressed and was taken aback by the warmth and hospitality of the whole family.

The young group conducted their interview tactfully and professionally, while the camera team filmed the group making decisions about their shots and preparing for interviews while walking along in the streets. The group filmed three families, two of which were in Jabaliya camp, each with devastating stories of loss and inspiring resilience. Abeer, the young girl directing the group, conducted most of the interviews while others assisted with photography and production work; it was a natural team with each one taking turns to manage the video shoot. Their short film, called *Walking towards the Truth* (2010), once edited, turned out to be a compelling documentary, intercutting witness testimony with introspective reflections among the group, unpacking the experiences of growing up in Gaza under constant war while considering how they can narrate these unspeakable concerns to an outside world.

Flying Paper and the Return to Seifa: Youth Experiences from Filmmaking and Journalistic Narratives

As the participatory media workshop in Jabaliya camp concluded, Abeer led a team of youth to work closely with us on the production of the feature-length documentary film *Flying Paper*. The film offered an opportunity to develop a playful subject, with children and adolescents as key characters doing what they loved most in their summers: making and flying kites. Abeer and her youth team from Jabaliya camp found this endlessly fascinating as they enjoyed learning how the young teenaged siblings Musa and Widad in al-Seifa had become such masterful kite makers.

In one of the opening scenes of the film, Widad challenges Musa to determine who is the best kite maker in the family, and the stakes of the sibling rivalry are set. The next day the brother and sister split into teams, building kites, and chal-

Boy holding his kite against the backdrop of destroyed buildings after the Israeli assault on Gaza in November 2012. Photo: Anne Paq / Active Stills, used with permission.

lenging each other on the nearby Waha beach at sunset to determine whose kite reigns supreme. Widad is confident the Palestinian children of Gaza will break the Guinness World Record, but first in her thoughts is proving who is the best kite maker in the family. Musa remains focused on how his designs could be improved from his first failed attempt with a newspaper-based kite. As the day ensues, Musa's kite flies majestically in the sky on Waha beach, but Widad's kite suffers many challenges from being poorly constructed and ends up crashing repeatedly in the sand. Widad retains her good humor, sharing her feeling of freedom that comes with kite flying, even if it fails to stay in the air.

The next day Musa demonstrates his latest construction, a huge six-meter-wide kite. When asked why he is building this kite, Musa replies frankly: "To attach a camera." Musa then blushes before giving the credit to his grandfather who is nearby trimming the strings. When asked when he learned to make kites, Abu Ziad laughs and replies, "Do you think I was born old, I was a kid like you when I learned. Kite making is like genes passed down and nothing changes."

In the field near the house the children gather to test the kite. Widad is lost in thought. In the horizon along the border an Israeli military jeep drives past. Widad looks to the dangerous area and mentions how the Israeli soldiers frequently come to her village from "that road" and detain the men while they search their homes, including hers. She changes her somber tone when asked about kite making and admits that she still needs help from her brother Musa, who's been mak-

Youth filmmakers conducting an interview with a family affected by the war in 2009, during production of their short documentary film titled *Walking towards the Truth* in Jabaliya refugee camp, Gaza. Photo: Nitin Sawhney.

ing kites since he was much younger. Musa manages to get his new camera kite in the sky and explains confidently that he will fly this kite in the competition the next day, after making some slight modifications.

During the kite festival, Abeer interviews Musa and Widad as they try to fly the large kite embedded with a camera to help film the festival from above. Their kite momentarily captures the scene with over seventy-five hundred other kites in the air, before spinning out of control and crashing due to the intensity of winds along the seashore. Moments later the UN announces the breaking of the Guinness World Record for the most kites ever flown simultaneously by children at the festival. Musa and Widad are exuberant about the outcome, despite losing their own kite along the way.

One year later, an older-looking Musa walks down the dirt road leading to his village carrying an old kite, as captured by Abeer in a closing segment of the film. Widad, now wearing a hijab on her head, looks on. A lot has changed in the last year for the siblings as they explain. Widad has become more religious, taken up volleyball, and seeks quiet places to read when not doing household chores. Musa has far more responsibilities that don't allow time to make kites, remaining consumed with school and working on the farm. Hence, a phase of playful childhood lives ends for many of these children as they transition to adolescence and roles of adulthood. However, this transition is further accelerated as they remain exposed to the risks of war and violence in their lives.

Outside his home Musa speaks of attacks that occurred recently when a missile landed in their fields, near their homes. Musa displays the missile casing, still intact, and fragments of a heavy shell fired from an Israeli tank across the border to his village. Musa reflects while sitting along the road leading to his village, talking about his dreams of travelling from Gaza to explore other places and cultures, and writing about them someday, mentioning his thoughts in the closing scene of the film, "Gaza is like a prison. I'd like to get out and see the world."

In the summer of 2014 as the war in Gaza raged, Abeer surveyed the destruction in her neighborhood and at times huddled with her family in their small home in the Jabaliya refugee camp, missiles falling around them. Our colleague Anne Paq, who had returned to Gaza as a photojournalist before the commencement of hostilities, worked closely with Abeer to help capture the experiences of young people in the midst of war, training her to use audio recordings to document witness testimony and her own experiences. They incorporated these visceral experiences and audio-visual testimony into *Flying Paper*'s short sequel, *Return to Seifa Village* (2014).

While the bombing intensified and the land invasion into Gaza began, Anne and Abeer bravely traveled across Gaza during very brief (and dangerous) ceasefires to document the devastation around them. On their return to al-Seifa (where they had filmed *Flying Paper* less than three years prior), they found a village destroyed. Ruins of homes dotted a broken landscape with which they had become familiar with during past visits. Returning to al-Seifa, the home of teenagers Widad and Musa and their grandfather Abu Ziad, was an emotional trip for the two women, who were not fully prepared for the level of destruction the village had endured. Musa, who had just begun his college studies, no longer spoke of his optimism for the future. The war had changed his tone as he showed them his destroyed bedroom, bluntly assessing the damage and stating his belief that "the home would surely be rebuilt, though it may be bombed again. . . . This is how it is."

On July 19, 2014, Abeer recorded a journalistic narrative in the midst of the war: "No place is safe in Gaza including Jabaliya camp and al-Seifa. I spoke with Musa and Abu Ziad about the situation in al-Seifa. The upper floor of their house has been bombed and one family member was injured. Now there are thirty people taking shelter on the first floor with nothing to survive on, with no food, water, or electricity. They were forced to feed on the birds they were breeding in order to survive. The [Israeli] tanks are stationed in front of their house and the farmland nearby was bombed. In Jabaliya camp, the UNRWA schools are over-

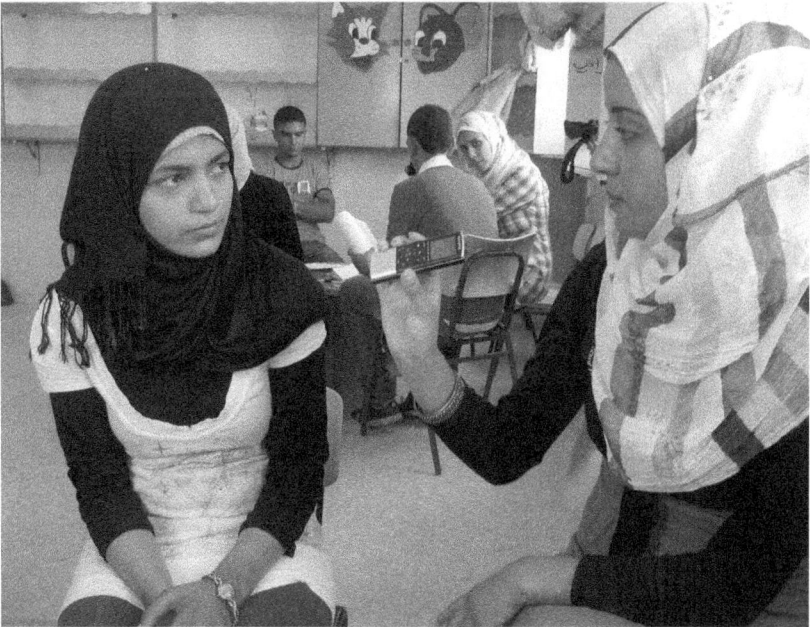

Young participants conducting peer-based audio journaling during the participatory media workshops conducted at the UN Women's Health Centre in Jabaliya refugee camp, Gaza, in July 2010. Photos: Nitin Sawhney.

crowded with people who fled their homes because of this horrific aggression on Gaza."

A few days later on July 24 Abeer shares more personal experiences in her journal: "This feeling of imminent death seems unimaginable and very surreal, every minute, every night wondering if you will become carnage and torn into pieces! Without electricity, the darkness of night is made more oppressive by the constant sounds of shelling. Dozens of families who were displaced from their homes have come to stay at our home in Jabaliya camp. Some of them I know, others I do not, scared faces seeking refuge; but what refuge can we give? At our home, we share mattresses and blankets while sleeping on the floor. All the children have fear imprinted on their faces as they hide in the embrace of their mothers. Their terror and panic amplified by the scenes of corpses and carnage in the streets."

Abeer channeled her narrative experiences in Jabaliya camp and her journalistic inquiry in al-Seifa into the short film she coproduced; this sequel, in contrast to *Flying Paper*'s uplifting message, captured a devastating snapshot of young lives and families in turmoil, adapting to the harsh realities of yet another violent disruption to their aspirations in Gaza.

Conclusions

From narrating their everyday experiences to undertaking journalistic inquiry, children in Gaza often employ narrative construction and creative agency in their lives to survive. The range of experiences that Abeer, Musa, and Widad have faced in the years that we have followed them, show to some extent how Palestinian children and adolescents in Gaza can develop ways to sustain their sense of self-expression, narrative imagination, and creative agency despite the extreme adversities they have continually faced. At other times, young Palestinians are also highly vulnerable to devastating psychosocial traumas and severe deterioration in their mental health and well-being. One of the themes emerging in our experiences with children in Gaza over the years is how the greater roles and responsibilities they undertake at a younger age may lead to accelerated transitions to adolescence and adulthood, while they must continue devising coherent narratives to explain the collective violence and injustices they face.

Through my work I've come to believe that being able to gain some agency in the midst of these struggles—through narration, peer-based cocreation, human rights advocacy, and assisting in reconstruction or developmental efforts in their communities—can strengthen mechanisms of resilience among young Palestinians in Gaza. Our experiences and ongoing assessment of these facets in the participatory media workshops and filmmaking initiatives point to the value of narrative construction and creative agency in the lives of such young people, as I have tried to elucidate in this chapter. However, with every ensuing war, loss of homes and family members, diminished educational and employment opportunities, and the destruction of the social and cultural fabric in the lives of young Palestinians, these mechanisms of coping continue to be challenged. This may lead to permanent traumas, displacements, and disruptions to their adolescence, which will be far more challenging to recover from if the world continues to remain silent to the unending injustices faced by yet another generation in Gaza.

NOTES

I want to thank my codirector Roger Hill and coproducers Anne Paq and Abeer Ahmed for our collaborative filmmaking efforts over the years. Thanks to Musa, Widad, Abu Ziad Al Ghoul, and all the young Palestinians who engaged in our participatory media programs and filmmaking activities in Gaza from 2010 to 2013. I wish to acknowledge the support of the United Nations Relief and Works Agency for Palestine Refugees in the Near East (UNRWA), the UN Woman's Centre in the Jabaliya refugee camp, the Gaza Community Mental Health Programme (GCMHP), and our Gaza study coordinators Wasseem El Sarraj and Samah Saleh. I also thank Nour Chamoun, Abe Assouli and Rula Awwad-Rafferty for assisting with Arabic translations.

1. Hashemi and Sánchez-Jankowski, "Children in Crisis."

2. Al-Seifa is an area northwest of Beit Lahia in the northern Gaza Strip, located in the buffer zone with Israel. The residents of al-Seifa, including the children we interviewed, often referred to their neighborhood in the agricultural area as a village, with many interrelated families residing there.

3. Betancourt et al., "Interventions for Children."

4. UNICEF, "Children in the State."

5. For more information on the humanitarian situation in Gaza, see Illan Feldman's *Life Lived in Relief.*

6. UNICEF, "Children in the State."

7. Amnesty International, "Israel/Gaza."

8. Amnesty International, "A Year On.

9. UN OCHA-OPT, *Situation Report.*

10. Defense for Children International Palestine, "Operation Protective Edge."

11. UN OCHA-OPT, *Situation Report.*

12. Hashemi and Sánchez-Jankowski, "Children in Crisis."

13. Sawyer et al., "Age of Adolescence."

14. Sawyer et al., "Age of Adolescence."

15. Carroll, "Teenage Brains Are Elastic."

16. Luthar, "Annotation."

17. Ungar, "Social Ecology of Resilience"; Ungar, *Social Ecology of Resilience*; Ungar et al., "Unique Pathways to Resilience"; Masten, "Resilience in Developing Systems."

18. Rutter, "Resilience as a Dynamic Concept"; Garcia-Dia et al., "Concept Analysis."

19. Ungar, "Social Ecology of Resilience."

20. Ungar.

21. Sousa et al., "Individual and Collective Dimensions."

22. Marie, Hannigan, and Jones, "Social Ecology of Resilience."

23. Marie, Hannigan, and Jones, "Resilience of Nurses Who Work."

24. Shalhoub-Kevorkian, *Incarcerated Childhood*.

25. Shalhoub-Kevorkian.

26. Nguyen-Gillham et al., "Normalising the Abnormal."

27. Barber, "Contrasting Portraits of War"; Betancourt and Khan, "Mental Health of Children Affected."

28. Thabet et al., "Prevalence and Mental Health Function."

29. Barber, "Contrasting Portraits of War"; Massad et al., "Rethinking Resilience for Children."

30. Ungar, "Social Ecology of Resilience."

31. Ungar, "Resilience across Cultures."

32. Barber, "Contrasting Portraits of War."

33. Betancourt et al., "Qualitative Study."

34. Huynh, D'Costa, and Lee-Koo, *Children and Global Conflict*.

35. Daiute, "Critical Narrating by Adolescents."

36. Daiute, "Critical Narrating by Adolescents."

37. Voices Beyond Walls participatory media program, http://www.VoicesBeyond Walls.org.

38. Sawhney, "Voices beyond Walls."

39. Whyte, *Participatory Action Research*; Baum, MacDougall, and Smith, "Participatory Action Research."

40. Sawhney, Graver, and Breitkopf, "Audio Journaling for Self-Reflection."

41. Higgins, Nairn, and Sligo, "Peer Research with Youth."

42. Sawhney, "Making Sense of Participatory Video."

43. The Gaza coastline is usually a very dangerous area due to the Israeli imposed siege. Israeli patrol boats regularly monitor Gaza's coastline and fire on Palestinian fishing vessels that go beyond the permitted distance of three nautical miles from the shore, killing many fishermen each year.

BIBLIOGRAPHY

Ahmed, A., N. Azez, F. Al Mabhoh, A. Moter, F. A. Asheba, M. Al Khateb, and M. Amar, dirs. *Walking towards the Truth. Voices Beyond Walls*, 2010. Duration: 11:00 minutes. https://youtu.be/4qBVPyRKeTU.

Ahmed, A., H. Afana, O. Ahmed, Y. A. Amsha, dirs. *I Wish I Were Deaf (Yaa Raitny Atrash)*. Voices Beyond Walls, 2010. Duration: 6:06 minutes. https://youtu.be/Dd _017W9W3A.

Amnesty International. "Israel/Gaza: Operation 'Cast Lead'—22 Days of Death and Destruction. Facts and Figures." *Amnesty International Publications*. July 2, 2009. Ref: MDE 15/021/2009.

———. "A Year On from Deadly Israel/Gaza Conflict, the Nightmare Continues."

November 14, 2013.https://www.amnesty.org/en/latest/news/2013/11/year-deadly
-israelgaza-conflict-nightmare-continues/.

Barber, B. K. *Adolescents and War: How Youth Deal with Political Violence*. New York: Oxford University Press, 2009.

———. "Contrasting Portraits of War: Youths' Varied Experiences with Political Violence in Bosnia and Palestine." *International Journal of Behavioral Development* 32, no. 4 (2008): 298–309.

Baum, F., C. MacDougall, and D. Smith. "Participatory Action Research." *Journal of Epidemiology & Community Health* 60, no. 10 (2006): 854–57.

Betancourt, T. S., and K. T. Khan. "The Mental Health of Children Affected by Armed Conflict: Protective Processes and Pathways to Resilience." *International Review of Psychiatry* 20, no. 3 (2008): 317–28.

Betancourt, T. S., S. E. Meyers-Ohki, A. P. Charrow, and W. A. Tol. "Interventions for Children Affected by War: An Ecological Perspective on Psychosocial Support and Mental Health Care. *Harvard Review of Psychiatry* 21, no. 2 (2013): 70–91.

Betancourt, T. S., L. Speelman, G. Onyango, and P. Bolton. "A Qualitative Study of Mental Health Problems among Children Displaced by War in Northern Uganda." *Transcultural Psychiatry* 46, no. 2 (2009): 238–56.

Carroll, K. "Teenage Brains Are Elastic: That's a Big Opportunity for Social-Emotional Learning." *EdSurge*, August 26, 2019. https://www.edsurge.com/news/2019-08-26-teenage-brains-are-elastic-that-s-a-big-opportunity-for-social-emotional-learning.

Daiute, C. "Critical Narrating by Adolescents Growing Up in War: Case Study across the Former Yugoslavia." In *Narrative Development in Adolescence: Creating the Storied Self*. Advancing Responsible Adolescent Development, edited by Kate C. McLean and Monisha Pasupathi, *207–30*. Boston, Mass.: Springer, 2010.

Defense for Children International Palestine. "Operation Protective Edge: A War Waged on Children." Defense for Children International Palestine (DCIP) Publications, April 16, 2015.

Feldman, I. *Life Lived in Relief: Humanitarian Predicaments and Palestinian Refugee Politics*. Oakland: University of California Press, 2018.

Garcia-Dia, M. J., J. M. Dinapoli, L. Garcia-Ona, R. Jakubowska, and D. O'Flaherty. "Concept Analysis: Resilience." *Archives of Psychiatric Nursing* 27, no. 6 (2013): 264–70.

Hashemi, M., and M. Sánchez-Jankowski. "Children in Crisis: Ethnographic Studies in International Contexts." *Routledge Advances in Sociology* 105 (2013).

Higgins, J., K. Nairn, and J. Sligo. "Peer Research with Youth: Negotiating (Sub)Cultural Capital, Place and Participation in Aotearoa/New Zealand." In *Participatory Action Research Approaches and Methods: Connecting People, Participation and Place*, edited by Sara Kindon, Rachel Pain, and Mike Kesby, 105–11. New York: Routledge, 2007.

Huynh, K., B. D'Costa, and K. Lee-Koo. *Children and Global Conflict*. Cambridge: Cambridge University Press, 2015.

Luthar, S. S. "Annotation: Methodological and Conceptual Issues in Research on Childhood Resilience." *Journal of Child Psychology and Psychiatry* 34, no. 4 (1993): 441–53.

Marie, M., B. Hannigan, and A. Jones. "Resilience of Nurses Who Work in Community

Mental Health Workplaces in Palestine." *International Journal of Mental Health Nursing* 26, no. 4 (2017): 344–54.

———. "Social Ecology of Resilience and Sumud of Palestinians." *Health* 22, no. 1 (2018): 20–35.

Massad, S., R. Stryker, S. Mansour, and U. Khammash. "Rethinking Resilience for Children and Youth in Conflict Zones: The Case of Palestine." *Research in Human Development* 15, nos. 3–4 (2018): 280–93.

Masten, A. S. "Resilience in Developing Systems: Progress and Promise as the Fourth Wave Rises. *Development and Psychopathology* 19 (2007): 921–30.

Nguyen-Gillham, V., R. Giacaman, G. Naser, and W. Boyce. "Normalising the Abnormal: Palestinian Youth and the Contradictions of Resilience in Protracted Conflict." *Health and Social Care in the Community* 16, no. 3 (2008): 291–98.

Rutter, M. "Resilience as a Dynamic Concept." *Development and Psychopathology* 24 (2012): 335–44.

Sawhney, N. "Making Sense of Participatory Video: Approaches for Participatory Content Analysis." In *The Handbook of Participatory Video*, edited by E-J Milne, Claudia Mitchell, and Naydene de Lange. Lanham, Md.: AltaMira Press, 2012.

———. "Voices beyond Walls: The Role of Digital Storytelling for Empowering Marginalized Youth in Refugee Camps." In *Proceedings of the 8th International Conference on Interaction Design and Children* (IDC '09), 302–5. New York: ACM, 2009.

Sawhney, N., C. Graver, and E. Breitkopf. "Audio Journaling for Self-Reflection and Assessment among Teens in Participatory Media Programs." In *Proceedings of the 17th Interaction Design and Children Conference (IDC '18),* 93–105. Trondheim, Norway: ACM, 2018.

Sawhney, N., and R. Hill, dirs. *Flying Paper.* Journeyman Pictures, 2013. Duration: 52 mins. http://www.FlyingPaper.org.

———. *Gaza from Within: Return to Seifa Village*, 2014. Duration: 10:49 mins. http://flyingpaper.org/gaza-from-within/.

Sawyer, S. M., P. S. Azzopardi, Dakshitha Wickremarathne, and George C. Patton. "The Age of Adolescence." *The Lancet Child & Adolescent Health* 2, no. 3 (2018): 223–28.

Shalhoub-Kevorkian, N. *Incarcerated Childhood and the Politics of Unchilding.* Cambridge: Cambridge University Press, 2019.

Sousa, C. A., M. M. Haj-Yahia, G. Feldman, and J. Lee. "Individual and Collective Dimensions of Resilience within Political Violence." *Trauma, Violence, & Abuse* 14 (2013): 235–54.

Thabet, A. A. M., A. Abu Tawahina, R. L. Punamäki, and P. Vostanis. "Prevalence and Mental Health Function of Resilience in Condition of Military Siege and Violence in a Palestinian Community Sample." *Journal of Psychiatry* 18, no. 3 (2015): 1–9.

Ungar, M. "Resilience across Cultures." *British Journal of Social Work* 38 (2008): 218–35.

———. "The Social Ecology of Resilience: Addressing Contextual and Cultural Ambiguity of a Nascent Construct." *American Journal of Orthopsychiatry* 81 (2011): 1–17.

———. *The Social Ecology of Resilience: A Handbook of Theory and Practice.* New York: Springer, 2012.

Ungar, M., M. Brown, L. Liebenberg, R. Othman, W. M. Kwong, M. Armstrong, and

J. Gilgun. "Unique Pathways to Resilience across Cultures." *Adolescence* 42 (2007): 287–310.

UNICEF. "Children in the State of Palestine." UNICEF *Report,* UN068305, November 2018.

United Nations Country Team. "Gaza in 2020: A Liveable Place?" *United Nations Country Team (*UNCT*) Report,* August 27, 2012.

UN Office for the Coordination of Humanitarian Affairs Occupied Palestinian Territory (UN OCHA-OPT). *Situation Report,* September 4, 2014. https://www.ochaopt.org /content/occupied-palestinian-territory-gaza-emergency-situation-report-4 -september-2014-0800-hrs.

Whyte, W. F., ed. *Participatory Action Research.* Thousand Oaks, Calif.: Sage Publications, 1991.

"I Did Something Big"

Crossing Emotional Frontiers
as a Palestinian Unchild

HEIDI MORRISON

> I long for my mother's bread
> Her coffee
> Her touch
> Childhood memories grow up in me
> Day after day
> I must be worth my life
> At the hour of my death
> Worth the tears of my mother.
>
> —excerpt from Mahmoud Darwish's poem "To My Mother"

In the above excerpt, acclaimed Palestinian poet Mahmoud Darwish uses the word "mother" as a metaphor for Palestine. The poem captures his feelings of love, respect, and anguish for his homeland, which in his childhood instilled in him many life-affirming tastes, smells, and sensations. The poem goes on to claim that his childhood memories motivate his behavior and actions on behalf of Palestine: "Use me as wood to feed your fire; / As the clothesline on the roof of your house." This poem illustrates how a child's deeply emotional relationship with his homeland has a profound impact on the course of his life.

In this chapter, I ask how children's emotional experiences can help us rethink conventional academic attitudes toward children's agency, a concept that in academic research is usually understood as the child's capacity to act independently and to make free choices. Scholars use the word "agency" without question, usually to mean that a child displays adult-like qualities of free will.[1] Agency all too often slips from being a conceptual tool to being an endpoint, inhibiting more analytically productive discussions.[2] As an unchallenged concept, agency locks the researcher into an adult-centric worldview with a Western, liberal definition of the individual. I seek to construct a different (child-centered) set of parameters for understanding children's agency. Instead of beginning with the question "What did the child do (or not do)?" I begin with the question "How and why did the child behave as he/she did?" The latter question formulates agency as something relative to the individual child. In Darwish's poem, the person acts in relation to his feelings: the taste and nourishment of childhood drive his quest to prove his worth to his people. In this chapter, I argue for a new understanding of children's agency, one that considers emotion as the launching point for actions and choices.

This chapter consists of three parts. First, I begin with a rough overview of the theoretical debates on agency, a concept that has been in widespread use among scholars for over a half-century. Second, I provide a portrait of a young adult Palestinian named Hani, who grew up during the second Palestinian intifada, a period of intensified violence from 2000 to 2006. Since childhood, Hani has been in exile, both inside and outside his home, and in his homeland. His life is enmeshed in the system of unchilding, defined as Israel's ongoing wounding of children and their dispossession from childhood.[3] Nonetheless, he transgresses the limits of acceptable behavior to try to find a way out of his marginalized status. The third part of this chapter connects the existing literature on agency with the portrait of Hani himself, paying particular attention to his emotions.

The chapter has three goals: 1) to avoid the conventionally flattening approach to children's agency that reduces agency to the binary categories of the powerful vs. the powerless; instead, I maintain that there are multiple forms of agency that can be accessed by engaging with the child's emotional world; 2) to demonstrate, through one in-depth case study, Israel's instrumentalization of the Palestinian child's emotions to affirm its control and achieve its political goals (unchilding); 3) to call attention to the child-oriented strategies one Palestinian boy used to traverse traumatic emotional situations.

Between 2010 and 2019, I visited Palestine numerous times, which included one year spent as a Fulbright scholar. I completed more than sixty multipart, in-depth oral life-history interviews with a cohort of eleven young adult Palestinians who had grown up during the second intifada. Instead of providing equal coverage of all interviewees, this chapter relies instead on micro-analysis, drawing from the life story of a single one of the Palestinians in my cohort.

Engaging with the Concept of Agency

In the 1960s and 1970s, scholars began documenting agency, in an effort to give voice to marginalized and neglected people. These scholars contested top-down (structural) views of power, arguing instead that ordinary people have the capacity to change their lives.[4] Working across a variety of academic disciplines, the agency movement focuses on oppressed groups, such as the enslaved, the poor, the colonized, women, and children. A guiding pillar of this important intellectual work was to "give the slaves back their agency," motivated by the contemporaneous growth of the civil rights movement and African American studies. To this day, agency theory remains a way to counter reductionist representations of marginalized groups as helpless victims.

By the early 2000s, however, some scholars began questioning the usefulness of the agency concept itself.[5] Critics range from those who want to replace the concept completely to those who want to reengage with its definition and purpose.[6] One of the fundamental problems with the scholarly concept of agency, as captured in Walter Johnson's pivotal 2003 article, is its ethnocentrism, or Western liberal conception of the individual. Scholars seeking to identify agency often do so through a narrow lens of how a human should act, that is, exercising free will. The focus on autonomous action obfuscates collective action, particularly the way in which people's everyday acts can operate together to effect change. For example, in terms of the history of slavery, Johnson argues that agency includes alliances and solidarity, such as providing refuge for someone or sharing in similar forms of prayer.[7] In gender studies, scholars such as Joan Scott argue that agency is created through situations, not independent choice, and Saba Mahmood shows that agency can include subordination in the face of power.[8] In children's studies, David Lancy argues that the mid- and upper-class Western model of agency assumes that a child must effectively challenge adults and have rights, whereas in other societies children earn their power and elevate their social position by being useful and mastering assigned responsibilities.[9] Exercising agency in the Western sense can come at a price for some children. Insisting that all people practice agency—let alone a Western form of it—leaves little room for divergent forms and analysis of the concept itself.

Another fundamental problem with the conventional scholarly concept of agency is the way some scholars appropriate it to serve themselves, despite their stated best intentions. The white-savior complex looms large behind the agency movement. For example, Johnson points out that white scholars in African American studies in the 1960s and 1970s often used agency to signal their goodwill toward their African American colleagues, an alignment that was not of pressing concern for the latter. He claims further that white scholars benefited from these gestures by using them to wipe away the sins of the past. Lynn Thomas claims that agency has become an easy and safe escape for scholars searching for an argument that won't be deemed politically incorrect.[10] For example, the resiliency narrative is popular among scholars of African women. Also highly problematic are some scholars' claims to cultural competency and their sense of entitlement to grant agency to another person. Gayatri Spivak's seminal article "Can the Subaltern Speak?" signals the power dynamics behind being heard, particularly the way in which elites mediate perspectives of the "Other" ultimately to create representations of themselves.[11] Lancy criticizes opportunistic scholars who seek to "liberate" children to advance their own agenda, political or career-wise. He says that agency dogma has become so institutionalized that it now even shapes research funding opportunities.[12] Thus, the quest to emphasize the agency of individuals can come at the expense of the individuals under study, as well as the integrity of one's research methodology.

In this chapter, I adopt two innovative analytical tools from the criticisms of agency described above. First, I seek to avoid the "agency trap" by refusing to rely on binaries such as strong vs. weak, good vs. bad, or powerful vs. powerless;[13] they are based on the simplistic notion that an individual is always able to act freely in the world. A binary worldview reinforces the misconception that hierarchies of power are monolithic and always transparent: a person is either free or oppressed. In reality, hierarchies contain multiple intertwining, interfacing, and masked dimensions, which individuals negotiate in various ways. The "child vs. adult" binary shapes conventional analysis of children's agency. Such analysis, born out of the children's rights movement, celebrates children's "voice," that is, speaking up for oneself and defending one's interests.[14] Although children's voice is important, the concept also has its limitations. It associates childhood with budding adulthood, or the inevitable progress toward maturity, rationality, and independence. It also assumes children to be powerless in relation to adults, leaving adult privilege intact. In order to understand children's worlds more fully, we must replace adulthood as the default point of comparison and reaching adulthood as the inevitable purpose of childhood.[15] Thus, this chapter operates from the assumption that adultlike actions are not the only framework through which to view children's agency.

Second, and building from the first point, this chapter intends to leave space for various meanings of children's agency. For this, I turn to Judith Butler's idea of intersubjective agency, the idea that agency occurs in relation to others and expresses internalized social norms.[16] This means that agency concerns social interactions and is a continuous process of situations within which one has to act.[17] When we take agency to be the navigation of relationships, then multiple identity markers (gender, age, race, ability, sexuality, etc.) come to bear. Like all people, children have many intersecting identities, in addition to just their age. As they face multiple forms of marginalization, they can create multiple forms of resistance: children's agency is multilayered in form, intent, and impact. What qualifies as children's agency is not always written or spoken, nor does it always consist of spectacular public acts of heroism. For example, children's agency can include silence, the performance of voice, or incoherent voices.[18] While it can include outright defiance of adults, it can also include adherence to social norms, such as gaining the approval of adults. It is important to consider what the children themselves understand as agency: it can look radically different across and within communities. Thus, I focus less on ascribing agency to the individual child, and more on unpacking the meaning of agency in its respective contexts.

The Emotional World of a Child

In order to account for multiple forms of agency, this chapter asks questions about how and why children act in the world. I do not seek to expose and define children's agency; instead, I seek to understand the motivations that guide action (or, in other words, the emotional world in which the child lives). This approach to children's agency privileges the emotions of the child, as expressed in his/her thoughts and experiences.[19] This approach to children's agency is based on the idea that "emotional patterns reflect and help sustain relationships of power."[20] Power is inextricably linked to a child's emotions because emotions are not fixed, but learned in relation to one's context and mediated through experience.[21] Adults have pinpointed childhood as the most intense period of shaping a person's emotions (i.e., in a process called emotional formation). This is not to say that children are blank slates or that there is a politics of intention everywhere.[22] But emotional formation has enormous political potential because there are competing interests in the emotional identity of a child.[23] Childhood is when we learn how to feel in a given situation and we learn how to negotiate different emotional spaces. Children are taught to express certain feelings in certain situations. Childhood is when we learn the feelings that align us with some people and against others.[24]

In this chapter, I engage specifically a part of a child's emotional formation called "emotional frontiers." An emotional frontier is the place where a child experiences mixed emotional demands.[25] As a basic example, children face an emotional frontier when the emotional prescriptions they learn at home collide with those they encounter among their peers. Or the clash could be between school and home or a religious institution and home. A child encounters a frontier when "there is a struggle within the child for primacy of an emotional regime."[26] An emotional frontier is a place of high stakes. A child may choose to navigate the frontier in a variety of ways. They may choose to break with expected emotional norms or hold conflicting emotional norms at once. Many children pass through emotional frontiers with ease on a regular basis, without notice; however, some frontiers register in the individual child through extreme discomfort, a stressful conscious shift, or a painful misunderstanding. Some frontiers produce violent confrontation between people. An emotional frontier is a place where a child can be pulled apart, disassembled, or find himself in emotional crisis.[27] Emotional frontiers are valuable windows allowing us to understand the how and why of children's thoughts and actions.

A child's experience at an emotional frontier is historically, culturally, politically, and socially contingent: that is to say, emotional frontiers are a product of their time and place, as well as a child's race, class, and gender. Children in underprivileged social positions face acute emotional boundaries. Take, for example, the situation of children subject to settler colonialism, which operates not only within the material world of children, but also in collisions involving emotional expectations. In colonial spaces, the child is constantly faced with competing power relationships pulling them in multiple directions. As an example, in Canada and Australia's long history of residential schools, the colonizer removed indigenous children from their homes to retrain them in European ways, to "take the Indian out of the child." As historians Karen Vallgårda, Kristine Alexander, and Stephanie Olsen describe it:

> They [children and young people] were taught habits of feeling derived from an emotional formation in contrast to the one according to which they were raised. No matter where they settled, missionaries and child welfare and education workers as well as social leaders never operated in a social or political vacuum; rather they encountered collaboration and adaption, but also subtle or fierce resistance from the people whose worldviews, ways of living and modes of feeling they sought to change. In this matter, children often became important symbols in battles among groups of adults in their attempts to shape the future of society.[28]

Thus, emotional formation must be understood in the context of such forces as race, class, and gender.

In terms of understanding the emotional world of children in Palestine, it is crucial to situate their experience in the context of unchilding, which (as mentioned above) can be defined as Israel's use of Palestinian children as expendable currency to affirm its control and achieve its political goals. Since birth (and even before, via fertility politics), Palestinian children serve as political capital in the hands of the state of Israel.[29] All spheres of Israeli violence against the Palestinian child involve emotions. Evicting children from their childhood includes the intention to disrupt their emotional formation, or their ability to learn the comportment and expression expected of them in given situations and by certain people. Gaining competency in the use of expected emotional codes constitutes healthy development in children. An important part of childhood is learning to adapt to and navigate emotional frontiers. The unchild experiences acute situations of emotional frontiers. In this chapter, emotional frontiers are used as access points into Palestinian children's worlds.

To enter these spaces effectively, creative techniques are required. I use a combination of oral history and portraiture to recreate the experience of a child to the extent possible.[30] Oral history allows us to hear ordinary people's voices and understand qualitatively their experiences with violence. Portraiture allows us to blend social sciences with art to understand life as it is lived and the web of forces shaping a person. My portraits are based on the oral history interview material I gathered in my multiyear research. This chapter includes one portrait, which although it does not provide equal coverage of all Palestinian children, does provide an in-depth look at one child's life experience. In the discussion that follows the portrait, I focus on one main emotional frontier from his life story (although the entire portrait is offered to provide context).

Portrait of Hani

Hani was eleven years old when he made his first "illegal" border crossing. At ten o'clock at night, without permission, he entered an Israeli settlement near his house in a Palestinian town under Israeli military occupation located just outside Jerusalem. Hani was desperate to escape a chronically abusive uncle at home. He hoped that an Israeli police officer would protect him. Israeli police jeeps quickly surrounded the vagrant Palestinian boy. At first the officers told Hani that his situation was outside their legal jurisdiction; then they said they would help him on the condition that he act as a Palestinian informant. He agreed.

By international law, Hani's crossing was hardly "illegal," since Israel built the Jewish-only settlement on land stolen from Palestinians. Nonetheless, as a Palestinian from the West Bank, Hani is prohibited from freely entering Israel's borders. The night Hani entered the settlement, his town was under an Israeli-imposed curfew that closed all Palestinian civil services. Most inhabitants of Hani's town, including Hani's family, hold Palestinian ID cards, which makes them ineligible to receive Israeli civil services. (Since 1967, there are three types of Israeli-issued compulsory Palestinian IDs: West Bank ID, Gaza ID, and Jerusalem ID. A carrier of a West Bank ID can only move around the West Bank, and rarely receives permits to enter Israel proper. The West Bank ID holder can be prosecuted in Israeli or Palestinian Authority [PA] courts.) Israel controls the "security" of Hani's hometown, but this mandate does not include affairs relating to the inhabitants' welfare. Even Palestinians from other parts of the West Bank must get permits from Israel to enter Hani's town to help.

Hani was a gentle child who built tree forts, cared for his rabbits, and longed to have a flock of sheep. Light-hearted, he enjoyed laughing and dancing with his sister. Hani intuitively knew that he did not deserve his uncle's abuse. The need for protection impelled Hani to cross to the "other side," becoming an informant against his own people. At the heart of the arrangement between Hani and Israeli police officers was a perverse logic: an oppressed Palestinian child sought refuge in the Israeli oppressor's arms. Born a nobody with many strikes against him, Hani decided at an early age that his only hope for achieving some form of dignity was to violate his community's norms and values. Although he did not know it at the time, Hani would repeat various permutations of this desperate behavior throughout his life.

The abuse Hani suffered at the hands of his uncle was part of a larger pattern: most of his family treated him as an outcast. Hani became acutely aware of this unfortunate reality at the age of seven, when his parents sent him to live with his elderly grandfather. Harmless childhood antics had triggered the banishment, but there was more to it than that: Hani's cousin had brought earthworms into the house and unfairly blamed it on Hani. The cousin's mother beat Hani with a phone charger, while Hani frantically jumped from sofa to table and back to dodge the blows. In Hani's aunts' and uncles' eyes, the worm incident confirmed what they already sensed: Hani was a bad influence on their children. Hani's parents were also concerned about their son because his behavior differed from that of his brothers. Hani sometimes liked to dress up as a girl, putting on his mother's apron and lipstick, prancing around the house, singing and pretending to dust furniture.

At his grandfather's house, Hani did housework and tended to the kind old man's needs. Hani admired his grandfather for having overcome many challenges in his life. The grandfather was illiterate until he taught himself to read and write at seventy years of age. Orphaned at age six, he became a street child until a mechanic took him in, teaching him his trade. The grandfather grew up to become a rich man and marry four different women (his first wife died in childbirth). During the Nakba, the grandfather fled with his family from their town near Jerusalem to Jordan. Hani's grandmother hid in a cave for a week to avoid Israeli soldiers hearing her baby's cry, then trailblazed the rest of the route to Jordan alone. When the family returned to their hometown a year later, they found it under Jordanian rule. The family home remained intact and unoccupied by Israelis, but surrounding areas had been overtaken. The Israeli encroachment on the town turned into full-blown occupation in the 1967 war, and continues until today.

Hani's grandfather passed away in the early 2000s, making it necessary for the eleven-year-old to move back to live at his parents' house. Almost immediately, the extended family ostracized Hani by prohibiting him from playing with their children, or even entering their homes. One uncle, Abed, was particularly mean to him; Hani recalls that his big hands felt like steel when they struck.

The deal the Israeli police made with Hani was to aid him in exchange for evidence that Abed was a security threat to Israel. Hani had no such evidence, but fabricated a convincing lie: he told the police that Abed had a gun hidden in his closet. They dressed Hani in protective gear (i.e., helmet and jacket) and told him to take them to Abed's building. They then ordered Hani to draw a map of the exact location of the gun. Hani directed the police to a gun he knew could be found in the closet of another uncle, Youssef, who was usually very nice to Hani. Hani planned to convince the police later that the gun belonged to Abed. The police closed down all the surrounding streets, brought in reinforcements (including dogs and ambulances), and stormed the building. Perched high up inside the Israeli police jeep, Hani watched the officers line up thirty Palestinian men against the wall, hands roped together. Hani was in disbelief, and recalls thinking, "What have I done? I did something big. Where did all these police come from?"

Hani tried to come down from the jeep to point out which one of the men was Abed, but the weight of the gear he was wearing made it difficult for him to move. Youssef magnanimously assumed ownership of the gun to spare all the other men trouble, and the police took Youssef away in handcuffs. When officers finally helped Hani down from the jeep, he informed them that they had taken the wrong man; they refused to listen. So Hani invented a second lie to try to rectify the matter. He told the police that there was another gun in Abed's house. The police turned Abed's house upside down, but found nothing incriminating there. They left at 3 a.m., failing to arrest Abed. The police dumped Hani off on the side of the road, on the outskirts of his town.

In a state of shock, Hani wandered around until he found himself back at his parents' house. His mother and father beat him severely, then his mother locked him in the bathroom for three days, hands and legs tied. He was without food and water, except for the few drops he could glean from the tap. The mother told Hani's brothers to urinate on him whenever they used the bathroom. In an effort to save face, given her son's treason, Hani's mother publicly bragged about the harsh punishment she had made him endure. One neighbor had pity on Hani and rescued him. Hani recalls that his mother swiftly retrieved him, slapping him with her shoe all the way home. He says his mother put him in the bathroom for one more day, then isolated him in a room for one week. Hani tried escaping a few times, but to no avail.

Hani's parents eventually sent him to live with his aging grandmother (from the other side of the family than the deceased grandfather). She was kind to Hani, and prepared him warm milk and a boiled egg each morning. Hani reciprocated her loving care, and stayed there until he was seventeen years old. When Hani's uncle Youssef got out of jail after nine months, he checked in on Hani. This show of concern angered Abed, who then transferred Hani to the worst school in the area. Although the grandmother was very poor, she offered Hani what she could in the form of love. She taught Hani how to grow a garden, tend to fruit trees, and cook various Palestinian dishes.

The incident with the Israeli police from the settlement occurred in 2004, the year that Israel assassinated Hamas leader Ahmed Yassin and Palestine Liberation Organization (PLO) leader Yasser Arafat. Chaos reigned all around Hani's town in the form of multiple school closures, roadblocks, curfews, and dust and noise from construction of the separation barrier. Men were stressed because they could not find work. Teachers were angry because Israeli soldiers patrolled the schools, sometimes pointing guns at children. Children feared that soldiers might shoot them from the control towers being erected alongside the new separation wall.

Hani had a bad reputation at school and in the neighborhood: children called him a girl or an Israeli spy. They refused to talk to him or walk with him. The fact that Hani was perpetually covered in red bedbug bites only intensified his ostracism. He lived in fear that an informant would give his name to the Israelis and he would end up in jail. At fourteen years of age, Hani lost his only friend, a bow-legged, overweight boy who suffocated in the street when he was unable to run fast enough to escape Israeli tear gas.

At age sixteen, in 2006, Hani came face-to-face with his own death. Hani's father caught him on the roof kissing another young man. The father said he was ashamed of Hani and disowned him, throwing his clothes into the sewer and destroying the computer he had bought for himself. The father dumped Hani shoeless on the outskirts of town and told him never to come back. Desperate, Hani once again decided to seek help in Israel. He jumped the Israeli separation barrier, which now completely encaged the town. He set off walking for Haifa, a liberal Israeli coastal town containing a mixture of Palestinians and Jews. Once Haifa was the main industrial port city of Palestinians until Zionists expelled its inhabitants to form the state of Israel in 1948. (The Palestinian-Arabs who remain there today, 9 percent of the population, are treated as second-class citizens.) Hani followed highway signs to Haifa and drank bits of water from discarded bottles on the side of the road.

After ten hours of walking in the summer sun, he lost the will to live, unable to summon up his usual optimism and inner strength. He threw himself in front of cars, but they swerved away. An Israeli police car picked him up, though the officers said they were unable to help a person with a Palestinian ID. The police dumped Hani back on the outskirts of his hometown. Hani called his uncle

Youssef to pick him up and bring him to his grandmother's house. When Hani
went to bed that night, he told his grandmother not to wake him in the morning.
Hani secretly overdosed on acetaminophen. The next morning, his grandmother
found him wailing from pain and vomiting in his sleep. Youssef rushed Hani to
the closest clinic, where a doctor said he needed the advanced level of care available only at Israel's leading hospital, Hadassah. Hospitals in the West Bank are
sometimes unequipped to deal with sophisticated medical procedures because
Israel permits only limited medical supplies to enter. Also, since the occupation
began, Israel has hindered development of various medical facilities, for example
turning the newly built and planned government hospital into the central police
station in the Sheikh Jarrah area.

Youssef drove Hani to the checkpoint into Jerusalem, but they were denied entry because of their Palestinian IDs. Palestinians from the West Bank attempting
to enter Israel without permit are often denied access to essential and life-saving
medical care. Border security was especially tight owing to Israel's war with Lebanon. Youssef detoured to a Palestinian hospital in Jericho, an hour away. No one
at the hospital knew how to treat Hani's condition; during the four days he spent
there, he received no overdose-reversal medicine. His liver was at a 90 percent
failure rate. Hani's mother suddenly showed up and arranged to have an ambulance take him to a hospital in Jerusalem. Hani's entry was again denied at Israeli
checkpoints. Finally, after many attempts, the ambulance received permission to
pass, but then the Israeli hospital would not admit him. Hani finally found a bed
in a less-than-reputable hospital in East Jerusalem, a predominantly Palestinian
area. (There are world-renowned Palestinian doctors in Israeli hospitals in West
and East Jerusalem, but most hospitals in East Jerusalem are understaffed and
undersupplied.) The doctor said that Hani would not survive; he would soon enter a coma and his body would waste away within a year. In one last effort to find
a course of treatment, the doctor consulted with a medical center in America. After twenty-one days of treatment, Hani's liver was functioning at a rate of 67 percent and the doctor said he could go home. Hani's mother had to sneak her son
out of the hospital, because she was unable to pay the 18,000-shekel bill.

Over the following year, Hani slowly rebuilt his strength. His grandmother
nourished his body with the healthiest food she could afford. After Hani finished
his last year of high school, he began work in a restaurant kitchen in another
part of the West Bank. He nurtured the culinary passion instilled by his grandmother. "I re-found my appetite to live through food and cooking," Hani recalls.
"The happy side of me will never die." Hani's love for animals encouraged him to
become a vegetarian. With dreams of attending a culinary school abroad, Hani
reached out to a distant uncle who had married an American woman and had re-

mained in the USA after their divorce. The uncle refused to help Hani, telling him that too many immigrants were cheating the American government.

Hani was deeply confused and disappointed, but decided not to give up on his dream. He turned to the persevering and resourceful part of his character that had always emerged in difficult situations. His common refrain is: "Shit is better than nothing." Hani decided to teach himself how to be an expert in the kitchen. He watched every episode he could find online of the world-renowned chef Jamie Oliver. He collected menus, talked to chefs, and bought cookbooks at flea markets. He visited elderly Palestinian farmers, trying to learn about heirloom seeds and traditional techniques for cultivating the land. Sometimes he jumped the separation wall to seek out in Israeli supermarkets ingredients that were otherwise unavailable in the occupied West Bank. Hani tried out new recipes as a volunteer chef in a Palestinian special-needs home. He made friends with foreigners, helping them host dinner parties in their lavish apartments.

For every door that had been slammed in Hani's face as a child, he earnestly opened new ones as a young man. He became part of the underground gay scene, occasionally dating men. He daringly pierced his ears and bleached his hair, a rare sight in the West Bank. At the urging of friends, he tried modeling. Sometimes he earned money as a pet sitter for foreigners. Other than cooking, his next greatest passion was home décor. He taught himself how to restore old Palestinian doors that dated from before Israel's founding. He regularly scoured flea markets and derelict houses for these antiques, lugging them across town and stashing them wherever he could find space. Each door he revived blew life back into his existence, and to a certain extent his Palestinian heritage as well. Hani opened doors to new horizons, even within the confines of the oppressive political situation. Nonetheless, he felt angry that Israel kept him trapped in the West Bank with so few opportunities. He often wondered why Israel considered a chef to be dangerous.

As much as Hani worked to make the best of his situation, he also refused to give up trying to escape. Escape had failed him on numerous accounts, from collaborating with Israeli police to his own suicide attempt; nevertheless he never stopped believing that he could achieve dignity by trespassing normal boundaries. Hani longed to live abroad, where open doors seemed more plentiful. He found such an opportunity through a middle-aged French journalist named Camille whom he met in the West Bank. She was fed up with reporting on a political situation that only seemed to worsen with time; she wanted to witness real change happening for Palestinians. On one trip home, she arranged the paperwork to bring Hani as her fiancé, with the hopes of eventually allowing him to acquire French citizenship via marriage. The situation between Hani and Camille turned sour in Paris, and Hani ended up spending only one month there. Before his departure, he signed up for a baking class at the Cordon Bleu. Since he lacked the means to pay for the class, the school let him attend on the understanding that he would pay later.

Back in his small village at the foot of Jerusalem's Mount of Olives, Hani used his newly acquired baking skills to develop a small business selling homemade goods. He brought his sister into the successful venture, teaching her everything he knew. Hani and his sister teamed with local olive and herb producers to infuse their baked goods with flavor and a sense of heritage. Ramallah's NGO-based economy, dependent on foreign aid, provided a small bubble for the business to thrive. (Their hometown afforded no market for their products.)

Like many of their young male counterparts, Hani's brothers struggled to find jobs other than the humiliating work offered in the Israeli settlements. Many of these young men were frustrated, and expressed their anger in troublemaking, such as fighting with each other in the street or throwing stones at the Israeli soldiers at checkpoints. (Hani's younger brother, for example, spent his last year of high school in an Israeli jail.) Hani did not feel welcome in his hometown and returned only occasionally to tend to his collection of antique doors. Hani remained largely estranged from his parents, but he and his mother developed a quiet bond over home décor; Hani would bring her special finds from the flea market. Nonetheless, Hani's mother criticized her son for "running around with atheists" and "having a different mentality" that she worried drew negative attention from locals.

As Hani became well known around some parts of the West Bank for his culinary talent, his piercings and dyed hair stood out all the more. He also became more confident in his sexuality, emerging as a leader in the local LGBTQ scene. At many of the hip cafés around town where he sold his products, he also met with activists to plan what they hoped would be the first ever gay pride parade in the West Bank. Hani and his peers were fed up with Israel's presenting of itself to the world as the freedom-loving gay haven of the Middle East while committing human-rights atrocities against Palestinians. Hani felt that Israel's hosting of Eurovision 2019, the world's largest "Gay Olympics" within the global music scene, was a shameful cover-up of Israel's gross indignities toward Palestinians. Unfortunately, Hani's activism and increasingly visible public persona created trouble for him. One night while he chatted with friends in front of a restaurant, a Palestinian man came up to him and said, "Are you Hani, the guy spreading gayness around Palestine and making a gay parade?" Before Hani could respond, the man attacked him violently. The incident was captured by the restaurant's security camera. Exactly the same incident happened to Hani two days later in front of a downtown juice shop. Hani reported the crime to Palestinian police, but no evidence was found and no one was charged. Hani does not know who the perpetrator of the crime was, and has not ruled out its being a Palestinian agitator paid by Israel.

Hani feared for his life in Palestine. With the help of foreign friends, he obtained a tourist visa to Greece, where he stayed past its expiration date to file for asylum. Hani remains in tenuous living conditions in Greece, along with more than a million other desperate migrants who have crossed the Mediterranean to Europe since 2015. While in Greece, Hani lost his mother to breast cancer. Their last tearful words were exchanged on Skype. Hani's sister continues to run the bakery business. Hani continues his "illegal" search for dignity.

Discussion

The purpose of this discussion is not to prove (or disprove) that the child has (or lacks) agency. Certainly the portrait could provide grounds for such black-and-white thinking. The informant incident could be viewed as a helpless, victimized boy selling out to his oppressor. Or, at the other extreme, it could be understood as the story of a resourceful boy trying to protect himself within the confines of an oppressive system. In reality, the incident is both of these things at once, and more. Opening our understanding to the gray zones of agency focuses on the complex emotional demands that children's worlds present. An emotion-based approach to agency raises an entirely different set of questions, namely: How does unchilding mark a child's emotional formation in the context of a structurally racist settler colonialism that escalates dispossession? How does unchilding complicate our notion of traumatic emotional frontiers? What tools do children use to survive difficult crossings of emotional frontiers?

How Does Unchilding Mark
a Child's Emotional Formation?

Before we can explore the impact of unchilding on Hani's emotional well-being, we must address the issue of homophobia in today's Palestine. It would be all too easy to blame Hani's child abuse solely on the stigmatization of queerness in Palestinian society. As in any part of the world, in Palestine people face different and intersecting forms of oppression. In Palestine, homophobia must be understood in the context of the Israeli military occupation, which controls virtually every aspect of Palestinian life. Israeli "pinkwashing" (depicting Israel as a safe haven for queer people and Palestine as not) attempts to distract from Israel's human-rights abuses in the Occupied Territories; it also attempts to justify Israel's military occupation of Palestine, as actions toward people needing to be subordinated in order to achieve emancipation from their backward culture. Such an

assertion denies the existence of a Palestinian queer movement existing both locally and transnationally.[31] Pinkwashing obfuscates intersectional framing of sexuality in Palestine and disavows the range of experiences of being queer in Palestine.[32] In reality, the struggle against Palestinian homophobia is a struggle against
Zionism, which perpetuates homophobia in Palestine in numerous ways. For example, Israeli intelligence undermines the indigenous Palestinian queer movement, through decades of threats to out queer Palestinians who don't serve as
informants and through attempts to co-op Palestinian queer voices.[33] A key organizing principle of the early Zionist movement was remasculinization of Jewish
identity; even today Israel relies on heightened toxic masculinity, much the same
as in Palestine.[34] Lastly, due in large part to the Israeli occupation, there is no system of sustainable public mental-health services in Palestine;[35] in its absence,
vulnerable groups lack proper supportive and protective social services and resources. The situation regarding homophobia in Palestine is similar to the situation in Kashmir, where India, an occupying power, perpetuates homophobia to
serve its interests.[36] Thus, while Palestinian homophobia played a role in Hani's
emotional trouble in childhood, it is certainly not its starting point.

Unchilding is the better place from which to begin, because it captures multiple intersecting forms of oppression that Palestinian children experience. At its
most basic level, unchilding is the use of Palestinian children as political capital
to advance Israeli state-building on political, economic, socio-temporal, and rhe-
torical levels.[37] As I argue in this chapter, unchilding also works on emotional
levels. It seeks to eliminate the next generation of Palestinians by treating Palestinian children as both *nobodies* who are unworthy of being granted global children's rights and as *dangerous and killable bodies* needing to be caged and dis-
membered. Shalhoub-Kevorkian elaborates:

> This "civilizing" power of settler colonial domination, entangled with the
> global racialized discourse of the "war on terror" (Shalhoub-Kevorkian, 2015a,
> 2015b), constructed the imaginary which relegated Palestinians and Palestin-
> ian children into uncivilized, "criminal," "terrorist" others, to unchild them
> through authorizing the deployment of moral, legal, and political violence
> against them.[38]

Israel defines Palestinian children along a continuum of "the helpless, uncivi-
lized, dangerous, and terrorist Other,"[39] in order to "create, direct, govern, transform, and construct colonized children as dangerous, racialized others, enabling
their eviction from the realm of childhood itself."[40] This definition sends a confusing message to Palestinian children as they grow up. Palestinian children receive from Israel the message that they are worthless criminals, which repudiates

their parents' expectations for them. In part, unchilding tries to cultivate in Palestinian children emotional scripts that are incompatible with those of their parents, which often creates traumatizing emotional frontiers (i.e., collisions of emotional expectations).

During the informant incident, the machinery of unchilding was in full force. In Hani's head, the colonizer was seen as his savior, and the colonizing state could "save" him from his abusive family. Unchilding operates by demonizing parents in the oppressed group as unable to nurture and protect their own children. The goal is to shift the responsibility for colonized children from their own community to the colonizing state, "all the while practicing its gendered and sexualized violation of children's bodies and lives through medical, educational, and welfare politics and technologies of 'saving' and 'caring'—and maintaining evicted children as captives in the hands of the state."[41] The informant incident reveals how the Israeli soldiers reproduced the stratification of colonial order via sexualized violence that pulled Hani into the control of the Israeli state. The Israeli soldiers' goal was not to protect Hani from family abuse, let alone combat the larger structural forces at its root. The Israeli soldiers effectively endorsed the uncle's homophobic violence, while sending the message that they were Hani's supposed protectors. Without access to citizenship and proper social benefits and protections, Hani was pushed to do the unthinkable (i.e., to commit treason) to guarantee his own survival.

In oppressive systems, the oppressor maintains hegemony by persuading the oppressed to collude with their own oppression. This is what Antonio Gramsci calls the "internalization of colonialism" by the colonized. Those who are oppressed in one context can become oppressors in the next.[42] (Jews decimated in the Holocaust could in their turn oppress Palestinians in the decades that followed.) When Hani aligned with the soldiers, he created for himself a sort of positional authority that the soldiers could exploit. The Israeli soldiers conditioned their help for Hani on his providing incriminating evidence against fellow Palestinians. In this "misplaced alliance," the interests of the involved parties (in this case, the Israeli police and Hani) differed. Misplaced alliances are defined as those when one party is the pawn in a chess game and the hegemonic arrangements benefit one particular group.[43] The exchange between the Israeli soldiers and Hani was not an exchange of equals. Appealing to the soldiers was not a "done deal" for Hani; it forced him to risk life and limb.[44] The soldiers dressed Hani in protective gear—again, sending the message of their supposed protection of him—yet ultimately used him to advance their tyranny over the community, as well as exercise divide-and-rule policies. Waking families in the middle of the night and arresting men without reason is a common Israeli practice in the

Occupied Territories. Israeli soldiers often storm family homes at night as a form of terror.[45] Israel also regularly uses informants to pit the colonized against each other.[46]

Unchilding interrupted Hani's emotional formation in childhood because it created debilitating emotional frontiers that he could not resolve successfully. In the informant incident, Hani had to choose between emotional loyalty to the state of Israel vs. to his people and himself. Generally speaking, a successful frontier crossing means the child experiences no more confrontation or unease when encountering different emotional scripts.[47] This was not the case for Hani. The way the incident played out furthered Hani's distress. Quite literally, the incident marginalized Hani even further: first he was dropped at the border, then locked in the bathroom of his home, and finally banished to his grandmother's house. The incident furthered Hani's being labeled as a danger and threat to his own community. It also reinforced the colonial master-slave dialectic, because the power differential between Hani and the Israeli soldiers reinforced his enslavement to them. Even Hani's attempt to commit suicide could be viewed as a way that the colonizer had encouraged the colonized to kill himself, as opposed to facing and fighting oppression.[48]

Unchilding is a battle over a child's emotional identity. As Hani's case shows, unchilding can place heavy emotional strain on children, pushing them into near-insurmountable emotional frontiers. Unchilding seeks to impair the emotional health of the next generation of Palestinians. The malleability of emotions is what makes emotions such a valuable target in war, and it is one of the reasons Israel engineered trauma and mass torture in the 2014 war on Gaza.[49] Critical race theorist Adrien Wing includes "emotional harm" in her definition of spirit injury, or the "slow death of the psyche, the soul, and the persona" of the Palestinian people due to many violations of their human rights, including exile, family dissolution, land dispossession, torture, imprisonment, and death.[50]

How Does Unchilding Complicate Our Notion of Traumatic Emotional Frontiers?

Children navigate emotional frontiers with ease many times during a day. In fact, a sign of healthy emotional formation is the ability to weigh mixed expectations without violence and turmoil. There is no one correct way to handle an emotional frontier: some children blend opposing expectations while others back away altogether. A child may take a very clear stand on an emotional frontier or seem indifferent; they might even construe the emotional codes incorrectly and have to make repeated attempts at crossing. A child can also live quite happily with some unresolved emotional frontiers. The self is always changing in relation to context, and what may be difficult one day could be easy the next. Emotional frontiers register in multiple ways in children, and overcoming challenges can also foster emotional growth. From an emotional-health perspective, concern arises when frontiers create trauma in the child. Toxic stress in the formative developmental years of life causes long-term physical and mental damage, including epigenetic changes.

In situations of unchilding, identifying trauma in children is very difficult because of the all-pervasive nature of the unchilding apparatus; one of its main characteristics is that it "maintains its machinery of dismemberment always and everywhere."[51] Palestinian children do not simply exist in a context of violence; they are the political capital upon which Israeli state crimes subsist. Israel cannot be Israel without using Palestinian children to effect its "state-building, employment, slavery, education, indoctrination, warfare, and health as well as security policies and practices."[52] Thus, trauma for Palestinian children does not occur in isolated incidents; it is a perpetual state. (Of course, Palestinian children find ways to manage and persist, but the narrative of resiliency has its own shortcomings.[53]) In Hani's childhood, his trauma preceded the informant incident by generations, starting with the Nakba, and continued up to and beyond the incident with perpetual wars and occupation. This trauma is embodied in the life experiences of Hani's past relatives who faced expulsion, and members of his extended family who face unemployment and incarceration. Many scholars have pointed out the deficiencies of individualized, Western, medicalized understandings of trauma that extract Palestinians from their context.[54]

If there are no hierarchies in oppression, how can we say there are hierarchies in the traumas that oppressions produce? No one trauma is more important than another. The focus should be less on delineating the signs of trauma in children, such as Hani, and instead on exposing its causes. An emotion-based approach to agency draws our attention to the system of unchilding that created the trauma in the first place. As Hani's portrait shows, what mattered most to him as a child (and arguably up until today) is living in dignity. At a fundamental level, indignity for Palestinians manifests in Israel's unremitting claim of ethnic exclusivity to the land (i.e., Israel as a Jewish-only state), which seeks to negate in Palestinians the "emotional and psychological symbolic value of belonging to the physical country—its hills, valleys, coasts, deserts, and fields."[55] Most Palestinian children are not consumed with the question of whether they are "victims" or "agents." Furthermore, such a binary frame of thinking leaves the system of unchilding intact, and also perpetuates the pathologizing of Palestinian trauma.

What Tools Do Children Use to Survive
Difficult Emotional Frontier Crossings?

It is crucial to listen to children to understand what they find useful in situations of perpetual emotional trauma. Palestinian children are capable of naming their abuse and recognizing the conditions that create their wounding; they demand the dismantling of the system of unchilding.[56] All too often in Palestine, humanitarian aid provided to children is based on outside agendas.[57] Until the goal of dismantling the system of unchilding is achieved, there are pragmatic ways to support Palestinian children using strategies they are already employing.

Children are not passive recipients of violence, but are constantly theorizing their own situation and acting to claim their right to a childhood, in ways specific to their age and maturity. As a child, Hani intuitively developed child-oriented strategies to try to safeguard his emotional formation. His child-oriented strategy centered on drawing strength from nurturing and protective adult relationships. Children in big families are well positioned to make useful alliances and mentorships with elders. Pinpointing childhood as the most significant life stage of emotional development, adults constantly seek ways to shape their children's emotional formation.[58] Research shows that social relations are a main factor promoting survival in Palestine.[59] In Judith Butler's latest work to imagine a less violent world, she poses the question, "But who actually stands on their own? We are all, if we stand, supported by any number of things."[60]

Thus, as much as Hani acted as a lone maverick in his childhood (i.e., assembling his own entourage of soldiers and braving illegal border crossings), we must not overlook that Hani grounded his resistance in kinship networks. His relationship with his kind uncle and grandparents, for example, was deeply significant for his emotional formation as a child. Hani's uncle Youssef treated him with compassion, standing up for him and checking in on him. Hani's grandfather, an orphan and refugee, modeled for his grandson *sumud* (steadfastness) and fortitude in the face of despair. The grandfather even learned to read at seventy years of age. Hani emerged from his childhood with an inspiring life motto: "The happy side of me will never die." Hani's grandmother cultivated in him a love for his endangered land and a link to disappearing Palestinian cultural traditions. It is common for Palestinian women to form a sense of togetherness in families through a combined reliance on family and awareness of a national legacy of oppression.[61] Hani would not settle for anything but a life of dignity, for himself and all of Palestine. Like all people in the Palestinian gay movement, Hani clings to the belief that queer liberation in Palestine cannot occur without liberation from Israel. For as much as unchilding seeks to destroy cross-generational bonds, Hani fortified himself through empowering emotional scripts from his grandparents. Ultimately, through his baking business, Hani helped pass on some of this empowering emotional script to his sister. They infuse their kitchen with locally produced goods that reinforce Palestinian heritage and ties to the land.

One could even argue that the abuse Hani suffered from his mother was a form of misguided love. There is a widespread belief in Arab society that homosexuality is socially constructed rather than biological. There is also a widespread belief that homosexuality prevents one from leading a fulfilling life. In some ways, Hani's mother sought to protect her son from what she perceived to be the dangers of being gay in Palestinian society. Hani's mother could be seen as trying to direct her little boy toward a better future. After the informant incident, his mother practiced inexcusable abuse by locking Hani in the bathroom; nonetheless, the public visibility she gave to her abuse was another desperate parental attempt to protect her son from societal stigma. To abate his community reputation as an informant, Hani's mother wanted to show everyone that he had received due punishment. This can be framed as a form of maternal love. Further, after his suicide attempt, Hani's mother saved her son's life. She escaped the hospital without paying the bill, again displaying her commitment to do what she thought best for Hani within her limited means. Although his mother never fully accepted Hani's sexuality, she found ways to bond with him through home décor, displaying a sort of shared understanding of his "feminine" side that she had shunned in him as a child. Hani said goodbye to his dying mother from a computer screen in Greece, where he was searching for a home and better life. His mother had always wanted the same for Hani, although her definition of what that entailed differed from his own. Over time, Hani's persistence in making a good life for himself reflects his internalization of the loving aspects of his mother's emotional script.

In addition to drawing strength from his caregivers, Hani's child-oriented strategy revolved around the neuroplasticity of the developing brain. Children have a remarkable ability to adapt to their environment, owing to the young brain's ability to modify its connections and rewire itself. People facing multiple forms of marginalization can use multiple forms of resistance. Facing violence, Palestinians as a whole demonstrate a remarkable ability to adapt to and sustain themselves within changing circumstances.[62] When Hani faced difficult emotional frontiers in his childhood, he often rerouted his navigation strategies (sometimes midcourse, such as jumping around the living room to avoid beatings, or changing his story when soldiers arrested the wrong uncle). Hani's plasticity was predicated on praxis, defined as reflection combined with action. Like all children, Hani cannot be pigeonholed as an impulsive and uncontrollable youth who acts in a sequential, as opposed to dialectical, manner. When we examine children in the context of their entire life (which is what the portrait allows us to do in one case), we see that they often manifest praxis over the course of time. During his childhood, Hani built upon life lessons, using his traumatic emotional frontiers to learn and reconstruct his self. For example, Hani processed his failed suicide attempt in such a way as to open new doors in the culinary arts for himself. His flea-market transactions testify to how he, both figuratively and literally, reframes life's discarded material into desirable treasures. He has continually sought to do the same for himself, that is, transform himself from an unchild into a child. His lifelong attempts to transgress restrictive national border laws are his attempts to restore his place on the map of human existence. National borders also represent the difficult emotional frontiers he continually faces and that pull him in different directions with respect to his emotional identity.

Hani emerged from his childhood wounded and scarred, no doubt, but he also created from the traumatic emotional frontiers an effective assemblage of emotional scripts that allow him to keep moving forward despite all odds. In the art world, assemblages are a collection of messy, awkward, unrelated, ugly pieces, whose beauty comes from their collision.[63] Hani used the disordered, fragmented emotional frontiers of his childhood to advance his quest for dignity. He integrated into this assemblage emotional scripts from across generations. He leaned on youthful skills to reboot and reorient himself during challenging times. Queerness, as understood as a contested site that expands rather than limits engagement with the world,[64] is part of Hani's toolkit for survival.

Conclusion

In the end, I have sought to engage with Palestinian children's emotional experiences in difficult situations. I have veered away from the conventional approach to agency, which all too often limits itself to the binary categories of helpless vs. hero or powerless vs. powerful. Such an approach to agency reifies existing forms of oppression, that a child must resemble an adult to be of value or that Western notions of autonomous free will define what counts as resistance. Agency depends on the person involved. I have used portraiture, that is, a detailed social-science-based yet artistic representation of a person's life, to explore the world from a child's view. Aesthetics are a part of life as well as a means to understand human emotions. Hani's life embodies an appreciation of beauty—in bread, coffee, and touch (to allude back to the opening poem excerpt): in Palestine itself. For all the ugly violence Hani endured as a child, he chooses to embrace beauty. He interrupts unchilding by insisting, both literally and figuratively, on his right to bread. Hani's bakery embodies multiple layers of meaning: the smell of home, with all its continuity and belonging; the sustenance it takes to (re)build a home-land; and the softness that emerges from melting hypermasculinity.

NOTES

This chapter was made possible by the support of the Fulbright Program, the National Endowment for the Humanities (NEH), the Palestinian American Research Center (PARC), the University of Wisconsin–La Crosse, and Tampere University's Center for Excellence in the History of Experiences. I am grateful to Nadera Shalhoub-Kevorkian and Stephanie Olsen for providing critical feedback on the chapter. I am most indebted to Hani for trusting me with his story.

1. Vuolanto, "The Case of Roman Childhood"; and Gleason, "Avoiding the Agency Trap."

2. Thomas, "Historicizing Agency."

3. Shalhoub-Kevorkian, *Incarcerated Childhood*.

4. Thomas, "Historicizing Agency," 325–27.

5. In this section, I lean heavily on the summary of these debates provided by Thomas's "Historicizing Agency" article.

6. Johnson, "On Agency," 113–14; Thomas, "Historicizing Agency," 324; Gleason, "Avoiding the Agency Trap"; Miller, "Children of the American Revolution."

7. Johnson, "On Agency," 113–24.

8. Scott, "Gender: A Useful Category"; Mahmood, *Politics of Piety*.

9. Lancy, David. "Unmasking Children's Agency," 4.

10. Thomas, "On Agency," 324–39.

11. Spivak, "Can the Subaltern Speak?"

12. Lancy, "Unmasking Children's Agency," 2.

13. Gleason, "Avoiding the Agency Trap," 446–59.

14. Alexander, "Agency and Emotion Work," 121–28.

15. Vuolanto, "The Case of Roman Childhood," 11–24.

16. Butler, *Gender Trouble*; Butler, *Giving an Account of Oneself*.

17. Vuolanto, "The Case of Roman Childhood," 11–24.

18. Spyrou, *Disclosing Childhoods*.

19. Alexander, "Agency and Emotion Work," 121–28.

20. Vallgårda, Alexander, and Olsen, "Emotions and the Global Politics," 20.

21. Boddice, *The History of Emotions*.

22. Vallgårda, Alexander, and Olsen, "Emotions and the Global Politics," 29.

23. Boddice, *The History of Emotions*, 178.

24. Vallgårda, Alexander, and Olsen, "Emotions and the Global Politics," 20.

25. Vallgårda, Alexander, and Olsen, 22–26.

26. Vallgårda, Alexander, and Olsen, 27.

27. Boddice, *The History of Emotions*, 178.

28. Vallgårda, Alexander, and Olsen, "Emotions and the Global Politics," 25.

29. "The Politics of Birth," 1188–89.

30. For more information about portraiture, see Lawrence-Lightfoot and Davies, *Art and Science of Portraiture*.

31. As recently as July 24, 2020, three Palestinian members of the Israeli Knesset voted in favor of gay rights (three voted against and three abstained). See Judy Maltz, "'They're Scared': LGBTQ Rights Divide Israel's Arab Lawmakers," *Haaretz*, July 24, 2020, https://www.haaretz.com/israel-news/.premium-they-re-scared-lgbtq-rights-divides-israel-s-arab-lawmakers-1.9016346.

32. Atshan, *Queer Palestine*, 4.

33. Atshan, 2.

34. Atshan, 9.

35. Giacaman et al., "Mental Health, Social Distress."

36. See, for example, Mirza Saaib Beg, "Pinkwashing Kashmir," TRT World, 2019. https://www.trtworld.com/opinion/pinkwashing-kashmir-30804.

37. Shalhoub-Kevorkian, *Incarcerated Childhood*, 19–24.

38. Shalhoub-Kevorkian, "Gun to Body," 137.

39. Shalhoub-Kevorkian, *Incarcerated* Childhood,12.

40. Shalhoub-Kevorkian, *i*.

41. Shalhoub-Kevorkian, 65.

42. Mayo, "Twentieth Anniversary of Paulo Freire's Death."

43. Mayo, "Hegemony, Migration, and Misplaced Alliances."

44. Mayo, "Hegemony, Migration, and Misplaced Alliances."

45. See, for example, Duaibis, "Devastating Effects of Night Raids."

46. See, for example, Fitsanakis, "Palestinian Informants."

47. Olsen and Vallgårda, "Historicizing Emotional Development."

48. This logic is similar to that expressed by suicide bombers who feel the immense violation of oppression. See, for example, the work of Nasser Abufarha.

49. Shehadeh, "The 2014 War on Gaza."

50. Wing, "Healing Spirit Injuries."

51. Shalhoub-Kevorkian, *Incarcerated Childhood*, 22.

52. Shalhoub-Kevorkian, 12.

53. Massad et al., "Rethinking Resilience for Children."

54. Meari, "Reconsidering Trauma"; Giacaman, "Reframing Public Health in War Time"; Sheehi "The Transnational Palestinian Self"; Lykes and Mersky, "Reparations and Mental Health"; Marshall, "Save [Us From] the Children."

55. Rouhanna, "Homeland Nationalism and Guarding Dignity."

56. Shalhoub-Kevorkian, "Gun to Body."

57. Marshall, "Save [Us From] the Children."

58. Vallgårda and Olsen, "Emotional Frontiers."

59. Kamal, "Neighborhood in Nablus City."

60. Quoted in Gessen, "Judith Butler Wants Us to Reshape our Rage."

61. Shalhoub-Kevorkian, "Counter-Spaces as Resistance."

62. Allen, "Getting by the Occupation."

63. Kelly, "The Anthropology of Assemblage."

64. Butler, *Bodies that Matter*.

BIBLIOGRAPHY

Alexander, K. "Agency and Emotion Work." *Jeunesse: Young People, Text, Cultures* 7, no. 2 (2015): 121–28.

Allen, L. "Getting by the Occupation: How Violence Became Normal during the Second Palestinian Intifada." *Cultural Anthropology* 23, no. 3 (2008): 453–87.

Atshan, S. *Queer Palestine and the Empire of Critique.* Stanford, Calif.: Stanford University Press, 2020.

Barber, B. K. "Annual Research Review: The Experience of Youth with Political Conflict—Challenging Notions of Resilience and Encouraging Research Refinement." *The Journal of Child Psychology and Psychiatry* 54, no. 4 (2013): 461–73.

Bed, M. S. "Pinkwashing Kashmir." https://www.trtworld.com/opinion/pinkwashing -kashmir-30804.

Boddice, R. *The History of Emotions.* Manchester, UK: Manchester University Press, 2018.

Butler, J. *Bodies That Matter.* New York: Routledge, 1993.

———. *Gender Trouble.* New York: Routledge, 1990.

———. *Giving an Account of Oneself.* New York: Fordham University Press, 2005.

Duaibis, S. "The Devastating Effects of Night Raids on Palestinians." +972 Magazine, August 31, 2015, https://www.972mag.com/the-devastating-effects-of-night-raids -on-palestinian-families/.

Fitsanakis, J. "How Does Israel Recruit Palestinian Informants in Gaza?" IntelNews.org, September 19, 2014, https://intelnews.org/2014/09/19/01-1558/.

Gessen, M. "Judith Butler Wants to Reshape our Rage." February 9, 2020. https://www .newyorker.com/culture/the-new-yorker-interview/judith-butler-wants-us-to -reshape-our-rage.

Giacaman, R. "Imprints on the Consciousness: The Impact on Palestinian Civilians of the Israeli Army Invasion of West Bank Towns." *European Journal of Public Health* 14, no. 3 (2004): 286–90.

———. "Quality of Life in the Palestinian Context: An Inquiry in War-like Conditions." *Health Policy* 81, no. 1 (2007): 68–84.

———. "Reframing Public Health in War Time: From the Biomedical Model to the 'Wounds Inside.'" *Journal of Palestinian Studies* 47, no. 2 (2018): 9–27.

Giacaman, R., Y. Rabaia, V. Nguyen-Gillham, R. Batniji, R.-L. Punamäki, and D. Summerfield. "Mental Health, Social Distress, and Political Oppression: The Case of the Occupied Palestinian Territory." *Global Political Health* 6, no. 5 (2011): 547–59.

Gleason, M. "Avoiding the Agency Trap: Caveats for Historians of Children, Youth, and Education." *History of Education* 45, no. 4 (2016): 446–59.

Grossman, Z. *Unlikely Alliances: Native Nations and White Communities Join to Defend Rural Lands.* Seattle: University of Washington Press, 2017.

Johnson, W. "On Agency." *Journal of Social History* 34, no. 1 (2003): 113–24.

Kamal, N. "Neighborhood in Nablus City: The Formation of a Social Safety Network During the Siege." *Middle East—Topics and Arguments* 14 (2020): 160–74.

Kelly, J. "The Anthropology of Assemblage." *Art Journal* 67, no. 1 (2008): 24–30.

Lancy, D. "Unmasking Children's Agency." *AnthropoChildren* 1, no. 2 (October 2012): 1–11.

Lawrence-Lightfoot, S., and J. Hoffman Davies. *Art and Science of Portraiture*. San Francisco, Calif.: John Wiley & Sons, 1997.

Lykes, B. M., and M. Mersky. "Reparations and Mental Health: Psychosocial Interventions Toward Healing, Human Agency, and Rethreading Social Realities." In *The Handbook of Reparations*, edited by Pablo de Grieff, 589–622. London: Oxford University Press, 2006.

Mahmood, S. *Politics of Piety: The Islamic Revival and the Feminist Subject*. Princeton, N.J.: Princeton University Press, 2005.

Marshall, D. J. "Save [Us From] the Children: Trauma, Palestinian Childhood, and the Production of Governable Subjects." *Children's Geographies* 12, no. 3 (2014): 281–96.

Massad, S., R. Stryker, S. Mansour, and U. Khammash. "Rethinking Resilience for Children and Youth in Conflict Zones: The Case of Palestine." *Research in Human Development* 15, nos. 3–4 (2018): 280–93.

Mayo, P. "Hegemony, Migration, and Misplaced Alliances: Lessons from Gramsci." In *Solidarity without Borders*, edited by Óscar García Agustín and Martin Bak Jørgensen, 135–49. London: Pluto Press, 2016.

———. "Twentieth Anniversary of Paulo Freire's Death (1997–2017): Freire's Relevance for Understanding Colonialism." *Postcolonial Directions in Education* 6, no. 2 (2017): 183–92.

Meari, L. "Reconsidering Trauma: Toward a Palestinian Community Psychology." *Journal of Community Psychology* 43, no. 1 (2015): 76–86.

———. "Sumud: A Palestinian Philosophy of Confrontation in Colonial Prisons." *The South Atlantic Quarterly* 113, no. 3 (2014): 547–78.

Miller, S. A. "Assent as Agency in the Early Years of the Children of the American Revolution." *Journal of the History of Childhood and Youth* 9, no. 1, (2016): 48–65.

Musleh, A. "The Shortfall of Development Policies to Address Youth Issues in Palestine." Working Paper No. 11, *Power2Youth*, May 2016.

Olsen, S., and K. Vallgårda. "Emotional Frontiers." In *The Oxford Handbook of Emotional Development*, edited by Daniel Dukes, Eric Walle, and Andrea Samson, 437–445. London: Oxford University Press, 2021.

Qouta, S., R.-L. Punamäki, and Eyad El-Sarraj. "Child Development and Family Mental Health in War and Military Violence: The Palestinian Experience." *International Journal of Behavioral Development* 32, no. 4 (2008): 310–21.

Rothberg, M. *The Implicated Subject: Beyond Victims and Perpetrators*. Stanford, Calif.: Stanford University Press, 2019.

Rouhana, N. "Homeland Nationalism and Guarding Dignity in a Settler Colonial Context: The Palestinian Citizens of Israel Reclaim their Homeland." *Borderlands eJournal* 14, no. 1, (2015): 1–37.

Scott, J. "Gender: A Useful Category of Historical Analysis." *The American Historical Review* 91, no. 5 (1986): 1053–75.

Shalhoub-Kevorkian, N. "Counter-Spaces as Resistance in Conflict Zones." *Journal of Feminist Family Therapy* 17, nos. 3–4 (2005): 109–41.

———. "Gun to Body: Mental Health Against Unchilding." *International Journal of Applied Psychoanalytical Studies* 17, no. 2 (2020): 126–45.

———. "Human Suffering in Colonial Contexts: Reflections from Palestine." *Settler Colonial Studies* 4, no. 3 (2014): 277–90.

———. *Incarcerated Childhood and the Politics of Unchilding*. London: Cambridge University Press, 2019.

———. "The Politics of Birth and the Intimacies of Violence Against Palestinian Women in Occupied East Jerusalem." *British Journal of Criminology* 55, no. 6 (2015): 1187–1206.

Sheehi, S. "The Transnational Palestinian Self: Toward Decolonizing Psychoanalytic Thought." *Psychoanalytic Perspectives* 15, no. 3, (2018): 307–22.

Shehadeh, S. "The 2014 War on Gaza: Engineering Trauma and Mass Torture to Break Palestinian Resilience." *International Journal of Applied Psychoanalytic Studies* 12, no. 3 (2015): 278–94.

Spivak, G. C. "Can the Subaltern Speak?" In *Marxism and the Interpretation of Culture*, edited by Cary Nelson and Lawrence Grossberg, 271–313. Urbana, Ill.: University of Illinois Press, 1988.

Spyrou, S. *Disclosing Childhoods: Research and Knowledge Production for a Critical Childhood Studies*. London: Palgrave MacMillan, 2018.

Swartz, R. "Educating Emotions in Natal Western Australia, 1854–65." *Journal of Colonialism and Colonial History* 18, no. 2 (2017).

Thomas, L. M. "Historicizing Agency." *Gender and History* 28, no. 2 (2016): 324–39.

Vallgårda, K., K. Alexander, and S. Olsen. "Emotions and the Global Politics of Childhood." In *Childhood, Youth, and Emotions in Modern History: National, Colonial and Global Perspectives*, edited by Stephanie Olsen, 12-34. London: Palgrave Macmillan, 2015.

Vallgårda, K., and S. Olsen. "Historicizing Emotional Development." *The Oxford Handbook of Emotional Development*, edited by Daniel Dukes, Andrea C. Samson, and Eric E. Walle, 146–56. London: Oxford University Press, 2021.

Vuolanto, V. "Experience, Agency and Children in the Past: The Case of Roman Childhood." In *Children and Everyday Life in the Roman and Late Antique World*, edited by Christian Laes and Ville Vuolanto. London: Routledge, 2017.

Wing, A. K. "Healing Spirit Injuries: Human Rights in the Basic Palestinian Law." *Rutgers Law Review* 54, (Summer 2002): 1087–1100.

Subjection of Palestinian Children's Political Agency
Beyond the Family

JANETTE HABASHI

The use of the term "political agency" in regard to children reflects larger thinking about children's abilities and responses to political discourse. This term recognizes that children are active in constructing and understanding political narratives and realities, regardless of continuous efforts to discredit their political agency. The idea that children exercise political agency is in opposition to their conventional portrayal as naïve and unable to understand the complexity of political discourse. This perception hinders not only the understanding of children's political agency in general, but it also substantially denies Palestinian children the right to have a voice regarding their own daily realities of oppression and colonization, which is intertwined with Israeli occupation and political discourse.

Typically, research on children in situations of political upheaval focuses on the notion of vulnerability, viewing them solely as victims. This omits any consideration of how such situations actually play a role in creating children's political agency. This is especially problematic in the case of Palestinian children who suffer from Israeli occupation, particularly, violence from settlers who live within their own communities and neighborhoods. A number of Palestinian children in the West Bank experience arrest, imprisonment, and deprivation at the hands of the Israeli occupying military, as well as from Israeli settlers' violent activities each year. According to Defense for Children International (DCI), in 2014 there were over 2,500 children between the ages of twelve and seventeen detained in Israeli prisons. Additionally, over six hundred Palestinian children under the age of seventeen have been killed in the past five years alone, as a direct result of the Israeli military and settler presence.[1] Hart and Forte point out numerous injustices against Palestinian children, including the fact that Israeli settlers attack Palestinian children on treks to and from school, and Israel tries Palestinian children in military courts rather than the civil courts they use for Israeli settler children, with the most common offense against Palestinian children being stone throwing.[2] The sentences for stone throwing can be up to twenty years in an Israeli security prison.[3] On top of all this, Israeli settlers in the West Bank essentially receive impunity for crimes committed against Palestinian children, largely due to a law passed by Israel's legislative branch in 1967 that grants "Israeli courts and authorities jurisdiction over any Israeli national accused of committing a crime that violates Israeli law."[4] All of these issues contribute to the harsh reality of unchilding in Palestine.

The political reality of Israeli occupation and its current extension of settler oppression shapes Palestinian children's well-being. This elicits a call for protection of these children and also attentive documentation and study of its impact on the children's political agency. Palestinian children's experiences under occupation help form their understanding of political discourse and its manifestation in their political agency. This chapter looks at how Palestinian children's political agency is formed within their everyday political and economic reality and their construction of the national narrative.

Unpacking Palestinian Children's Political Agency

The premise of children's agency is the rejection of the idea that children are inactive receivers of their cultural, social, and political settings and that children are unable to deconstruct and respond to political discourse.[5] The research of Habashi, Horschelmann, and Katz provides evidence and examples of children's political agency, or the ability to deconstruct and respond to social and political circumstances.[6] In the Palestinian context of war and violence, children's political agency, or resistance to Israeli occupation, demonstrates that factors such as the child's subjective and psychological well-being must be taken into account.[7] Palestinian children adapt to unchilding and violence, integrating resistance to it into their daily lives. For Palestinian children, political involvement includes political graffiti, posters and shrines dedicated to martyred children who have been killed as a result of the conflict, and role-playing games of the "occupier and occupied in the streets with sticks and plastic guns."[8] Palestinian children are rooted in their living conditions, engaging as agents with others and society.

One challenge facing adults' ability to identify children's political agency is limited familiarity with its various forms and expressions. Adults tend to perceive children as a work in progress seen in the notion of becoming not being.[9] Therefore, children's political agency is not always something that is endorsed, supervised, or regulated by adults. While certain adult-controlled platforms for involving children in politics have seen some positive results,[10] there are numerous ways in which children act politically outside of official arenas such as schools or government-based programs.

Political agency is rooted within local and global discourses. Children are "subjected to and acting as a subject" of political discourse, meaning "young people's political 'agency' cannot take place outside of a careful examination of the myriad networks of power within which they are caught."[11] Children are subjects of their family, community, and nation, all the while subject to geopolitics. Multiple narratives are part of children's political socialization that connects and forms children's "acting." Within this context, "acting" refers to moments of children's independence, manifested in their responses to the subjugation framed within their social political narratives.[12] It is this interconnected relationship of being both subject and subjugated that forms Palestinian children's political agency. Their political narrative is rendered in their lived resistance, as well as the larger conditions of Israeli oppression.

Children's political agency is based on the complex ecology of children's everyday life, which does not follow a linear progression. A constant interaction of the macro- and microsystems define children's lives.[13] Palestinian children's political agency renders, captures, and responds to the interactions of regional and international discourse and its impact on the Palestinian community.[14] This means children's lives must be understood as beyond the control of the adults in both their immediate communities and families. Such an understanding of interactions cannot be captured or analyzed in a linear perspective, nor are they dominant in traditional Western theories of development, which tend to be structured, and rely, on positivist empirical research.[15] This method does not always take into account children's political agency, and also tends to neglect "influences of history, culture, and politics on child development."[16] The ubiquity of such a notion assumes that children can develop in isolation from political interaction. To endorse such a view would not shed light on "normal" childhoods, but rather create disconnects between the child's living reality and theory. This premise ignores children's political interactions because it standardizes development as something formed outside local and global discourse.[17] This perspective further contributes to the unchilding of Palestinian children and the perception of them as empty vessels, creating a false understanding of children's development in Western and non-Western societies alike. Reconceptualization of children's political agency requires considering the nuances of children's moments of independence as they interact with local global discourse. Pain and Hopkins argue that interactions, whether within the same age group or within multiple generations, are significant in shaping a child's political agency.[18] Interactions of minority children are not the same as the majority; furthermore, minority children's interactions are shaped by gender, community discourse, class, and other factors. Therefore, assuming political agency is the same for all children is a mis-representation of children's interactions with their family, community, and global discourses.

Taking into account social and political interactions assists in understanding Palestinian lived resistance and political agency today. This is especially import-ant given that Palestinian children's daily interactions are not confined to those with the Israeli army and the Palestinian community. They are also shaped by their close proximity to Israeli settlers in the West Bank and by settlers' global advocates. Settlers, with the support of the Israeli government, expel Palestinian families from their homes, confiscate land, and rob and divide the Palestinian community.[19] This can be seen clearly in the case of the Old City of Hebron in the West Bank. The Hebron Protocol of 1997 divided the Old City into two sec-tors (H1 and H2) in an attempt to aid in the withdrawal of Israeli Defense Forces. H1 is governed by the Palestinian Authority, while H2, which had a 98 percent population of Palestinians at the time of the agreement, is controlled by the Is-raeli military.[20] The numerous settlers in H2 have no limitations on settlement expansion and they maintain a multitude of security measures, which serve to restrict Palestinian movement. Palestinians living in the area face settler violence on a regular basis. In a complicated political situation such as Hebron, a Palestin-ian child's political agency must be viewed from many angles. Israeli oppression does not discriminate in targeting adults over children but impacts the entire Pal-estinian community. Therefore, assuming that adults can control the impact of oppression on children risks diminishing the impact of Israeli settler violence on children's daily lives and invalidates their lived resistance.

Presumed Family Subjugation

Conventional literature on children's agency conveys families as child armor, or the front line that filters information, adjusts behavior, and modifies responses.[21] This idea is particularly prominent in the concept of the role model, which im-plies children learn by directly observing and imitating the behavior of others, in-cluding all that relates to politics.[22] This idea of adult role models in the political education of children assumes children are powerless recipients and victims of parental governing, unable to act with purpose, and the idea that children should be supervised at all times by adults in order to ensure that they are molded with the same values and views as the parents.[23] Certainly, the value of parental in-volvement is not to be ignored, but it should not preclude children's political agency. Harker and Skelton indicate that policy makers have used the concept of the powerless child to silence children's views and speak on their behalf.[24]

This silencing exercise practiced by adults on children is not something new, as it is connected to a complex concept of denying children's ability to construct politics, which is reflected in research dating back as far as the 1960s that depicts parents as being the biggest influence of political attitudes among children, assuming adult supervision is a main factor in this process.[25] Such studies do not recognize children's political agency and focus merely on the parents' ability to regulate outside influences, and in a way, to silence children's views. It assumes family members are solely responsible for teaching children social and cultural processes. This is without any consideration of outside factors, especially political discourse, which impacts every individual, regardless of age, through social and cultural interactions.[26] Even in the 1980s with the rise in importance of children's studies and a new conceptualization of children's political agency, some adult-centric elements of politics remained. The "new" sociology of childhood acknowledged ways in which children are able to make sense of their surroundings, that is, exert agency within their family or express perspectives different than adults.[27] But this approach still prioritized the family's role in controlling children's political agency.

Some researchers are critical of the assumption that families are the architects of children's political agency, often implying that interactions outside the social and cultural processes of the family have a major influence on children's political views.[28] To endorse a limited concept of children's political agency that is engineered in a narrow dimension is to promote the idea that families act as a buffer to children's interactions with the outside world and hence can artificially construct children's political agency. This mindset often finds support from policy makers and educators.[29] It was evident, for example, in the aftermath of September 11, 2001, when there was a call by many parents in the United States for families to avoid discussing the catastrophic event with children as a means of avoiding further trauma.[30] The explicit assumption is that parents can control their children's political narrative, as well as their political views. Allen and Bang hold that family political orientation is one factor that shapes children's political views and behavior.[31] Likewise, Beck and Jennings's research in the 1980s finds that parents and children tend to share the same political orientations.[32] This assumption is also supported by McDevitt and Kiousis, who argue "parents do not directly shape political orientations; instead, they share with children environments that reinforce parent attitudes in diffusive orientations such as trust in institutions."[33] Jennings, Stoker, and Bowers's support for this notion changed as a result of their multigenerational family study, which did not yield a continuation of similar political views.[34] The second generation of children were surveyed in 1982, after their parents were first surveyed in 1973, and the third-generation children were surveyed in 1997. The findings revealed that the second generation's political views are comparable with the first generation; however, this did not continue on to the third generation. The explanation of the results relates to changes in media and in family structure. Apparently, the pattern of interaction with the environment was similar in the first and second generations. The third generation's living conditions and interactions with the outside environment resulted in a deviation of political views from the previous generations.

Another weakness in an exclusively family-based approach to children's political orientation is that children actually impact their parents' orientation.[35] For example, Wong and Tseng find that low-income immigrant children can influence their parents' political thinking.[36] Bloemraad and Trost find that children in 2006 mobilized their parents to advocate for immigrants and to participate in rallies.[37] Another factor to consider is that children are often more familiar with technology compared to their parents, which provides access to political discourse outside parental supervision.[38] Therefore, the illusion that parents exclusively control children's political subjugation is neither accurate nor realistic.

This is especially the case for Palestinian children since the political reality of Israeli oppression and colonization activities are intertwined in every element of living. Spellings, Barber, and Olsen studied youth involvement in political activism in Palestine during the first intifada (1987–93).[39] Their study takes various factors into account, such as parental activism and expectations, individual feelings of self-worth, socioeconomic status, gender, and religiosity, in order to discover whether or not and why youth engage in activism. Their findings indicate that while parental involvement in activism, and the expectation for their children's involvement in activism, did significantly impact youth activism, much of the youth's activism was voluntary and not a result of standard parenting behaviors, such as parental support and psychological control. Families cannot always oversee children's constructions of political agency, although family is a component that plays a role. Family discourse is intertwined with the community and local politics, and it is also framed within the multigenerational narrative. Palestinian political agency is influenced by collective memory, not based just on school textbooks, but also on the narrative shared at home from different generations, community discourse, and most of all contemporary responses to political discourse. Some Palestinian children are third-generation refugees, but that does not negate their identity of being a refugee, especially since refugee camps are part of continued Palestinian living conditions.[40] Children and families do not live in a vacuum; thus, assuming children's political agency adheres only to social and cultural processes denies that such processes are constantly evolving alongside politics. Children's political agency must be situated within multiple interactions, including local and global politics.

Subjugation of Local and Global Discourse

Situating children's political agency within the local/global discourse is an acknowledgment that their unchilding and lived reality is not confined to family interactions. Children's lives are complex, interconnected, and cannot be divided into simple compartments. They should be understood within the ecological interactions of both micro- and macrosystems.[41] Ecological interactions are embedded in many areas of local and global discourse. For example, global economic trends, political ideology, and international social politics shape the welfare and development of children and their lived resistance. As Solhaug and Kristensen note, children display a complex pattern of politicization that is intertwined with globalization.[42] The World Health Organization, United Nations Development Program (UNDP), and other international humanitarian organizations have been documenting the impact of different policies, disasters, and wars on children for many years.[43] Although these concepts seem distant from children's realities, they have a direct and implicit effect. Cheney provides a potent analysis of how international policies are integrated in international child adoption and surrogacy policies, concluding that there needs to be more protection of the rights of the adoptee at an international level.[44] Another example of the impact of local and global interaction on children's lives is the United States' policy of abstinence-only based sexual education. The United States spends millions of dollars to fund abstinence-only based domestically. Despite the failure of such programs, the United States also pushes its abstinence-only programs onto international partners, with disregard to local cultures.[45]

Cases such as the two aforementioned assume the relationship of global to local is one-directional, that is, the global dictates the local. Yet, in some cases, local discourses push back against global impositions. Such an assumed top-down directional approach parallels the traditional model of families teaching children about politics without recognizing the dynamic interaction embedded in the relationship. Children's political agency debunks top-down notions. Habashi and Worley's 2014 study on Palestinian children transcending local political affiliation provides a critical example.[46] The study analyzed a 2001 survey of 1,187 Palestinian children attending 30 schools, grades 5–7. Almost 70 percent of participants were aged 11–12, 18 percent were aged 9–10, and 10 percent were aged 13–15 years old. The questions focused on children's knowledge about dominant political parties in their neighborhoods, and which political parties they will join in the future. Seven political parties were listed, and 41.3 percent of the participants identified with Palestinian Islamic Jihad (PIJ) as the dominant party, while 29.7 percent recognized that Hamas is dominant. However, this knowledge of political parties did not correspond with which political party they would join as adults. Almost 91.4 percent of participants wanted to join a political party in the future and 63.3 percent of the participants identified Hezbollah as a political party to join. Another 15.3 percent expressed interest in Fatah, while 12.8 percent revealed the PIJ as the political party they wanted to join as adults. Palestinian child participants did indicate that they identify with a local party too but opted to join a regional one in the future. One of the reasons for such identification is that the local political parties did not achieve any victory against Israeli oppression compared to Hezbollah.[47] Hezbollah is Lebanon's political party but was in conflict with Israeli Defense Forces following occupation in a security zone located in Lebanon, and it successfully placed pressure on Israel to achieve its own goals. Hezbollah is the only party in the neighboring countries that Israel considers a major threat.[48] The results of Habashi and Worley's research might be surprising, especially for individuals who deny children's political agency. Hence, the research findings of Palestinian future political membership are contrary to the research that children's political views are a proxy to their parents.[49]

Children should be perceived to have political agency with the ability to actively construct and respond to political discourse. The linear perspective denies the broader interactions within the macrostructure and its influence on children's political agency, and more importantly, the interaction between the local and global discourse.[50] Holloway, Holt, and Mills explain the significance of understanding the local and global impact on children's constructions of political agency and emphasize that such interaction exists in all societies and is not confined to Western countries.[51] Political agency should not be perceived as a binary construct, or a spatial structure, but as a unit intertwined in the social, economic and political discourses that have a demonstrated impact on adults' and children's daily living. For example, international organizations are changing the Palestinian approach to early childhood education in Palestine by promoting education that adheres to international donor agendas rather than focusing on local issues such as community political aspirations and cultural contexts.[52] These international organizations seem to want to implement the curriculum for, and conceptualization of early childhood in, Western countries.

As another example of this disconnect, after the Oslo agreement between the Palestinian Liberation Organization (PLO) and the Israeli government in 1993, international donors forged policies that focused on Palestinian nongovernmental organizations (NGOs) and instituted a funding criterion that does not support projects founded on Palestinian community interests but opted to fund proposals that would support the Israeli agenda of colonization. One important example is the overwhelming funding for "human rights" workshops in the West

Bank, where children are taught about issues related to human rights. The irony is that these children receive classroom lessons about human rights while simultaneously experiencing a lack of human rights in their daily existence.

These examples are a reflection of how local and global concepts are not in opposition but are involved in a dialectic relationship and pose a challenge to the way we construct children's political agency. Not perceiving local and global as binary provides a spatial mobility for understanding children's input in the present and future. Katz explains such a relationship in a study of Sudanese children living in two continents (Africa and North America), in which such dialectic interactions between local and global political discourse has shaped three forms of children's political agency: resistance, resilience, and reworking.[53]

Settlement Subjugation and
Palestinian Political Agency

The current extension of the Israeli occupation is embedded in the expansion of Israeli settlements in the West Bank, which have created harsh political realities for the Palestinian community, including the children. Prior to 1948, Palestine was under the rule of the British Mandate. In 1948, the Zionist movement with the help of the British government, established the state of Israel, which resulted in forcefully expelling 70 percent of the Palestinian people and colonizing 77 percent of the land.[54] In 1967, the Six-Day War resulted in the Israeli occupation of the West Bank and the Gaza Strip, which were once just a small portion of historic Palestine and the British Mandate lands of Palestine. Israel created a military administration to oversee the Palestinian Occupied Territories, drastically altering the laws of the land, specifically in regard to land registration, so as to control "unregistered" land.[55] Since this time, especially in the late 1970s, Israeli settlements, with the support of Israeli government policies, have expanded to control almost 40 percent of the West Bank land.[56] These continuous subversive Israeli actions, which are against international law, shape the formation of Palestinian national discourse and identity that in turn influences children's political agency. The expression of Palestinian identity in the twentieth century was primarily linked to the Israeli military government and occupation. However, in the contemporary moment, especially in the era of Abbas, Palestinian children's national identity is also heavily linked to Israeli settlements and the aggression of Israeli settlers in the West Bank.[57]

Settlements are strategically located in the West Bank to control resources and to create disjointed enclaves of Palestinian populations.[58] This settlement expansion plan is maintained by Israeli military checkpoints, and a dual legal system (one for Israeli settlements under the Israeli criminal court and one for Palestinians that is overseen by the Israeli military).[59] Settlements are illegal under international law and often condemned by the United Nations as in violation of the Fourth Geneva Convention.[60] Nonetheless, the number of settlements continues to grow. According to the Israeli Information Center for Human Rights in the Occupied Territories (B'Tselem), there have been more than 200 settlements established since 1967, 127 of which are recognized by the Israeli Ministry of the Interior, and 100 of which have been constructed without authorization, but with the support and aid, of the Israeli government. A report by the United Nations Conference on Trade and Development found that, "The cumulative economic cost of the Israeli occupation ... during the 2007–2018 period is estimated at $16.7 billion." Aside from the assistance provided by the Israeli government, which itself is bolstered by American tax dollars, settlements also enjoy funding and support from private donors from such outside countries as the United States.[61] Weirich notes there are numerous private charities in the United States that provide tax-exempt, financial support for building settlements in Israel, which not only aids in the development of illegal settlements but also hinders the peace process between Israel and Palestine.[62] Furthermore, Gorenberg discusses the fact that as the settler population grows, they become more powerful, whereby now even the Israeli government is struggling to control their expansion, as they are fearful of civil unrest.[63] Settlers have a significant impact on governmental activities by utilizing their "penetration into the governing apparatus, their disproportionate power within important institutions and organizations, and consequently, their influence on state practices."[64] The blending of politics and ideologies coincide with Israeli citizens moving into the settlements in the West Bank because the houses are cheaper, bigger, and are supported by funding from international groups.[65] New Israeli immigrants are encouraged to spend at least two years living in a settlement before residing in Israel proper.[66] Though the initial creation of settlements in the West Bank was based on secular ideology, it has since shifted to be more religious in nature.[67] Settlers, specifically those residing in illegal settlements or those made without the authorization of the Israeli government, are, by majority, "composed of religious ideologues," as they want the West Bank to be included as part of "Greater Israel."[68] In ancient biblical terms, the area we now know as the West Bank was Judea and Samaria. The religious dimension of the Israeli settlements is attracting zealous newcomers to Israel.[69] In addition, the Birthright trip, which aims to build loyalty among young Jews, especially in the United States, offers them a free ten-day trip to Israel.[70] Traditionally, such trips focus on building relationships between foreign Jewish people and Jewish people within Israel, excluding the West Bank. For the last decade, these trips have included trips to West Bank settlements. Some settlements are in the heart of the Palestinian communities, such as settlement de-

velopments that confiscate houses in the Old City of Jerusalem and Hebron. Political ideology has driven Israelis to take over these historical places and rename
them with biblical names in order to attract newcomers.[71]

This global interaction with Israeli settlements is not only changing the local
makeup of the Palestinian community but also altering their political identification, specifically with regard to children. Israel's consideration of illegal settlers
to be Israeli citizens dismisses the fact that the settlement project violates international law. Furthermore, the settlement project claims that part of the West
Bank is actually a part of Israel and that any attacks on settlers is an act of terrorism because it is an attack on civilians rather than occupiers. Due to the fact
that Palestinians must live side by side with the Israeli settler population, settlers have become integrated in Palestinian local communities, as well as Palestinian children's concept of political agency. For example, in the Palestinian village of al-Tuwani, located in the South Hebron Hills, Palestinian children must
pass through two Jewish settlements in order to reach their school. On this trek
to school, the children suffer verbal and physical attacks from Jewish settlers. Palestinian adults that accompany and attempt to protect or defend the children are
often arrested by Israeli authorities.[72] Other ways in which Palestinian children
are impacted by the settlements include "denial of access to clean water, exposure to toxic waste, demolition of homes, prevention of family reunification, and
destruction of parental livelihoods precipitating exploitative employment of the
young."[73] Additionally, Palestinian children are denied their right to visit family
members due to the fact that their houses are in close proximity to a settlement.[74]

The evolving global-local reality of Israeli settlements is associated with Palestinian land confiscations of 1967, as well as global, financial, and political support for such colonial activities that undermine the international community's
consent to create a Palestinian sovereign state. Israel's expansion of settlements
makes it impossible to have a cohesively connected Palestinian community
across the West Bank. It is anticipated that the continuation of Israeli settlements will hinder the peace process and create difficulty in obtaining Palestinian statehood. Thus, an alternative call for a one-state solution (encompassing
Israeli and Palestinian-Arab minorities) has started to emerge within the global
arena. Although this reality has been building for the last fifty years, the attitude
of Palestinian children differs from this solution, in that their responses are primarily focused on the Palestinian narrative of establishing an independent state
of Palestine and maintaining a sense of national identity.[75] There is no illusion
that global discourse is isolated from the Palestinian local reality and renders the
shape of children's political agency, lived resistance, and unchilding. Considering
Palestinian children's political agency in context with local and global discourse,

as well as their daily realities that are intertwined with Israeli oppression and oc-cupation, is crucial to the understanding of children's political agency as a whole.

NOTES

1. Palestinian Central Bureau of Statistics, *Status of the Rights.*

2. Hart and Forte, "Mandated to Fail?"

3. Hall, "To Throw a Stone in Palestine"; Horton, "Advocating for Palestinian Children"; Joronen, "Politics of Precarious Childhood"; Mason and Falk, "Assessing Nonviolence."

4. Omer-Man, "Separate and Unequal," 18.

5. Matthews, "Window on the 'New' Sociology."

6. Habashi, "Palestinian Children: Authors"; Hörschelmann, "Landscapes of Critical Geopolitics"; and Katz, *Growing Up Global.*

7. Veronese, Pepe, Jaradah, Murannak, and Hamdouna, "'We Must Cooperate.'"

8. Steffen, "Beyond Child Participation.'"

9. Huang, "Being and Becoming."

10. Kallio and Häkli, "Tracing Children's Politics."

11. Hörschelmann, "Landscapes of Critical Geopolitics," 588.

12. Habashi, *Political Socialization of Youth.*

13. Spellings, Barber, and Olsen, "Political Activism of Palestinian Youth."

14. Habashi, *Political Socialization of Youth.*

15. Diessner, Yazdani, and Richel, " Developmental Stage Theories."

16. Bucx, "Child Development: Theories," 306.

17. Rubin and Menzer, "Culture and Social Development."

18. Hopkins and Pain, "Geographies of Age: Thinking Relationally."

19. Dugard and Reynolds, "Apartheid, International Law."

20. Andoni, "Redefining Oslo."

21. Bloemraad and Trost, "It's a Family Affair."

22. Rico and Jennings, "Formation of Left-Right Identification."

23. Kuczynski, Harach, and Bernardini, "Psychology's Child Meets Sociology's Child."

24. Harker and Skelton, *Conflict, Violence, and Peace.*

25. Tedin, "Assessing Peer and Parent Influence"; Davies, "Family's Role in Political Socialization."

26. Milstein, "Politics Is Also 'Child's Play."

27. Matthews, "Window on the 'New' Sociology."

28. Kallio and Häkli, "Tracing Children's Politics"; Katz, *Growing Up Global.*

29. Zimmerman, "Child and Family Well-Being."

30. Williamson, Creswell, Butler, Christie, and Halligan, "Parental Responses to Child Experiences."

31. Allen and Bang, "Ecological Contexts and Youth."

32. Beck and Jennings, "Family Traditions, Political Periods."

33. McDevitt and Kiousis, "Active Political Parenting: Youth Contributions," 20.

34. Jennings, Stoker, and Bowers, "Politics Across Generations: Family Transmission."

35. McDevitt and Chaffee, "From Top Down to Trickle-Up Influence."
36. Wong and Tseng, "Political Socialization in Immigrant Families."
37. Bloemraad and Trost, "It's a Family Affair."
38. Pinquart and Silberesien, "Transmission of Values from Adolescents."
39. Spellings, Barber, and Olsen, "Political Activism of Palestinian Youth."
40. Habashi, "Palestinian Children: Authors."
41. Spellings, Barber, and Olsen, "Political Activism of Palestinian Youth."
42. Solhaug and Kristensen, "Political Learning among Youth."
43. Hart and Forte, "Mandated to Fail?"
44. Cheney, "Preventing Exploitation, Promoting Equity."
45. Mauro and Joffee, "Religious Right."
46. Habashi and Worley, "Children's Projected Political Affiliation."
47. Ibid.
48. Aran, "Containment and Territorial Transnational Actors."
49. Beck and Jennings, "Family Traditions, Political Periods"; Allen and Bang, "Ecological Contexts and Youth."
50. Habashi, *Political Socialization of Youth.*
51. Holloway, Holt, and Mills, "Questions of Agency."
52. Habashi, "[Im]possibilities of Reinvention."
53. Katz, *Growing Up Global.*
54. Beinin and Hajjar, "Palestine, Israel."
55. Orpett, "The Archaeology of Land Law."
56. Dugard and Reynolds, "Apartheid, International Law."
57. Habashi, "Palestinian Children: A Transformation."
58. The World Bank, "West Bank and Gaza."
59. Omer-Man, "Separate and Unequal."
60. Abu Zayyad, "Legalizing the Illegal."
61. UNCTAD, "Israeli Occupation Cost Gaza."
62. Weirich, "Hijacking the Charitable System."
63. Gorenberg, "The Other Housing Crisis."
64. Haklai, "Religious—Nationalist Mobilization," 734.
65. Sarsar, "Jerusalem's Housing Crisis."
66. Hirschhorn, "Origins of the Redemption?"
67. Tenenbaum and Eiran, "Israeli Settlement Activity."
68. Haklai, "Religious—Nationalist Mobilization," 720.
69. Ellis, "Three Discursive Dilemmas."
70. Ben Hagai, Whitlatch, and Zurbriggen, "'We Didn't Talk About the Conflict.'"
71. Blenkinsopp, "The Bible, Archaeology and Politics."
72. Hart and Forte, "Mandated to Fail?," 629.
73. Ibid., 632.
74. Habashi, *Political Socialization of Youth.*
75. Ibid.

BIBLIOGRAPHY

Abu Zayyad, Z. "Legalizing the Illegal." *Palestine-Israel Journal of Politics, Economics, and Culture* 20, no. 2/3 (2015): 59–63.

Allen, L., and H. J. Bang. "Ecological Contexts and Youth Civic and Political Engagement in Paris, France." *Journal of Applied Developmental Psychology* 39 (2015): 34–43.

Andoni, L. "Redefining Oslo: Negotiating the Hebron Protocol." *Journal of Palestine Studies* 26, no. 3 (1997): 17–30.

Aran, A. "Containment and Territorial Transnational Actors: Israel, Hezbollah and Hamas." *International Affairs* 26, no. 4 (2012): 835–55.

Beck, P. A., and K. Jennings. "Family Traditions, Political Periods, and the Development of Partisan Orientations." *The Journal of Politics* 53, no. 3 (1991): 742–63.

Beinin, J., and L. Hajjar. "Palestine, Israel and the Arab-Israeli Conflict." *Middle East Research and Information Project*. Lokayat, 2014. https://lokayat.org.in/books/palestine.pdf.

Ben Hagai, E., A. Whitlatch, and E. Zurbriggen. "'We Didn't Talk About the Conflict': The Birthright Trip's Influence on Jewish Americans' Understanding of the Israeli-Palestinian Conflict." *Peace and Conflict: Journal of Peace Psychology* 24, no. 2 (2018): 139–49.

Blenkinsopp, J. "The Bible, Archaeology and Politics; or The Empty Land Revisited." *Journal for the Study of the Old Testament* 27, no. 2 (2002): 169–87.

Bloemraad, I., and C. Trost. "It's a Family Affair." *American Behavioral Scientist* 52, no. 4 (2008): 507–32.

Bolin, A. "Children's Agency in Interprofessional Collaborative Meetings in Child Welfare Work." *Child & Family Social Work* 21, no. 4 (2016): 502–11.

B'Tselem: The Israeli Center for Human Rights in the Occupied Territories. "Settlements." November 11, 2017. https://www.btselem.org/settlements.

Bucx, F. "Child Development: Theories and Critical Perspectives." *Journal of Family Theory and Review* 10, no. 1 (2018): 304–8.

Cheney, K. "Preventing Exploitation, Promoting Equity: Findings from the International Forum on Intercountry Adoption and Global Surrogacy 2014." *Adoption and Fostering* 40, no. 1 (2016): 6–19.

Davies, J. "The Family's Role in Political Socialization." *The Annals of the American Academy of Political and Social Science* 369, no. 1 (1965): 10–19.

Diessner, R., M. Yazdani, and T. Richel. "Western and Middle Eastern Developmental Stage Theories." In *Psyche and Eros: Bahá'í Studies in a Spiritual Psychology*, edited by R. Diessner, 35–54. Oxford, UK: George Ronald Publishers, 2007.

Dugard, J., and J. Reynolds. "Apartheid, International Law, and the Occupied Palestinian Territory." *European Journal of International Law* 24, no. 3 (2013): 867–913.

Ellis, D. "Three Discursive Dilemmas for Israeli Religious Settlers." *Discourse Studies* 16, no. 4 (2014): 473–87.

Gorenberg, G. "The Other Housing Crisis: Why Can't Israel and the Palestinians Make Peace? There Are Many Complicated Reasons, but the Facts on the Ground Point to a Simple Answer: It's the Settlements, Stupid." *Foreign Policy* 170, no. 170 (2009): 56–58.

Habashi, J. "[Im]possibilities of Reinvention of Palestinian Early Childhood Education."

In *Reconceptualizing Early Childhood Care and Education: Critical Questions, New Imaginaries and Social Activism*, edited by M. Mimi Bloch, B. Swadener, and G. Cannella, 303–11. New York: Peter Lang, 2014.

———. "Palestinian Children: Authors of Collective Memory." *Children and Society* 27, no. 6 (2013): 421–33.

———. "Palestinian Children: A Transformation of National Identity in the Abbas Era." *Fennia* 197, no. 1 (2019): 77–93.

———. *Political Socialization of Youth: A Palestinian Case Study*. New York: Palgrave Macmillan New York, 2017.

Habashi, J., and J. Worley. "Children's Projected Political Affiliation: Transcending Local Politics." *Children's Geographies* 12, no. 2 (2014): 205–18.

Haklai, O. "Religious—Nationalist Mobilization and State Penetration: Lessons from Jewish Settlers' Activism in Israel and the West Bank." *Comparative Political Studies* 40, no. 6 (2007): 713–39.

Hall, C. "To Throw a Stone in Palestine: The Principle of Proportionality and Children in the Israeli Military Justice System." *Denver Journal of International Law and Policy* 46, no. 2 (2018): 91–122.

Harker, C., and T. Skelton. *Conflict, Violence, and Peace*. Singapore: Springer, 2017.

Hart, J., and C. Forte. "Mandated to Fail? Humanitarian Agencies and the Protection of Palestinian Children." *Disasters* 37, no. 4 (2013): 627–45.

Hirschhorn, S. Y. "The Origins of the Redemption in Occupied Suburbia? The Jewish-American Makings of the West Bank Settlement of Efrat, 1973–87." *Middle Eastern Studies* 51, no. 2 (2015): 269–84.

Holloway, S. L., L. Holt, and S. Mills. "Questions of Agency: Capacity, Subjectivity, Spatiality and Temporality." *Progress in Human Geography* 43, no. 3 (2019): 458–77.

Hopkins, P., and R. Pain. "Geographies of Age: Thinking Relationally." *Area* 39, no. 3 (2007): 287–94.

Hörschelmann, K. "Populating the Landscapes of Critical Geopolitics—Young People's Responses to the War in Iraq (2003)." *Political Geography* 27, no. 5 (2008): 587–609.

Horton, G. "Advocating for Palestinian Children in the Face of the Israeli Occupation." *Critical and Radical Social Work* 1, no. 1 (2013): 111–15.

Huang, J. "Being and Becoming: the Implications of Different Conceptualizations of Children and Childhood in Education." *Canadian Journal for New Scholars in Education* 10, no. 1 (2019): 99–105.

Jennings, M. K., L. Stoker, and J. Bowers. "Politics across Generations: Family Transmission Reexamined." *The Journal of Politics* 71, no. 3 (2009): 782–99.

Joronen, M. "Politics of Precarious Childhood: Ill Treatment of Palestinian Children under the Israeli Military Order." *Geopolitics* 21, no. 1 (2016): 92–114.

Kallio, K., and J. Häkli. "Tracing Children's Politics." *Political Geography* 30, no. 2 (2011): 99–109.

Katz, C. *Growing Up Global*. London: University of Minnesota Press, 2004.

Kuczynski, L., L. Harach, and C. S. Bernardini. "Psychology's Child Meets Sociology's Child: Agency, Influence and Power in Parent-Child Relationships." In *Contemporary Perspectives on Families*. Vol. 1 of *Through the Eyes of the Child: Re-visioning Children* as *Active Agents of Family Life,* edited by F. M. Berardo, and C. L. Shehan, 21–52. Stamford, Conn.: JAI Press, 1999.

Mason, V., and R. Falk. "Assessing Nonviolence in the Palestinian Rights Struggle." *State Crime Journal* 5, no. 1 (2016): 163–86.

Matthews, S. "A Window on the 'New' Sociology of Childhood." *Sociology Compass* 1, no. 1 (2007): 322–34.

Mauro, D., and C. Joffee. "The Religious Right and the Reshaping of Sexual Policy: An Examination of Reproductive Rights and Sexuality Education." *Sexuality Research & Social Policy* 4, no. 1 (2007): 67–92.

McDevitt, M., and S. Chaffee. "From Top Down to Trickle-Up Influence: Revisiting Assumptions about the Family in Political Socialization." *Political Communication* 19, no. 3 (2002): 281–301.

McDevitt, M., and S. Kiousis. "Active Political Parenting: Youth Contributions during Election Campaigns." *Social Science Quarterly* 96, no. 1 (2014): 19–33.

Milstein, D. "Politics Is Also 'Child's Play.'" *Teaching and Teacher Education* 26, no. 1 (2010): 136–43.

Omer-Man, E. "Separate and Unequal: Israel's Dual Criminal Justice System in the West Bank." *Palestine-Israel Journal of Politics, Economics, and Culture* 21, no. 3 (2016): 16–21.

Orpett, N. "The Archaeology of Land Law: Excavating Law in the West Bank." *International Journal of Legal Information* 40, no. 3 (2012): 344–92.

Palestinian Central Bureau of Statistics. *The Status of the Rights of Palestinian Children 2014.* April 2015. https://www.pcbs.gov.ps/Downloads/book2147.pdf.

Pinquart, M. and R. Silberesien. "The Transmission of Values from Adolescents to Their Parents: The Role of Value Content and Authoritative Parenting." *Adolescent* 39, no. 153 (2014): 83–100.

Rico, G., and M. Jennings. "The Formation of Left-Right Identification: Pathways and Correlates of Parental Influence." *Political Psychology* 37, no. 2 (2016): 237–52.

Rubin, K., and M. Menzer. "Culture and Social Development." In *Encyclopedia on Early Childhood Development,* edited by R. E. Tremblay, M. Boivin, and R. Peters, 1–14. Quebec: Centre of Excellence for Early Childhood Development, 2010.

Sarsar, S. "Jerusalem's Housing Crisis." *Washington Report on Middle East Affairs* 31, no. 7 (2012): 18.

Solhaug, T., and N. Kristensen. "Political Learning among Youth: Exploring Patterns of Students' First Political Awakening." *Citizenship, Social, and Economics Education* 12, no. 3 (2013): 174–85.

Spellings, C., B. Barber, and J. Olsen. "Political Activism of Palestinian Youth: Exploring Individual, Parental, and Ecological Factors." *Journal of Marriage and Family* 74, no. 5 (2012): 1084–1100.

Steffen, B. "Beyond Child Participation in the Occupied Palestinian Territories: The Case for 'Protective Solidarity.'" *Law, Social Justice and Global Development Journal* 16, no. 2 (2011): 1–16.

Tedin, K. "Assessing Peer and Parent Influence on Adolescent Political Attitudes." *American Journal of Political Science* 24, no. 1 (1980): 136–54.

Tenenbaum, K., and E. Eiran. "Israeli Settlement Activity in the West Bank and Gaza: A Brief History." *Negotiation Journal* 21, no. 2 (2005): 171–75.

The United Nations Conference on Trade and Development. "Israeli Occupation Cost Gaza $16.7 Billion in Past Decade—UNCTAD Estimates." November 25, 2020. https://unctad.org/news/israeli-occupation-cost-gaza-167-billion-past-decade-unctad-estimates.

Veronese, G., A. Pepe, A. Jaradah, F. Murannak, and H. Hamdouna. "'We Must Cooperate with One Another against the Enemy': Agency and Activism in School-Aged Children as Protective Factors against Ongoing War Trauma and Political Violence in the Gaza Strip." *Neglect* 70, (2017) 364–76.

Weirich, M. "Hijacking the Charitable System: An Examination of Tax-Exempt Status for Charities That Support Israeli Settlements." *Journal of Gender, Race and Justice* 14, no, 1 (2010): 327–58.

Williamson, V., C. Creswell, I. Butler, H. Christie, and S. Halligan. "Parental Responses to Child Experiences of Trauma Following Presentation at Emergency Departments: A Qualitative Study." *BMJ Open* 6, no. 11 (2016): 1–10.

Wong, J., and V. Tseng. "Political Socialization in Immigrant Families: Challenging Top-Down Parental Socialization Models." *Journal of Ethnic and Migration Studies* 34, no. 1 (2008): 151–68.

The World Bank Group. "West Bank and Gaza: The Economic Effects of Restricted Access to Land in the West Bank [PDF]." Washington, D.C.: World Bank Group. October 21, 2008. https://documents.worldbank.org/en/publication/documents-reports/documentdetail/654801468176641469/west-bank-and-gaza-the-economic-effects-of-restricted-access-to-land-in-the-west-bank.

Zimmerman, S. "Child and Family Well-Being in States with Different Political Cultures. (Policies Affecting Individuals And Families)." *Families in Society: The Journal of Contemporary Social Services* 84, no. 2 (2003): 275–84.

PART 2

The Violent and Carceral Practices of Unchilding

The Violent Circulation of Affects and Necropenological Unchilding

NADERA SHALHOUB-KEVORKIAN

The occupation [the Israeli state] does not see our children as children, nor do they feel their pain . . . the state wants to silence their pain . . . but . . . our children live in daily fear that one morning they will wake up to find out that another friend or relative was killed or burned alive. Our children do not mean anything to them; [to them] they are not children, they are bodies to be killed.

—Ayman's mother

The case of Mohammed Abu Khdeir and his burning alive made all Ghassan's school classmates feel deep humiliation. Let me remind you that all those young children who got angry after his burning alive were arrested, and we as parents needed to silence our children's pain, to protect them, prevent their injury, arrest or death . . . but, this is wrong, one can't silence a child crying loudly from pain . . . can you, can I? Can we? Was the state of Israel able to deprive my son from feeling deep sadness following the burning alive of a child his age?"

—Ghassan's mother
(conversing with the author and
other parents who lost their children,
following the death of Ayman,
in Ayman's family home)

The above quotes are voices of two mothers, Ayman's and Ghassan's, who lost their sons, both of whom were about to turn fifteen years old. Israeli Occupying Forces shot and killed Ayman near Al-Aqsa Mosque in August 2019, and Ghassan in the Pisgat Ze'ev settlement in Beit Hanina near Jerusalem in 2015. The mothers insisted that, in the eyes of the Israelis, "children are not children" in the Occupied Palestinian Territories and that feelings of loss and pain, like the land, are under military occupation. They described how the settler state, in wounding their children, also attempts to govern and occupy their emotions and feelings. In detailing the ways their sons witnessed state violence, the mothers exposed the deep layers of daily oppression endured by children under occupation. Ghassan and Ayman's siblings explained how they fear expressing their anguish and deep agony at school, or among friends and relatives. One of their sisters remarked: "If I tell my friends at school that I am having bad dreams since I lost my brother, or share with my teachers or relatives my anger and missing my brother, our school can be invaded, and my house can be searched by the military and security people." Ghassan's younger sister explained to me: "You see, they only consider us terrorists." More than the failure of the state to govern children's feelings, Israeli state power in fact aims to silence their pain and sadness by treating their inner and collective emotions as terrorism against the state.

The cases of Ayman and Ghassan, which I examine by engaging with their families' ordeals and listening to their narrations, reveal how the Israeli state uses a "governance of emotions" to intensify its colonial rule, especially over children. State modalities of violence not only objectify and unchild children while turning them into disposable terrorists in life and death, but also use the dead body of the child as a tool for disciplining and punishing the colonized, an affective apparatus I call "Necropenology." By paying close attention to the cases of Ghassan and Ayman, I make visible what I see as the circulation of the Israeli state's affective governance power through a necropenological regime of unchilding. Tracing the characteristics of a necropenological regime of unchilding illustrates the political work of affects as state violence. The regime enables state terror to exert its power through and around slain children's bodies and their community's affects. But it also gives rise to modes of resistance that have the capacity to interrupt unchilding. This chapter builds on my past work on childhood and unchilding, necropenology, and the occupation of the senses.[1] It draws from evidence from my involvement with eleven bereaved Palestinian families. I accompanied them to demonstrations, public and family meetings, and while anxiously awaiting their children's dead bodies to be returned to them by Israeli authorities. I focus on the governance of affects to examine the ways in which the settler state kills children and then manipulates and abuses bereaved families' and their community's emotions. Observing the dynamics between Israeli authorities and heartbroken family members, I came to notice how the state uses affects of sudden loss in unknown but violent circumstances to maintain, circulate, and further activate its eliminatory power.

This chapter combines theoretical and fieldwork insights to investigate the "circulating affects" of families whose children's bodies are killed, kidnapped, and withheld in freezing morgue refrigerators. The encounters I share demonstrate that the colonial state forcibly requires bereaved families to adhere to colonial sovereignty over their land, lives, and bodies. Further, the colonial state's concern with Palestinians' "circulating emotions," "public moods," and sentiments is managed through mundane acts of control. This combined with legal and securitized punitive structures of colonial governance over mourning render the colonized disposable in life and ungrievable in death.

Settler-State Strategies to Manage
Dead Palestinian Bodies, Burials, and Death

As of 2018, according to the National Campaign for the Retrieval of the Bodies of Palestinian and Arab War Victims, and the disclosure of the fate of those missing since its launch in 2008, over four hundred cases of slain Palestinians were documented.[2] The Palestinian human rights NGO al-Haq found that, as of March 13, 2018, eighteen Palestinian bodies remain in Israeli custody since 2016; all were killed by the Israeli military for alleged attacks.[3] In March 2018, the Israeli government passed a law sanctioning the withholding of dead bodies by police. The law imposes constraints on the families of the deceased, including restrictions on the burial of the bodies and limitations on the funeral's location and number of attendees. The withholding of Palestinian bodies by the Israeli government is a violation of international law,[4] and an initiative by the UN Convention against Torture in 2016 has advised Israel to return Palestinian bodies to be buried in accordance with religious customs and tradition.[5] In some of those cases, Israel conditioned freeing the bodies on the family's commitment to bury them outside of their family plots in Jerusalem. The state's policies vary from family to family, further increasing the unpredictability and uncertainty of their situation and how they respond to the withholding of their loved one's imprisoned dead body.[6] Some families receive official letters with Israel's conditions for negotiating the release of the bodies. Those families view such practices by the state, in addition to the letters and phone calls from authorities, as threats intended to terrorize and punish them and their communities, as well as to disrupt their communal and familial kinship. In September of 2019, while fifty-one bodies of Palestinians were being held by Israel, the Israeli Supreme Court, in a three-to-three decision, supported Israel's continued holding of the bodies as bargaining chips.[7]

The official Israeli legal position on the withholding of Palestinian corpses, turning them into objects for political negotiation, and the divergent positions held by Israeli politicians regarding what to do with dead bodies, have been expressed in public debates and the media. Then–prime minister Benjamin Netanyahu and former minister of public security Gilad Erdan insisted on withholding the bodies and not returning them to their families as a punitive measure against alleged Palestinian attacks, in addition to preventing funerals, because Erdan believes they encourage incitement. At the funerals, religious and political slogans are chanted, which are, for Erdan, "inadmissible by all standards and measurements everywhere, and more so in the capital Jerusalem."[8] The image of Palestinian funerals being violent is part of the bigger Israeli stigmatization of Palestinians as "Muslim terrorists" who subscribe to a "culture of death."[9] The head of the Israel Security Agency (Shabak), Yoram Cohen, also saw "advantages in keeping the bodies in Israel."[10]

Leveraging the imprisonment of dead bodies has been the topic of conversation in the Knesset. In a discussion that took place on November 4, 2015, Minister of Defense Moshe Ya'alon opposed the withholding of Palestinian bodies. On November 27, 2019, Minister of Defense Naftali Bennett "ordered all bodies of Palestinians, who attacked or who are alleged to have attacked Israelis, to be withheld and not returned to their families."[11] The above discussion reveals that not only are the Israeli military and police empowered to enforce sacralized power over Palestinians and their dead, but state authorities can freely conduct these practices because no policy against them is in place. At the same time, the Knesset and state officials perform "democratic debate" to maintain the appearance that they are addressing the issue.

Similar to most people around the world, many Palestinians dispose of their dead with rituals developed through spiritual and community traditions. Proper burial of the dead ensures dignity to the deceased and the living mourners. In Islam, it is fundamental that the body be buried quickly after the death, usually no more than twenty-four hours. Common Islamic burial practices include collective bathing of the body with heated water within hours after death, the minimization of fluid leakage in case of physically damaged corpses, enshrouding the corpse, allowing well-wishers to pass on their respects and condolences, funeral prayer requesting forgiveness for the dead, and burial of the dead body (without a coffin) in a grave perpendicular to the direction of Mecca. Martyrs, those who died in wartime or defending their property, are to be unbathed and buried in the clothes in which they were killed. The respectful treatment of dead bodies is a vital aspect to psycho-familial, national, and religious human behaviors. In the case of martyrs, the sacredness of burial and retrieval of the body is heightened because of the nature of the death. By ridiculing the Palestinian body, neglecting religious-traditional rites, and dispossessing a family and community of its basic human right to mourn and part with loved ones, the settler colony defines and memorializes its power on the bodies of the colonized dead. The practice of holding captive Palestinian corpses in Israeli morgues exemplifies the colonizer's efforts to render the deaths of these Palestinians impersonal. When families and communities cannot mourn their loved ones in an intimate and dignified setting, the dead are reduced from kin who are beloved by their families to mere numbers, to an anonymous racialized "offender." Yet, in a twisted way, the treatment of the bodies of the deceased by the settler-colonial state produces the colonized

subject as "the living dead." By identifying the dead Palestinian body as "terrorist," regardless of political affiliation or acts, it is inherently dangerous and always
feared.[12] Stripping the family of every possible relic of unique personhood justifies various modes of racialized violence against living and dead Palestinians.

Theorizing the Settler State and Circulating Affects

As I have argued in previous work, and following scholars of indigenous and settler-
colonial studies, securitized and governmental structures of the Israeli state produce and reproduce Jewish supremacy and Palestinian dispossession not only in
the sphere of land, but they also intimately penetrate the lived experiences of Palestinians in the sphere of senses—smell, taste, touch, sight, sound, and affects.[13]
I have described the ways in which the Israeli state uses sensory stimuli as a con-
frontational tactic with the goal of invading, governing, and dispossessing the
colonized community within their spaces of belonging as the "occupation of the
senses."[14] The "occupation of the senses" identifies state-sponsored sensory and
material production and reproduction of colonial racialized, religio-nationalist
hegemony, distinction, and exclusivity through technologies that manage what
Rancière calls the "distribution of the sensible."[15] I illustrate this sensory assault
by showing how public ceremonies, marches, parades, and festivities—seemingly apolitical, mundane "cultural" or "artistic" activities—become key vehicles
for maintaining forms of sensory imposition over Palestinian neighborhoods in
Occupied East Jerusalem (OEJ). At the same time, sensory power produces new
spaces solely available to the colonizer and excludes the material, historical, and
cultural presence of Palestinians that is tied to the land. The compounded and
manifold invasions of the senses, on a daily and hourly basis, relentlessly broadcast the colonizer's force and systems of power into native places. Noises, smells,
lights, and more are imposed by the colonizer and interpreted, internalized, and
resisted by the colonized.

This chapter sees sentiments, emotions, and situated experiences as sites in
themselves to be interpreted as dependent on structural conditions that embody
their own discourses of power.[16] Expanding the understanding of the relationship between subjective experiences, personal emotions, collective affects, and
sentiments and state power has long been central to the work of feminist scholars.[17] Sara Ahmed theorizes "affective economies" as the circulating of emotions
in society that are mediated by bodies and signifiers that participate in the consti-
tution of particular attachments and differentiations between individual and social bodies.[18] Judith Butler makes a distinction between those who are grievable,
"whose lives are seen to matter and to be worthy of grief after death, and those
who are not," who fall into the category of "ungrievability."[19] Studying the grief

and the emotional climate of populations under conditions of violence, siege, and military occupation can help us uncover not only the political work of the violation of pain, the transmutation of grief and anger, but also its modes of operation and its penetration of the dead and living.[20] Punishing the living, by capturing dead bodies and torturing them in death, while simultaneously casting them into ungrievability as nonchildren and nonhumans, renders them, as Butler explains "destructible" and "lose-able," precisely because their lives are framed as being "already lost or forfeited."[21]

The state's production and invasion of affects is particularly evident in colonial and settler-colonial contexts, as well as in areas with political violence and conflicts.[22] Ann Stoler weaves the thread between the seemingly discordant categories of "state" and "sentiments," arguing that sentimental, rather than rational concerns were central to the establishment of the colonial state. In Stoler's work, she argues that sentiment was required for the maintenance of control by Dutch colonial institutions over natives in the East Indies. She explains, "Striking in the nineteenth century Dutch archives of colonial Indonesia—in its more public as well as its secret documents, official and private correspondence, commissioned reports, guides to good health, economic reform, household management, primary education, and belles-lettres—is not the rule of reason but what might be (mis)construed as its very opposite: namely, a discursive density around sentiments and their subversive tendencies, around private feelings and public moods and their political consequences, around the racial distribution of sensibilities, around assessments of affective dispositions and their beneficent and dangerous political effects." The process of "state-craft," Stoler argues, was driven by state practices of "assessing appropriate sentiments and in fashioning techniques of affective control." The governance of the "affective self" of the targeted populations was constituted by "educating their desires, directing affective judgments, severing some affective bonds and establishing others . . . and by adjudicating what constituted moral sentiments." These tactics "educat[ed] the proper distribution of sentiments and desires," all with the aim of disciplining the native to conform to the ideological underpinnings of the state.[23]

In OEJ, colonial governance's specific coupling of the education of desire and the logic of elimination occurs in ways that prompt myriad questions: Does the settler-colonial state expect the families of the deceased to ally with their discourses of power, embodied in their governance of affects and modes of punishment? Is the state concerned with "educating the desires" of the bereaved families? Is it interested in maintaining the ungrievability of their loved ones? Is this affective targeting another modality of elimination? Or is it all of the above? In order to investigate the Israeli state's involvement in the "culturally standardized organization of feeling and sentiment" among Palestinians, we need to delineate the particular politico-ideological structure that the settler state works to legitimize.

The settler-colonial structure of the Zionist project, with its primary motivation of access to territory, shapes the contours of Israeli state power.[24] The state enacts elimination through multiple modes, during different historical eras and across geographies, even attempting to eliminate Palestinian affects in spaces of death and times of grief. The strategies the settler state uses to manage dead Palestinian bodies, burials, and death—to the point of obsession—constitutes part of its necropenological regime, whereby it regulates its biopolitical engineering through extending discipline and punishment into the realm of death. Necropenology is the performance of power that marks both living and dead bodies as disposable. Necropenology is also a form of carcerality masked by a structurally instituted racialized regime, authorized by a colonial legal system, and manifested through marking and conquering the flesh, body, and land. State-sponsored assaults on death, dead bodies, and grief result in a carcerality with ever-changing penalties that entrench an already-eliminatory social order, keeping the bereaved captive in their loss.

Withholding Kin as a Political Weapon

On October 12, 2014, Ghassan and his cousin Ahmad walked to a settlement just five minutes from their homes in Jerusalem, informing their family they were going to look for a video game. Later, Ghassan's mother learned Israeli police shot and killed her son on the spot, while his cousin was badly wounded. In the aftermath of the shooting, Israelis could be heard shouting the words "Die, you son of a whore, die!" at Ahmad while he lay on the ground bleeding and in agony.[25] October 2014 marked a period of intensified violence in Jerusalem, with the loss of many lives and loved ones. With the support of Prime Minister Benjamin Netanyahu, the Israeli security cabinet approved Public Security Minister Gilad Erdan's proposal to withhold the bodies of Palestinians killed by security forces after allegedly committing violence against Israelis,[26] and Ghassan's body was one of them. Ghassan's father remembered, "First they shot them without any mercy, then they dragged, humiliated, and tortured them after death, leaving them bleeding in the streets while others were watching . . . and now they kidnapped their dead bodies. . . . Refusing to free them, refusing to return them to us, and preventing us from burying them with dignity in Jerusalem."

This story is one of many in which bereaved Palestinian families were further agonized by witnessing the bodies of their deceased loved ones go through a violent procession that begins with the act of extrajudicially killing and abducting the body of their son or brother, withholding him in Israeli freezers, negotiating his release and burial with the state, and finally the policing, surveillance, and micromanagement of his funeral.

This section investigates the political significance of the Israeli courts and military disrupting and stealing the natural bereavement and mourning process that the family goes through as the body of their murdered son or brother is withheld from them. Without manufacturing and manipulating populations and individual's affects, state-crafting is impossible. The Israeli settler-colonial state's survival relies on multiple registers of fear to maintain its rule, all in the name of "security." It is through a racialized ideology that the state's security becomes sacred, protecting the "superior" ethno-religious group (with muddled secular and biblical claims) against the profane other (the displaced from time and space Palestinian Arab). The Israeli state produces a security theology along these lines, accompanied by a colonial "common sense" that generates laws, policies, and practices of suspecting and accusing all Palestinians of ahistorical violent motivations.[27] Securitized common sense entangles with the colonizer's political economy of fear and works through legal, political, economic, spatial, and corporeal spheres, as well as targeting affective, emotional relations. On one hand, securitized common sense casts racialized suspicion over all Palestinian subjects and spaces (including death), on the other, it causes daily harm to the colonized by denying these always-already "suspects" of their own sentiments of fear, anguish, love, loss, anticipation, hope, and despair.

The act of preventing the right of a family to grieve properly and see their child's body after death is justified by the settler state as a "security" measure. Yet, these "security concerns," as the bereaved tell us, are implicated in the state's political ethos toward the Palestinian population in general, and function as part of the intentional debilitation of the colonized Palestinian community.[28] Families whose deceased loved ones are taken away experience disrupted and disjointed relations. In one case, the youngest sister in a family refused to go back to school for over a month following the loss of her brother. She shared her fears with me: if her parents couldn't even bury her brother, how could they protect her on her way to school? She was extremely angry with her parents and refused to communicate with her father, believing that he was not doing his best to bring back the dead body of her martyred brother. In another case, a grandmother suffered from depression and withdrawal. She refused to leave her house or allow family members inside and refused when they tried to bring her medicine or gather during feasts or holidays. She continued to refuse until she witnessed the release and burial of her grandson's body. The ten-year-old sibling of a dead Jerusalemite child explained the violence of withholding their loved one's body as "soul torture." Soul torture manifests in mundane, everyday micropolitics across the community, as they wait in uncertainty while children's corpses are held frozen in state morgues.

Waiting:
Incomplete Grief, Ambiguous Loss,
and Its Terrorizing Affects

This section analyzes the circulating emotions and sentiments of Jerusalemite family members subjected to waiting for their deceased loved ones, drawing on in-depth interviews and conversations with both Ayman's and Ghassan's family members. Across my fieldwork, Jerusalemite families expressed that being robbed of these moments created a painful state of uncertainty, confusion, and lack of narrative as they waited while state authorities withheld their loved one's body. Scholars studying the psychological effects of death on kin speak to the immense difficulties facing family members who lose loved ones under unclear circumstances. Family members struggle more acutely when they cannot comprehend their loss, know the details of it, the how, why, and in what way their loved ones perished, or respond to their inner feelings of guilt when questioning their ability to prevent the death. As family counselors Gabrielle Betz and Jill M. Thorngren explain: "For the family who experiences ambiguous loss, the situation is stressful and oftentimes cruel in its ongoing torment. Because the loss is intangible or uncertain, the mourning process for family members becomes complicated. Ambiguous loss is characterized by factors that inherently impede the grieving process."[29] Insofar as the Israeli state stages a governance of affects around Palestinian children as ungrievable, the process of grieving ambiguous loss becomes even more traumatizing for the bereaved.[30] This power over the circumstances of loss extends the state's techniques of torturing the family and maneuvers around their affects to reestablish the ungrievability of the colonized child. The torture of waiting for the returned body of a child corresponds with the casting of Palestinian children as criminals who are undeserving and imprisonable even after their deaths.

Family members expressed severe psychological pain as a result of the agonizing process and knowledge that the state was using the dead bodies of their loved ones as political tools, depriving them of their right to mourn the dead. Referring to her child, a bereaved mother explained: "I was praying for his release from the Israeli refrigerators. I wanted him out, I wanted him free, I hated his cold incarceration in their prisons, even as a dead body. The fact that we did not bury our children, and the fact that they are prisoners of the Israelis even as dead bodies—this kills us all every day . . . I feel I die a hundred times every day. He appeared in my dreams. He was begging me, '... Mom ... please take me back home.' They are telling us, 'You are under our control, in life and in death. ... We decide when and how you die, whether your children can be buried in Jerusalem, and even whether you have the right to breathe.'"

These voices reveal how the state invades not only the visceral experience of a bereaved parent, but also the innate senses of the colonized. The testimonies of family and community members suggest that we see the colonizer as intentionally forcing families to feel, to the greatest extent possible, humiliation, loss, and defeat, and that in that defeat, they should wait for the Israeli authorities to free the bodies of their children. Their ability to pay their respects, hug, kiss, see or talk to their child for the last time is dependent on the regime's "goodwill." When Israeli officials withhold Palestinian children's dead bodies, they sever necessary physical human bonds that constitute a family's intimate relations during loss, and impose an unending uncertainty on grief, "a waiting for what is not comprehendible," as Ghassan's mother reiterated. The imprisonment of Ghassan and Ayman's bodies by the Israeli state—and thus the denial of their loved ones seeing and touching them—produced a sharp psychological trauma for their siblings and parents, causing a lack of closure and coherent narrative. The colony's power to invade even the most intimate senses, such as feelings of loss and bereavement, and the vast power they wield to influence the emotions of the family serves the regime in establishing a new lever for controlling and dominating Palestinians.

Over time, the state's control confiscates even the emotions of the bereaved. Parents expressed their deep sorrow and agony in both private and public meetings when they shared, for example: "I feel I can't sense my own feelings, as if feeling stopped." One father explained: "When Baha'a [the deceased son] used to get sick, I used to go crazy. I think back to those times when my agony over him being sick, having a cold, having a pimple, used to cause me so much pain. Now, I lost him totally, and he is there in prison, in that fridge." In death, taking the time to grieve, to comprehend the loss of a loved one, and to let go and come to terms with loss, is deeply meaningful and essential to mental health.

In making Ayman's family wait for their child's body and negotiate his return with those who killed him, Saeda, Ayman's twelve-year-old sister, realized how through these securitized procedures, her community's emotions are managed by the political power of her colonizer. She asked, "Are our emotions a game (lu'beh) in their hands?" Saeda conveys her pain at witnessing the execution of her brother on the Israeli security cameras, and how that pain was amplified once his body was taken from them and "imprisoned in their refrigerators" as they "tried his dead body in their court." Anan, Saeda's seventeen-year-old sister, elaborated on her words, "People's emotions are weapons in their hands, they are games to silence us, to defeat and hurt us." Ayman's sisters' grieving was full of ambiguity. They were anxiously waiting to see him again, but the state prevented them from transmitting their grief corporeally, turning their loved one into a ungrievable other.

The sense of not knowing while at the same time inhabiting the shock over the loss of a child swells the pain of the bereaved family. Ghassan's mother was questioning if Ghassan was "for sure gone" to those who came to pay their condolences, and she insisted: "I can still hear his voice in the house, as if he is still sleeping in his bed, maybe he will return, maybe it is a lie and my son is calling for help. I keep on hearing him calling me Yamma, Yamma [mama] . . . why can't I see him, show me that he is dead, show me . . . bring him to me . . . am I not his mother?" Ghassan's sister kept putting her hands on her chest, pointing to the heaviness she felt, as she expressed: "I can't believe he is gone . . . I can't wait . . . I can't breathe . . . my eyes are blinded from agony and pain . . . I don't want to wait anymore." Ayman's sisters, too, voiced how their urgent need to grieve was foreclosed. They communicated their inability to do anything, even move from the bed or the sofa, let alone breathe. Another sister, Laila, said: "My legs are not listening to me . . . how long should we wait?" Saeda insisted: "I refuse to wait . . . I will go get him . . . myself . . . yes, alone . . . they think our emotions are a game in their hands . . . I can't take a breath (Mish adri akhod nafas)."

In the case of the loss of a child at the hands of the military occupation, waiting becomes a violent colonial technique. Waiting for the military-occupied senses to meet the facts of loss, the body, the blood, the wound, the sound and smell of death. Waiting for the Tasrih [the official Israeli approval to access the court, the graveyard, the investigation room], waiting in the cells of the colonizer for undefined and constantly expanding periods of time. Waiting in the freezers, waiting to return to life, to land, to humanity. Waiting without control strikes at the core of the Palestinian experience, emotionally and viscerally. It is one more way the settler state suspends the life of the colonized, and extends its power to hold the community hostage to its scrutinizing gaze. As Ghassan's mother talked about the day of her son's killing, she mentioned how the pervasive political and military violence in Jerusalem made her afraid for her son when he ventured out of the house for benign reasons, like getting a haircut. Crying she said, "I, like all mothers in Jerusalem, fear for my children, I worry about them all the time, and can't relax until I see them all around me here, at home. . . . I never thought I would lose Ghassan that way . . . such a calm boy, outstanding in his studies. . . . and this way . . . with no information . . . no proof . . . without seeing his body . . . hearing his breathing . . . smelling him . . . without even burying him . . . waiting and waiting . . . hearing his voice at night screaming for help . . . and waiting more . . . begging them to release his little body."

Waiting for her son to come home was already a painful daily routine for

Ghassan's mother. Waiting with fear that he will not return home persists now that he is dead. This form of torture blurs the boundaries between life and death; the mother is tormented daily as she fears for her son's life, and when dead, she begs for his body. In both cases, she wants her son to come home to safety, but is denied that by the state. Ayman's mother could not handle the politics and organization of waiting, because "waiting is not only shaped by the person waiting, it is also shaped by those who are providing whatever one is waiting for."[31] She was moving restlessly in her house, snapping at those who came to pay their condolences. She told me: "I can't bear this feeling of not knowing what happened to my son, where is he, how is he . . . my son is very young . . . he is only 36 kilos. . . . Please understand me, I am agonizing . . . can't breathe . . . his sister fainted yesterday. . . . She can't breathe either . . . it is torture . . . I woke up this morning, and started crying and sobbing, and asked my husband to call the lawyer . . . I talked to the lawyer at 7:00 a.m., asked him to tell me where is my son, who took him, what happened to him, why did they kill him. . . . I asked him to tell me what is going on . . . why is he imprisoned in their refrigerators. . . . He answered me like he talks to an object, like I am nothing, a table, a chair . . . nothing . . . please help me . . . bring back my son please . . . can't wait . . . I [am] dying . . . dying from waiting . . . torture . . . this is torture." Similarly, Ayman's mother's yearning to know the location of her son, to receive, hug, and smell him, and to "apologize to him that I failed to protect him," reveals a deep sense of torture. She insisted that they are being tortured by the state, being objectified by the lawyer, and being abandoned by the Palestinian Authority (PA). She felt disrespected as a mother, when the state, the lawyer, and the PA, asked the family to accept the torture of waiting.

The agony of waiting permeated Ghassan and Ayman's classmates and community. Young girls and boys in the neighborhood wore T-shirts with the boys' names and photos to send the message that, as a young girl in the neighborhood explained, "they are not gone, and we are not waiting for them to release him . . . he is here [pointing to her heart] . . . here in my heart." For family and community members, knowing the boys' bodies were waiting in the morgue, and had been "thrown" into the freezers to preserve their flesh in a frozen space, exacerbated the sense of loss. The inflicted waiting sent a violent message to the community that they have no right to grief and that their dead children are "frozen waste," subjected to torture even in death. But this same state-crafted politics of waiting used against the colonized became an active mode of resisting the settler-colonial logic and politics of elimination.

"Corpse Messaging":
State Power over the Human Flesh

What can you tell a state that wants to sculpt pain over children's dead bodies?
—Ghassan's fourteen-year-old cousin

The voices of Ayman's and Ghassan's families reveal the violent impact of the state's confinement of the frozen flesh of the deceased, which further oppresses living colonized bodies. The Israeli authorities' treatment of Ghassan's dead body and his family members' reactions show the brutality of the state's necroeconomy of withholding corpses, delaying burial, and suspending mourning and grief. The hyperpolitical violence embodied in security and legal logics and court processes inscribes state power over dead bodies. The site of punishment and anticipation in the frozen, dead flesh resonates with Alexander Weheliye's suggestion that flesh should be the focus of racial analysis.[32] Weheliye offers the generative analytical framework of "living enfleshment," a concept that helps to map the biopolitical, geopolitical, and necropolitical work of settler states by centering the flesh within the oppressive racializing assemblages over the bodies of the colonized. Palestinian bodies become "waste that can be stepped on," as a community member suggested. These experiences bring back memories of displacement and uprooting, which keep Palestinians "captive even in death." Ayman's and Ghassan's cases illustrate the political work and symbolic role of punishing the colonized by imprisoning their dead in new carceral spaces of erasure. In looking closely at the performativity of withholding dead bodies, we start to see how the colonial state and its bureaucracies reproduce a necropenological regime of dispossession that marks the living and dead colonized as nonhuman and disposable.

Ghassan's mother, in pain, told me, "My son is in prison. . . ." Her daughter interjected, "But mom, he is dead. . . . He is not in prison." Her mother replied, "No . . . he is in prison, he is in a prison called the refrigerator, and he will stay in prison, because they are preventing me from burying him inside Jerusalem. Poor, poor man. . . . He lived all his life handcuffed, he is dying in that cold, freezing prison, and will suffer and die more and more. . . . They want us to bury him outside Jerusalem." Ghassan's mother's voice speaks about her son's incarceration and unchilding, and his father added that the imprisonment of his son's slain body caused him "to die more and more." The occupation of Ghassan's parents' emotions, as they endured the state-sanctioned separation from their dead son, pushes us to read beyond nongrievability, toward recognizing how the body of a dead child, and the soul and emotions of bereaved families, become penetrable, woundable, and killable in life and in death.

Mbembe's theorization of necropolitics as the colonial sovereign's simple and brutal right to kill parallels the legal negation of indigenous land ownership. He explains, "The ultimate expression of sovereignty resides in the power and capacity to dictate who may live and who may die," in other words, "to exercise sovereignty is to exercise control over mortality and to define life as the deployment and manifestation of power."[33] In Mbembe's terms, colonial state sovereignty is determined through its necropological mechanisms of establishing "death zones," whereby the native is exposed to social, cultural, political, and corporal death. These spatial practices relegate natives into the realm of "disposable others." Yet, the colonial state's withholding of dead bodies goes beyond Mbembe's necropolitics. Carceral death exposes how the necropenological regime operates over the flesh of the dead to further produce the sites of eviction and disposability. Mbembe discusses the political economy of death as an expression of colonial sovereignty. In the case at hand, the Israeli state enhances its geographical sovereignty through regulating and bounding bodies in a liminal site between life and ungrievable death; bodies that are trapped in a frozen uncertainty. In this way, the refrigerators used to store bodies involved in police investigations become new sites of torture that extend the sense of occupation to further manipulate the affects of Palestinian families and the Palestinian community.

The withholding and eventual return of Ghassan's and Ayman's bodies is a form of political communication. The imposed waiting becomes vital to the legitimation of colonial authority. It is the colonial regime telling its subjects, "I have your sons' bodies, I can keep them or give them back as I see fit." As the state is constantly objectifying and unchilding children in their lives as criminals undeserving of life, so does it declare their bodies after death as undeserving of dignified burial. Withholding a child's body carries the message that there will never be a future Palestine, because the next generation does not exist in life or death. The performative instrumentalization of the body to demarcate sovereignty is reminiscent of the Mexican cartel practice of affective and performative inscriptions of power through acts of public execution and mutilation of victims, what Andrew Lantz analyzes as "corpse messaging."[34] Whereas in Mexico corpse messaging is about hypervisibilizing abuses and extra-state power, the processes described in this chapter are more about maintaining the slain child as invisible, and keeping the body imprisoned, hidden in freezers, buried from sight, and away from the public. The commodification and use of bodies becomes a mode of drawing boundaries, demarcating who deserves dignity in life and death.

The use of dead bodies as tools to draw geographies of power was clear in the case of Mustafa al-Khatib, a seventeen-year-old high school student from East Jerusalem, who was shot dead at the end of 2015 in the area of Lion's Gate (Bab-al-Asbat). Mustafa's body was released after three months, and only upon the condition that he would not be buried in his hometown of Jerusalem, but instead in the Ramallah area.[35] As his parents explained, the Israeli authorities demanded they bury his body outside of Jerusalem, as a way of displacing him even after death. "Corpse messaging" was apparent in the use of Mustafa's body to mutilate his connection to Jerusalem, and evict his dead body from the city that carries intimate familial, religious, and national meanings. His mother stated, "Now, in his death certificate, they can't write that he died in Jerusalem." Even in death, the colonizer's efforts to evict the native perpetuate Palestinians in a constant state of dying by deferring, delaying, and refusing the closure of a peaceful burial in one's own city. The Palestinian is abused in his last passing, another violent checkpoint in a life dominated by borders.

For one mother describing the cold body of her son, her pain was unintelligible. She was unable to express the depth of her hurt or sadness brought on by the psychological impact of imagining her son's body in "their refrigerators." She fixated on the coldness of the body and the degradation of even the basic sanctity of his corpse. For Palestinian corpses in Israeli custody, the preservation of the body requires draining it of all fluids, so they return to their families blue and unrecognizable. In this process, overseen by the colonial authorities, the dead are unable to fully die. They are preserved through cryogenic technology yet deprived of their natural state. Even after death, colonization continues to operate through the violation of the sanctity of the body and treatment of the frozen flesh as captive.

Corpse messaging through the bodies of dead Palestinian children was also transmitted through the innumerable bullets that filled their flesh. Ayman's mother remembered, "I was kissing his slain body, and counting the bullets. . . . Each wound, every bullet I saw was meant to kill us all . . . to step on our agony of loss more and more . . . hurt us more . . . and I counted the bullets. . . . Why would they shoot a child with so many bullets . . . he is not the terrorist they claim . . . they are the terrorists . . . yes . . . a terrorist state." Ghassan's father stated: "They wanted to humiliate us further . . . they returned his body frozen . . . his little eyes frozen . . . his face . . . I saw blood on it. . . . You think he was alive when they threw him in that big black bag? Was he struggling to get out? . . . I am sorry, son. . . . I am sorry, I did not hear you . . . did not prevent their rifles from penetrating your little body . . . their hands to injure you that much. . . . Forgive me son."

Unchilding can be read in the number of bullets penetrating the body and the psyche of the slain child. Unchilding was apparent when family members discussed the black bags used to contain the slain body, as one mother said during our meeting: "Please . . . do not let them put him in those big black bags . . . like trash . . . he is a child, a child they killed, they executed in public. . . . This is my child ... I speak from my wound. ... I won't be able to bear seeing him in their black plastic bag. ... I beg you ... he is a child ... human ... my son ... I beg you." The mother used my interview to speak back to Israeli officials, and to ask me to find a way out of the plastic bag. Using her voice, and with the help of local feminist activists, lawyers, human rights organizations, Palestinian officials, and other interventions, we managed to bring her son back, without the plastic bags, and with as much dignity as possible.

The violence of the black bags, the bullets, the freezers, and the degrading objectification of children's slain bodies seeps into moments of mourning and proliferates in silence and pain. Family and community members sit, frozen in their shock and horror, for hours, in pain, in silence, just looking at each other, as if they fear to speak their pain. I watched a mother counting on her fingers, pressing on them, and crying, shaking with her flowing tears. I hugged her, and asked whether I could do anything, maybe bring her water, but she just looked at me and said: "I am counting the bullets. ... How dare they ... he is just a child."

The Governance and Policing of
Burials as Emotional Torture

After the suffering of waiting for the body's return, families then had to plan their child's funeral under the harsh conditions set by the Israeli military. "How can they control the funeral"? asked a sibling. A community member observed, "They have cameras all over the place, they watch the movements of our breathing ... they get pleasure in preventing us from having a burial ... what other power do they have?" The Israeli state surveils and controls these funerals not only to disrupt traditional rites of death and grieving, but to regulate these rites as part of its construction and governance of affects that legitimate its regime of unchilding.

The way the state obsesses over the regulation of the burial of children—all of them accused of violence—works to solidify their identity as "terrorists," and portrays their families as "the families of the terrorists." Israeli officials' and the media's manipulation of the family's mourning is then twisted into nationalist political symbols.

Once these racialized affects have been established, the state practices torture on Palestinian families by imposing conditions on the return of their loved ones. A bereaved mother recalled, "I was so traumatized, and in so much pain when I learned about the conditions that they imposed on us to bury our son. We were so shocked when they [the Israeli authorities] called us, but we wanted our son to rest in peace. We wanted him outside their refrigerators, but the Israeli

Mukhabarat [Intelligence] called us in the morning and informed us that they would free my son's body and told us to await their orders. They asked for a list of thirty people who would be allowed to participate in my son's funeral. They told us that if we failed to abide by their rules, we would pay a fine of 20,000 shekels."

The accounts of the demands placed on families in order to receive their children's bodies further reveal the cruelty of marking juvenile dead bodies as sites of terror. Such necropenological unchilding can be partially explained with Ann Stoler's term the "microphysics of rule."[36] Within the racialized distinctions of colonial rule, she identifies "microsites" where sentiments of loss are informed by patterns of biopolitical governance. Limiting funeral attendees to thirty people forces the family to create a hierarchy of importance and exclusion. They must decide who from the community can gain access to mourn the dead. These state-imposed conditions—as I have explained in my previous research on death and dying—are tactics that seek to fragment and disintegrate the community, turning the burial, something painful, sacred, personal, bonding, and reconciling, into an administrative task that is controlled by and accountable to the state's authorities.

Palestinian parents shared how the Israeli regime manufactures spaces of unending dispossession for living and dead Palestinians, even in the most intimate and minute moments during or after the loss of a child. The aunt of a killed child reflected, "We were at the funeral, thirty people with about three hundred [Israeli] military and police persons present. His sister was with him in school—they [the martyr and his sister] went to a school for children with special needs. But her name was not on the list, and the police refused to allow her to participate. She was nervous, anxious, and started begging to go with us to the cemetery. Everything was painful, and burying him in the dark [he was buried at midnight] was extremely hurtful." Then, the mother explained, "There was no other choice, we needed to agree to their conditions, and their conditions were humiliating. But this is it—this is military occupation. We do not understand their language, we do not understand their laws, and no one explained the conditions to us. So we agreed."

The state imposes an environment of humiliation, surveillance, and further pain on what should be an intimate, healing, and peaceful ceremony. As one young mother told me, "Is there anything harder than losing a child? Show me a mother in the world who wants to bury her own children. Nothing is as torturous and painful as losing a child." To the family of the deceased, the letter of the restrictions around burial is written in Hebrew, a language with a different alphabet than Arabic and one that the majority of families do not read, speak, or understand. The letter begins by discussing the individual case and the context of the death. Throughout their entirety, these letters refer to the deceased as a "terrorist." All the letters outline a set of instructions that the deceased's family must follow precisely in order for the bodies to be returned, specifying the exact details of what the families can and cannot do to mourn the loss of their loved ones. The authorities require families to pay large monetary deposits to receive and bury the bodies, with the stipulation that these sums will only be returned if they obey the colonizer's orders regarding the size, time, and setting of the funeral and the location of the burial. In the case of Ahmad Abu Shaaban, the family's letter from the authorities began: "On 14/10/2015, the terrorist stabbed a woman in the central bus station in Jerusalem. Police who arrived on the scene shot the terrorist before he managed to stab additional people." Not only was the deceased labeled a "terrorist" twice in a short section of text, but elsewhere in the letter, his family was also referred to as "the family of the terrorist." The state here not only created the category of the "terrorist" but also the category of "family of the terrorist," an accusation saturated with racialized and extrajudicial judgement. The official documents sent to the family reflect a conclusive state narrative of what occurred during the events that led to the death of Ahmad, a twenty-two-year-old from Ras al-Amoud, who was executed at the central bus station in West Jerusalem for allegedly trying to kill an Israeli. The family is not allowed to challenge or alter this record, which legally memorializes the family's child as a terrorist in perpetuity. The implications of this official narrative, as reflected in the document, impose conditions on the burial, communicating the state's control over the body, family, place, time, and much more. The conditions imposed on the family's mourning included:

1. The dead body will be handed over to the family in the coming four days.
2. It will be transferred between 00:30–1:30 am.
3. The police will inform the family two hours ahead of time.
4. To meet the police, four members of the family should arrive to receive the body.
5. At the moment they receive the body, the body will be directly transferred to the burial in Golden Gate (Gate of Mercy).
6. Participants in the funeral should be gathered in the burial area to receive the body.
7. Participants are not allowed to stop or park in any other places.
8. In the cemetery, only 50 members of the family can be present.
9. During the burial, participants are not allowed to use language to incite.
10. The burial should be completed in one-and-a-half hours from the time the family receives the body [in the middle of the night].

11. Upon completion of the burial, participants should leave the site without making public displays and return to their homes.
12. To ensure that the above conditions are met, family members must pay a deposit of 20,000 shekels.
13. If the family abides by the conditions, the money will be returned.

The state's calculation of a deposit required from the families is intended to further dehumanize the deceased Palestinian, putting a price on the return of the body and the right to mourn. These letters effectively charge a price for the right to practice grief—a price that many families cannot pay. Other parents noted that the death certificates of their sons who were killed by the Israeli police and army were issued by Israel, exacerbating their pain. The parents discussed the state's control over their mourning process, sharing with us that Israel imposed conditions similar to those imposed upon Abu Shaaban's parents. One parent described the letter they received: 1) Only thirty people can participate; 2) 20,000 shekels fine if the family violates the rules; 3) No photographs . . . "and they took all of our cellphones away from us so that we could not take photos"; 4) All thirty people who participated underwent a body search.

Yet despite the strict preconditions, Israel also polices the funerals. One mother explained, "Even when there were only thirty people, the number of police and military officials present was immense. Between each one of us, they had five to ten police officers . . . we could not even mourn him. . . . We were so worried, so afraid to violate the rules and end up paying a large fine when we have no income and no power to handle further suffering." The heavy policing at the funerals impedes the family's ability to mourn fully and freely. As one mother stated, "Can I cry loudly? Can I talk to him? Can I smell him? Would I be able to touch him when he is freezing, coming from their refrigerators?" The policing of dead and living bodies has, as the voices speak to, not only incarcerated the dead but also created a prison of the senses for the bereaved family. If they act, speak, touch, or smell freely, they might violate the state's stringent rules. A mother exclaimed, "Believe me . . . between us in the funeral, there were around three hundred to four hundred soldiers and police." She paused briefly before revealing that even in her deep sorrow, she was afraid and confused. "I could not do anything. I only kissed my son in fear, in pain. The soldiers were all around us, I could not bid him farewell."

Counter Discourses: Life after Death

His body was filled with bullets . . . the number of bullets in his little
body broke my heart . . . I felt it in my own body, I even heard it in my
dreams. . . . but we freed him from their refrigerators . . . and I kissed him.
—Saeda, Ayman's twelve-year-old sister

They burned our hearts with pain. . . . We never knew how they killed him, what
happened to his body, how many bullets killed him, was he tortured. . . .
I wanted to feel his body, count the bullets, and kiss each wound to remove
the pain caused by the bullets . . . but, I could not [silence]. . . . I dream
about walking and searching for him, I dream about kissing his wounds, and
pulling out their bullets. . . . I counted the bullets . . . I did it in my dreams.
—Ghassan's mother

In Ayman's, Ghassan's, and other bereaved family members' voices, we can hear the
sounds of emotional torture. They narrate losses that debilitate intimate relations
and punish the entire community. The waiting for the body, the criminalization of
the loved one, the regulations on the return of the corpse, and the restrictions on
burial extract the psychological power of family members following the loss of a
child. The state's securitized theology justifying these families' emotional torture
perpetuates their suffering in ways that inflict technologies of pain, which engineer the wounds of the soul. Ghassan's sister described her feelings like this: "The
occupation wanted to decide for us how to feel, what to feel, how to react, how to
scream, cry, stand, mourn . . . they tried to engineer our feelings. . . . They can't. . . . I
write his name every morning, when I wake up, to remind myself that my feelings
are not under their military occupation." His mother said:

> [T]hey deprived us from sleep, heaviness was all I sensed when waking and
> sleeping, not knowing when he will be dignified and buried, I sensed coldness
> in my veins . . . as if I was telling Ghassan, I feel you . . . I am with you. . . . by
> you. . . . and I did. . . . I felt him, talked to him while sleeping. . . . It is tor-
> ture not only to lose your child, but not even to know what happened and
> how he was killed . . . or when you will bury him . . . pure torture. . . . You feel
> guilty to close your eyes, eat, smile, help your other children to dress and go
> to school . . . you feel guilty that you are alive . . . you walk with such heaviness,
> questioning yourself . . . the feeling of loss . . . major loss . . . but, then I hear his
> voice telling me, Yamma . . . this is what I wanted to do, please carry it with
> pride not with pain. . . . As my children always stress, no one can occupy or
> control our feelings, they are a private matter.

The state's torture confused the families and made them vulnerable, but the
cruel mechanisms of governing their grief also opened awareness of their oc-

cupied context and their emotional journey. The state deprived them of information, and tortured them at home, in their own beds, while sleeping by their loved ones, in ways that engineered feelings and provoked outrage. While the state attempts to discipline bereaved families, govern their relations with their deceased loved ones, and pervert the perception of themselves and their community, families nonetheless reject the racist accusations of them as dangerous security threats.

In spite of the debasement of their mourning rites in the media and by politicians, and the state-sponsored violent targeting of their funerals and grief, families defied the efforts to occupy their emotions and feelings. Families insisted that no one has the capacity to militarily occupy feelings, and the state cannot govern or dictate what and how they feel. In fact, even in the confined and regulated spaces of their profound sadness, they found hope, growth, closeness, and resilience. Anthropologist Michael Taussig observes, "The space of death is preeminently a space of transformation: through the experience of death, life; through fear, loss of self and conformity to a new reality; or through evil, good."[37] At the funeral of Ayman, which I attended, I noticed the textured simultaneity of life and death. As something died in that community, something else was being born, a different consciousness of life. As Ayman became a *shahid* [martyr], the funeral marked not only an end, but a beginning of an eternal colorful assemblage of togetherness. The funeral itself becomes a claim to sovereignty against the colonial necropenology of unchilding. The funeral transformed the space of death into a space where new meanings were constructed, countering the "culture of terror" with a "culture of life" and continuity.

Ghassan's father refused to accept the body of his son from the Israeli authorities, stating that he was frozen: "The occupation took him hot, and now they gave him back to us cold. How can I bring him to his mother in this condition? How would his mother and sister see him, when he is not the same . . . cold . . . freezing cold . . . filled with blood . . . everything is cold. . . . Do I know how my son was killed? I guess they want us all frozen, in refrigerators." Ghassan's father was unable to protect his son from death, and unable to protect his dead body from the treatment it received from the Israeli police. He describes the failures of the police to investigate the killing of his son and the lack of accountability for the perpetrators.[38] Ghassan's mother describes her son's frozen body with unbearable pain—the depth of her hurt and sadness caused her to fixate on the coldness of the body, viewing freezing as degradation of even the basic sanctity of the body. In his refusal to accept his son's body, Ghassan's father attempts to exert a final shred of dignified agency, to comfort his wife's agony, and protect his family from experiencing more anguish at witnessing the state of their son's unrecognizable body. After they received Ghassan's frozen body, his father sent it back to the Israelis, a message that interrupted the state's governance of feelings, and resisted its necropenological unchilding of the slain child. Returning their child's frozen body to the colonizer, as an act of resistance, transformed the family's uncontrollable suffering into a more controlled one.

Children and families were aware of the regime's intention to torture the soul and harm the body and psyche. They were able to read the state's assertion of power over their bodies and affects, and they looked for ways to defy it. In fact, they challenged it, by refusing to wait for dead bodies, writing the names of their deceased siblings daily, exchanging feelings of guilt with feelings of respect and pride, maintaining sentiments of anger and determination, and creating a community of parents and siblings that meet regularly to support each other. They invested in understanding Israel's colonial laws in order to negotiate their rights as bereaved families, and read their national history to find inspiration and methods to resist colonial oppression. Families' emotions that were targeted by the state were also sites of struggle. Countering the sentiments of helplessness and submission generated the creation of new sentiments of communal togetherness and knowledge and the development of collective strategies to dignify their children, both alive and dead.

Conclusion

The cases of Ghassan and Ayman speak loudly against the settler state's circulation and governance of affects within a necropenological regime of unchilding. The imprisonment of their slain bodies and the state-imposed suffering on their community suggest that affects are zones where violent governance and torture is permissible and mobilized in the settler colony. The waiting for their return home caused deep wounds in their loved ones. More than just constructing affects, the kidnapping and captivity of their young bodies work to show the "occupation of emotions," just as the state militarily occupies the land. The state's control over grief and grieving sought to evict Ayman and Ghassan from childhood, punish their communities, and deepen their bereaved families' pain. The state's obsession with manipulating and exploiting bereaved families' affects is evidence of a flexible, expanding, and dynamic regime of state terror and state-crafting that seeks to consolidate its grasp by occupying affects.

The management of grief, the denial of the right to closure, the robbery of knowledge and information, the captivity of dignity, and the withholding of the warmth of the body in colonial freezers all are part of a calculated state apparatus of a necropenological regime of unchilding, relying on racial enfleshment and the circulation of affects that proliferate in the community and across generations. The circumstances of Ayman's and Ghassan's life after death brought up old memories of pain and dispossession. While waiting for the release of their children, parents shared family stories of the loss of loved ones, of land, of state violence, and unending colonial atrocities.

As the experiences of Ayman and Ghassan illustrate, there is terror and torture in waiting for the nongrievable. Waiting is a state of pain. It causes an unseen wound for the colonized that the colonial authorities continuously keep open. Waiting and its political work permeate the everyday emotional lives of Palestinians in the West Bank, Jerusalem, and Gaza. The multitude of checkpoints, the request for approval to pass, cross, access services, the mode of "must-wait-for-the-colonizer's-approval" is an ongoing, violent psychological instrument in the colony. Waiting within the necropolitical regime of unchilding that "engineers" affects was written on Ayman and Ghassan's corpses by the settler's state governance. The sudden captivity of the dead bodies of loved ones serves the performance of superiority of the colonizer's body, politics, and power. State terror was inscribed through corpse messaging in the refrigerators, which operate as new prisons to hold Palestinian bodies and violate family and community religious and social rites. The sense of loss experienced by Palestinians is more and more managed and policed through the technique of freezing children's bodies, with legal restrictions, policies, and procedures around burial, all constituting an enfleshed politics of waiting.

While the state's incarceration and control of the dead Palestinian body allow the state to "play" with bereaved families' emotions, memorialize colonial power, and further facilitate the process of colonization via the circulation of specific affects, Palestinians challenge that control by asserting the impossibility of "engineering" their feelings and occupying their affects. Families defied this engineering by reframing their own inner trauma and pain of loss, negotiating the bodies' return and burial, holding demonstrations, and producing pamphlets, posters, and T-shirts that call for the bodies' release. The families refused to let the inhuman obstacles surrounding burial distract them from exposing the unjust cause of their children's murders.

If we follow the story of Ayman and Ghassan's unchilded corpses and their family's narratives, we begin to comprehend that emotions are major sources of knowledge. Sentiments and sensibility are not outside but at the center of politics. Bereaved families' sentiments were understood by the state as dangerous political forces and sites of resilience and resistance. When the colonizer insisted on refusing to allow the dead to rest, bereaved families contested this move by calling for "freedom for the bodies." The slogan "We want our children بدنا ولدنا [Bidna Wladna]" echoed from homes and neighborhoods, resisted the state's torturous governance of affects, interrupted the state's regime of necropolitical unchilding, and maintained parents' and the community's ownership over their loss, defying the state's claims over dead bodies and living affects.

NOTES

1. Shalhoub-Kevorkian, *Security Theology, Surveillance*; Shalhoub-Kevorkian, "Necropenology."

2. Aruri, "Families Demand Return of Bodies."

3. Al-Haq, "Law to Withhold the Bodies."

4. Ledford, "A Form of Psychological Torture."

5. UN Committee Against Torture, "Convention against Torture."

6. Masarwi, *Bereavement of Martyred Palestinian Children*.

7. Adalah, "Israeli Supreme Court Reverses Earlier Ruling."

8. Ma'an News Agency, "Israeli Minister Orders Bodies."

9. Asad, "Thinking about Terrorism and Just War."

10. Harel, "Returning Bodies of Terrorists."

11. Adalah, "Israeli Supreme Court Reverses Earlier Ruling."

12. Adalah. "Adalah Responds to Israeli Defense."

13. Shalhoub-Kevorkian, *Security Theology*; Shalhoub-Kevorkian, "The Occupation of the Senses."

14. Shalhoub-Kevorkian, "The Occupation of the Senses."

15. Rancière, *The Politics of Aesthetics*.

16. Butler, *Precarious Life*; Butler, *Frames of War*.

17. Lutz and Abu-Lughod, *Language and the Politics of Emotion*; Harding, "Representing Fundamentalism"; Stoler, *Race and the Education of Desire*; Feldman, *Formations of Violence*; Butler, *Frames of War*.

18. Ahmed, *The Cultural Politics of Emotion*.

19. Butler, *Precarious Life*, 2004.

20. Scheper-Hughes, *Child Survival*; Scheper-Hughes and Bourgois, *Violence in War and Peace*; James, *Democratic Insecurities*.

21. Butler, *Frames of War*, 31.

22. Taussig, "Culture of Terror—Space of Death"; Martín-Baró, *Writings for a Liberation Psychology*; Shalhoub-Kevorkian, "The Politics of Birth."

23. Stoler, "Affective States," 4–5.

24. Wolfe, "Settler Colonialism," 388.

25. Addameer, "PHROC Stands in Solidarity."

26. Addameer, "Negating High Court Decision."

27. Shalhoub-Kevorkian, *Security Theology, Surveillance*.

28. Ibid.

29. Betz and Thorngren, "Ambiguous Loss and the Family."

30. Boss, *Ambiguous Loss: Learning to Live*.

31. Hage, *Waiting*, 3.

32. Weheliye, *Habeas Viscus*.

33. Mbembe, "Necropolitics."

34. Lantz, "The Performativity of Violence." Lantz takes the term "corpse messaging" from Jules Gibbs's poem, http://www.fishousepoems.org/corpse-messaging/.

35. Al-Haq, "From Death to Burial."

36. Stoler, "Tense and Tender Ties."

37. Taussig, "Culture of Terror—Space of Death," 75.

38. Addameer, "PHROC stands in solidarity."

BIBLIOGRAPHY

Adalah—The Legal Center for Arab Minority Rights in Israel. "Adalah Responds to Israeli Defense Minister Naftali Bennett's Order to Withhold all Palestinians Bodies."
November 11, 2019. https://www.adalah.org/en/content/view/9865.

———. "Israeli Supreme Court Reverses Earlier Ruling, Authorizes Israel to Hold Bodies
of Palestinians as Bargaining Chips." June 9, 2019. https://www.adalah.org/en/content
/view/9808.

Addameer. "Negating High Court Decision, Israeli Public Security Minister Seeks Sus-
pension of Return of Palestinian Bodies." May 25, 2016. http://www.addameer
.org/news/negating-high-court-decision-israeli-public-security-minister-seeks
-suspension-return.

———. "PHROC Stands in Solidarity with the Manasrah Family for Refusing to Receive
their Son's Frozen Body." March 23, 2016. https://www.addameer.org/news/phroc
-stands-solidarity-manasrah-family-refusing-receive-their-sons-frozen-body.

Ahmed, S. *The Cultural Politics of Emotion.* Edinburgh: Edinburgh University Press,
2004.

Al-Haq. "From Death to Burial: Israel's Failure to Respect International Law, The Cases
of Mustafa Al-Khatib and Fadi 'Alloun." January 20, 2016. http://www.alhaq.org
/advocacy/topics/right-to-life-and-body-integrity/1009-from-death-to-burial-israels
-failure-to-respect-international-law-the-cases-of-mustafa-al-khatib-and-fadi-alloun.

———. "Newly Adopted Law to Withhold the Bodies of Palestinians Killed Breaches
International Law, Must be Repealed." March 14, 2018. http://www.alhaq.org/advocacy
/topics/right-to-life-and-body-integrity/1197-newly-adopted-law-to-withhold-the
-bodies-of-palestinians-killed-breaches-international-law-must-be-repealed.

Aruri, F. "Feature: Palestinian Families Demand Return of Bodies in War with Israel."
XinhuaNet. August 30, 2018. http://www.xinhuanet.com/english/2018-08/30/c
_137428975.htm.

Asad, T. "Thinking about Terrorism and Just War." *Cambridge Review of International
Affairs* 23, no. 1 (2010): 3–24.

Betz, G., and J. M. Thorngren. "Ambiguous Loss and the Family Grieving Process." *The
Family Journal: Counseling and Therapy for Couples and Families* 1, no. 4 (2006):
359–65.

Boss, P. *Ambiguous Loss: Learning to Live with Unresolved Grief.* Cambridge, Mass.:
Harvard University Press, 2000.

Butler, J. *Frames of War: When is Life Grievable?* New York: Verso, 2009.

———. *Precarious Life: The Powers of Mourning and Violence.* New York: Verso, 2004.

Feldman, A. *Formations of Violence: The Narrative of the Body and Political Terror in
Northern Ireland.* Chicago: University of Chicago Press, 1991.

Hage, G., ed. *Waiting.* Carlton: Melbourne University Press, 2009.

Harding, S. "Representing Fundamentalism: The Problem of the Repugnant Cultural
Other." *Social Research* 58, no. 2 (1991): 373–93.

Harel, A. "Returning Bodies of Terrorists." [in Hebrew] *The Marker.* February 11, 2015.
https://www.themarker.com/misc/themarkersmartphoneapp/.premium-1.2766194.

James, E. C. *Democratic Insecurities: Violence, Trauma, and Intervention in Haiti.* Berkeley: University of California Press, 2010.

Kubovich, Y. "Officials Slam Defense Minister: Withholding Bodies Won't Help Return Israelis Held in Gaza," *Ha'aretz*. December 17, 2019. https://www.haaretz.com/israel-news/.premium-officials-slam-defense-minister-withholding-bodies-won-t-help-return-israeli-mias-1.8284272.

Lantz, A. "The Performativity of Violence: Abducting Agency in Mexico's Drug War." *Journal of Latin American Cultural Studies* 25, no. 2 (2016): 253–69.

Ledford, M. L. "A Form of Psychological Torture: Why Israel's Refusal to Return the Bodies of Palestinian Soldiers Is a Violation of International Law." *North Carolina Journal of International Law*. June 9, 2018.

Lutz, C., and L. Abu-Lughod, eds. *Language and the Politics of Emotion*. Cambridge, UK: Cambridge University Press, 1990.

Ma'an News Agency. "Israeli Minister Orders Bodies of Palestinians to be Withheld." *The Palestine Chronicle*. May 24, 2016. http://www.palestinechronicle.com/24311/.

Martín-Baró, I. *Writings for a Liberation Psychology*. Cambridge, Mass.: Harvard University Press, 1988.

Masarwi, M. *The Bereavement of Martyred Palestinian Children: Gendered, Religious, and National Perspectives*. Cham: Palgrave Macmillan, 2019.

Mbembe, A. "Necropolitics." *Public Culture* 15, no. 1 (2003): 11–40.

Rancière, J. *The Politics of Aesthetics*. Translated by Gabriel Rockhill. London: Bloomsbury Academic, 2013.

Scheper-Hughes, N., ed. *Child Survival: Anthropological Perspectives on the Treatment and Maltreatment of Children*. Dordrecht: D. Reidel, 1987.

Scheper-Hughes, N., and P. Bourgois. *Violence in War and Peace: An Anthology*. Malden, UK: Blackwell Publishing, 2004.

Shalhoub-Kevorkian, N. "Necropenology: Conquering New Bodies, Psychics, and Territories in East Jerusalem." *Identities* 27 (2020): 285–301.

———. "The Occupation of the Senses: The Prosthetic and Aesthetic of State Terror." *British Journal of Criminology* 57, no. 6 (2016): 1279–1300.

———. "The Politics of Birth and the Intimacies of Violence against Palestinian Women in Occupied East Jerusalem." *British Journal of Criminology* 55, no. 6 (2015): 1187–1206.

———. *Security Theology, Surveillance, and the Politics of Fear*. Cambridge, UK: Cambridge University Press, 2015.

Stoler, A. L. "Affective States." In *A Companion to the Anthropology of Politics*, edited by David Nugent and Jon Vincent, 4–20. Malden, UK: Blackwell Publishing, 2007.

———. *Race and the Education of Desire: Foucault's History of Sexuality and the Colonial Order of Things*. Durham, N.C.: Duke University Press, 1995.

———. "Tense and Tender Ties: The Politics of Comparison in North American History and (Post) Colonial Studies." *The Journal of American History* 88, no. 3 (2001): 829–65.

Taussig, M. "Culture of Terror—Space of Death. Roger Casement's Putumayo Report and the Explanation of Torture." *Comparative Studies in Society and History* 26, no. 3 (1984): 467–97.

UN Committee Against Torture. "Convention against Torture and Other Cruel, Inhuman or Degrading Treatment or Punishment." June 3, 2016. https://docstore.ohchr.org/SelfServices/FilesHandler.ashx?enc=6QkG1d%2FPPRiCAqhKb7yhsmEKqN

hdzbzr4kqou1ZPE79BvBJe97SSM1KP2v4ng3Dhx74ohsby7x4AlEgvGhwtvav7rPvZ
mtwpwObldkyK%2BM9cNY7svWLlYmp6PB4chW8O.

Weheliye, A. G. *Habeas Viscus: Racializing Assemblages, Biopolitics, and Black Feminist Theories of the Human.* Durham, N.C.: Duke University Press, 2014.

Wolfe, P. "Settler Colonialism and the Elimination of the Native." *Journal of Genocide Research* 8, no. 4 (2006): 387–409.

Guilty by Default
The Legal Process of Unchilding Palestinians

SHAHRAZAD ODEH

A Tale of Two Justice Systems

In Jerusalem, both Jewish Israeli and Palestinian children are known to take part in stone throwing. In 2013, a fifteen-year-old Jewish boy joined three other minors in throwing stones at vehicles of Palestinian residents.[1] That same year, a fifteen-year-old Palestinian boy similarly joined three minors in throwing stones at an Israeli police jeep transporting Jewish settlers to their homes in Kidmat Zion, a settlement neighborhood in East Jerusalem.[2] Both boys faced similar charges, and both cases were examined by the same judge. The Jewish boy was detained for several days and sent to nine months of house arrest, during which he underwent three alternative correctional programs and rehabilitation services. The judge's verdict, delivered a year after his arrest, determined that although the boy had admitted to his actions under a plea bargain, he would be acquitted.[3] The Palestinian boy was not as lucky: he spent a month in detention and was then put under house arrest. The same judge delivered his verdict four years after the boy's offense—during which the boy was still kept under house arrest.

This study argues that these cases, among others it examined, represent a systematic process of "unchilding" of Palestinians in Jerusalem. This gradual process stands on three pillars: declaring the child as unworthy of rehabilitation; maintaining that they are a danger to the public; and convicting them without fair due process.

The author examined data from the years 2013 to 2018, a period characterized by intense political violence following the 2014 Gaza war and the 2015 "knife intifada" in Jerusalem. To explain its findings, the chapter begins with background on Israel's political and legal violence toward Palestinian residents of Occupied East Jerusalem. It will then discuss developments in Israel's legislation regarding stone throwing, followed by a review of cases of child arrests related to the offense in Jerusalem in 2013 and 2014. In doing so, this chapter argues that the Israeli legal system carries out the unchilding of Palestinians by securitizing and prosecuting them, and deeming them undeserving of special treatment or protection, in stark contrast to Jewish children. This unchilding in Israeli courtrooms—manifested through the high incrimination, conviction, and incarceration rates of Palestinians—is used to justify measures of state control and surveillance over Palestinian homes and to infiltrate the intimate lives of Palestinian families. These microprocesses, in turn, enable Israel to assert structural dominance and control over the wider occupied Palestinian population.

Equality for the Similar, Inequality for the Different

The process of unchilding begins with the birth of the Palestinian child—the day they are automatically regarded as a demographic threat, and categorized as a person unworthy of enjoying full or equal rights under the Israeli state. For Palestinian Jerusalemites, this treatment manifests in great part through the state of limbo created by their status as "permanent residents"—a legal category conferred under the 1952 Entry into Israel Law—rather than as citizens.[4] Following Israel's establishment in 1948, Israel effectively rendered the Palestinian nationality invalid;[5] until 1967, the legal status of Palestinians in Jerusalem was either determined by Israel, which controlled the western part of the city, or by Jordan, which controlled the eastern part. With Israel's occupation of East Jerusalem in 1967, Palestinians who were able to remain under its newly annexed municipal boundaries were censused and required to apply for an Israeli-issued Jerusalemite residency in order to retain their right to live, work, and travel in the city. This status provides them with access to certain social services and the right to vote in Jerusalem's municipal elections, but not in the national parliamentary election.

The Entry into Israel Law grants the Israeli minister of interior the authority to revoke the permanent residency status from individuals and eventually deport them. The grounds for revocation and other restrictions have broadened over the years, including if Palestinian residents failed to prove their "center of life" is in the city, or if they were involved in political activities deemed hostile to the state.[6] With the constant changes in Jerusalem's metropolitan map, the erecting of the separation wall, and the demolition of homes, Palestinian Jerusalemites find themselves in a constant battle to prove their center of life is in Jerusalem, let alone to actually live and exist in their city.[7]

Scholars observed that violence in colonial contexts—which uproots native societies by dispossessing their land and invading their intimate lives—

can be manifested through "incarceration, criminalization and institutionaliza-tion."[8] Through these means and more, the colonial encounter, Thobani writes, produces "a world divided: on the one side, a world of law, privilege, access to wealth, status, and power for the settler; on the other, a world defined in law as being 'lawless,' a world of poverty, squalor, and death for the native."[9] The pursuit of the native's elimination further creates what Shalhoub-Kevorkian defines as the "entrapment" of communities—a form of violence that is often enacted and enforced by the criminal justice system.[10]

It is within this oppressive context that many Palestinian children in Jerusa-lem see themselves as part of a wider liberation struggle, seeking to break Israel's entrapment of their bodies both as a national group and as individual children. As such, many Palestinian children are willing to practice forms of political resis-tance against the colonial regime. This includes throwing stones—perceived both as a form of symbolic resistance and as a physical interruption against the occu-pier's violence—even at the risk of state punishment.[11] But while these conditions generate resistance, the state of limbo produces structural obstacles for Palestin-ian Jerusalemites facing criminal charges in Israeli courts, which are sharply evi-dent in this chapter's case studies.

The divided colonial world is exemplified by Israel's two parallel justice sys-tems in the Occupied Territories: a military system for Palestinian noncitizens, and a civil system for Israelis, including settlers.[12] The treatment of Palestin-ian noncitizen residents, however, is not as clear-cut. Indeed, conventional le-gal studies around the question of equality in Israel are often at a loss to explain this exception to the misleading binary, neglecting the settler-colonial values on which the legal system is built.[13] Justice Aharon Barak,[14] the former president of Israel's Supreme Court, argues that once a person is a citizen, the state should not act in a discriminatory manner against them;[15] that is, to enjoy equality, the in-dividual should be "inside the house" of the Israeli polity.[16] Judge Yuval Shadmi, however, argues that citizenship does not guarantee equal treatment by the Is-raeli court—effectively confirming, as Viterbo argues, the deeply embedded in-stitutionalized discrimination in Israel's justice system.[17]

If we are to follow Barak's argument, Palestinian Jerusalemites, as residents of a city annexed by Israel yet who are not *citizens* of the state, are treated as less worthy of equality.[18] "Citizenship," critical scholars argue, is a selective legal sta-tus used by elites to legitimize class-, race-, and masculine-based political orders in Western democratic states,[19] dividing groups and individuals as worthy or un-worthy of entering a society.[20] Ajzenstadt explains that the Israeli juvenile jus-tice system, which is shaped by Zionist ideology,[21] *de facto* divides children and youth into different ethnic categories,[22] with the state's treatment of some groups often deriving from perceptions of them as "primitive" or "undeserving" of full rights.[23] In the case of Palestinians, socio-legal studies extensively show that Israel subjects them to methods of control and surveillance that are not applied to Jews, including by characterizing their relations to the state as "security" matters.[24]

Official statistics suggest there is a higher level of criminality among Palestinian youth versus Jewish youth in Israel, despite the former being a numerical minority. But as Khoury-Kassabri, Khoury, and Ali explain, this disproportionate representation can be partly attributed to discriminatory treatment by the police and justice system.[25] Palestinian youth are more likely to receive harsher treatment from law enforcement than Jewish youth, including being arrested, kept in detention during interrogation, or referred to juvenile court.[26] Although Israel adopted the 1971 Youth Law and added extensive amendments to ensure maximum protection for children under criminal law, these statutory rights are easily denied to Palestinian children.[27]

This differentiation based on identity, according to Ajzenstadt, splits society into "normal insiders" and "deviant outsiders."[28] The division is manifested in a wide range of state practices, and is apparent in the public, professional, and governmental discourse on crime and juvenile delinquency.[29] The classification of "deviant" identities invokes Fanon's description of the settler-colonial logic of eliminating the native, which in this case, formulates the Palestinian child as a dangerous "other" who poses a security threat to the social-political order, and who therefore must be combatted, contained, and defeated.[30]

The "permanent residency" of Palestinian Jerusalemites raises questions over how the state should deal with them when accused of "security offenses." As Shalhoub-Kevorkian describes, Israeli civil laws enable the state to inflict violence in a "legal" and "rational" manner against Palestinian natives,[31] who are perceived as "born terrorists,"[32] while justifying human rights violations as means of protecting Jewish civilians from Palestinians.[33] Zureik et al. further stress that the courts' different treatment of Palestinians and Jewish Israelis is rooted in the state's political ideology, which asserts that Israel is, first and foremost, a Jewish state.[34] This was further enshrined in July 2018 with the passing of the Jewish Nation-State Basic Law, declaring as a constitutional value that, among other things, "the right to exercise national self-determination in the State of Israel is unique to the Jewish people."[35] This commitment to Jewish superiority surpasses other social commitments, including equality.[36] This agenda is similarly manifested through incarceration and criminalization,[37] with Palestinian children as key targets.[38]

Methodological Notes

This study uses thematic content analysis, per Klaus Krippendorff,[39] to identify analytical categories relevant to its research question. Content analysis is a fitting method for understanding the motives of political and judicial elites who, scholars argue, are the main architects determining citizenship rights and criminal policy.[40] The study's data sources include: (1) court verdicts and other court decisions concerning Palestinian and Jewish juveniles in Jerusalem accused of stone throwing during the years 2013–14—to select these cases, the author gathered 54 court decisions and verdicts relating to the study's focus published in the Israeli legal engines Nevo, Takdin, and PsakDin between the years 2011 and 2018;[41] (2) interviews with prosecutors in the Jerusalem district during April–August 2018; (3) and police records from 2016–17, which were requested under the Freedom of Information Law. This data was juxtaposed with relevant information from local and international media, reports of human rights organizations, and protocols of Knesset meetings discussing child arrests and juvenile justice. This methodological combination helped to identify recurrent themes that elucidated Israel's treatment of Palestinian Jerusalemite children. The collected materials were in Arabic, Hebrew, and English (all translations here are the author's).

Israel's Unchilding of Palestinians

POLITICAL-LEGAL CONTEXT

East Jerusalem's centrality to the Israeli-Palestinian conflict plays a significant role in the social, political, and legal affairs of the city's Palestinian residents.[42] In 2014,[43] three Israeli teenage settlers were kidnapped and killed by Palestinian militants, which sparked a series of violent events that summer. Before finding their bodies on June 30, Israel launched a military operation to find the teenagers, arresting hundreds of Palestinians.[44] Between June and August, Israel conducted 767 raids in the West Bank and East Jerusalem,[45] with 507 reported clashes between Palestinians and Israelis.[46] In July 2014, Mohammed Abu Khdeir, a sixteen-year-old Palestinian Jerusalemite, was abducted and burned to death by Israeli settlers.[47] During riots in the city, Israeli forces used sponge-tipped bullets, tear gas, skunk water, and physical force, injuring hundreds of Palestinian civilians.[48] In the following two months, Israel carried out a destructive war in Gaza dubbed "Operation Protective Edge."[49]

These violent contexts had a clear effect on the Israeli legal system, including in juvenile justice. As the 2014 escalations intensified, the Israeli government translated the political tensions into new law enforcement legislation. These included Knesset Decisions 1775 and 1776, which enabled new legal measures to deter and punish people accused of stone throwing in East Jerusalem.[50] In July 2015, the Knesset enacted the Penal Law (Amendment No. 119),[51] which added the offense of throwing stones or other objects at a police officer or police vehicle, punishable by up to five years' imprisonment; at a civilian vehicle, punishable by up to ten years' imprisonment; and with intent of hitting a vehicle passenger or person in the vicinity, punishable by up to twenty years' imprisonment.[52]

The Counter-Terrorism Law,[53] passed in July 2016, expanded the state's police powers and its definitions for terrorist organizations, while imposing harsh penalties and sentencing guidelines. More changes were made with Amendment 22 to the Youth Law in August 2016,[54] which allows the imprisonment of minors convicted of stone throwing even if they are below fourteen years of age. Amendment 22 marks a significant break from Israeli civil and military law, which previously accorded with international standards by prohibiting custodial sentences against children under fourteen.

The Knesset approved additional penalties against the parents of children convicted of throwing stones or committing a "security offense" with amendments to the Youth Law and National Insurance Law: the first imposes on parents "a fine, legal expenses, and compensation," and the second punishes parents by "denying payment of social welfare benefits."[55] These amendments reflect an Israeli legal mindset that views all sectors of Palestinian society as culpable for their children's acts due to supposed societal negligence or encouragement of such behaviors.[56]

THE TOOLS OF JUSTICE AND THE PALESTINIAN CHILD

Armed with these political-legal tools, Israel's legal system operates as a frontier between equality and ethno-supremacy over the Palestinian child,[57] with the courts determining what is in greater need of legal protection—the rights of the child, or "public safety"—and whether both can be maintained. In many of this study's cases, the juvenile courts even stressed that their rulings are based solely on evidence, and that the court is "color blind" or "racially blind."[58]

Despite this declaration, the Israeli legal system routinely strips Palestinians of their childhood in the early stages of their criminal case. In fact, as Viterbo details, the language of "rights of the child" can even be used *against* Palestinian defendants; arguments favoring harsher punishment to ensure "public safety," for example, are not seen by the courts as conflicting with the Palestinian child's rights.[59] The courts' offer of "protection" is also skewed by Israel's varying definitions: while the Jewish child is to be protected from criminality, the Palestinian child is to be protected from their family and society. Interviews with prosecutors further revealed that in many cases, a Palestinian family's socioeconomic background, their inability to provide bail money, or a perceived inability to change their familial relationship can influence courts to decide against the child's rehabilitation or against releasing them until the end of proceedings. The cases in this chapter also revealed that the court would only work with the Palestinian family and the parole officer to provide rehabilitation as a last, rather than first, resort.

Although 64 percent of Jewish Israeli children, according to Viterbo, are denied the right to have their parent present during an interrogation by police (in violation of Israeli law), a study by B'Tselem suggests that Palestinian children are systematically deprived of their right to have an adult companion during both arrest and interrogation, leaving law enforcement agencies free to coerce the children into confession early on.[60] Many detained minors involuntarily sign confessions (either false or written in a language they do not understand), which are then used as the basis for indictments.[61] Since 2014, Israeli authorities have more frequently held minors in detention for prolonged periods, or kept them in house arrest under harsh conditions, until the end of legal proceedings.[62]

This encourages defendants to reach a plea bargain and confess to the charges,[63] in the hope that the time already spent in prison will count toward their sentence.[64] Such plea bargains are often used as a tool of extortion against defendants who believe they have no better option.[65] Courts themselves would often hint to defendants that it is better to agree to a bargain, thus compelling them to admit guilt rather than investigating their case in depth.[66] A defendant who agrees to a bargain is also seen as a positive player who shows consideration for the preciousness of the court's time.[67] This growing tendency to reach a plea bargain without hearing evidence is liable to cause damage to the right to due process.

DOUBLE STANDARDS AND LACK OF DUE PROCESS

Article 21 of the Israeli Youth Act indicates that even when a child defendant's criminal liability is determined, the court is not authorized to automatically convict the child; rather, it can only declare that the defendant has committed the offense, or can acquit them.[68] Theoretically, rehabilitation is a core value when it comes to minors, and the Youth Act and Article 401 of the Penal Law set strict rules that place conviction as a last resort—only after the court is convinced there is no possibility for treatment or rehabilitation.

This study, however, reveals a worrisome picture whereby Israeli courts appeared to have little hesitation in incriminating and convicting Palestinian children of throwing stones compared to Jewish children, which, according to prosecutors interviewed in this study, is partly a consequence of the courts' refusal to provide rehabilitation opportunities for the children.[69] While in the past decade the Israeli judiciary has emphasized the need to rehabilitate children, in practice the offers to Palestinian children are very limited, and when they are provided, take place under Israeli terms of what Palestinian rehabilitation should entail. The opposite was true for Jewish Israeli children accused of the same offenses.[70]

Unchilding through the Trial

The study extracted three interconnected themes from Israeli court decisions, which demonstrate the process of unchilding: Rehabilitation; Danger to the Public; and Conviction and Due Process.

I. DENYING REHABILITATION

The Israeli legal system asserts that it is the community's duty to take part in rehabilitating minors involved in criminal acts, and to contribute to their return to society. The Penal Law and the Israeli High Court of Justice emphasize that rehabilitation, or a child's willingness to pursue it, can be a consideration for minimizing punishment.[71] The court further details that it is the society's duty to reintegrate the child and allow them to regain a normal life.[72] This process does not rely solely on the courts' decision; both the Youth Law and Penal Law emphasize the family's role in rehabilitation, and urge courts to discuss family ties and parental-child relationships before issuing any decision.[73]

Despite these stipulations, the study's data reveals a contradiction between the Israeli legal system's rhetoric around child rights and rehabilitation (as applied to Jewish Israeli children),[74] and its securitized discourse that constructs Palestinian children as a permanent threat unless they abide by the judiciary's definition of rehabilitation—a discourse that ultimately strips away the Palestinian child's rights and removes them from their family and surroundings.[75]

During a meeting of the Knesset Committee on Child Rights held on December 27, 2016, Arab Member of Knesset (MK) Osama Saadi discussed the state's discriminatory behavior toward Palestinian juvenile prisoners, raising the fact that close to half of Palestinian minors in Israeli prisons had not yet been sentenced and 42 percent were being detained until the end of proceedings. According to MK Saadi, over 50 percent of the children in Israeli custody were imprisoned for politically motivated acts as defined by the state.[76] The committee chair, MK Yifat Shasha-Biton, replied that the Palestinian children were incited by their surroundings, and therefore rehabilitation requires that they be removed from their community so that they will not return to the "crime cycle" in which they were raised.[77]

Many prosecutors echo this rhetoric. In fact, some prosecutors will actually argue that a child's decision to participate in stone throwing is a result of the Israeli authorities' negligence of the Palestinian community, making the "streets" an afterschool playground where children can engage in deviant behavior like stone throwing as a way of passing the time; this is in addition to "ideological" (nationalist) reasons and peer pressure to throw stones.[78] From this premise, however, prosecutors will then argue that the community is unsafe and unqualified for rehabilitating minors. The opposite is true for Jewish Israeli children: even when their criminal involvement is conducted under similar conditions of a low socioeconomic background or induced by political motives, the child's actions are considered as individual incidents.

This securitized view of Palestinian children was present in the study's cases. In CC 53368,[79] the probation officer's report on Defendant 1, a Jewish minor accused of throwing stones at a moving vehicle, gave a positive review of the defendant; the officer concluded that the child was suitable for rehabilitation and was less likely to be a threat to others, even though he had an additional criminal case in court for another offense. Meanwhile, in CC 7511, two Palestinian children who were accused of throwing stones at a military jeep were charged, under a plea bargain, of attempting aggravated assault and attempting to cause damage in *mala fide*. Although the probation officer believed the Palestinian defendants learned much during their house arrest and detention, and although both defendants and their families were committed to the process, the officer concluded that it was better to convict them. Judge Moshe Drori—who presided over the two cases above—adopted the probation officer's recommendations in both cases. In August 2014, the judge acquitted the Jewish minor and ordered rehabilitation. In January 2015, he convicted the two Palestinian minors without an adequate rehabilitation program—even though they were accused of a less severe offense than the Jewish minor.

Obedience to authority also factors into the courts' analysis of a child's behavior. The study's cases show that Jewish families are given opportunities to work on their relationship with the child and to rebuild their authority over them. For example, Jewish Defendant 3 in CC 15634 had divorced parents and maintained minimal ties with the father, yet was offered a rehabilitation framework that allowed both parents to reset boundaries for him.[80] Jewish Defendant 7 of CC 35801 projected violent behavior toward his mother and siblings, but the probation officer worked with his boarding school to provide a program to address his violence and assist rehabilitation with his family. In CC 35801—a case involving eight Jewish children accused of throwing stones at Palestinians—the court recognized that the defendants' parents and siblings had also suffered the ramifications of the child's offense, particularly during house arrest.[81]

In contrast, the courts' denial of rehabilitation for Palestinian children begins with the debilitation, rather than engagement, of the parents. Because many Palestinian parents in Jerusalem don't have the financial means to pay bail, and others cannot provide supervision for house arrest because of work schedules and the lack of state services, courts are more likely to view the parents as unable to reintegrate the child into society.[82] Unlike Jewish Israeli children whose house arrests will often include formal or vocational education, Palestinian house arrests are mostly confined to imprisonment only.[83] Other times, rehabilitation is not provided because the defense lawyers themselves do not request such alternatives,[84] knowing the difficulty in achieving them for Palestinian children.[85] Indeed, the low odds are seen as so predictable that, in one court hearing, a defense lawyer simply asked the family straightforwardly, "Do you want him to go back home [to house arrest] so that his time in the house is not counted [reduced from his future sentence]?"[86]

The space for informal rehabilitation is also hampered by the exclusion of parents from the proceedings altogether. Upon arrest, Palestinian parents are no longer treated as persons entitled to protect their children.[87] They are given little information about their children's rights and conditions, and are usually granted only one visit every two weeks (as in the case of Defendant 1 in CC 37040),[88] or even less in other cases. In courtrooms, the family, many of whom may not be fluent in Hebrew, are often seated away from the arrested child, who is surrounded by guards. The families, without a translator, end up relying on the explanation of the lawyer, who is busy working the case. Each movement or attempt by the family to contact the child is blocked by the guards or the judge, and requests to hug or kiss the child are either denied by the judge or even dismissed by the defense lawyer.[89]

Palestinian defendants (especially those under house arrest) and their parents are therefore denied the opportunity to enroll in rehabilitation programs and improve their family relationships. Even when Palestinian parents are actively involved in the child's life, the court does not consider this as an adequate factor in reducing the child's supposed danger. This enforces the perception that Palestinian parents are incapable of teaching their children to obey authority; yet, by placing Palestinian children under house arrest without rehabilitation, the court still expects parents to act as the children's jailers.

II. DANGER TO THE PUBLIC

The courts' assessment of a child defendant's risk factor involves a combination of the components described above alongside other elements. For example, the court considers Jewish parental supervision and "normative" families as an adequate means of eliminating the danger of the Jewish child, making a pardon more likely. In CC 15634, the court noted the functionality of the three Jewish defendants' families, describing the first defendant as having a distant relationship with his father, but with all three having close relationships with the mothers.

Palestinian children, in contrast, were viewed as requiring interventions from state institutions rather than their parents, regarding them as riskier and posing a greater danger to society.[90]

Israeli courts tended to view Palestinian children who throw stones as inherently more dangerous to the public than their Jewish counterparts, primarily because their offenses are viewed as contributing to political escalations, whereas the Jewish children's offenses are seen as isolated and irregular incidents.[91] As one prosecutor said, they would often consider "statistics on minors' involvement in stone throwing in [East] Jerusalem—in that case we see that consideration of public safety and deterrence would prevail."[92] While the courts expressed understanding of the political environment's impact on Jewish children and acquitted them (as in CC 15634), with Palestinian children accused of the same offense under identical circumstances, the court saw them as dangerous persons who should be kept under arrest (as in CC 37149).[93]

In CC 35801—a case involving nine Jewish children accused of throwing stones at moving vehicles belonging to Palestinians on different occasions in 2013—the court ruled that the evidence did not establish a profound reasoning for implementing Israel's Danger to the Public Act, even though all defendants were held responsible for acting in *mala fide*.[94] Meanwhile, in CC 7511—two Palestinian minors accused of being involved in throwing stones at a military jeep transferring settlers to their neighborhood—the court adopted the prosecutor's opinion that throwing even a single stone at a military vehicle is a threat to public security, even describing the acts as a "city plague." The verdict for the Jewish children was issued in 2015, two years after their actions; the verdict for the Palestinian children was issued in 2017, four years after the act and following the new political-legal changes in Jerusalem.[95]

When explaining their actions, many of the Palestinian defendants told the court that they were motivated by peer pressure (such as proving masculinity or showing off to girls). However, the indictments and the court asserted that the Palestinian children acted solely out of racist intentions, basing this claim in part on the defendants' acceptance of guilt in their plea bargains. Notably, some Palestinian minors who were acquitted did not throw stones but only acted as lookouts or observers, yet were still arrested for at least a month before being placed under house arrest until the end of proceedings, as with Defendant 2 in CC 43972 and Defendant 1 in CC 37149.

This incrimination is also expressed in subtle ways. In CC 53368, Judge Drori wrote that "some incidents are more crucial than others, especially when the incident occurs in places of worship such as the Temple Mount." The judge continued: "There is no difference between a Jew or an Arab (victim). Nevertheless, the rulings suggest that when the stone or Molotov cocktail throwing is directed at security personnel, then the offense is much more severe; and sometimes the defendant is charged with a stone throwing offense in addition to assaulting a police officer."[96] In other words, although Drori tried to emphasize that there is no difference between the two groups, he used specific words to describe offenses more likely to be conducted by Palestinians by referencing a Jewish holy site and Israeli security forces. In doing so, he made a clear distinction of the places and situations that are more worthy of protection.

III. HIGH CONVICTION, LACKING DUE PROCESS

Israeli courts' case overload and lack of judges specialized in juvenile delinquency is another obstacle in accessing justice, pressuring many judges to rush their decisions without sufficient inquiry.[97] As a result, only a few cases are granted meaningful time for consideration, while most others are either closed by an administrative decision or drag on for years.[98]

As mentioned previously, the Youth Law sets strict rules for discussing the criminal liability of minors. Although the probation officer's report is nonbinding, the court cannot rule on methods of punishment or rehabilitation without it, and must turn to conviction only as a last resort.[99] Notwithstanding these guidelines, the judiciary is required to balance between rehabilitation and considerations of public interest, deterrence, and retribution.[100] While rehabilitation is central, the severity of the offense often decreases the weight of the rehabilitation component, and in this case the components of public interest and deterrence prevail.[101]

This study's cases reveal that the courts weighed these considerations very differently on similar cases: it was more understanding and forgiving of Jewish minors,[102] but more punitive toward the Palestinian minors. As one prosecutor said, the court "would rule arrest until the end of proceedings for this one [the Palestinian] and would release the other [the Israeli] for alternative to arrest, because it's easier to suggest such alternatives. At the end of the day, the indictments would be different, because in general the court won't imprison back a minor that was sent to alternatives for arrest."[103] For example, a Palestinian child was accused of throwing a single stone at Israeli vehicles in May 2014 without causing damage, acting alongside others; in September 2014, Judge Drori found the defendant responsible and convicted him.[104] In comparison, in March of the same year, a Jewish boy alongside two adults threw stones and attacked Palestinians who were working on their land near the Ramat Migron settlement, injuring the Palestinians.[105] While the court convicted the adult defendants, it acquitted the minor despite holding him responsible for his actions. Despite the multivariabilities in the Jewish case compared to the Palestinian one, the court still decided to be more tolerant toward the Jewish child.

The cases also show that Palestinian children—who are regularly detained before, during, and after the end of legal procedures, or put under harsh house arrest conditions—are often charged for serious offenses, making the benchmark for negotiating a plea bargain higher. Since most Palestinian children plead guilty as part of the bargain—in part due to their lack of faith in the Israeli justice system—it is impossible to know who was falsely criminalized based on the court decision alone. Lawyers, too, often encourage Palestinian defendants to "seal the deal" in a plea bargain to end the "limbo" of arrest or house arrest.

During 2013–14, Palestinian children were arrested at higher rates but indicted at lower rates, while Jewish Israeli children were arrested at lower rates but indicted at higher rates. This may suggest that during those years, Palestinian children were policed and arrested on charges for which the Israeli police did not necessarily have evidence to support an indictment (or the arrest itself); whereas Jewish Israeli children were more frequently arrested for crimes for which the police had more evidence to support indictments.[106]

Official police data presented in State of Israel v. Anonymous et al., CC 37040–05–14 (D.C. 2014) revealed that the number of incidents of throwing stones and Molotov cocktails in the first three months of 2014 alone stood at 994, while the total number in the previous year stood at 1,010 incidents. When comparing children arrested for stone throwing in Jerusalem specifically, we find an overrepresentation of Palestinian minors: police records show that in 2014, 95 percent of the stone throwing cases involved Palestinian minors; in 2013, they accounted for 87 percent.[107]

Although Jewish children, like Palestinian ones, also plead guilty in plea bargains, their admittance is seen by the probation officer and the court as taking responsibility for their actions. The courts subsequently either decide to acquit them, or to give them a minimal punishment while maintaining their rehabilitation.[108] As seen in the case of eight Israeli defendants in CC 35801, the court claimed that one of the reasons for the prolonged trial was to provide the defendants with adequate time for rehabilitation, and to work individually with each defendant toward accepting the consequences of their actions. Thus, the legal system paves the way for Jewish defendants to reach a better plea bargain, leading to a better verdict.

As such, the indictments against Jewish children featured less serious offenses than those of Palestinian children. Even among Jewish defendants who were convicted of stone throwing, 75 percent were sent to community service while 25 percent had small sentences such as fines. Palestinians who were charged with similar offenses, however, faced harsher sentences with a detention rate of 60 percent and community service rate of 20 percent.[109] While the "deterrence" factor played a major role in the courts' decisions to convict Palestinian children, with little nuance for conceptualizing their responsibility, the courts seemed to be more understanding of the ramifications of the political situation on the acts of Jewish children, perceiving the incident as a "one-time thing" that ignores the act as criminal behavior.

This systematic discrepancy reveals that the Israeli courts do in fact abide by Supreme Court guidelines for juvenile cases,[110] but with a twist: the rights of the individual are the highest value when the child is Jewish, and the public's "safety" prevails when the child is Palestinian. Consequently, the courts do not treat the Palestinian public as worthy of protection, but extend almost automatic protection to the Jewish public.[111] Palestinian defendants are thus effectively excluded from the rule of law, making every Palestinian case an inherent exception to the Youth Law—as if guilt is the Palestinian child's legal default, and as if the Palestinian child is not enough of a child to enjoy the protection of the law.

This discrepancy in arrest and conviction rates between Palestinians and Jewish Israelis goes beyond the Jerusalem court: as Viterbo explains, Palestinians across the board, whether citizens or noncitizens, have higher incarceration and conviction rates.[112] During the war on Gaza in May 2021, the Israeli police launched a military-style "Operation Law and Order" that targeted Palestinian citizens and residents of the state, many of whom participated in protests against the war;[113] the operation did not see Jewish Israelis as a primary target, including those who were filmed lynching Palestinians on the streets or participated in other violent crimes.[114] The operation ended in June 2021 with 2,142 arrests, about 91 percent of whom were Palestinian citizens and residents, with 184 indictments filed against 285 persons.[115]

Discussion and Conclusion

Legalized state violence, Pugliese writes, is based on a biopolitical caesura that marks its targets as nonhuman animals, believing that "the state's target subjects are, as the embodiment of ungovernable violence, at once anathema to and beyond law and thus outside of any ethical consideration."[116] This study demonstrates that such legalized state violence is systematically deployed by Israel against Palestinian children in East Jerusalem, who are subjected to institutionalized discrimination throughout the legal procedure compared to Jewish children,[117] despite being subject to the same civil law. The study shows that to understand the discrepancies in the Israeli criminal justice system, we must shed light on how the Palestinian child is securitized, "othered," and unchilded by that system.

The eviction of Palestinian juveniles from their legal rights and protections, in both rhetoric and practice, reveals how the Israeli legal system constructs Palestinians as unwanted persons, as nonchildren, and as an eternal threat to the governing power. As such, we should recognize how the political environment feeds the thoughts and actions of decision-makers, legislators, and judges operating in the Israeli justice system. The study demonstrates that the securitization and unchilding of Palestinians is a multilayered process, identified firstly in the legal amendments enacted after the escalations of 2014 that primarily targeted and framed Palestinian children as a security threat, and secondly in the Israeli court decisions in cases of child stone throwers.

This chapter discussed three modes of unchilding practiced by the Israeli courts: the denial of rehabilitation, the framing of the child as a danger to public, and the high conviction rate with lack of due process. Palestinian Jerusalemite children are not provided with the same opportunities for rehabilitation as their Jewish counterparts, nor do they face the same arrest period or arrest restrictions. The children's and parents' identity as Palestinians contributed to their portrayal as less normative persons because they were seen as being less integrated with Israeli society, and were therefore deemed less worthy of rehabilitation. The courts' racialized othering of Palestinian children further generated the view that they were dangerous subjects,[118] which was used to justify the legal system's approaches to imposing control and restricting the child's liberty. As such, the judicial and welfare system jointly invaded intimate spaces and social bonds, thereby serving as the legal arm of unchilding Palestinian minors.

Taken altogether, these systemic disadvantages against Palestinian children cannot be analyzed solely as a matter of inequality in a deeply divided society, but as a direct product of the dominating, asymmetric process of "othering" the Palestinian native by Israel as a settler-colonial regime.[119] The state's ideology is evident in the decisions and practices of the legal system, which sees the Palestinian child as a "security threat" and "enemy of the state" in a "war game," while the Israeli child is considered a victim to be protected. As Shalhoub-Kevorkian explains, such unchilding operates "with wounding regulations and nonregulations inherent in a geography of power within settler-colonial contexts that is inherently and necessarily preoccupied with children."[120]

In his elaboration of equal treatment and due process in CC 35801, Judge Drori claimed that the ideology behind the throwing of a stone does not change the consequences of the actions, since the victim can be equally damaged by a stone thrown by a Jew or an Arab. And yet, Drori also explains that, in terms of correctional policy, the court should still consider the motives behind the actions, and give special legal weight to racially motivated crimes.[121] The result is that the Israeli criminal justice system constructs Palestinians as a securitized threat in constant need of control, incarceration, and incapacitation,[122] while maintaining an image of a democratized system that "believes" in due process for Palestinian children.

The contradictions of Judge Drori's ruling open the door to discrepancy and lack of due process for Palestinians in the juvenile court system. These discrepancies create a pervasiveness of indifference and neglect of the Palestinian child,[123] which Rana identified as central to the development of the settler colony and its institutions.[124] Although both Palestinian and Jewish children in this chapter's case studies committed stone throwing offenses in the same years, and during political escalations, the Israeli courts were clearly more eager to lighten the consequences for Jewish children compared to Palestinians.

NOTES

Part of the findings were first published in: Shalhoub-Kevorkian, Nadera, and Shahrazad Odeh. "Arrested Childhood in Spaces of Indifference: The Criminalized Children of Occupied East Jerusalem." *Canadian Journal of Women and the Law* 30, no. 3 (2018): 398–422.

1. State of Israel v. Anonymous, CC 53368-05-13 (D.C. Jerusalem, 2014).

2. State of Israel v. Anonymous CC 7511-01-14 (D.C Jerusalem, 2016).

3. The articles mentioned in the court decisions and/or verdicts are of the *Penal Law*, 5737–1977, unless stated otherwise.

4. Israel: Law No. 5712–1952, Entry into Israel Law, September 5, 1952.

5. Tamari, "The Phantom City," 1.

6. Stein, "The Quiet Deportation Continues"; see the recent case of Salah Hamoury in Human Rights Defenders, "Israel-OPT: [Follow Up] Ongoing Judicial Harassment of Salah Hamouri," FIDH: International Federation for Human Rights, July 8, 2021; Azulay, Moran. "Interior Minister Revokes Residency of 4 East Jerusalem Terrorist." Ynetnews, January 21, 2016. https://www.ynetnews.com/articles/0,7340,L-4756044,00.html.

7. Kadman, Szlecsan, and Cohen, *Temporary Order?*

8. The author chose the word native because it has an immediate connection to the land. Thobani, *Exalted Subjects*; Razack, *Dying from Improvement*, 112.

9. Thobani, *Exalted Subjects*, 38.

10. Shalhoub-Kevorkian, *United Nations Security Council Resolution 1325*.

11. J. Kuttab, "The Children's Revolt"; Viterbo, *Problematizing Law, Rights, and Childhood*, 55.

12. Viterbo, *Problematizing Law, Rights, and Childhood*, 28–31.

13. Odeh, "Two Stones, One Law," 55–58.

14. Barak, "Some Reflections."

15. Ibid.

16. Ibid.

17. State of Israel v. John Doe (Minor), 6255-01-09 (November 11, 2009), found in Viterbo, *Problematizing Law, Rights, and Childhood*, 321–22.

18. Odeh, "Two Stones, One Law."

19. Fujiwara, "The Impact of Welfare Reform," 82; Orloff, "Gender and the Social Rights," 303; Quadagno, *The Color of Welfare.*

20. Fujiwara, "The Impact of Welfare Reform," 82; Orloff, "Gender and the Social Rights," 303; Quadagno, *The Color of Welfare*; Rosenhek, "Migration Regimes, Intra-State Conflicts."

21. Ajzenstadt, "Crime, Social Control," 585.

22. Ibid., 586.

23. Ibid., 588.

24. Koren, "The Criminalization of Political Conflict," 157.

25. Khoury-Kassabri, Khoury, and Ali, "Arab Youth Involvement in Delinquency," 577.

26. Ibid.

27. Viterbo, *Problematizing Law, Rights, and Childhood*, 307–8.

28. Ajzenstadt, "Constructing Juvenile Delinquency."

29. Ibid.

30. Fanon, *The Wretched of the Earth*; Shalhoub-Kevorkian and Odeh, "Arrested Childhood."

31. Shalhoub-Kevorkian, "Palestinian Children as Tools."

32. Shalhoub-Kevorkian and Odeh, "Arrested Childhood."

33. Odeh, "Two Stones, One Law."

34. This in contrast to Barak, who argues that the state's Jewishness does not negate its democratic values; see Barak, "Some Reflections"; Zureik, Moughrabi, and Sacco, "Perception of Legal Inequality," 423–428.

35. Harris, "The Knesset, Basic Law."

36. Shamir, "Legal Discourse, Media Discourse."

37. Wolfe, "Structure and Event."

38. Tauri and Porou, "Criminal Justice as a Colonial Project"; Odeh, "Two Stones, One Law," 55–58; Razack, *Race, Space, and the Law*; Berg, "Geographies of Identity I."

39. Krippendorff, *Content Analysis.*

40. Moyser and Wagstaffe, *Research Methods for Elite Studies*; Hafner-Burton, Hughes, and Victor, "Cognitive Revolution and the Political Psychology."

41. To find stone throwing verdicts specifically, the following codes were used in the search engines (in Hebrew): "stones," "minor," "protest," "public disobedience," and "riots." The results mostly consisted of cases of Palestinian defendants, and less of Jewish Israelis. Therefore, different coding in the search engines was used to find cases of Israeli defendants, such as adding the potential targets of stone throwing acts such as "police," "Arabs," and "Palestinians," or dates of the incidents such as "Shabbat" (Saturday), or "Yom Kippur."

42. Hasson, *Jerusalem.*

43. Ibid.; OCHA-OPT, *Fragmented Lives, Humanitarian Overview 2014*; Peter Beaumont, "Video Footage Indicates Killed Palestinian Youth Pose No Threat," *The Guardian*, May 20, 2014. https://www.theguardian.com/world/2014/may/20/video-indicates-killed-palestinian-youths-no-threat-israeli-forces.

44. OCHA-OPT, *Humanitarian Bulletin, Monthly Report.*

45. Ibid.

46. Ibid.

47. Peter Beaumont, "Three Israelis Confess to Killing Palestinian Teenager," *The Guardian*, July 7, 2014. https://www.theguardian.com/world/2014/jul/07/reported -confessions-israel-mohammed-abu-khdeir-killing#:~:text=Three%20Israelis%20 accused%20of%20kidnapping,the%20murder%20for%20the%20authorities.

48. OCHA-OPT, *Protection of Civilians, Weekly Report*.

49. OCHA-OPT, *Fragmented Lives, Humanitarian Overview 2014*.

50. The governmental decisions included an updated version of the *Attorney General Instruction* No.2.19 (December 24, 2019), which enables the imprisonment of those suspected of stone throwing for nationalist motives until the end of proceedings, in addition to increasing the punishment and including a prolonged active prison term, as well as imposing a fine or compensations on parents of children accused of stone throwing. Prime Minister's Office, "Decision 1775" [translated by author]. In Decision 1775's protocol, the prime minister's office portrayed Palestinian children as violent criminal offenders and Jewish settlers as unprotected citizens victimized by the other.

51. *Penal Law*, 5737-1977.

52. *Penal Law*, Amendment No. 119, 5775-2015 (Israel). See Alyan and Russo, "Arrested Childhood."

53. *Counter-Terrorism Law*, 5776-2016; Jonathan Cook, "Israel's Anti-Terror Law 'Dangerous' and 'Anti-Arab.'" *Al-Jazeera*, June 19, 2016. https://www.aljazeera.com/ news/2016/6/19/israels-anti-terror-law-dangerous-and-anti-arab.

54. *The Youth Law*, Amendment No. 22 (hereinafter: The Youth Law).

55. *The Youth Law*, Amendment No. 22; Alyan and Russo, "Arrested Childhood," 8. *National Insurance Law*, Amendment No. 163; see Alyan and Russo, "Arrested Childhood," 8.

56. Viterbo, *Problematizing Law, Rights, and Childhood*, 93–94.

57. Sampson and Lauritsen, "Racial and Ethnic Disparities in Crime."

58. State of Israel v. Anonymous et al., CC 35801-10-13 (D.C. Jerusalem, 2016).

59. Viterbo, *Problematizing Law, Rights, and Childhood*, 143–44.

60. Stein, *Unprotected*.

61. Ibid.

62. After the murder of Mohammed Abu Khdeir, the Israeli courts adopted a stricter policy of detaining minors until the end of the proceedings or until the release of the disciplinary officer's report, which takes about a month. See Addameer, "Imprisonment of Children."

63. See interview with attorney Mohammad Mahmoud, Addameer, "Imprisonment of Children."

64. Addameer, "Imprisonment of Children."

65. Weiss and Zohar, "Plea-Bargain Game."

66. Friedman et al., "Symposium: Judicial Supervision."

67. Interviews with prosecutors from Jerusalem district in April–August 2018.

68. In CrimA 2669/00, Supreme Court Justice Ayala Procaccia set clear guidelines for the criminal trial and declared that, in accordance with Article 24 of the Youth Act, it is only after a minor meets with a probation officer and receives the officer's report that the

court can decide on a conviction and decree, or treatment, or exemption. See State of Israel v. Anonymous, CrimA 2669/00 LIV (3) 685 (S.C.J., 2000).

69. Viterbo, *Problematizing Law, Rights, and Childhood*, 142–47.

70. Interviews with prosecutors from Jerusalem district in April–August 2018.

71. Article 401X of the Penal Law suggests that rehabilitation, or a child's willingness to pursue it, can be a consideration for minimizing punishment.

72. Justice Procaccia in Anonymous v. the State of Israel, CrimA 10715/05, (S.C.J., Not Published, Sep. 4, 2007) (paragraph 12); in CrimA 5048/09 (S.C.J., 2010), Supreme Court Justice Hendel ruled that rehabilitation "is much more valued in minor delinquency cases than adult delinquency cases. In fact, it is not another consideration, rather it is a purpose in the criminal procedure." See Anonymous v. The State of Israel, CrimA 5048/09 (S.C.J., 2010).

73. According to the Youth Law and Article 401V of the Penal Law, the court is expected to discuss family ties and parental relationships, and the child's rehabilitation prospects, as factors affecting its final decision; under Article 40X1(2), the court should also consider the implications of the offense on the child's family. Under Article 12A of the Youth Law, the court should also consider rehabilitation not solely as an alternative to punishment, but as a central part of the legal process.

74. Viterbo, *Problematizing Law, Rights, and Childhood*, 161–62.

75. Ibid.

76. Odeh, "Two Stones, One Law," 45; Protocol No. 120, "Meeting protocol the Committee on Child Rights," 20th Knesset, https://m.knesset.gov.il/Activity/committees/Pages/AllCommitteesAgenda.aspx?Tab=3&ItemID=2010696. (Access date September 28, 2023.)

77. Odeh, *"Two Stones, One Law,"* 45; Protocol No. 120, "Meeting protocol the Committee on Child Rights," 20th Knesset.

78. Interviews with prosecutors from Jerusalem district, May–July 2018.

79. State of Israel v. Anonymous, CC 53368–05–13.

80. State of Israel v. Anonymous et al., CC 15634–07–14 (D.C. Jerusalem, 2015).

81. State of Israel v. Anonymous, CC 35801-10-13 (D.C. Jerusalem, 2016, Chapter XVII, paragraph 377.

82. Interviews with prosecutors from Jerusalem district May–July 2018.

83. Nadera Shalhoub-Kevorkian and Amir Marshi, "Iron Caging the Palestinian Home: Child House Arrest in Occupied East Jerusalem as Lawfare." *Jerusalem Quarterly* 85 (2021): 106–124.

84. Interview with prosecutor Y.Z., Jerusalem district, July 30, 2018.

85. Interview with prosecutor S.S., Jerusalem district, May 1, 2018.

86. Court watch in Jerusalem Magistrate's Court, March 27, 2018 (12:00–14:00). No further information will be shared for the safety and security of the minor.

87. Stein, "Unprotected."

88. State of Israel v. Anonymous et al., CC 37040-05-14.

89. Based on court watch of fifteen cases conducted by the author and fellow lawyer between March–May 2018 and July 2019.

90. Shalhoub-Kevorkian and Odeh, "Arrested Childhood"; Viterbo, *Problematizing Law, Rights, and Childhood*, 8–18.

91. Interviews with prosecutors from Jerusalem district, May–July 2018.

92. Interview with prosecutor R.K., Jerusalem district, July 17, 2018.

93. State of Israel v. Anonymous, CC 37149-05-14.

94. A similar decision can be found in State of Israel v. Anonymous et al., CC 39422-06-14.

95. Although most cases of stone throwing reported to prosecutors are by Palestinians, this high representation can be the result of the heavy police presence in Palestinian neighborhoods, or due to the fact that incidents of stone throwing in the Jewish Israeli community, like throwing at vehicles during the sabbath, are not as heavily reported. Interviews with prosecutors from Jerusalem district, May–July 2018.

96. State of Israel v. Anonymous, CC 53368-05-13.

97. See Judge Beijsky in Friedman et al., "Symposium: Judicial Supervision," 34.

98. Ibid.

99. See Justice Procaccia in CrimA 2669/00, at LIV (3) 685.

100. Interview with prosecutor G.Z., Jerusalem district, April 25, 2018.

101. Ibid.

102. State of Israel v. Anonymous et al., CC 15634-07-14.

103. Interview with prosecutor G.Z., Jerusalem district, April 25, 2018.

104. State of Israel v. Anonymous, CC 7614-05-14.

105. State of Israel v. Yousef Weinberg et al., CC 58199–03–14.

106. Odeh, "Two Stones, One Law," 24.

107. Ibid.

108. Interviews with prosecutors from Jerusalem district, April–August 2018.

109. The other 20 percent were not yet declared in the published decision.

110. State of Israel v. Anonymous, CrimA 2669/00, and State of Israel v. Anonymous, CrimA 9262/03.

111. Viterbo, *Problematizing Law, Rights, and Childhood*, 323; Odeh, "Two Stones, One Law."

112. Viterbo, *Problematizing Law, Rights, and Childhood*, 313–15.

113. Adalah, "Adalah Demands Israeli Police End."

114. Khoury, "Israeli Police Aren't Seeking Law."

115. Adalah, "New Israeli Government Must Confront."

116. Pugliese, *State Violence*, 7.

117. Stein, "Unprotected."

118. Nunn, "The Child as Other"; Shalhoub-Kevorkian, "Palestinian Children as Tools," 38; Nadera Shalhoub-Kevorkian, "Childhood," 36; Ward, *The Black Child-Savers*.

119. Zureik, "Colonialism, Surveillance, and Population Control."

120. Shalhoub-Kevorkian, *Incarcerated Childhood*, 17.

121. State of Israel v. Anonymous et al., CC 35801-10-13, Chapter XIII, 317, 319 (2016).

122. Razack, *Race, Space, and the Law*.

123. Shalhoub-Kevorkian and Odeh, "Arrested Childhood."

124. Rana, "Colonialism and Constitutional Memory."

BIBLIOGRAPHY

Adalah—The Legal Center for Arab Minority Rights. "Adalah Demands Israeli Police End Mass Arrests of Palestinian Citizens." May 27, 2021. https://www.adalah.org/en /content/view/10334.

———. "New Israeli Government Must Confront Police Violence and Impunity." June 21, 2021. https://mailchi.mp/adalah/adalahs-news-21-june-2021.

Addameer—Prisoner Support and Human Rights Association. "Imprisonment of Children." July 2017. https://www.addameer.org/the_prisoners/children.

Ajzenstadt, M. "Constructing Juvenile Delinquency: The Socio-Legal Control of Young Offenders in Israel, 1920–1975." In *Constructing Social Work Practices, edited by A. Jokinen, K. Juhila, and T.* Pösö, 196–97. Aldershot, UK: Ashgate, 1999.

———. "Crime, Social Control, and the Process of Social Classification: Juvenile Delinquency/Justice Discourse in Israel, 1948–1970." *Social Problems* 49, no. 4 (2002): 585–604.

Alyan, N., and M. Russo. "Arrested Childhood: The Ramifications of Israel's New Strict Policy Toward Minors Suspected of Involvement in Stone Throwing, Security Offenses, and Disturbances." Association for Civil Rights in Israel (ACRI). February 21, 2016. www.acri.org.il/en/2016/02/21/prohibited-childhood/.

Azulay, M. "Interior Minister Revokes Residency of 4 East Jerusalem Terrorists." Ynetnews, January 21, 2016. https://www.ynetnews.com/articles/0,7340,L-4756044,00 .html.

Barak, A. "Some Reflections on the Israeli Legal System and Its Judiciary." *Electronic Journal of Comparative Law* 6, no. 1 (2002).

Beaumont, P. "Video Footage Indicates Killed Palestinian Youth Posed No Threat." *The Guardian*, May 20, 2014. https://www.theguardian.com/world/2014/may/20 /video-indicates-killed-palestinian-youths-no-threat-israeli-forces.

Berg, L. D. "Geographies of Identity I: Geography, (Neo)Liberalism, White Supremacy." *Progress in Human Geography* 36, no. 4 (2012): 508–17.

Fanon, F. *The Wretched of the Earth.* New York: Grove Press, 1963.

FIDH: International Federation for Human Rights. "Israel-OPT: [Follow Up] Ongoing Judicial Harassment of Salah Hamouri." July 8, 2021. https://www.fidh.org/en/issues /human-rights-defenders/israel-opt-follow-up-ongoing-judicial-harassment-of-salah -hamouri.

Friedman, D., M. Bejski, R. Gavison, and M. Kremnitzer. "Symposium: Judicial Supervision on the Criminal Justice System—Decision on Prosecution and Pardon." 5 HAMISHPAT 4, 35 (1995)(Hebrew). https://www.nevo.co.il/books/תעש20%‏ י בתכ /כ י בתכ/תעש20%/טפשמה/כ דר ד20%ג/hamishpat-03–015.pdf. (Author's translation.)

Fujiwara, L. H. "The Impact of Welfare Reform on Asian Immigrant Communities." *Social Justice* 25, no. 1(71)(1998): 82–104.

Hafner-Burton, E. M., D. A. Hughes, and David G. Victor. "The Cognitive Revolution and the Political Psychology of Elite Decision Making." *Perspectives on Politics* 11, no. 2 (2013): 368–86.

Harris, H. R., trans. "The Knesset, Basic Law: Israel—The Nation of The Jewish People." The Knesset, 2022.

Hasisi, B. "Police, Politics, and Culture in Deeply Divided Society." *The Journal of Criminal Law and Criminology* 98, no. 3(2008): 1119–46.

Hasson, S., ed. *Jerusalem: The Challenge of Transition.* Jerusalem: The Floersheimer Institute for Policy Studies, 2007.

Kadman, N., A. Szlecsan, and S. Cohen. *Temporary Order? Life in East Jerusalem under the Shadow of the Citizenship and Entry into Israel Law.* Jerusalem: HaMoked Center for the Defence of the Individual, 2014.

Khoury J. "Israeli Police Aren't Seeking Law and Order, but to Silence Arab Citizens." *Haaretz,* May 28, 2021. https://www.haaretz.com/israel-news/.premium-israeli-police -aren-t-seeking-law-an-order-but-to-silence-arab-citizens-1.9853398.

Khoury-Kassabri, M., N. Khoury, and R. Ali. "Arab Youth Involvement in Delinquency and Political Violence and Parental Control: The Mediating Role of Religiosity." *American Journal of Orthopsychiatry* 85, no. 6 (2015): 576–85.

Koren, A. "The Criminalization of Political Conflict: Crime Among Arab Citizens in the Fifties." *Plilim* 8 (1999) (Hebrew).

Krippendorff, K. *Content Analysis: An Introduction to its Methodology.* Thousand Oaks, Calif.: Sage Publications, 1980.

Kuttab, D. "A Profile of the Stonethrowers." *Journal of Palestine Studies* 17, no. 3 (1988): 14–23.

Kuttab, J. "The Children's Revolt." *Journal of Palestine Studies* 17, no. 4 (1988): 26-35.

Moyser, G., and M. Wagstaffe, eds. *Research Methods for Elite Studies.* London: Allen & Unwin, 1987.

Nunn, K. B. "The Child as Other: Race and Differential Treatment in the Juvenile Justice System." DePaul L. Rev. 51 (2001): 679.

Odeh, S. "Two Stones, One Law: The Israeli Legal System and the Palestinian Child." LL.M diss., The Hebrew University of Jerusalem, 2019.

Orloff, A. S. "Gender and the Social Rights of Citizenship: The Comparative Analysis of Gender Relations and Welfare States." *American Sociological Review* 58, no. 3 (1993): 303–28.

Prime Minister's Office. "Israeli Government Decision 1775–1776." June 26, 2014.

Pugliese, J. *State Violence and the Execution of Law: Biopolitical Caesurae of Torture, Black Sites, Drones.* New York: Routledge, 2013.

Quadagno, J. *The Color of Welfare: How Racism Undermined the War on Poverty.* New York: Oxford University Press, 1996.

Rana, A. "Colonialism and Constitutional Memory." UC Irvine L. Rev. 5, no. 2 (2015): 263.

Razack, S. H. *Casting Out: The Eviction of Muslims from Western Law and Politics.* Toronto: University of Toronto Press, 2007.

———. *Dying from Improvement: Inquests and Inquiries into Indigenous Deaths in Custody.* Toronto: University of Toronto Press, 2015.

———. *Race, Space, and the Law: Unmapping a White Settler Society.* Toronto: Between the Lines, 2002.

Rosenhek, Z. "Migration Regimes, Intra-State Conflicts, and the Politics of Exclusion and Inclusion: Migrant Workers in the Israeli Welfare State." *Social Problems* 47, no. 1 (2000): 49–67. https://doi.org/10.2307/3097151.

Sampson, R. J., and J. L. Lauritsen. "Racial and Ethnic Disparities in Crime and Criminal Justice in the United States." *Crime and Justice* 21 (1997): 311–74.

Shalhoub-Kevorkian, N. *Incarcerated Childhood and the Politics of Unchilding*. Cambridge, UK: Cambridge University Press, 2019.

———. "Palestinian Children as Tools for 'Legalized' State Violence." *Borderlands* 13, no. 1: 1–24.

———. *The United Nations Security Council Resolution 1325: Implementation in Palestine and Israel 2000–2009*. Jerusalem: Norwegian Church Aid, 2010.

———. "Childhood: A Universalist Perspective for How Israel is using Child Arrest and Detention to further its Colonial Settler Project." *International Journal of Applied Psychoanalytic Studies* 12, no. 223 (2015).

Shalhoub-Kevorkian, N., and S. Odeh. "Arrested Childhood in Spaces of Indifference: The Criminalized Children of Occupied East Jerusalem." *Canadian Journal of Women and the Law* 30, no. 3 (2018): 398–422

Shamir, R. "Legal Discourse, Media Discourse, and Speech Rights: The Shift from Content to Identity—the Case of Israel." *International Journal of the Sociology of Law* 19(1) (1991): 45–65.

Sherer, M. "Delinquent Activity among Jewish and Arab Junior and Senior High School Students in Israel." *International Journal of Offender Therapy and Comparative Criminology* 53, no. 5 (2009): 535–55.

Stein, Y. "The Quiet Deportation Continues." B'Tselem: The Israeli Center for Human Rights in the Occupied Territories and HaMoked Center for the Defence of the Individual, 1998. https://www.btselem.org/sites/default/files/sites/default/files2/the_quiet_deportation_continues.pdf.

———. "Unprotected: The Detention of Palestinian Teenagers in East Jerusalem." B'Tselem: The Israeli Center for Human Rights in the Occupied Territories and HaMoked Center for the Defence of the Individual, 2017. https://www.btselem.org/sites/default/files/publications/201710_unprotected_eng.pdf.

Tamari, S. "The Phantom City," in *Jerusalem 1948: The Arab Neighborhoods and Their Fate in the War,* 2nd ed., ed. Salim Tamari,1. Jerusalem and Bethlehem: Institute for Jerusalem Studies and Badil Resource Center for Palestinian Residency and Refugee Rights, 1999.

Tauri, J. M., and Ngati Porou. "Criminal Justice as a Colonial Project in Contemporary Settler Colonialism." *African Journal of Criminology and Justice Studies* 8, no. 1 (2014): 20–37.

Thobani, S. *Exalted Subjects: Studies in the Making of Race and Nation in Canada*. Toronto: University of Toronto Press, 2007.

United Nations Office for Coordination of Humanitarian Affairs—Occupied Palestinian Territory (OCHA-OPT). *Protection of Civilians, Weekly Report 1 July–7 July 2014*. July 11, 2014. https://www.ochaopt.org/sites/default/files/ocha_opt_protection_of_civilians_weekly_report_2014_7_11_english.pdf.

———. *Humanitarian Bulletin, Monthly Report*. June–August 2014. https://www.ochaopt.org/sites/default/files/ocha_opt_the_humanitarian_monitor_2014_10_03_english.pdf.

———. *Fragmented Lives, Humanitarian Overview 2014*. March 2015. https://www .ochaopt.org/sites/default/files/ocha_opt_the_humanitarian_monitor_2014_06_24 _english.pdf.

Viterbo, H. *Problematizing Law, Rights, and Childhood in Israel/Palestine*. Cambridge, UK: Cambridge University Press, 2021.

Ward, G. K. *The Black Child-Savers: Racial Democracy and Juvenile Justice*. Chicago: The University of Chicago Press, 2012.

Weiss, U., and Y. Zohar. "Is The Plea-bargain Game a Bribe Game?" In *Justice in the Legal System : Criminal Law and Criminal Procedure in Israel: Problems and Challenges*, edited by Alon Harel, 183–215. Tel Aviv: Buchmann Faculty of Law, Tel Aviv University, 2017.

Wolfe, P. "Structure and Event: Settler Colonialism, Time, and the Question of Genocide." In *Empire, Colony, Genocide: Conquest, Occupation, and Subaltern Resistance in World History*, edited by A. D. Moses, 102–32. Oxford: Berghahn Books, 2010.

Zureik, E. "Colonialism, Surveillance, and Population Control." In *Surveillance and Control in Israel/Palestine: Population, Territory and Power*, edited by Elia Zureik, David Lyon, and Yasmeen Abu-Laban. New York: Routledge, 2011.

———. "Crime, Justice, and Underdevelopment: The Palestinians under Israeli Control." *International Journal of Middle East Studies* 20, no. 4 (1988): 411–42.

Zureik, E., F. Moughrabi, and V. F. Sacco. "Perception of Legal Inequality in Deeply Divided Societies: The Case of Israel." *Journal of Middle East Studies* 25, no. 3 (1993): 423–42.

LEGAL CODES

The Counter-Terrorism Law, 5776–2016.

The Penal Law, 5737–1977.

The National Insurance Law [Combined Version], 5755-1995.

The Youth Law, (Adjudication, Penalizing and Manners of Treatment), 5731-1971.

VERDICTS

Anonymous v. The State of Israel, CrimA 9262/03 (S.C.J., 2004).

Anonymous v. the State of Israel, CrimA 10715/05 (S.C.J., Not Published, Sep. 4, 2007).

Anonymous v. The State of Israel, CrimA 5048/09 (S.C.J., 2010).

State of Israel v. Anonymous, CrimA 2669/00 (S.C.J., 2000).

State of Israel v. Anonymous, CrimA 2669/00 LIV (3) 685 (S.C.J., 2000).

State of Israel v. Anonymous, CC 53368-05-13 (D.C. Jerusalem, 2014).

State of Israel v. Anonymous, CC 1179-09-13 (D.C. Jerusalem, 2014).

State of Israel v. Anonymous, CC 7614-05-14 (D.C. Jerusalem, 2014).

State of Israel v. Anonymous et al., CC 37040-05-14 (D.C. Jerusalem, 2014).

State of Israel v. Anonymous, CC 37149-05-14 (D.C. Jerusalem, 2015).

State of Israel v. Anonymous et al., CC 39422-06-14 (D.C. Jerusalem, 2015).

State of Israel v. Anonymous et al., CC 15634-07-14 (D.C. Jerusalem, 2015).

State of Israel v. Anonymous et al., CC 39422-06-14 (D.C. Jerusalem, 2016).

State of Israel v. Anonymous et al., CC 43972-07-14 (D.C. Jerusalem, 2016).

State of Israel v. Anonymous et al., CC 35801-10-13 (D.C. Jerusalem, 2016).

State of Israel v. Anonymous, CC 4450-04-15 (D.C. Jerusalem, 2016).

State of Israel v. Anonymous, CC 1815-01-14 (D.C. Jerusalem, 2016).

State of Israel v. Anonymous, CC 7511-01-14 (D.C. Jerusalem, 2016).

State of Israel v. Yousef Weinberg et al., CC 58199–03–14 (D.C. Jerusalem, 2017).

Childhood behind Bars
Palestinian Children in Israeli Detention

MOHAMMED ALRUZZI, VALENTINA
MARCONI, AND YOUSEF M. ALJAMAL

In December 2017, the story of seventeen-year-old Palestinian child activist and icon of resistance Ahed Tamimi hit the headlines of Arab and international media. Israeli soldiers arrested Ahed at 4:00 a.m. in her West Bank village of Nabi Saleh after a video of her kicking and slapping two Israeli soldiers went viral. Israeli soldiers took her mother and cousin into custody as well. The detentions took place the same day that an Israeli soldier hit Ahed's cousin, fifteen-year-old Mohammed Tamimi, at close range with a rubber bullet. Ahed eventually signed a plea deal and served an eight-month prison sentence.[1] The arrest of Tamimi could be viewed as part of the process of "unchilding" that many other Palestinian children go through, stripping them of their childhood.[2]

Ahed comes from a politically active family that is relatively well known in international solidarity circles, which contributed to the global reach of her case. However, her arrest brings to light the reality that thousands of similar stories about Palestinian children pass without appeal or resonance in foreign media. In fact, child detention is a practice that Israeli authorities have been carrying out for decades, and Israel is the only country in the world that prosecutes children systematically before military courts, a practice that has only intensified since the military courts' inception in 1967.[3]

The objective of this chapter is to explore the situation of Palestinian children in the Israeli military detention system, focusing particularly on its widespread, systematic, and institutionalized abuse of international law. This detention system affords Palestinian children different rights and treatment than their Israeli peers living in the West Bank settlements. In fact, Palestinian civilians in the West Bank, including Palestinian children, are tried before military courts, unlike their Israeli counterparts,[4] who live in the same area, who are tried before civil courts, a practice that has been described by Human Rights Watch in April 2021 as a form of apartheid.[5] This results in two different legal and social constructions of childhood, operating side by side in the occupied West Bank.[6]

The chapter starts with an overview of the typical phases of child detention, from arrest to the moment of release and beyond, and then situates child detention in the context of international law. The chapter argues that detention is a tool of settler colonialism with widespread implications for Palestinian society, and that child detention is integral to the logic of elimination, which is at the core of the Israeli settler-colonial project in the Occupied Territories.[7] Finally, the chapter offers a way to look at the issue beyond a linear interaction between colonizer and colonized. In fact, we show that colonized children manage to find ways of empowering themselves within these same practices that seek their elimination. This results in Palestinian children assuming agency and playing a role in political life, often receiving recognition from the community.

This chapter is based on fieldwork that took place in the West Bank in March 2016 and included interviews with twelve Palestinians, aged fourteen to nineteen, who were arrested and/or detained and then released after serving their sentences. Face-to-face semistructured interviews were organized with each of the children separately in community centers, and sometimes, at the house of the child.[8] The chapter also uses interviews with child prisoners collected in the book *Dreaming of Freedom: Palestinian Child Prisoners Speak.*[9]

The Context

Imprisonment has been a constant in the lives of the Palestinians in the Occupied Territories. Starting from 1967, most families have been going through this experience either directly or indirectly. During the first Palestinian intifada (uprising), between 1987 and 1993, 100,000 families were affected.[10] In general, it is estimated that more than 800,000 Palestinians have been in Israeli detention since 1967.[11] Much of the stone throwing by Palestinians has been carried out by Palestinian children, making them a target for the Israeli military over the years.

Children's administrative detention is accompanied by high sentences and heavy fines. Approximately one thousand children from the West Bank are arrested every year, according to *Haaretz* newspaper.[12] Israel transfers a fifth of the arrested children to the Palestinian Authority (PA). More than five hundred children are tried in military courts. These figures do not include the 800–1,100 Palestinian children arrested in East Jerusalem every year, who are usually tried in Israeli civil courts.[13] At the moment of writing, the number of Palestinian child prisoners stood at 198, and 26 of them were under the age of sixteen.[14] More than 12,000 Palestinian children have been detained since 2000.[15] During 2019, the Israeli authorities arrested 880 children, 84 of whom were under the age of twelve, the youngest of them three-year-old Nader Hejazi from Nablus.[16] Subsequently, under the pretext of incitement on Facebook, Israel arrested nineteen more children, eight of them shot and wounded upon arrest.[17] For example, Mahmoud Hussein Salah, a fifteen-year-old from Bethlehem, was seriously injured in the feet, transferred to an Israeli hospital, and one of his legs was amputated from below the knee.[18]

THE ARREST

The Israeli army undertakes arrests in a range of locations, including houses, streets, or checkpoints, and in a range of situations, including en masse or while the suspect is presumed to be committing an *alleged offense*. In many cases, children are arrested from their homes in the middle of the night. In this case, the Israeli army usually begins by surrounding the building and then searching the premises. The arrest can entail damage to the family's property and theft of household valuables by the Israeli army.[19] The Israeli army tends to be physically and verbally violent to not just the child but also the family.[20] In the account of a seventeen-year-old child we interviewed:

> At the beginning they [the soldiers] knocked. We took some time to open so they broke the house door and got in. They were looking for me . . . and my family was very scared that they are coming to arrest me. They were terrorized. They [the soldiers] brought me out, then they blindfolded and handcuffed me.[21]   —Ali, Alarroub Camp, March 2016

Children who are subject to street arrest, or arrest at the scene of the alleged offense, report beatings, threats, and verbal harassment. For example, a sixteen-year-old child we interviewed reported that the violence at his arrest was so excessive that his body went numb.[22] Another technique the Israeli army uses to take children into custody is mass arrests, which can take the form of street roundups or public announcements demanding children assemble at a predetermined location.[23]

In the majority of cases, children are charged with throwing stones. Other charges have included membership of, or activity in, proscribed associations, throwing Molotov cocktails, and possession, trade, or use of firearms.[24] Some other charges revolved around the act of holding a flag or publishing material of "a political significance."[25]

THE INTERROGATION

At arrest, children are usually handcuffed and blindfolded, then transported in military vehicles to interrogation centers, sometimes via transition centers.[26] The

interrogation includes intimidation, threats, and physical violence, with the evident aim of pressuring the child to confess. Israeli soldiers physically restrain
children, in some cases tying them to a chair.[27] Such practices can last for extended hours, resulting in bodily pain. Israeli soldiers threaten children with
death, physical violence, solitary confinement, and sexual assault, against themselves or family members.[28] A sixteen-year-old child described the violence
during the interrogation as follows:

> They started to interrogate me. I was stubborn and did not answer their ques-
> tions. They took me to another room in which there were no cameras and they
> started beating me . . . they beat me all over my body. Literally, they stepped all
> over me. Then they took me back to the interrogation room. I was not cooper-
> ating, so they took me again to the other room.[29]
>
> —Yousef, Dheisheh Camp, March 2016

Interrogation centers are commonly located in Israel itself or the Israeli settlements of the occupied West Bank. This exacerbates the isolation of the child because Israel forbids or heavily restricts Palestinians' access to both these areas.
Israel forbids the presence of the child's lawyer and family members during the
interrogation. In addition, Israeli interrogators do not properly inform children
about their rights, especially the right against self-incrimination.[30]

TRIAL AND SENTENCING

After the interrogation, children are brought before an Israeli military court for
a hearing. They enter the courtroom in leg chains and shackles, wearing prison
uniforms. Most children meet their lawyers for the first time when they are taken
to court. Weak evidence against the children is permissible in the courtroom.
For example, a child can be incriminated by a testimony given by another child,
or sometimes a single source will suffice. Five boys from the West Bank's village of Hares were sentenced to fifteen years in jail based on one Israeli driver's
account.[31] In the majority of cases, the main evidence against children is their
own *confession*, which is often obtained under duress.[32] As a result, at the end of
the interrogation, most children accept to sign a form, although they often lack
a proper understanding of its content.[33] This is especially so because, in most
cases, the forms are in Hebrew, which the majority of children do not understand. In this sense, children are not fully informed about the consequences of
their confessions, especially because many of them are obtained after promis-
ing the children that confessions are the only way to be released. Although many
children state that confessions were the result of ill-treatment, only a small number of them bring the issue before the court because they fear that their com-

plaints would entail longer sentences, even though international law forbids the use of evidence collected under duress. According to a 2013 UNICEF report, "almost all children plead guilty in order to reduce the length of their pre-trial detention. Pleading guilty is the quickest way to be released."[34] In this situation, children are not given the opportunity to defend themselves. In addition, two of the three prisons managed by the Israel Prison Service, where most of the Palestinian children are detained, are inside Israel. This makes the visits of the Palestinian families, and the Palestinian lawyers, extremely difficult because of the restrictive regulation on entry from the West Bank to Israel. This is especially true as the bureaucratic procedure for granting a permit is very lengthy.[35]

Finally, during the detention period, children have limited access to education. They can select some subjects from the Israeli curriculum, instead of studying the curriculum of the Palestinian Authority. This results in many children having difficulties when rejoining schools after being released.[36]

THE PSYCHOLOGICAL CONSEQUENCES
OF CHILD DETENTION

Article 37 of the United Nations Convention on the Rights of the Child (UNCRC) stipulates that "no child shall be deprived of his or her liberty" and that "[t]he arrest, detention or imprisonment of a child shall be in conformity with the law and shall be used only as a measure of last resort and for the shortest appropriate period of time." These provisions have been put in place to avoid the long-lasting social and psychological consequences of child arrest and imprisonment. This is true especially when such arrest and detention involve excessive abuse, ill-treatment, and deprivation, all happening in the context of political violence. In fact, both being separated from the family and being verbally and physically abused entail different forms of traumatic experiences.

Many of the children we interviewed reported having experienced insomnia, nightmares, and flashbacks during and after the detention. These symptoms extend beyond the period of imprisonment and include withdrawal and avoidance symptoms. For example, one of the children we interviewed continued to have nightmares and experience a deterioration in his psychological well-being. When he was asked, "What would you do if we told you that there are soldiers in the street?" he answered, "I'd run away and hide myself."[37] Another child stated that he avoids taking specific roads that remind him of the experience of arrest. Imprisonment often initiates a psychological downturn for children. For example, upon release, many of them drop out of school, develop different forms of aggressive behavior, and/or disengage with family and friends. A. A., a then-fifteen-year-old, was arrested by Israel in 2015, and following release from prison, dropped out of school, due to his inability to catch up with peers. Speaking of the experience, he noted:

> I was transferred to the interrogation center where they left scars of torture on my body. They used threats and intimidation to achieve their goals and made me confess to baseless accusations under torture. They asked me about things I didn't know and people I had either never heard of, or rarely met. Every time I denied something, they would hit me and threaten me with worse things. I spent five months in that dark prison where the sun could not be seen, and the moon could not light my summer nights.[38]

Some of these forms of psychological distress are addressed by local nongovernmental organizations. Yet the fact that prisoners in the Palestinian community, including child prisoners, are treated as heroes makes talking about providing them with psychological support a controversial issue. Recommendations for mental health care are perceived by many Palestinians as an insult.[39] Wounds are both physical and psychological; the latter materialize as the "wounds inside" that deprive Palestinian children of a normal life as a result of having been placed in Israeli detention.[40]

THE LEGAL FRAMEWORK

International legal instruments have established minimum standards and protections with regard to children in detention. Israel has ratified both the Convention on the Rights of the Child and the Convention against Torture; however, in its treatment of Palestinian children, Israel has been violating and continues to violate many principles embedded in these two core treaties.[41] For example, while depriving children of liberty can only be used as a measure of last resort (article 37 of the UNCRC), Israeli military courts only rarely allow Palestinian minors to be released on bail.[42] In addition, as we saw earlier, physical and verbal abuses are common experiences during the arrests and interrogation,[43] although the use of degrading treatment is forbidden, and the UNCRC establishes the obligation to treat children with humanity.[44]

Moreover, in violation of international legal instruments, Israeli incarceration policies and practices entail discriminatory measures that grant fewer rights and protections to Palestinian minors in comparison with their Israeli peers.[45] Indeed, a situation of institutionalized legal discrimination is in place in the West Bank where Palestinians of all ages are subject to Israeli military legislation, while Israeli settlers are subject to Israeli domestic law.[46] Consequently, two different legal constructions of childhood, carved along ethnic lines, are operating side by side. For example, for a long time, Israel considered Palestinians to be minors until age sixteen, while their Israeli counterparts would become adults at age eighteen. Although the age of legal majority of Palestinians has been raised to eighteen, this was merely a token reform. According to Viterbo, this "reform" has not changed Israel's treatment of Palestinian children, evidenced in the maximum sentence periods or the actual sentences imposed.[47] In addition, until the present day, the Israeli legal system in the Occupied Territories constructs Palestinian childhood, in contrast to Israeli childhood, through a number of subcategories with different sets of rights and protections.[48] For example, children between twelve and thirteen years old can be sentenced to imprisonment for up to six months, while for children between fourteen and fifteen years old the maximum imprisonment can reach twelve months, unless the offense entails a maximum penalty of five years. In reality, all common charges against Palestinian children are more than five years, which means that this maximum sentence limitation almost never applies.[49] Throwing stones, the most common charge against Palestinian children, is punishable under military law by up to twenty years in prison.[50] Finally, children from sixteen to eighteen years old are treated as adults, although tried in separate courts, and maximum penalties are stipulated according to the offense, in violation of the Convention on the Rights of the Child. It is worth noting that a Palestinian child's sentence is decided on the basis of the child's age at the time of sentencing, and not at the time when the alleged offense was committed. Thus, a child who is accused of committing an offense when he or she is fifteen years old will, therefore, be punished as an adult if he or she turns sixteen while awaiting sentencing. Furthermore, as Viterbo's research shows, Israeli military judges explicitly treat young age not as a mitigating but as an aggravating sentencing factor.[51] In other words, Palestinian children are sentenced more harshly because of their young age. According to the Israeli judges, this punitive approach is meant to deter not only other Palestinian children but also adults who allow children to break Israel's military law.[52]

In recent years, partly due to pressure by international and local human rights organizations, Israel carried out a number of reforms, which unfortunately still fall short of equalizing treatment between Palestinian children and Israeli children living in the same areas of the West Bank.[53] Despite these reforms, children still appear before military judges in military courts (for young people). As explained before, these changes did not result in granting children their rights as in the UNCRC.[54] Notwithstanding the reform, structural problems persist, particularly in relation to the judges' qualifications or the prosecutors' wide authority to suspend protections for children.[55] In fact, these "reforms" increased the isolation of Palestinian children. The growing separation of Palestinian children from adults, in military court hearings, in detention, and in prison, expose children to greater harm and deprive them of valuable support, and enable Israel to revoke rights and fragment Palestinian society.[56]

Children's Detention in the
Context of Settler Colonialism

International human rights organizations tend to focus on the humanitarian and legal aspects of incarceration.[57] Following this approach, lawyers and professionals examine the adherence, or lack thereof, of the Israeli policies and practices to international laws and assess the humanitarian conditions in which prisoners live. This approach falls short of analyzing the political context in which these practices take place. To complement this approach, we suggest addressing children's incarceration within the theoretical framework of "settler-colonialism."[58] In drawing the lines between classical forms of colonialism and settler colonialism, Wolfe argues that, unlike the former, which were "primarily established to extract surplus value from indigenous labour," the latter is "premised on displacing indigenous [peoples]. . . from the land."[59] For him, settler colonialism is a structure and not a one-off event, with the logic of elimination at its core.[60] The elimination in question is principally motived by the access to territory, and not race, religion, ethnicity, and so forth, per se. In his words, "[t]erritoriality is settler colonialism's specific, irreducible element."[61]

The Zionist movement pre-1948 and Israel proper are part of a settler-colonial project. For Veracini, policies of criminalization and incarceration are an integral part of any settler-colonial project, as will be explained here.[62]

The Criminalization of Palestinian Children

Israel constructs Palestinian children as security threats.[63] Or, as one child in our study so aptly commented:

> They [Israeli authorities] think whoever is born [among the Palestinians] is impacted by the surroundings, be he an adult or a child it does not matter, they think that Palestinians are a lifelong threat for their State. . . . Of course the army is scared of us . . . I am sure of it . . . they are scared of us.[64]
> —Tariq, Alarroub Camp, March 2016

Nadera Shalhoub-Kevorkian, a leading scholar on the conflict, argues that Israel perceives Palestinian children in "zoological terms," "situating them as unwanted others."[65] This entails a process of dehumanization, in which children are pushed out of childhood. In doing so, children lose their rights, as defined in international legal instruments and frameworks.[66] For example, their right to resist the illegal Israeli occupation often results in incarceration. These children find themselves in spaces of death, being criminalized for being Palestinian, in places like East Jerusalem, where Israeli state violence serves as a colonial tool of suppression. In the story of Rasha and Samer, a Palestinian couple from Jerusalem, who had to get a permit to bury their baby, who was suffocated to death by Israeli tear gas fired in their neighborhood, the mother recalled: "The area was packed with soldiers, and it took us a while to convince them to allow us to take her to the hospital. I carried her out, took her to the street, showed the soldiers that she is not breathing, that she needs a hospital. I ran with her in the middle of a street filled with military jeeps, soldiers, and police cars, but we were late, too late. She died in my arms. I couldn't do anything to help her."[67] From this story and many others, it appears evident that these children are criminalized for the mere fact of being Palestinian.

Incarceration, Transfers, and Depoliticization

Israeli incarceration of Palestinians often entails practices that are in violation of international law. This includes torture and transfer to Israeli-controlled areas largely inaccessible to family members living in the West Bank.[68] According to Anadolu News Agency, Israel detains Palestinian children in Ofer Prison in the West Bank, and Hasharon and Megiddo Prisons inside Israel. Detaining children outside the occupied territory violates international law and the Geneva Conventions and lies at the heart of settler colonialism, which is premised on the need to push the indigenous population out of their territory while bringing settlers in.[69] In this context, "unchilding" becomes a racialized process, in the framework of a dispossession produced by settlers that impacts children as a group.[70]

In the context of the West Bank, incarceration not only involves the transfer of a vital part of the population away from their community and the temporary breaking down of family and communal ties; it also, and more importantly, entails an attempt at depoliticizing the younger generations, not only on a temporary basis during the period of incarceration but also permanently after their release. Practices related to depoliticizing children and their families range from inculcating fear to attempts at recruiting minors as informants for the Israeli security apparatus.[71] It is important to note that children are the bearers of values for the next generation of Palestinians. Thus, depoliticization is a technique to eliminate nationalist ideals, such as the right to exist or to self-determination as a *people*. As Kimmerling puts it, Palestinians face *politicide*, or "the dissolution of the Palestinians' existence as [a] legitimate social, political, and economic entity."[72]

The ordeal of Palestinian child prisoner Ahmad Manasrah holds a particular significance in the practices Israel imposes on child prisoners, especially solitary confinement. Arrested in 2015 in Jerusalem after being shot, humiliated, and left to bleed by Israeli settlers for a long time, Manasrah became a national hero after footage of his interrogation was revealed in which an Israeli integrator screamed at him, accusing him of not telling the truth, as the child repeatedly said, "I can't remember." Manasrah has spent much of his nine-and-a-half-year sentence in solitary confinement and Israel refused to early-release him or move him out of solitary confinement, although his psychological condition has worsened, claiming that he was arrested on "terrorism charges." Ahmad's cousin, Hassan, was killed next to him after a group of Israeli settlers accused them of attempting to carry out a stabbing attack, an accusation the family completely refuses.

Examples from our fieldwork indicate that many formerly detained and incarcerated children say they would abstain from committing the same acts for which they were taken to prison. Children report that their run-ins with the law create a new form of pressure to not *put themselves and their family in danger*, which can be read as a form of depoliticization. As one of the children we interviewed reported: "I do whatever it takes not to end up in the prison again, I'll never get involved in politics."[73] However, arrest and detention do not depoliticize all children. Some children become even more politicized by joining political movements or by becoming active in cultural centers in the camps. This was the case for Yazan Al-Sharbati, from Hebron's Shuhada Street, a particularly tense area of Hebron where Israeli settlers are known to be more violent. Arrested at the ages of fourteen and seventeen, he notes: "They scream at us and beat us. All of this disturbs the tranquility of our lives from the day we come into this world. Arresting me without committing any crime gave me more determination to continue to exist here. I still live in my family's house in my street, in my little neighborhood. I will never leave."[74] Israel's practices against Palestinian children, especially those living near Israeli settlements, make Palestinian children aware of the nature of settler colonialism from a young age.[75]

A Vicious Cycle to Serve Settler Colonialism

Criminalization is connected to incarceration in two ways. First, dehumanizing representations of children pave the way for the use of harsh and disproportionate coercive state practices against them. Second, high incarceration rates perpetuate the stereotypical image of Palestinian youngsters as criminals, especially in the eyes of Israeli society and the international community. Moreover, as Veracini explains, in settler-colonial settings, the indigenous population is subsumed by the narrative of criminalization, which transforms the political value of indigenous acts into criminal behavior.[76] Therefore, the image of indigenous people is recoded according to a new language that erases the intrinsically political character of their resistance to the settler-colonial project.

This vicious cycle applies to the whole indigenous population; however, children are particularly important targets. Children and young people play an important role in Palestinian society and, consequently, in Israel's calculations as a settler-colonial state. Children compose more than 40 percent of the population of the Occupied Territories. This makes the Palestinian society very young and, therefore, represents a potential obstacle to Israel's settler-colonial expansion and to the logic of elimination at the core of settler colonialism. Israel fears that, in case of official annexation, the demographic weight would turn in favor of the Palestinians inside its own official borders.[77] For example, Trump's peace plan, revealed in February 2020, envisions the annexation of the largest possible portion of the West Bank to Israel without its Palestinian population. It also includes the transfer of small portions of land in Israel with some 350,000 Arab-Israeli citizens who currently live on it to the proposed Palestinian state.[78] For Israel, there is strategic importance to demographic policies.

Shalhoub-Kevorkian explains that child incarceration is a tool "that advances Israel's biopolitical aims, just as positing Palestinian infants and children as demographic security threats advances the Zionist project."[79] Violence against children can pass unquestioned as "these persons' bodies and the territories they inhabit always-already signify violence."[80] Israel justifies its abuse and killing of Palestinian children on the grounds of self-protection. As Dunbar-Ortiz notes, "Settler colonialism, as an institution or system, requires violence or the threat of violence to attain its goals. People do not hand over their land, resources, children, and futures without a fight, and that fight is met with violence."[81]

The incarceration phenomenon is not just one revolving around demographic *power*. It also relates to Israel's public relations campaign. Palestinian children play an active role in exposing Israeli injustices in the Occupied Territories. The case of Ahed Tamimi, for example, stirred both admiration and controversy in international media. One CNN headline read "Ahed Tamimi: Palestinian heroine or dedicated troublemaker?"[82] Her story challenges the normative Western image of childhood as a period of play and joy without economic, social, or political burdens.

Children arguably compose a politically active group that represents a challenge to the successful realization of a settler-colonial project. Israel, one could say, intensifies its practices against children for strategic reasons.[83] In fact, children are the natural *successors* in the struggle against occupation, and their actions, when they grow up, are going to be determinants of the future of the colonial project. Thus it becomes useful for Israel to suppress this tendency to political activism, which represents a challenge to settler colonialism's logic of elimination. The political activity of children is indeed a reminder that national anticolonial discourses are still alive and are being passed on to the younger generations. The mere presence of Palestinian children and their "play" poses a threat to the project of Israeli settler colonialism in Palestine.[84]

Detention and the Reconstruction of Childhood

It is common for Palestinian prisoners to receive a warm welcome by their communities upon their release and to be portrayed as heroes.[85] Children are no exception and in fact they receive more sympathy due to their age and the additional courage required for resistance compared to adults. As demonstrated by the local and international media coverage of Ahed Tamimi's release (on July 29, 2018), children are met with celebrations that are centered around the praise of their qualities of steadfastness and courage. In the context of these celebrations, families and neighbors usually march in the streets toward Israeli checkpoints to meet newly released children. Once the child is out of the checkpoint, family, friends, and supporters carry them to their family's house, in some cases to be received by political figures, where more events are organized to celebrate their release. One of the children described the moment when he was released as follows:

> When we got out, people carried us on their shoulders. We had the press and the family and the flags [waiting for us].[86]
>
> —Ali, Alarroub Camp, March 2016

Another child reported:

> Everyone in the neighborhood was waiting for me in front of the checkpoint. Also, the press and the political leaders were there.[87]
>
> —Baraa, Alarroub Camp, March 2016

These celebrations reflect the status these children enjoy within their community, not just upon release, but also later on in life. Former child detainees are often invited to events in appreciation of their time in Israeli jails, such as in the case of child prisoner Shadi Farrah from Jerusalem, who was twelve when he was arrested by Israel in 2015. Since Shadi's release, along with his politically active mother, he has taken part in political events and talks organized throughout the West Bank, including in his hometown in Jerusalem. A Palestinian child who has been sentenced for disturbing the public order or security and has been detained for a civil offense in a Palestinian juvenile center would not receive the same kind of recognition.

Sociological Impact of Detention

The celebratory reception of the child is a demonstration of communal appreciation. Such praise also occurs at the microlevel in the child's family. Children report becoming closer to their nuclear family after being released. They say they receive long-lasting favorable treatment in the home due to their imprisonment experience. Former child prisoners we interviewed say their parents were more willing to listen to them and take their ideas seriously. The praise also manifests in increased emotional and material support. As one child puts it:

> My mother now prepares breakfast for me, and [gives me] pocket money. The family takes more care of me and treats me better.[88]
>
> —Yousef, Dheisheh Camp, March 2016

Children attributed this change to two main reasons. The first comes from the family's understanding that the child went through an exceptionally traumatic and difficult experience and that they have been deprived of family warmth for a considerable period of time. Therefore, this affection becomes a form of compensation for what the child missed during the period of detention. The second reason is that the released detainees are no longer seen as young children. Instead, they are treated as mature adults due to their experience of imprisonment, which does not much differ from that of older imprisoned Palestinians.[89] According to Farehan Farrah, the mother of child prisoner Shadi Farrah, who was the youngest child prisoner at the time of his detention in 2015, "Child prisoners get better treatment by their families and friends because of their imprisonment experience. Families and friends feel proud that one of their children was detained by Israel while resisting it. These children are treated like adults rather than children, as prisons are 'hubs for making men.' It is no longer acceptable to treat children other than as adults."[90] The children we interviewed confided that they acquired a higher status in the social structure of the Palestinian society, due to the political work they performed that is normally done by adults.

Changes in peer groups' dynamics are one of the manifestations of this "upgraded" status. At least two of the children we interviewed reported that they made new friends (older in age than them) after being released, and that their ties with the previous peer group (younger children) have diminished or faded altogether. One of the children said:

> After being released, I made new friends.... I started to hang out with new people.... They are older than me.... My old friends were the same age as me.[91]
>
> —Mustafa, Alarroub Camp, March 2016

Another child reported being treated better by people around him not only in the family but also by neighbors, other children, and relatives. In Palestinian society, the main adulthood markers include physical puberty, marriage, economic independence, and political activism.[92] These social markers form a "checklist"; the more items a child checks, the more likely it is that he/she will be perceived as an adult. In attempting to understand child labor in the context of the Gaza Strip, Alruzzi elsewhere argues that many children drop out of school and work not only to overcome the economic hardships but also to negotiate their status in the family and within society, where they are socially marginalized.[93] Therefore, children's work, and by extension, economic independence, becomes a means through which children disassociate themselves from childhood, and abandoning school becomes a manifestation of the same desire. Palestinian children seek to turn the unfavorable circumstances of their childhood into something that can empower them: they do so, by leveraging the status and recognition from their political activism to be perceived and treated as adults.

Both the prison experience and the transition process from childhood to adulthood are gendered experiences.[94] At the level of national discourse, girls' political activity is welcomed and appreciated, but this does not translate into a fast-track transition into adulthood. Political activism and imprisonment are activities and experiences attaining to the public realm, which is traditionally associated with manhood and masculinity. Women are expected not to break this gender role, otherwise they might be considered disrespectful of family honor and reputation.[95] In the case of women/girls, political activism does not translate into a reinforcement of the social ideals of womanhood or femininity. However, the celebration of female participation in politics can be more pronounced when the woman comes from an already well-known, politically active family (such as in the case of Ahed Tamimi) or during a tense political moment.[96] This is true for women's (and girls') involvement in the Palestinian liberation movement throughout contemporary history, where a lot of women who are active politically come from well-known families. Since 1967, more than 10,000 female political prisoners have been jailed in Israeli military detention.[97]

There are intergenerational dynamics between children and adults that determine each group's respective experiences. Alanen argues that the relations between adults and children are equivalent to those happening between other constructed groups and structures (class, gender, race and ethnicity, etc.).[98] For Alanen, it is key to tackle children-related phenomena not only through the lens of childhood as a social construction but also through a structural generational perspective.[99] The experience of childhood cannot be fully understood only as a reflection of how childhood is constructed in a given spatial and temporal moment but is also influenced by the structural relations between children and adults at that moment. Building on that, political activism and the consequences of detention are not only understood as a reflection of a culture with a heritage of political activism (or through the interaction between the colonized and colonizer), but also as a consequence of child/adult relations in the society. These theorizations are at the core of the *new sociology of childhood* and the field of childhood studies, which attend to children's agentic aspects.[100]

Child political activism in the context of the West Bank can be seen as a practice of agency and a means of challenging the existing social structure. The children we interviewed expressed awareness that detention rendered them adults in their society's eyes, although they remain children.

Conclusion

Detention and incarceration of Palestinian children reflects a consistent Israeli practice against Palestinians throughout decades of occupation. Conventionally, the issue of incarceration in the Occupied Territories has been tackled from an international law perspective, weighing it against international standards and legal instruments. Although this type of analysis has the merit of shedding light on the humanitarian and legal complexity of the issue, it does not provide a comprehensive understanding by situating it in its political context. Understanding Israeli detention and incarceration of Palestinian children requires the framework of settler colonialism.[101] In the context of the Occupied Territories, settler colonialism's policies and practices contribute to the criminalization, and/or dehumanization, of Palestinian children, and their incarceration. These are practices aimed at *elimination*, a key component of the settler-colonial project.

Israeli military detention entails grave violations of human rights, and results in psychological and emotional distress both for the children and their families. However, analyzing children's detention and incarceration only in the context of Israeli settler colonialism creates a limiting colonizer-colonized divide that does not do justice to the lived experiences of children. In considering the dynamics of Palestinian society, it is important to highlight that Palestinian children are not passive recipients of colonialism. In Palestinian society, imprisonment reinforces Palestinian children's association with the markers of masculinity and adulthood, and children leverage this added social capital for their own benefit.

NOTES

1. Zaman, "From Murad Awaisa to Ahed Tamimi."
2. Ben-Natan, "Above and Beyond Denial."
3. Netland, "Exploring 'Lost Childhood.'"
4. In the 1960s and 1970s, some Jewish citizens of Israel were tried before military

courts. Since then, Israeli military courts have retained jurisdiction over Israelis, but they exercise this power only to review administrative orders issued by the military against certain settlers.

5. Human Rights Watch, *A Threshold Crossed.*

6. Aljamal, "Dreaming of Freedom."

7. Shalhoub-Kevorkian, "Childhood: A Universalist Perspective."

8. We thank Ms. Iman Dawoud for organizing and facilitating the fieldwork in the West Bank as the researchers were not able to have access to the West Bank.

9. Hashim and Aljamal, *Dreaming of Freedom.*

10. Bornstein, "Palestinian Prison Ontologies."

11. Addameer, "Palestinian Political Prisoners in Israeli Prisons."

12. Ahituv, "'Endless Trip to Hell.'"

13. Viterbo, *Problematizing Law, Rights, and Childhood.*

14. DCIP, "Military Detention Statistics"; the majority of children in detention are boys.

15. Addameer, "Imprisonment of Children."

16. Tadamun, *A Report on the Situation.*

17. Tadamun, *A Report on the Situation.*

18. Tadamun, *A Report on the Situation.*

19. Issacharoff and Cohen, "IDF Soldiers Suspected of Stealing."

20. Hashim and Aljamal, *Dreaming of Freedom.*

21. Interviews conducted by a researcher in the West Bank with former child prisoners in March 2016. Pseudonyms are used to protect the identity of the interviewees.

22. From fieldwork, Yousef, Dheisheh camp, the West Bank, March 2016.

23. Cook, Hanieh, and Kay, *Stolen Youth.*

24. Viterbo, *Problematizing Law, Rights, and Childhood,* 57, 90; Cook, Hanieh, and Kay, *Stolen Youth.*

25. Human Rights Watch, *Born Without Civil Rights.*

26. Cook, Hanieh, and Kay, *Stolen Youth*; UNICEF, *Children in Israeli Military Detention.*

27. DCIP, "Palestinian Forces Detained 22 Children."

28. UNICEF, *Children in Israeli Military Detention*; Viterbo, *Problematizing Law, Rights, and Childhood.*

29. Interviews conducted by a researcher in the West Bank with former child prisoners in March 2016. Pseudonyms are used to protect the identity of the interviewees.

30. UNICEF, *Children in Israeli Military Detention.*

31. Hashim and Aljamal, *Dreaming of Freedom,* 120.

32. DCIP, "How Was 2014 for Palestinian Children?"

33. DCIP, "How Was 2014 for Palestinian Children?" According to the recent Military Court Watch report, Hebrew documents were used in 71 percent of cases. MCW, UNICEF bulletin, 2015.

34. UNICEF, *Children in Israeli Military Detention,* 13, DCIP, "Palestinian Forces Detained 22 Children."

35. UNICEF, *Children in Israeli Military Detention.*

36. UNICEF, *Children in Israeli Military Detention.*

37. UNICEF, *Children in Israeli Military Detention.*

38. Hashim and Aljamal, *Dreaming of Freedom*, 37.

39. UNICEF, *Children in Israeli Military Detention*.

40. Giacaman, "Reframing Public Health in Wartime," cited in Shalhoub-Kevorkian, "Unchilding and the Killing Boxes," 491.

41. Israel claims, controversially, that international treaty law—including these two treaties—does not apply to its actions in the West Bank and Gaza Strip. Viterbo, *Problematizing Law, Rights, and Childhood*, 30–32.

42. Viterbo, *Problematizing Law, Rights, and Childhood*, 73–74; Bisharat, "Courting Justice?"

43. Viterbo, *Problematizing Law, Rights, and Childhood*, 234–5.

44. UN, United Nations Convention on the Rights of the Child (UNCRC).

45. Viterbo, *Problematizing Law, Rights, and Childhood*, 307–26.

46. Viterbo, "The Age of Conflict"; Shalhoub-Kevorkian, "Stolen Childhood."

47. Viterbo, *Problematizing Law, Rights, and Childhood*, 133–36.

48. Khoury-Kassabri, Haj-Yahia, and Ben-Arieh, "Adolescents' Approach toward Children's Rights."

49. Viterbo, *Problematizing Law, Rights, and Childhood*, 139.

50. In 2015, Israel criminalized stone throwing under its civil law, with a maximum penalty of twenty years' imprisonment. Although this provision formally applies to all Israeli residents, the then–prime minister Benjamin Netanyahu asserted publicly that it was specifically targeted at East Jerusalemites. Viterbo, *Problematizing Law, Rights, and Childhood*, 58–59.

51. Viterbo, *Problematizing Law, Rights, and Childhood*.

52. For more on the logic of incarceration of young children, see Viterbo, "The Age of Conflict," and Viterbo, *Problematizing Law, Rights, and Childhood*, 88–94.

53. UNICEF, *Children in Israeli Military Detention*.

54. Addameer, "Imprisonment of Children."

55. Ronen, "Blind in Their Own Cause."

56. Viterbo, "Rights as a Divide-and-Rule Mechanism."

57. Cook, Hanieh, and Kay, *Stolen Youth*.

58. Veracini, *Settler Colonialism*; Wolfe, "Settler Colonialism and the Elimination." The concept started to appear in the literature in the context of Palestine after being used by the Research Center of the Palestinian Liberation Organization to establish relationships with other anticolonial movements all over the world. Salamanca, Qato, Rabie, and Samour, "Past Is Present."

59. Wolfe, *Settler Colonialism and the Transformation*, 1–2.

60. Wolfe, "Settler colonialism and the Elimination."

61. Ibid., 388.

62. Veracini, *Settler Colonialism*.

63. Shalhoub-Kevorkian, *Incarcerated Childhood*.

64. Interviews conducted by a researcher in the West Bank with former child prisoners in March 2016. Pseudonyms are used to protect the identity of the interviewees, especially being children.

65. Kovner and Shalhoub-Kevorkian, "Child Arrest, Settler Colonialism"; Shalhoub-Kevorkian, "Childhood: A Universalist Perspective."

66. Shalhoub-Kevorkian, "Childhood: A Universalist Perspective."

67. Shalhoub-Kevorkian, "Criminality in Spaces of Death."

68. Korn, "Rates of Incarceration."

69. Pictet, "The New Geneva Conventions."

70. Razack, "Race and Unchilding," 486.

71. These claims were reported during the fieldwork by many children.

72. Kimmerling, *Politicide*, 3.

73. From fieldwork, Ali, sixteen-year-old, Alarroub camp, the West Bank, March 2016.

74. Hashim and Aljamal, *Dreaming of Freedom*, 30.

75. Boudreau, "Radicalization of the Settlers' Youth."

76. Veracini, *Settler Colonialism*.

77. Toft, "Differential Demographic Growth in Multinational States"; Yonah, "Israel's Immigration Policies."

78. White House, "Peace to Prosperity."

79. Shalhoub-Kevorkian, "Childhood: A Universalist Perspective," 238. See also Kanaaneh, *Birthing the Nation*.

80. Da Silva, "No-bodies: Law, Raciality, and Violence," 213.

81. Dunbar-Ortiz, *Indigenous People's History,* 8.

82. Lee, "Ahed Tamimi."

83. Shalhoub-Kevorkian, *Incarcerated Childhood*.

84. Marshall, "Save (Us from) the Children."

85. Baroud, *These Chains Will Be Broken*.

86. Interviews conducted by a researcher in the West Bank with former child prisoners in March 2016. Pseudonyms are used to protect the identity of the interviewees.

87. Ibid.

88. Ibid.

89. Rosenfeld, "Power Structure, Agency, and Family."

90. Farrah, Farehan. "An interview with Farehan Farrah, mother of child prisoner Shadi Farrah, via e-mail."

91. Interviews conducted by a researcher in the West Bank with former child prisoners in March 2016. Pseudonyms are used to protect the identity of the interviewees.

92. Alruzzi, *Children's Work and Education*.

93. Ibid.

94. More than 99 percent of Palestinian political prisoners aged eighteen years and over are men, and nearly 99 percent of those under the age of eighteen years are boys. Viterbo, *Problematizing Law, Rights, and Childhood*, 64.

95. Erez and Berko, "Palestinian Women in Terrorism."

96. Ghanem, "Palestinian Women Political Prisoners."

97. Addameer, "Occupied Lives."

98. Alanen, "Generational Order"; Alanen, "Childhood and Intergenerationality."

99. Alanen, "Generational Order."

100. James, Jenks, and Prout, *Theorizing Childhood*; Jenks, *The Sociology of Childhood*.

101. Veracini, *Settler Colonialism*; Veracini, "The Other Shift"; Wolfe, *Settler Colonialism and the Transformation*; Wolfe, "Settler Colonialism and the Elimination."

BIBLIOGRAPHY

Addameer—Prisoner Support and Human Rights Association. "Imprisonment of Children." December 2017. http://www.addameer.org/the_prisoners/children.

——. "Occupied Lives: Imprisonment of Palestinian Women and Girls." July 3, 2016. http://www.addameer.org/publications/occupied-lives-imprisonment-palestinian -women-and-girls.

——. "Palestinian Political Prisoners in Israeli Prisons." June 2013. https://www .europarl.europa.eu/meetdocs/2009_2014/documents/dplc/dv/palestinianpolitica lprisoners/palestinianpoliticalprisonersen.pdf.

Ahituv, N. "'Endless Trip to Hell': Israel Jails Hundreds of Palestinian Boys a Year. These Are Their Testimonies." *Haaretz,* March 16, 2019. https://www.haaretz.com/israel -news/.premium.MAGAZINE-israel-jails-hundreds-of-palestinian-boys-a-year-1. 7021978.

Alanen, L. "Childhood and Intergenerationality: Toward an Intergenerational Perspective on Child Well-Being." In *Handbook of Child Well-Being: Theories, Methods, and Policies in Global Perspective,* edited by A. Ben-Arieh, F. Casas, I. Frønes, and J. E. Korbin, 131–60. New York: Springer, 2014.

——. "Generational Order." In *The Palgrave Handbook of Childhood Studies,* edited by Jens Qvortrup, W. A. Corsaro, & M.-S. Honig, 159–74. London: Palgrave Macmillan, 2009.

Aljamal, Y. M. "Dreaming of Freedom: Palestinian Child Prisoners Speak." *Türkiye Ortadoğu Çalışmaları Dergisi* 4, no. 1 (2017): 187–90.

Alruzzi, M. *Children's Work and Education in the Context of Political Activism, State Building, and Foreign Aid: The Case of the Gaza Strip.* PhD diss., University of Fribourg, 2017.

Baroud, R. *These Chains Will Be Broken: Palestinian Stories of Struggle and Defiance in Israeli Prisons.* Atlanta: Clarity Press, 2019.

Ben-Natan, S. "Above and Beyond Denial: Incarcerated Children in Israel/Palestine." *Journal of Genocide Research* 23, no. 3 (2020): 478–85.

Bisharat, G. E. "Courting Justice? Legitimation in Lawyering under Israeli Occupation." *Law & Social Inquiry* 20, no. 2 (1995): 349–405.

Bornstein, A. "Palestinian Prison Ontologies." *Dialectical Anthropology* 34, no. 4 (2010):459–72.

Boudreau, G. B. "Radicalization of the Settlers' Youth: Hebron as a Hub for Jewish Extremism." *Global Media Journal: Canadian Edition* 7, no. 1 (2014): 69–85.

B'Tselem: The Israeli Information Center for Human Rights in the Occupied Territories. "Minors in Jeopardy: Violation of the Rights of Palestinian Minors by Israel's Military Courts." March 2018. https://www.btselem.org/sites/default/files/publications /201803_minors_in_jeopardy_eng.pdf.

Cook, C., A. Hanieh, and A. Kay. *Stolen Youth: the Politics of Israel's Detention of Palestinian Children.* London: Pluto Press, 2004.

Da Silva, D. F. "No-bodies: Law, Raciality, and Violence." *Griffith Law Review* 18, no. 2 (2009): 212–36.

DCIP, Defense for Children International Palestine. "How Was 2014 for Palestinian Children?" December 2014. https://www.dci-palestine.org/how_was_2014_for _palestinian_children_1.

———. "Military Detention Statistics." 2019. https://www.dci-palestine.org/military _detention_stats.

———. "Palestinian Forces Detained 22 Children Using Improper Procedures in First Half of 2018." Ramallah, Palestine. November 14, 2018. https://www.dci-palestine.org /palestinian_forces_detained_22_children_using_improper_procedures_in_first _half_of_2018.

Dunbar-Ortiz, R. *An Indigenous People's History of the United States.* Boston: Beacon Press, 2014.

Erez, E., and Berko, A. "Palestinian Women in Terrorism: Protectors or Protected?" *Journal of National Defense Studies* 6, no. 6 (2008): 83–110.

Ghanem, H. "Palestinian Women Political Prisoners: A Sociological Perspective." *Palestine-Israel Journal of Politics, Economics & Culture* 2, no. 3 (1995): 32–36.

Giacaman, R. "Reframing Public Health in Wartime: From the Biomedical Model to the 'Wounds Inside.'" *Journal of Palestine Studies* 47, no. 2 (2018): 9–26.

Hashim, N., and Y. M. Aljamal. *Dreaming of Freedom: Palestinian Child Prisoners Speak.* Kuala Lumpur: Gerakbudaya, 2016.

Hashim, N. *The Prisoners' Diaries: Palestinian Voices from the Israeli Gulag.* Malaysia: Wise Word Publishing, 2013.

Human Rights Watch. *Born Without Civil Rights: Israel's Use of Draconian Military Orders to Repress Palestinians in the West Bank.* December 17, 2019. https://www.hrw.org /report/2019/12/17/born-without-civil-rights/israels-use-draconian-military-orders -repress.

———. *A Threshold Crossed: Israeli Authorities and the Crimes of Apartheid and Persecution.* April 27, 2021. https://www.hrw.org/report/2021/04/27/threshold-crossed/israeli -authorities-and-crimes-apartheid-and-persecution.

Issacharoff, A., and G. Cohen. "IDF Soldiers Suspected of Stealing Palestinian's Gold in West Bank Raid." *Haaretz*, April 11, 2012. https://www.haaretz.com/1.5213077.

James, A., C. Jenks, and A. Prout. *Theorizing Childhood.* Cambridge, UK: Polity Press, 1998.

Jenks, C. *The Sociology of Childhood: Essential Readings.* London: Batsford Academic and Educational, 1982.

Joronen, M. "'Refusing to Be a Victim, Refusing to Be an Enemy': Form-of-Life as Resistance in the Palestinian Struggle against Settler Colonialism." *Political Geography* 56 (2017): 91–100.

Kanaaneh, R. A. *Birthing the Nation: Strategies of Palestinian Women in Israel.* Oakland: University of California Press, 2002.

Khoury-Kassabri, M., M. M. Haj-Yahia, and A. Ben-Arieh. "Adolescents' Approach toward Children's Rights: Comparison between Jewish and Palestinian Children from Israel and the Palestinian Authority." *Children and Youth Services Review* 28, no. 9 (2006): 1060–73.

Kimmerling, B. *Politicide: Ariel Sharon's War against the Palestinians.* London: Verso, 2003.

Korn, A. "Rates of Incarceration and Main Trends in Israeli Prisons." *Criminal Justice*, 3, no. 1 (2003): 29–55.

Kovner, B., and N. Shalhoub-Kevorkian. "Child Arrest, Settler Colonialism, and the Israeli Juvenile System: A Case Study of Occupied East Jerusalem." *The British Journal of Criminology* 58, no. 4 (2017): 886–905.

Kuttab, D. "A Profile of the Stonethrowers." *Journal of Palestine Studies* 17, no. 3 (1988): 14–23.

Lee, I. "Ahed Tamimi: Palestinian Heroine or Dedicated Trouble-Maker?" January 8, 2018. https://edition.cnn.com/2018/01/05/middleeast/ahed-tamimi-palestinian-activist/index.html.

Mabuchi, K. "The Meaning of Motherhood during the First Intifada: 1987–1993." M.Phil. thesis, University of Oxford, 2003.

Marshall, D. J. "Save (Us from) the Children: Trauma, Palestinian Childhood, and the Production of Governable Subjects." *Children's Geographies* 12, no. 3(2014): 281–96.

Military Court Watch. "Progress Report 12 Months On." March 31, 2014. https:/www.militarycourtwatch.org/files/server/UNICEF%20REPORT%20-%2012%20MONTHS%20ON%20-.pdf.

Muhanna, A. *Agency and Gender in Gaza: Masculinity, Femininity, and Family during the Second Intifada*. Surrey, UK: Ashgate, 2013.

Netland, M. "Exploring 'Lost Childhood': A Study of the Narratives of Palestinians Who Grew Up during the First Intifada." *Childhood* 20, no. 1 (2013): 82–97.

Pictet, J. S. "The New Geneva Conventions for the Protection of War Victims." In *The Development and Principles of International Humanitarian Law*, edited by Michael N. Schmitt and Wolff Heintschel von Heinegg. Berlin: Routledge, 2017.

Qvortrup, J. "Varieties of Childhood." In *Studies in Modern Childhood*, edited by J. Qvortrup, 1–20. New York: Palgrave Macmillan, 2005.

Razack, S. H. "Race and Unchilding." *Journal of Genocide Research* 23, no. 3 (2020): 486–89.

Ronen, Y. "Blind in Their Own Cause: The Military Courts in the West Bank." *Cambridge Journal of International and Comparative Law* 2, no. 4 (2013): 739–63.

Rosenfeld, M. "Power Structure, Agency, and Family in a Palestinian Refugee Camp." *International Journal of Middle East Studies* 34, no. 3 (2002): 519–51.

Rosenfeld, M. *Confronting the Occupation: Work, Education, and Political Activism of Palestinian Families in a Refugee Camp*. Stanford, Calif.: Stanford University Press, 2004.

Salamanca, O. J., M. Qato, K. Rabie, & S. Samour. "Past Is Present: Settler Colonialism in Palestine." *Settler Colonial Studies* 2, no. 1 (2012): 1–8.

Shalhoub-Kevorkian, N. "Childhood: A Universalist Perspective for How Israel Is Using Child Arrest and Detention to Further Its Colonial Settler Project." *International Journal of Applied Psychoanalytic Studies* 12, no. 3 (2015): 223–44.

———. "Criminality in Spaces of Death: The Palestinian Case Study." *British Journal of Criminology* 54, no. 1 (2014): 38–52.

———. *Incarcerated Childhood and the Politics of Unchilding*. Cambridge, UK: Cambridge University Press, 2019.

———. "Stolen Childhood: Palestinian Children and the Structure of Genocidal Dispossession." *Settler Colonial Studies* 6, no. 2 (2016): 142–52.

———. "Unchilding and the Killing Boxes." *Journal of Genocide Research* 23, no. 3 (2021): 490–500.

Tadamun, The International Association in Solidarity with Palestinian Prisoners. *A Report on the Situation of Palestinian Prisoners in Israeli Jails in 2019*. Lebanon, 2020.

Toft, M. "Differential Demographic Growth in Multinational States: Israel's Two-Front War." *Journal of International Affairs* 56, no. 1 (2002): 71–94.

UN. United Nations Convention on the Rights of the Child (UNCRC). November 20, 1989. http://www.ohchr.org/en/professionalinterest/pages/crc.aspx.

UNICEF. *Children in Israeli Military Detention: Observations and Recommendations*. March 6, 2013. https://www.unicef.org/oPt/UNICEF_oPt_Children_in_Israeli _Military_Detention_Observations_and_Recommendations_-_6_March_2013.pdf. https://www.unicef.org/sop/reports/children-israeli-military-detention.

UNICEF. "Children in Israeli Military Detention: Observations and Recommendations." February 2, 2015. https://www.unicef.org/sop/media/216/file/Children%20in%20 Israeli%20Military.pdf.

Usher, G. "Children of Palestine." *Race & Class*, 32, no. 4 (1991): 1–18.

Veracini, L. "The Other Shift: Settler Colonialism, Israel, and the Occupation." *Journal of Palestine Studies* 42, no. 2 (2013): 26–42.

———. *Settler Colonialism: A Theoretical Overview*. London: Palgrave, 2010.

Viterbo, H. "The Age of Conflict: Rethinking Childhood, Law, and Age through the Israeli-Palestinian Case." In *Law and Childhood Studies*, edited by M. Freeman, 133–55. Current Legal Issues 14. Oxford: Oxford University Press, 2012.

———. *Problematizing Law, Rights, and Childhood in Israel/Palestine*. Cambridge, UK: Cambridge University Press, 2021.

———. "Rights as a Divide-and-Rule Mechanism: Lessons from the Case of Palestinians in Israeli Custody." *Law & Social Inquiry* 43, no. 3 (2018): 764–95.

White House. "Peace to Prosperity: A Vision to Improve the Lives of the Palestinian and Israeli People." *The White House*, February 2020. https://trumpwhitehouse.archives .gov/peacetoprosperity/.

Wolfe, P. "Settler Colonialism and the Elimination of the Native." *Journal of Genocide Research*, 8, no. 4 (2006): 387–409.

———. *Settler Colonialism and the Transformation of Anthropology*. London: Cassell, 1999.

Yonah, Y. "Israel's Immigration Policies: The Twofold Face of the 'Demographic Threat.'" *Social Identities* 10, no. 2 (2004): 195–218.

Zaman, W. *From Murad Awaisa to Ahed Tamimi: The Experiences of Palestinian Children Under the Israeli Military Justice System in the Occupied Palestinian Territories*. PhD diss., University of Essex, 2019.

PART 3

Parenting, Activism, and Resistance under Occupation

Youth Discourse, Objectives, and Strategies under Occupation

Palestinian Children's Political Activism in the
East Jerusalem Village of Silwan, 2008–2015

AMNEH BADRAN

While Jerusalem is the focal point of international discourse on the Palestinian-Israeli conflict, the small neighboring village of Silwan is locally at the forefront of the struggle against Israeli policies of control, colonization, and domination. On one hand, the Israeli occupation power seeks to colonize the territory and Judaize the identity of the space while pushing the Palestinian community in Silwan out of it through different strategies. On the other hand, children's activism in Silwan makes it difficult for the Israelis to move on with their plans quietly and freely.

This study examines Palestinian children's political activism in Silwan village (East Jerusalem) as a "re-emerged phenomenon" that became part of daily life between 2008 and the youth protests that began in October 2015. Children's activism is studied as a component of Palestinian civil society operating in the context of settler-state colonization, alongside three related aspects (political discourse, objectives, and strategies). Such activism also occurs in the context of the implicit presence of the Palestinian Authority (PA),[1] the political entity that was established after the signing of the Oslo Accords between the Palestine Liberation Organization (PLO) and the state of Israel. The PLO and the PA have no formal public presence in East Jerusalem but they function in an informal manner through their factions' members and partisan civil society organizations.

This qualitative research showed positive causal relationships between the intensive and provocative presence of Israeli-Jewish settlers and police and increasing political activism among children, and between the vacuum in Palestinian leadership and a weakened Palestinian civil society in Silwan and Jerusalem and the children's various activities. Often impulsive and lacking clear aims and strategies, such activities failed to serve a well-defined national objective. Nevertheless, the children insisted their activism had spread the discourse of freedom, resistance, steadfastness, defense of land and home, and sacrifice for Silwan, Jerusalem, Al-Aqsa Mosque, and personal houses, and believed their achievements, albeit limited, were worthy. They live/d the experience of "unchilding" and practice/d "lived resistance," both of which are explored on theoretical and empirical levels in this chapter.

Research Approach

Existing literature on children in conflict areas typically emanates from human rights organizations that tend to publish reports that depict Palestinian children as passive subjects responding to their environment, not as actors or agents actively shaping their environment. Examples of reports include the Defense for Children International Palestine (DCIP) overview issues from the year 2000 onward, which focus on violence against children, settler violence, military detention, and juvenile justice; the Community Action Center of AlQuds University reports about its Human Rights Clinic and success stories; Amnesty International's "Urgent Action: Children Administratively Detained"[2] and "Palestinian Residency Revoked as Punishment"; and Addameer Prisoner Support and Human Rights Association's "Imprisonment of Children" report.

While recognizing the interdisciplinary origins of the field of children's studies, this study nonetheless approaches children primarily through a political science lens.[3] This study examines children's political activism from a perspective that considers what James and Prout refer to as "youth political agency" (for a larger discussion of the current debates regarding children's agency, see Morrison's chapter of this volume).[4] This chapter views agency "in proportion to the effects and dynamics that spark off, alter, or oppose certain politicized or politicizing processes."[5] Such an approach takes a holistic view of children, situating them in their generational and social class context as well as civil, economic, cultural, and racial context. A critical aspect of that context for Palestinian children is settler colonialism, which "requires and produces settlers as racially superior and thus entitled to the land, and Palestinians as racially inferior and disposable. This intrinsic link between land theft and race is something we readily see when we focus on the treatment of children."[6] A critical feature of settler colonialism is unchilding, or the authorized eviction of children from childhood, the construction of children as nonchild-like, through multiple means that penetrate their lives, bodies, and intimate spaces.[7]

In the East Jerusalem village of Silwan, children challenge not only existing spheres of political power but also the social traditions of the Arab family. Conservative norms hold that adult men, and not children, involve themselves in the public sphere and children obey parents and the elderly. It is often assumed that family is responsible for raising, educating, and to a great extent controlling children's political orientation. This premise ignores the fact that children are also affected by their living conditions, which shape and develop their political agency outside family control.[8] In Silwan, parents do not endorse their children's political activism; they try to stop them, but they do not succeed. One mother says, "I have never met a mother or a father who accepts for their child to participate in protest actions."[9]

This research aimed first to understand the situational context in which the children of Silwan were living. The second stage sought to describe and illuminate challenges facing Palestinian civil society. The third sought to address the discourse, objectives, and strategies of children active in opposing Israeli policies, while the fourth stage was to interpret results and develop conclusions. Originally, it had planned to use both quantitative and qualitative methods of research, and had started by developing a questionnaire that addressed the main issues to be examined. However, after trying to distribute this to the children, it soon became clear that questionnaires were not effective tools, due to the complexity of the subject, the age of the children, their level of education, and, most particularly, the political sensitivity of the subject. Instead I decided to meet the children in focus groups where I could ask questions and engage them in discussion.[10] The ages of the child participants were between twelve and eighteen. One third of them were female. One focus group included a number of released child prisoners, who at the time of our meeting were aged up to twenty-one years.[11] Focus groups were organized by and conducted in the presence of Suha Abbassi, coordinator of the Wadi Hilwa Information Center. Ms. Abbassi introduced me and I led the discussion while an assistant took notes. Students were given free space to answer my questions and each one was given the floor to comment and/or add an element to the points discussed.

In addition, I conducted interviews with leading figures in Silwan to understand the subject from the perspective of those adults who were active in the public life of the village.[12] Thus, in terms of methodology, it was in the end feasible to use qualitative research methods only, and to discard quantitative methods. The primary data was collected through focus group discussions and interviews, while secondary data was collected from available literature, whether produced locally or internationally, such as by human rights organizations, research institutions, and other scholarly sources that addressed the Jerusalem question.

I. Political Context of Children's Activism in Silwan

Since 2008, the phenomenon of children's political activism has once again spread throughout East Jerusalem.[13] The village of Silwan, which is located to the south of the Old City of Jerusalem, has produced the most frequent incidences of children's resistance activities toward the policies of the Israeli municipality, army, police, and Jewish settlers. This village lies at the heart of the so-called "Holy Basin," an area located to the southeast of the Old City of Jerusalem, which Israel considers of such religious and political importance to Israelis that it must be treated differently from other parts of East Jerusalem in terms of Jewish control, presence, and in any peace deal. This area is targeted by Israel through its policies of Judaization of territory, space, and identity, at physical and symbolic levels. For example, successive Israeli governments have worked actively to alter the demographic balance of the area by displacing Palestinian residents with Jewish Israeli settlers. Judaization policies are a manifestation of the settler colonialism that prevails throughout the whole of historical Palestine. Like other settler-colonial projects, Jewish settler colonialism regards the indigenous population as a threat; thus children are framed as a primary component of the demographic problem that must be monitored and controlled, to sustain the settler-colonial project and its view that the native people "must always be disappearing."[14]

In this political context, children in Silwan became active in response to the daily harassment activities derived from legally justified policies of discrimination, separation, and domination. Children say: "We protest against checkpoints, [the] takeover of Palestinian homes, police harassment [of] us on our way to school and back, house demolitions, and settlers' raids of Al-Aqsa Mosque" (focus group meeting with children aged ten to sixteen). According to Israeli law, which was imposed on East Jerusalem after the state of Israel had illegally captured and annexed it in the 1967 war, Palestinian Jerusalemites were granted permanent residency status. They became residents, not citizens, of the state of Israel and have therefore found themselves under constant threat of losing their residency status, particularly since and due to the "center of life" policy practiced by the Ministry of Interior in violation of international law.[15] They are stateless in their own city and face a structured regime that relegates them to a "zone of nonbeing."[16] The colonial state, to address the fact that they exist while it denies them, imposes a system of subjectivity against them, a system of political structuring of the psyche, which Fanon refers to as subjectification.[17] It is a product of oppression and alienation. The latter fits with the state's definition of being a Jewish state with Jerusalem as the capital of that state, which automatically undermines the "non-Jews," that is, the indigenous population. At the same time, state apparatuses consolidate their efforts to develop the presence, identity, and control of the dominant group in power—the Jewish Israelis. This being the case, there is a discrepancy in citizenship between the dominant and the dominated group, which is reflected by their lack of citizenship status.

From the beginning of the occupation in 1967, permanent residency status restricted the rights of Palestinian Jerusalemites to those specifically tailored by the occupiers. Two and a half decades later, following the establishment of the PA in 1994, East Jerusalemites were again left in limbo. They were not granted Palestinian citizenship, compared to the Palestinians living in the West Bank and Gaza. According to the Oslo Accords in 1993, the "Jerusalem Issue" was to be left for the final status negotiations, which failed to materialize. To minimize the Palestinian presence in the city and secure it as an "eternal united Jewish capital of the state of Israel," the government of Israel and the Jewish municipality of Jerusalem developed a structure whereby Palestinian control of land was reduced to 13 percent of East Jerusalem territory, with less than 9 percent zoned for housing.[18] At the same time, systematic policies of domination were put in place, at the core of which was, and is, oppression. This has been intertwined with the adoption of the politics of fear vis-à-vis the indigenous population, who are thereby reduced to a security threat.

To further lessen the Palestinian presence in the city, the municipality of Jerusalem has made it very difficult and very expensive for any Palestinian to obtain a permit to build a house; thus, a high percentage of Palestinians build on their private land without permits. In Silwan village this is the norm, and the municipality's response has been to demolish houses and facilitate the incursion and presence of settlers in Silwan. Between 1987 and 2011 nearly one-third (31 percent) of the participants from East Jerusalem had lost a home or land.[19] By 2014, Jewish settlers managed to capture or to purchase in the heart of Silwan 80 houses or apartments, while the number of settlers living among 40,000 Palestinian inhabitants had increased to almost 400.[20] This followed from, and led to, the intensive presence of Israeli army personnel, police, and private security guards throughout the village, to protect the settlers and their properties and to enhance an advanced system of control in the area.

As an arm of the Israeli control system, the Israeli police took on the role of protecting state policies of Judaizing territory, space, and identity. In this context, the Israeli police forces undermined Palestinians' feelings of safety, not only in their neighborhood but also in their own homes (focus group meeting with children aged ten to sixteen). Michael Dumper addresses the role of the police in divided cities where the police are in control of security. In areas where ethnopolitical conflict on the national level is evident, the police serve the community that is in power and thus lose legitimacy among the dominated community.[21] This has been the case in East Jerusalem including Silwan.

II. Palestinian Civil Society and Children's Activism

Palestinian civil society weakened during the Oslo period and afterward, due mainly to the PA's policies, intra-Palestinian identity crises after the establishment of Hamas, and changes in the formation of Palestinian civil society's work.[22] On the one hand, the PA developed a competing relationship with Palestinian civil society organizations that were aiming to control the national discourse, and sought to minimize their funds and ways of spending. This enhanced the fragmentation of efforts in both sectors of society (the formal and the informal). On the other hand, the establishment of Hamas in late 1987 enhanced an existing identity crisis among Palestinians. Hamas elevated the Islamic component of Palestinian identity over other components and managed to reach out and mobilize a substantial portion of Palestinian society around a different political platform and strategy for liberation.[23] Hamas's success in galvanizing support for its religious platform and strategies reflected a loss of confidence in the new PLO/Fatah platform, which fit with that of the Oslo Accords and normalization with Israel. This created political division and a reality that later manifested itself in the decline of the PLO's agenda and influence among the public. Consequently, Palestinian civil society became divided and lost direction compared to the period of the 1980s when a national (mainly secular) agenda had geared the work of this sector toward an agreed-upon agenda and strategies. Thus, two parallel civil society organizations operated separately, each with a different agenda and priorities.

In the case of the secular institutions, the focus was on "development and state-building, and confrontations with Israeli occupation policies were contained within the sphere of documentation alone. Some redressed this balance in later years, while others did not, leading to de-politicization and marginalization."[24] Islah Jad refers to "The NGO-isation" of social movements, including women's movements, in Palestine, where civil society organizations/groups gradually lost connection with people at the grassroots level and acted as professional organizations focusing on project planning and implementation.[25] The Hamas-affiliated organizations worked independently, serving a different social and political agenda from that of the secular ones. This had a negative effect on people's feelings of loyalty toward common national aims, and strengthened their devotion to conservative ideas and a family-oriented patriarchal system.[26]

The weakness of Palestinian civil society became evident in East Jerusalem, which was almost cut off from the rest of the West Bank during that period. The fact that children have come to the front line of protest in East Jerusalem during the past few years is an indication of this weakness. The limited actions of civil society groups and their ineffectiveness toward the daily Israeli violations of Jerusalemites' rights contributed to children filling the vacuum and acting. In this context, it is important to note that civil society groups and organizations have historically been linked to branches of the Palestinian political factions. The latter lost, to a great extent, their connection with their grassroots affiliates and could not develop new ones since the establishment of the PA in 1994. The space of civil society was largely contained by the formal sector as mentioned earlier. Also, individually undertaken actions by youth against Israeli policemen and settlers are evidence of the weakened Palestinian civil society in terms of its ability to reach out, recruit, organize, and mobilize.

III. Political Agency, Objectives, Discourse, and Strategies

The escalating tension between the occupying state of Israel, represented by the city's municipality and its apparatuses, and the Palestinian residents of Jerusalem translated into political activity led by children against both the municipality's policies and the settlers and their supporters. This activity increased in 2010, after Israeli orders to demolish eighty-eight homes in the Bustan neighborhood in Silwan—a directive that triggered a wave of confrontations between Palestinian children and the Israeli army, police, settlers, and the settlers' guards. The order involved the largest number of homes to be demolished in East Jerusalem, and in effect meant eradicating an entire neighborhood. One thousand five hundred Palestinians live in it.[27] Children of the families in this neighborhood took the lead in demonstrating against the order, saying they felt they had to defend their own homes.[28] As resistance to Israeli policies, the children went into the streets, obstructing Israelis' movement with rocks, setting tires alight, and throwing stones at the police and the settlers' vehicles. Images of masked children became part of the daily scene, and imprisonment of children by the Israeli police became a daily practice, with lasting consequences. Children as young as twelve were sentenced and fined.[29] Here is one child's experience:

> "Mahmoud" came home to see a letter with his name on it, instructing him to come to the Russian Compound prison facility in Jerusalem. The fifteen-year-old Palestinian resident of the Silwan neighborhood of Occupied East Jerusalem went to the prison with his father, mother, and aunt. He was interrogated for seven hours. "I felt nervous," said Mahmoud, as he quietly explained what happened to him to the office of the Wadi Hilweh Information Center, a news and information center run by Silwan residents. "They took me to a lawyer, then they took my clothes," he recalled. "It wasn't a good situation." Mahmoud spent one week in the Russian Compound interrogation center in a room with four other teenagers. Israeli police claimed that he threw stones at an Israeli

police car and Israeli settler cars passing through Silwan. He wholly denies the charge. "I didn't know how long I would be in the prison. I kept thinking, 'Will I go home or not? Will I go home or not?' It was very bad," Mahmoud said. "A lot of my friends are in jail. It's normal," he added. "But I always think that I will go back [to prison]. I'm afraid of the soldiers and the police."[30]

Another child said:

> The way they entered our house was barbaric, they had dogs with them, they were screaming and breaking the furniture all the way to the bedrooms. They handcuffed me and blindfolded me in front of my family. The soldiers hit me in the jeep and I was forbidden to raise my head. In prison cells in the Russian Compound, I was asked to sit on my knees in the corner while facing the wall. I was left for hours without water [and wasn't] given a chance to go to the toilet. The interrogation lasted for hours, and the interrogator didn't stop swearing at me, insulting my mother and sisters. There was a lot of physical and psychological pressure, hitting, slapping, and pushing. I felt humiliated. When I got out of prison, I felt important and proud but at the same time I feel lost; especially, because I wasn't able to finish high school and I can't find a job. (Interview with Z.A.)[31]

According to the files on child arrest and/or interrogation assembled by a local NGO, DCIP, out of thirty-one testimonies by children from East Jerusalem in 2012, 97 percent had endured some form of physical abuse and 90 percent suffered humiliation and intimidation.[32] It is important to note that children under the age of twelve are usually arrested for a short period only, during which they are interrogated about their actions and the actions of the older ones. In terms of impact, the children I interviewed who had experienced arrest and interrogation expressed feelings of fear, emphasized that their education had been disrupted, and stated that they suffered from financial burdens due to the fines that their families had been obliged to pay.

Activities that were organized by the various political factions followed,[33] rather than caused, the children's spontaneous protests/resistance activities: "For most of the children, no one organizes them—they protest in their personal capacities, then they get imprisoned, and there they get recruited."[34] Children's protests took, and have continued to take, civil forms: for example, ad hoc and/or planned demonstrations and sit-ins, as well as participation in social activities that are arranged by local organizations and address children's needs or provide services to the local community. It is important to note that many of these children belong to families with political history, being active in different sorts of activism in the previous two intifadas.

While children's activism in Silwan continues to be mostly spontaneous, activities are initiated by youth leaders and members of the three major political factions: Fatah, Hamas, and the Popular Front for the Liberation of Palestine. They do not act according to unified, interfactional plans of action, nor to agreed-upon strategies with clear objectives. Their actions are fragmented, unsustainable, and in many cases reactionary. Still, they are keen to organize activities that commemorate national events. In this context, it is important to point out that organizations and individuals use a variety of social media to call for activities or to disseminate Silwan news.

The vacuum resulting from the lack of any credible formal leadership in East Jerusalem has weakened political factions and their ability to coordinate children and youth in any systematic and sustainable manner. The Fatah-Hamas division has also had a negative impact on the political morale of children and youth and of activism in general. A young twenty-two-year-old activist from the Bustan neighborhood in Silwan, who had been imprisoned twenty-eight times, observed that "the street unites us while the leaderships divide us."[35] Most of the children interviewed expressed strong feelings of disappointment toward the Palestinian leadership and felt isolated and marginalized. Still, they continued in their activism of resistance to the Israeli policies.

The children expressed their objectives in their discourse on activism. They stressed that their political activism was meaningful. They emphasized words of freedom, resistance, steadfastness, defense of land, home, and personal houses, sacrifice for Silwan and Al-Aqsa Mosque, protest against wars on Gaza and the murder of Muhammed Abu Khdeir.[36] "They say a stone will not liberate a country, yes, but it can liberate 2 cm or so. It can irritate the state of Israel and the settlers" (focus group meeting with children aged ten to sixteen). They stress that their presence in certain areas and their activism also aimed to save sensitive areas from settlers' incursion in terms of control, acquisition or living, especially in the Bustan area (focus group meeting with children aged twelve to eighteen).

In terms of achievement, they underlined the fact that they had managed to achieve small gains (focus group meeting with children aged twelve to eighteen). First, enhancing steadfastness in the Bustan neighborhood, which delayed the demolishing of houses: "Our protest enhanced the pressure exerted by the international community, especially the EU, which postponed so far the implementation of the order."[37] Second, raising national awareness among the young generation: "The presence of children in the Bustan Sit-In Tent raised their national awareness, it was a learning experience . . . associated activities motivated children to confront the Israeli police and settlers."[38] "We defend our rights, we don't need a permit to do that. They enter Al-Aqsa Mosque without our permission. . . . By protesting we raise the awareness of our generation, . . . the old (Palestinians) died but the young did not forget" (focus group meeting with children aged twelve to eighteen). Third, sending an advocacy message against Israeli violations of their rights: "Our activism highlighted the case of Silwan, being exposed to an intensive Israeli plan to control and Judaize because of its location being the closest area to the Al-Aqsa Mosque" (focus group meeting with children aged twelve to seventeen). Fourth, sending a message to the occupier that they did not accept normalization with the occupation: "The occupier assumes that we normalized with the occupation, but this is not true, we teach it [the occupier] that we refuse to normalize with [the] occupation . . . The youth of Silwan are aware of what freedom is" (focus group meeting with children aged sixteen to twenty-one). Fifth, irritating the settlers and making their life difficult in Silwan was an important goal: "The Israeli police and the settlers provoke us, we throw stones at their cars . . . the setters can't live a normal life in Silwan" (focus group meeting with children aged sixteen to twenty-one). "The guards of the settlers killed two residents of Silwan. They can't live safely in Silwan without the presence of their security guards, which protect them and their settlements projects."[39] Sixth, at certain points, the children felt they contributed to forcing Netanyahu to send extra forces to Silwan to control it. "We managed to make Silwan uncontrollable for a period of time or even a month" (focus group meeting with children aged twelve to seventeen).

Despite these expressed feelings of accomplishment, the children admitted that they had not managed to alter Israeli policies in Silwan. Due to the lack of an influential civil society at the Palestinian national level and especially in East Jerusalem, this was hardly surprising.[40] Also, we need not underestimate the existing asymmetry of power between the occupied and the occupier.

Conclusion

This research shows the "lived resistance" model that Palestinian children in Silwan practice/d in their daily life. It shows the hardships and the "unchilding" process they live through and its impact on them. It manifests a model of political agency that, despite its limited results in changing the structure of power, managed to develop a narrative of resistance among children and youth that refuses to normalize with the occupation.

The research concludes that there is a positive causal relationship between Israel's settler-colonial regime and the targeting of Palestinian children by the intensive presence of settlers and Israeli police and their provocations, as well as the increase in children's political activism. There is also a positive causal relationship between the political history of a child's family and his/her involvement in political activism during the previous two intifadas. In addition, there is a causal relationship between the leadership vacuum and the nature of the activities that children carry out, these being, in many cases, reactionary and without clear objectives and strategies, and thus unable to serve a clear national objective. The researcher also wonders whether the existing grassroots leaders have set clear objectives and strategies for themselves.

This research suggests several new perspectives on the phenomenon of Palestinian children and youth activism and protest. The level of disappointment experienced by children toward the Palestinian leadership is strongly articulated—they feel isolated and marginalized by the leaders. They express a belief that they can contribute to the struggle against the occupation (as a manifestation of the settler-colonial system), to protecting Al-Aqsa Mosque, and to making Silwan ungovernable. They think that their protest contributes to a process of raising awareness, and they refuse to allow the occupation to become normalized into their consciousness. My observation is that they are full of energy and hope, despite the fact that the effects of activism on children are evident in the numerous cases of imprisonment, dropping out of school, and psychological problems.

This fits with the conclusions arrived at by researchers as a result of other case studies. Studying the impact of trauma on children in Ein Shams refugee camp in Tulkarm, Veronese and Castiglioni concluded that children continue to display positive functioning in terms of adjustment to trauma, while Shalhoub-Kevorkian confirmed that although the subjects of her research experienced *qahr*, that is, subjugation, fear, sadness, and at times were depressed and angry, at other times they felt they had the power to resist.[41] Children are both victims and active protestors.

The political division between Fatah and Hamas and the weakened civil society have affected them deeply and have further undermined the credibility of Palestinian leadership/s in their eyes. In answer to my question "Do you feel a need for leadership to guide you in your struggle?" one child aged twelve replied: "No, because if there is one [leadership], it will split." This research challenges top-down political models of socialization. It proves that grassroots political socialization could be effective if well organized and planned. As such, several questions arise from it. What can be done to rebuild Palestinian civil society and what role is expected from children and youth? Since children and youth personify great potential, what are the best policies to invest in human development while living under a settler-colonial regime but striving for liberation? What further threats can a settler-colonial regime inflict on children and their future, and how can these be addressed—locally, nationally, and internationally?

NOTES

1. Hilal, "Civil Society in Palestine," 10.

2. This report/appeal explains the case of three minors from Silwan and Jabal Mukaber neighborhoods who were administratively detained in November 2015. They are accused of throwing stones and calling for actions through social media.

3. Rothstein, "How Childhood Has Changed!"

4. James and Prout, *Constructing and Reconstructing Childhood*, 39.

5. Dean, "Introduction: the Interface of Political Theory," 20.

6. Razack, "Race and Unchilding," 1.

7. Shalhoub-Kevorkian, *Incarcerated Childhood*, 92–122.

8. For a detailed look at this phenomenon, see Habashi's *Political Socialization of Youth*. The tension between young men's activism and its challenge to conservative family norms and power arrangements is explored in Peteet's "Male Gender and Rituals of Resistance."

9. Interview with Sahar Abbassi, coordinator of the Women and Children Project at the Mada Center.

10. Aware of the general guidelines of institutional review boards, I was conscious of the need to protect the "human subjects" of my research, i.e., children under the age of eighteen, in addition to youths aged over eighteen. Therefore, my interviews with them were coordinated with the administrative staff of two child- and youth-oriented institutions in Silwan. The "subjects" were interviewed inside the premises of the two institutions, using a focus group setting. I explained the objectives of the research to them, and made sure that confidentiality was safeguarded and that their names were not revealed. The interviews were documented, and random nonidentifying initials were used when referring to any of the respondents.

11. According to the United Nations Convention on the Rights of the Child, a child is defined as being under eighteen years of age (see UNICEF Guiding Principles, August 2017). Nevertheless—and again according to the UN—the definition of youth as an age group refers specifically to young individuals aged between fifteen and twenty-four years. This is also the formal specification of the World Bank, the Arab League, and the Palestinian Bureau of Statistics. (See Al-Batnieji, "Al-shabab . . . dirasa fi al-mafhum," 9). Thus the ages of children and youths overlap by several years.

12. As a resident of Abu Tor, one of the neighborhoods of Silwan, I am familiar with the community of activists in the area.

13. Previous children's activism occurred during the first intifada (1987–93), a period during which the chairman of the Palestine Liberation Organization (PLO), Yasser Arafat, applied the term "The Children of the Stone." Children and youth were at the forefront of the uprising and "the images of skinny, *keffiyeh*-masked youngsters throwing stones at Israeli soldiers and tanks . . . flooded the world's TV screens." A recent study reveals that over 80 percent of young men and 50 percent of young women participated in different types of actions in the first intifada as part of their struggle for self-determination, dignity, and basic rights (see Barber et al., "Whither the 'Children of the Stone'?" 78).

14. Shalhoub-Kevorkian, *Security Theology, Surveillance*, 7.

15. The "center of life" policy has been applied since 1995 by the Israeli Ministry of Interior on the basis that permanent residency status is not like citizenship, but rather is a matter of daily reality, i.e., residing within demarcated municipality borders. Thus, when that particular reality changes, the license to this status is no longer valid. Consequently, all East Jerusalem Palestinians who have not lived in the city for seven or more years (whether they are in the West Bank or abroad) automatically lose their right to live in their city. This policy ignores the fact that many of them were born and have lived in Jerusalem for years, and have no home or legal status elsewhere. Unlike foreign nationals who choose to live in Israel, it was the State of Israel that entered East Jerusalem and applied its law there. According to B'Tselem records (2023), 14,643 Palestinian Jerusalemites have lost their residency rights since 1967. (B'Tselem, "Statistics on Revocation of Residency.")

16. Shalhoub-Kevorkian, *Security Theology, Surveillance*, 2.

17. Fanon, *Black Skin, White Masks*, 112–18.

18. Shalhoub-Kevorkian, *Security Theology, Surveillance*, 4.

19. Barber et al., "Whither the 'Children of the Stone'?," 91.

20. Figures from the Wadi Hilweh Information Center indicate that 50 percent of Silwan's Palestinian residents were under the age of eighteen, and 75 percent of these children were living below the poverty line in 2010 (Kestler-D'Amours, "Targeting Silwan's Children"). Wadi Hilweh Information Center, "Israeli Settlers Takeover Apartment."

21. Dumper, "Policing Divided Cities," 5–8.

22. Badran, "Women, Peace-Building, and Political Development in Palestine," 11.

23. 'Abd al-'Ati, "Al-shabab al-filistini," 20–21.

24. Salem, "Civil Society in Palestine," 5.

25. Ishaq and Salman, "Al-Quds watahadiyyat tams al-hawiyya," 8–9.

26. 'Abd al-'Ati, "Al-shabab al-filistini," 20–21.

27. Interview with Sahar Abbassi.

28. Interview with Sahar Abbassi, the coordinator of the Women and Children Project at the Mada Center in Silwan. She belongs to one of the biggest families in Silwan and she resides there. She is considered a credible person who children and their families trust.

29. Figures from DCIP indicate that between five hundred and seven hundred children are detained and persecuted every year.

30. Kestler-D'Amours, "Targeting Silwan's Children."

31. This child from Silwan was imprisoned many times as a young boy. He was twenty-one when interviewed.

32. DCIP, "Arrest and Abuse by Israeli Police."

33. This situation is different from that occurring during the first intifada, when political factions took the lead in mobilizing all sectors of society—albeit in the absence of a common or a specific strategy concerning the city (see Latendresse, *Jerusalem, 1967–1994*, 51).

34. Interview with Adnan Ghaith.

35. Interview with Z.A., a longtime child activist who was detained many times.

36. Abu Khdeir was a sixteen-year-old child from East Jerusalem who was beaten and burnt alive by Jewish extremists on July 2, 2014.

37. Interview with Sahar Abbassi. She frequently repeated a statement by the children that their activism made it difficult for the Israeli municipality and government to go ahead with the demolishing order.

38. Interview with Riham Hamdallah, twenty-two years old.

39. Interview with Adnan Ghaith.

40. It should be noted that when the components of Palestinian civil society are discussed, Palestinian political factions are integral elements of it. In the Palestinian context, political factions historically took the lead in organizing the Palestinian people around the liberation agenda; they also established many organizations, some of which continue as leading NGOs and unions.

41. Veronese and Castiglioni, "When the Doors of Hell Close," 13; Shalhoub-Kevorkian, "Political Economy of Children's Trauma," 337–39.

BIBLIOGRAPHY

PRIMARY SOURCES

Focus Group Meetings

Four such meetings took place between the author and children in Silwan:

6 children aged 10–16, on February 5, 2015
5 children aged 12–17, on February 25, 2015
10 children aged 12–18, on April 13, 2015
8 children aged 10–15, on March 14, 2015
4 children aged 16–21, on April 2015 (These last were ex-prisoners.)

One focus group took place in the Mada Community Center in Wadi Hilweh neighborhood; the others were held at the Silwan Sports Club. All focus group meetings, except that with the ex-prisoners, included both female and male children.

Interviews

Sahar Abbassi, coordinator of the Women and Children Project at the Mada Community Center. February 25, 2015.
Adnan Ghaith, secretary of the Fateh movement in the Jerusalem area. March 26, 2015.
Riham Hamdallah, youth sector supervisor, Silwan Sports Club. March 19, 2015. (She is 22 years old.)
Jawwad Siam, director of Wadi Hilweh Information Center, Silwan. February 19, 2015.

SECONDARY SOURCES

'Abd al-'Ati, S. "Al-shabab al-filistini bayn al-tahadiyyat w'al bada'il [Palestinian Youth between Challenges and Alternatives]." *Siyasat*, no. 37–38, (2016): 20–21, 19–50.
Addameer Prisoner Support and Human Rights Association. "Imprisonment of Children." December 2017. http://www.addameer.org/the_prisoners/children.
Al-Batnieji, A. "Al-shabab . . . dirasa fi al-mafhum [Youth: Study of the Concept]." *Siyasat*, no. 37–38 (2016): 9, 9–18.
Al-Modallal, W. *The Israeli Settlements in Jerusalem: A Study of Settlement Patterns and*

Processes and their Impact on Peace and Security in the Region. Saarbrucken, Germany: LAP Lambert, 2011.

Amnesty International. "Palestinian Residency Revoked as Punishment." January 3, 2020. https://www.amnesty.org/en/documents/mde15/037/2014/en/.

Anderson, J. "Imperial Ethnocracy and Demography: Foundations of Ethno-National Conflict in Belfast and Jerusalem." In *Locating Urban Conflicts: Ethnicity, Nationalism, and the Everyday*, edited by Wendy Pullan and Britt Baillie, 195–213. Basingstoke, UK: Palgrave Macmillan, 2013.

Association for Civil Rights in Israel (ACRI). "The Failing East Jerusalem Education System." ACRI Annual Status Report, Jerusalem. September 2013. http://www.acri.org.il /en/wp-content/uploads/2013/09/EJ-edu-report-2013.pdf.

Badran, A. "Women, Peace-Building, and Political Development in Palestine." *International Journal of Social Sciences and Economic Research* 4, no. 5 (2019): 3742–56.

Barber, B., C. McNeely, C. Allen, R. Giacaman, C. Arafat, M. Daher, E. El Sarraj, M. A. Mallouh, R. F. Belli. "Whither the 'Children of the Stone'? An Entire Life under Occupation." *Journal of Palestine Studies* 45, no. 2 (2015–16): 77–108.

Ben-Natan, S. "Above and Beyond Denial: Incarcerated Children in Israel/Palestine." *Journal of Genocide Research* 23, no. 3 (2020): 478–85.

B'Tselem. "Statistics on Revocation of Residency in East Jerusalem." August 2023. https://www.btselem.org/jerusalem/revocation_statistics.

Child Rights International Network (CRIN). "Israel-OPT: Silwan Children Abducted from Their Bedrooms." 17 June 2011. https://archive.crin.org/en/library/news-archive /israel-opt-silwan-children-abducted-their-bedrooms.html?ID=25302&flag=news.

Cook, J. *Disappearing Palestine: Israel's Experiments in Human Despair*. London: Zed Books, 2008.

Dean, J. "Introduction: the Interface of Political Theory and Cultural Studies." In *Cultural Studies and Political Theory*, edited by Jodi Dean, 1–22. Ithaca, N.Y.: Cornell University Press, 2000.

Defense for Children International Palestine. "Arrest and Abuse by Israeli Police Part of Life for Children in Silwan." February 22, 2014. http://www.dci-palestine.org/arrest _and_abuse_by_israeli_police_part_of_life_for_children_in_silwan.

———. "Number of Children (12–17) in Israeli Military Detention." http://www.dci -palestine.org/children_in_israeli_detention.

———. "Violence against Children, Military Detention, Juvenile Justice and Settler Violence." January 3, 2020. https://d3n8a8pro7vhmx.cloudfront.net/dcipalestine/pages /1296/attachments/original/1433985444/DCIP_settler_violence_2010_report_0.pdf ?1433985444.

Dumper, M. "Policing Divided Cities: Stabilization and Law Enforcement in Palestinian East Jerusalem." *International Affairs* 89, no. 5 (2013): 5–8.

———. "Security and the Holy Places of Jerusalem: The 'Hebronisation' of the Old City and Adjacent Areas." In *Locating Urban Conflicts: Ethnicity, Nationalism, and the Everyday*, edited by Wendy Pullan and Britt Baillie, 76–92. Basingstoke, UK: Palgrave Macmillan, 2013.

Fanon, F. *Black Skin, White Masks*. Black Cat edition. New York: Grove Press, 1968.

Fuqaha, N. "Palestinian Civil Society Organizations and the Palestinian National Authority." *Palestine-Israel Journal of Politics, Economics, and Culture* 18, nos. 2/3 (2012): 31–35.

Gilligan, C. "'Highly Vulnerable'? Political Violence and the Social Construction of Traumatized Children." *Journal of Peace Research* 46, no. 1 (2009): 119–34.

Habashi J. *Political Socialization of Youth: A Palestinian Case Study.* New York: Palgrave Macmillan, 2017.

Hilal, J. "Civil Society in Palestine: A Literature Review." Paper presented at *Research on Civil Society Organizations: Status and Prospects*, a conference organized by *Foundation for the Future, Jordan,* January 2010. www.foundationforfuture.org.

Ishaq, J., and N. Salman. "Al-Quds wa tahadiyyat tams al-hawiyya [Jerusalem and challenges facing Palestinian identity]." Jerusalem: Applied Research Institute (ARIJ), 2004.

Islah, J. "The NGO-isation of Arab Women's Movements." 2014. https://www.ikhtyar.org /wp-content/uploads/2014/06/Jad-Islah-The-NGO-isation-of-Arab-Womens -Movements.pdf.

James, A., and A. Prout. *Constructing and Reconstructing Childhood: Contemporary Issues in the Sociological Study of Childhood.* 2nd ed. London: Routledge Falmer Press, 1997.

Kestler-D'Amours, J. "The Tactic of Arresting Palestinian Children." *Al-Jazeera.* July 8, 2011. http://www.aljazeera.com/indepth/opinion/2011/07/20117211922998201.html.

———. "Targeting Silwan's Children." *The Electronic Intifada.* December 1, 2010. https:// electronicintifada.net/content/targeting-silwans-children/9126.

Khoury, H. "Civil Society: From Advocacy to Social Change." *Palestine-Israel Journal of Politics, Economics, and Culture* 18, nos. 2/3 (2012): 66–70.

Klein, M. *The Shift: Israel-Palestine from Border Struggle to Ethnic Conflict.* New York: Columbia University Press, 2010.

Latendresse, A. *Jerusalem: Palestinian Dynamics, Resistance, and Urban Change, 1967–1994.* Jerusalem: Palestinian Academic Society for the Study of International Affairs (PASSIA), 1995.

Nasasra, M. "From Damascus Gate to Shaikh Jarrah: The Palestinian Sovereignty Protests in East Jerusalem." *Protest* 1, no. 2 (2022): 329–45.

Palestinian Academic Society for the Study of International Affairs (PASSIA). "The Old City, 1944 & 1966." http://passia.org/maps/view/54.

Peteet, J. "Male Gender and Rituals of Resistance." *Journal of the American Ethnological Society*, 1994.

Razack, S. "Race and Unchilding." *Journal of Genocide Research* 23, no. 3 (2020): 486–89.

Rothstein, E. "How Childhood Has Changed! (Adults, Too)." *New York Times*, February 14, 1998. https://www.nytimes.com/1998/02/14/books/how-childhood-has-changed -adults-too.html.

Salem, W. "Civil Society in Palestine: Approaches, Historical Context and the Role of the NGOs." (Civil Society Challenges, Focus 2). *Palestine-Israel Journal* 18, nos. 2 and 3 (2012). https://pij.org/articles/1437/civil-society-in-palestine-approaches-historical -context-and-the-role-of-the-ngos.

Shalhoub-Kevorkian, N. *Incarcerated Childhood and the Politics of Unchilding.* Cambridge, UK: Cambridge University Press, 2019.

———. "The Political Economy of Children's Trauma: A Case Study of House Demolition in Palestine." *Feminism and Psychology* 19, no. 3 (2009): 337–39.

———. *Security Theology, Surveillance, and the Politics of Fear.* Cambridge, UK: Cambridge University Press, 2015.

United Nations. "Convention on the Rights of the Child." 1989. https://www.unicef.org
/child-rights-convention/convention-text.

———. "Convention on the Rights of the Child, UNICEF Guiding Principles." August
2017.

Veronese, G., and M. Castiglioni. "When the Doors of Hell Close: Dimensions of Well-
being and Positive Adjustment in a Group of Palestinian Children Living amidst Military and Political Violence." *Childhood* 22, no. 1. December 10, 2013. https://journals
.sagepub.com/doi/10.1177/0907568213512692.

Wafa: Palestine News and Info Agency (referring to Wadi Hilweh Information Center).
"Israeli Settlers Takeover Apartment in East Jerusalem." December 3, 2012. https://
english.wafa.ps/Pages/Details/116166.

E-Fathering
Constructing Life in Spaces of Death

ABEER OTMAN

> My son, my soul, and my bond,
> Here I am, far from, but close to, your cradle, your throne, your holy shrine, and your eternal immaculate body. I am still alive, breathing, and resisting, with the help of the beat of your tender heart and your rebellious soul that shines above us. . . . And let me, my friend and companion . . . acknowledge and confess, as we approach the commemoration of the ninth anniversary of your death (departure), that this early and forced departure is still tragic and painful for all of us, we, your family and your lovers. The pain of loss, my son, is an open and deep wound. It is more difficult and more painful than any other wound, it never heals with the passage of time, and it cannot be bandaged or lessened by elegant words, and artificial pride or circumvented by equivocation. . . . However, despite the harshness of the experience, and the difficulty . . . we had to derive from your short life, your good and rich life, from your flowing and fervent spirit, from your great dream that you carried, patience, determination, and renewed will, to continue the life we deserve thanks to your sacrifice. . . . Yes, we are still living and breathing by your breath my son . . . and we will keep the promise and stay faithful to the same dream you were lost for, the dream of a free homeland and a better life.
> —Samir

The above 2020 Facebook (FB) post was written and shared by Samir, a bereaved Palestinian father, to his deceased son, who was shot and killed by the Israeli occupation forces in Occupied East Jerusalem (OEJ) when he was only fifteen years old. Via this post, Samir mourns in cyberspace his son's sudden loss. He shares his continuous and deep wounding, which does not heal and cannot be circumvented. He points to the feeling of unending suffocation resulting from the forced loss of his son. Such forced loss invaded Samir's powers to father, depriving him of his fatherhood. Samir shows the agony he encounters in his memory, a suffering that cannot be lessened. Although deprived of his son and disempowered, in this post, Samir reveals that he still resists to survive his loss, to face and cope with his wounds. He rebels against his dispossession by insisting on living, breathing, and pushing back against the pain. He tells his son, publicly, that his new power flows and stems from his son's death.

While this private pain made visible to others in an FB post, and many others like it, provides Samir with a space to mourn and memorialize his martyred son, the significance of Samir's FB post for this chapter is threefold. First, it shows how the Israeli military occupation operates through not just unchilding, but unfathering. Unchilding, as Shalhoub-Kevorkian argues, is racialized violence that constructs and governs colonized children as dangerous others, thereby enabling their eviction from the realm of childhood itself.[1] It is a form of necropolitics that determines who gets to be born and live, and who is left to die.[2] Unchilding results in unfathering, the dispossession of the father's power, right, and license to protect and father his children. Second, this post shows that despite Israel's unfathering of Samir through the murder of his son, he finds innovative ways to carry on his fathering practices via electronic fathering. Bereaved fathers display tenderness, love, and care toward their children, all too often obfuscated by the criminalization of Palestinian men.[3] Third, there is a politics of resistance to sharing personal grief through public online forums, despite the fact that social media in the Occupied Palestinian Territories, and around the world, can serve as "repression technology," strengthening governance and autocratic control in the name of security.[4] Palestinian fathers' FB interactions reveal that, in spite of the heavy surveillance on Palestinian activities via cyberspace as well as the ongoing arrests of Palestinians who post allegedly criminal and terrorist posts on FB and other cyberspaces, bereaved fathers express their own feelings and thoughts cautiously, as a form of liberation and agency.

Samir's FB post, coupled with other bereaved fathers' FB activities, invites us to examine fathers' mourning posts as a rich and insightful social phenomenon. A detailed analysis of Samir's post reveals multiple layers of fatherhood suffering and resistance, including ongoing wounding and never-ending pain, in addition to a complex father-son bond and challenges to livability in a settler-colonial context. Fatherhood implies responsibility, love, care, and attention toward one's children and family, in addition to protection of them and provision for them. Nevertheless, the specifics of how all that is carried out, along with conceptions of fatherhood itself, vary by context. Sometimes fatherhood roles can be fulfilled in surprising and contradictory ways, including through struggles and failures.[5] This chapter focusses specifically on Jerusalemite Palestinian bereaved fathers' whose sons were killed by Israeli occupation forces.[6] How do they use social media to mourn unchilded, martyred sons while facing ongoing unfathering, and how does mourning on social media aid their coping as well as assist their survival and alleviate their pain? I am going to answer these questions by centering fathers' experiences of loss in the settler-colonial context of the ongoing Israeli occupation of OEJ. I apply thematic textual analysis to over four hundred of the fathers' FB posts and activities, which I collected in 2018–2019 after receiving permission to "dig into" their respective pages.

Fatherhood and Fathering in
Politically Violent Colonial Contexts

Colonial policies in countries such as Canada, Australia, South Africa, and the United States have been enormously destructive to indigenous cultures and have massively undermined traditional community and family practices.[7] Forced-assimilation processes such as boarding schools, land theft, and cultural denigration continue to create psychological difficulties for indigenous communities, reflected in family violence, sexual abuse, child abuse, alcoholism, depression, and suicide.[8] Accordingly, violent colonial policies produce fissures in the sociocultural transmission of fatherhood roles across generations and create challenges for indigenous fathers' sustained involvement with their children while challenging their roles of protecting, providing, and building a home.[9]

In Palestine, Israeli colonial violence undermines gender hierarchies and challenges parenting practices, particularly affecting fathers' roles and culture itself.[10] Under occupation, Palestinian fathers face a range of challenges every day, such as poverty, lack of mobility, decreased access to social and health services, and violence, which strongly mitigate against the fulfillment of their responsibility to protect their children.[11] The protection hierarchy typified by the parent-child relationship tends to be leveled off between fathers and their children, mediated by the occupation.[12] Shalhoub-Kevorkian notes that the Israeli authorities take all measures to incapacitate parents and make them powerless while the child is exposed to his parents crying and begging the Israeli military not to harm him.[13]

Additionally, I show elsewhere how the Israeli regime and its bureaucracies operate to handcuff, "muffle," and exclude fathers as the main protectors of their children, homes, and families.[14] Israel invades and penetrates family spaces of safety and togetherness, making fathers constantly fear for their families, both every day and during incidents of intensified violence. Shalhoub-Kevorkian argues that Palestinian fathers who suffer the brutal incarceration of their children and violent invasion of their houses experience unfathering as they are put in a situation wherein their intervention not only cannot protect their children but constructs them as helpless others.[15] All the while, Palestinian fathers insist on offering innovative modes of protection that subvert the structures that strip them of their powers.[16]

Political Martyrdom in Palestine

In order to understand the FB posts, it is essential to understand the meanings of martyrdom in Palestinian society. A Palestinian who is killed by the Israeli occupation forces becomes a *shahid*, or martyr, in the eyes of Palestinians. Martyrdom is a political and/or religious act that is valorized because it contains historical layers of practice and mythology, and sedimentations of both nationalist and religious ideologies.[17] Political-national martyrdom in the context of Palestine is a manifestation of one's sacrifice for the sake of one's homeland, fighting the occupation's powers and resisting for freedom and dignity regardless of religious affiliation. Throughout the Palestinian Nakba, and specifically during the first and the second intifadas, Palestinians sought to memorialize martyrs through rituals that included funeral marches, posters, and political communiqués.[18] Martyrdom is a form of resistance against Israel's practice of necropolitics, or Israel's absolute control over which Palestinians get to live and which must die.[19]

Martyrdom in Islamic theology is not just a sacrifice. Its literal translation is that of witnessing, suggesting that martyrs testify to the violations brought upon them by the Israeli state.[20] In two verses of the Qur'an, believers are instructed not to think of "those dead in Allah's path" as dead, but as eternally living. In both nationalist and religious understandings of martyrdom, the status of the martyr is a mark of deep respect, and elevates the families of those who were killed by the Israeli occupation socially and politically.[21] National solidarity and national intimacy in Palestine have been created through martyr memorialization and the culture associated with martyrdom.[22] Indeed, martyrs' posters and other visual commemoration play a pivotal role in acts of resistance that can accompany more visible acts of demonstrations and strikes.[23] Moreover, some commemorative activities set heroism and nationalism aside, honoring the personal grief of the families of the dead.[24] All these kinds of community actions are mostly welcomed and expected by martyrs' families.[25]

Political Loss and Bereavement on Social Media

In postmortem situations, social-media users incorporate in their networks their own belief systems about afterlife and death.[26] Death in the world of social media is never a singular event, but part of the grieving process and part of the trajectory of meaning-making through social engagement.[27] Continuing emotional bonds with the deceased postmortem is a way to effectively cope.[28] Carroll and Landry note that online memorializing is important to many as it also forms an important narrative of legacy as a type of public memory, since individuals' online selves persist after their bodies have gone.[29] Others use social media to make sense of death, framing and containing it within myths, beliefs, stories, moralities, and emotions that are part of what sensate human beings do.[30] Getty et al. suggest that bereavement posts seek collective support, as users will know where to look for the sort of support they need or wish to offer, be it information about a memorial service or stories from others.[31] The Internet allows intimate communication to take place between strangers and potential friends.[32]

Little research exists on bereavement in the context of political violence through social media; what does exist focuses mainly on collective upheaval rather than individual trauma.[33] De Choudhury's and others' observations on the widely circulated hashtag of #BlackLivesMatter on Twitter indicate that trauma causes people to seek collective identity and reduce psychological distancing, to connect socially, support, cope, and engage with each other as a community that has experienced collective abuse but transcends incidents of police brutality.[34] Lawson emphasizes that African American mothers' grief over the violent and unexpected death of a child is "public motherhood" rather than a private expression of pain because they are driven, in part, by economic and racial injustice as well as a need to articulate their own political subjectivity about justice.[35] Likewise, in Kashmir, Zia finds that mourning in public is a form of political engagement.[36] Reparation practices are performed in both public space and cyberspace as part of bereaved families' coping and healing processes.[37] Lykes and Mersky demonstrate how reparation practices such as exhumation and truth testimonies create an experience of justice for bereaved families and enable individuals to mourn their murdered relatives and reestablish relations among the living and the dead.[38] Reparation processes create public spaces in which survivors can articulate their individual narratives and heal as a nation.[39] Indigenous communities in Mexico are using low-budget platforms like social media to make indigenous haunting visible, to counter notions of indigenous disposability and invisibility, and further to demand that the dead are found, counted, and named.[40]

Social media networks are sometimes used as alternatives in political situations in which other channels are blocked, monitored, or restricted by the state.[41] Social media and technologies under political violence, oppression, and militarization have made visible the everyday acts of the oppressors as well as the everyday coping strategies of the oppressed, and have aided in bringing the voices and daily struggles of the silenced to the forefront.[42] Aouragh notes that Palestinians use Internet infrastructures to allude to the absence of independent territorial places and free infrastructures necessary for free debate, mobility, and democratic decision-making to create new spaces for resistance.[43] Further,

Shalhoub-Kevorkian argues that many technology users challenge domination through counter-technologies of resistance, which she calls e-resistance.[44] Bonilla and Rosa reveal that the increased use and availability of these technologies have provided racialized populations, such as African Americans, with new tools for opposing state-sanctioned violence and contesting media representations of racialized bodies and marginalized communities. Bonilla and Rosa suggest that it is surely not coincidental that the groups most likely to experience police brutality, to have their protests disparaged and misrepresented as rioting or looting, are precisely those turning to digital activism.[45] The hashtag #BlackLivesMatter on Twitter represents a general statement about the inherent value of Black life in the face of state-sanctioned racial violence. The hashtag also reflects ways that social media can reevaluate Black materiality and give African Americans a space to rematerialize their bodies in alternative ways.[46]

Fathering a Martyred Son in Cyberspace

The Palestinian [bereaved] parents are not desperate or looking for warmth and peace in the middle of all that pain; they will definitely find it in the ray of hope emitted from the message of their martyred children, the message of life.

—Jamal

Jamal, a martyr's father in his sixties, lost his nineteen-year-old son three years ago. Jamal is one of many fathers who constantly use FB to write about his thoughts and feelings concerning his son's loss. Jamal tells his FB friends that he, like other bereaved parents, suffers great pain but finds comfort in the warmth he receives from fathering a martyr and sharing it with others through social media. Jamal takes his pain from the intimate, private space of the chest to the public space of the Internet. Jamal's FB page is a space that he controls and maintains by writing, sharing, and circulating his feelings with and among others, therefore it is a space where he creates autonomy in a context of constant invasion and dispossession.

Husam, in his forties, lost his son three years ago, when he was shot and killed at age fifteen. Husam uses FB frequently to vent his feelings:

As-salam 'alaykum my son,
You know today I imagined that you were traveling (as a student) . . . and I imagined that I am writing a letter to you. Every time I gather my words to write them down to you, they shock me. . . . I wrote to you asking to please let me know how you are, about your dorm, your studies. . . . I wrote that I miss you and that I imagine you enjoying your time with your friends and that you have forgotten about your family. . . . . . Oh my boy, I imagined many things.

—Husam

Husam's son was bleeding to death in his arms while he was driving him to the hospital after he was shot by Israeli soldiers. Like Jamal, Husam uses his own FB space to expose his great pain. In return, Husam, like Jamal, gets people to acknowledge and ease his irreversible suffering. More importantly, by addressing his son, Husam creates an alternative space where he can speak and even admonish his dead boy. Cyberspace enables Husam to create a different space that allows him to maintain his connection as a father with his dead boy, temporarily escaping his dispossession in a militarized colonial reality.

Like Husam, Samir, the father mentioned in the opening of this chapter, is a bereaved father who also addresses his martyred son on FB:

> A letter to a brave boy:
> My child, my friend, my dear son, my letter to you today is dedicated to your Memorial Day. . . . I am pleased to tell you . . . that a couple of days ago I started a series of events that suit you and your Memorial Day. I wish to see it as the most glorious, as I was working on it for a long time. . . . I am sure my friend that you will enjoy it and you will be happy about it . . . but to have it in the greatest way I need your friends' support. I am sure that your friends will not hesitate to give the best they can for children, women, and men that sacrificed their lives and painted with their blood the way to freedom, liberation, and life. . . . Here I am sending a message to the whole world and especially to your friends. . . .   —Samir

Samir is a father in his fifties whose son was shot and killed six years ago when he was only fifteen years old. Samir, like Husam, uses a direct call, "my child, my friend, my dear son," to build a space on FB wherein he maintains direct connection to his son without being prevented by the fact that his son has been dead six years. In this space, Samir addresses his son as a brave boy, illustrating that he is a proud father. Samir tells us that his pride also comes from his son's glorious martyrdom. Being a proud father, Samir works hard to organize a series of memorial events as glorious as his son. His efforts to memorialize his martyred son illustrate fatherly protection, as he protects his son's name, bravery, and sacrifice, to be remembered as glorious against the settler-colonial mechanism of unchilding. Samir's efforts to set up such events to make his son happy also manifest his fatherly care and love, as he is attentive to his son's needs even when he is dead. In doing so, Samir is telling us that he regains his fatherhood over his son against the settler-colonial unfathering. In this post, Samir effectively declares, "Here I am, the martyred father, I am doing things for him—I provide, I care, I am proud, and I protect amidst the settler colonial dispossession." In a situation where ordinary fathering modes are not possible, Samir bonds with his son in cyberspace, suggesting that bereaved fathers create their own new electronic modes of fathering, "e-fathering," while facing constant dispossession. E-fathering reflects the best that fathers can do, even if with limited success, showing that fathering the dead is not just possible but also accessible and applicable in spaces of ongoing dispossession. One of the comments that Samir got about this text was from another martyr's father:

> The message of the martyrs is to make their memory an opportunity for giving, working, and promoting the "culture of life." . . . Continue my friend to be loyal to martyrs and to your son.   **—Ali**

Ali, in his fifties, is the father of a martyr who died four years ago. Ali's comment on Samir's post tells us about the connection and bond martyrs' fathers have and how they share it through FB space. Fathers are together in bereavement, and they use FB as a space where they produce and share a common language and further build their autonomous network and support mechanism in public amidst the ongoing unfathering context. Ali tells Samir in his comment that he is not alone in his struggle to carry his son's message, conveying an additional level of electronic bonding: fathers use FB as an incubating environment to share joint suffering and survival. Dispossessed fathers understand each other's pain and new father-to-father bonds emerge from e-fathering.

Ali's comment is also about supporting and strengthening Samir's ongoing process of meaning-making. Ali agrees and emphasizes that memorializing the martyrs is about being loyal to their message and keeping it alive. Fathers of martyrs share the same understanding of the martyred sons' message, as they create their own symbol of the martyrs' deaths by calling them the "culture of life," which implies that the message of the martyrs is about life and not death. Circulating together the "culture of life" meaning-making paradigm is part of father-to-father e-bonding, as the fathers demonstrate a fatherly loyalty to all martyred sons. Palestinian fathers create new spaces, modes, and languages of fathering, building together resistance, hope, and life to challenge the settler-colonial machinery of unchilding as it confronts the dehumanization and the criminalization of their sons.

Ahmad is a martyr's father in his sixties whose son was killed three years ago. He writes this on his FB page:

> To Rami's supporters everywhere
> And to those who are looking for freedom
> It is out there look for it
> Even if you are chained
> Always remember this
>
>   **—Ahmad**

Ahmad directly addresses his son's supporters and friends, remembering them with Rami's message of freedom. Ahmad, like Samir, doesn't stop fathering after losing his son. In fact, he uses cyberspace to continue his duty to protect his son's legacy from disappearing. Furthermore, Ahmad's post reveals that bereaved fathers use FB to maintain and nurture their fathering of other sons. Ahmad expands his fatherhood duties to his FB friends, implying that the father of a martyr is a father to all Palestinians and freedom-seekers. His new expanded fatherhood role includes the responsibility of spreading awareness, cultivating hope, and teaching that freedom is possible, close, and achievable by looking, searching, and seeking, and remembering that chains can be broken. Killing the son is like handcuffing the father; however, Ahmad and other fathers unlock their chains by reproducing their fatherhood in new spaces, modes, and meanings, suggesting that e-fathering contains new duties expanded to other martyrs and supporters, and implying that e-fathering contains "public fathering." Palestinian fathers push their fatherhood capacities in cyberspace far beyond the notion of blood relations of their dead sons and create new complex psychosocial relations, that is, electronic fathering lineages.

The following are two comments about Ahmad's post written by two different fathers of martyrs:

> I wish to you a morning full of hope, determination, and drive that won't be broken and whoever goes on your son's path is invincible.

And,

> I wish to you a morning full of strength, and I wish that your [second] son be released [from Israeli arrest] soon.

Fathers feed each other and exchange determination and drive to strengthen their resilience. Accordingly, cyberspace gives bereaved fathers of martyrs a place to expand their fathering powers to feeding, loving, and supporting each other. E-fathering is also about fathering the other bereaved and dispossessed fathers. Even if the world does not widely acknowledge fathers' pain with support and warmth, e-fathers provide it for one another.

Fathers use FB space to challenge their fatherhood dispossession and their sons' deaths, as Jamal explains:

> Maybe some friends wonder about martyrs' families who write about their sons and share their sons' photos daily. Is it because of the memories that refuse to leave us?! Is it the endless pain?! Is it the fire of yearning that cannot be extinguished?! Is it the inexorability of eternal absence? Maybe it's this and that, but it is also ringing the bell so his sound doesn't fade, and making ripples

in the pond so it does not stagnate. Isn't this our sons' message? Ringing bells and making ripples? —Jamal

Another martyr's father responded:

Definitely . . . this is true.

Jamal's post is about him and the other martyrs' families', parents', and fathers' writings on FB. Jamal explains that writing on FB is a choice they make out of pain, as FB is their space to reveal their burdens and tell about their longing for their eternally absent sons, which helps to both air and alleviate their pain. However, Jamal tells us that it's not only this but the need to make a noise, to disrupt the cruelty of silence, so that neither their sons nor their cause ever fades from public consciousness. He uses his son's story to muddy the clear water, to interrupt the routines of life under settler colonialism.

Jamal's post reveals that writing on FB is a political act to resist the fading of martyred sons' messages of freedom and dignity. Writing and sharing on cyberspace is about preventing his son's death from becoming forgotten, and consequently, preventing the settler-colonial unchilding to be normalized under the everyday oppression of settler colonialism. Accordingly, unfathered fathers' FB activities are their mundane electronic mode of lived resistance. Fathers' e-lived-resistance practices in cyberspace seek to interrupt their sons' unchilding and disposability and resist their own unfathering. Fathers resist by making fatherhood flexible and elastic so that they can expand it and create new meanings and roles, via cyberspace, to never stop being fathers even for dead sons. Hence, e-fathering is about resisting unfathering and unchilding and further creating life out of death.

E-Fathering in Realities of Death

In colonial regimes of death, dead bodies are arenas for restructuring the sovereign relationships between the colonizer and the colonized.[47] Studies that examine death rituals and bereavement ceremonies reveal that they constitute meaningful sites for analysis of the colonial dynamics in Palestine.[48] Scholars note that Israel positions Palestinians as the "disposable other," thus framing Palestinian deaths within the discourses of "security threats" and "terrorism," which contradict the Palestinian narrative of sacrifice and fighting for dignity and freedom.[49]

Bereavement and grief studies suggest that the bereaved should accept death, and cope with it either by "continuing emotional bonds," or by establishing a new, sometimes closer, relationship postmortem.[50] Such studies on grief do not account for situations of unchilding, settler colonialism, and martyrdom, as explored in this chapter. Palestinian fathers constantly fear for their children's safety under the unchilding racial violence of settler colonialism, which constructs, directs, governs, and transforms colonized children as dangerous, racialized others, thereby enabling their eviction from the realm of childhood itself and even from humanity.[51] Therefore fathers find it challenging to protect their children's safety in their homes and in public spaces.[52] As was stated earlier, fathers in OEJ experience "handcuffing," meaning that under continuous violence, Palestinian fathers feel they cannot protect their families, homes, and even themselves in daily life, let alone in confrontations with armed Israeli soldiers and police.[53] As a result, Palestinian fathers experience daily "unfathering" such that neither fathers' intervention nor their nonintervention can protect their children.[54] Such situations push fathers to invent new spaces and technologies through which they can father and protect their children daily, even during arrest and incarceration and after death.[55] Paying attention to the intimate, detailed examination of fathers' writings on FB tells us about fathers' constant struggle to father through their counternarration of loss and death.

The death of a beloved compels bereaved family members to find new meanings in a permanently altered reality, one that leads to activism to change unjust social relations.[56] War survivors/victims show agentic modes in the public sphere and in social media through historical, social, cultural, and political processes as a potential tool for "rehumanizing" the victims/survivors in their societies, where they may often have been stigmatized and criminalized.[57] In addition, Viaene posits that permanent loss implies a pain that cannot be relieved because the loss is irreparable.[58] Such pain is unable to be healed, but what can be done instead is to "repair/mend" the current social/ familial/ psychological tissue. According to fathers' cyber activities and writings shared above, in which fathers suffer but refuse their fatherhoods' and their sons' disposability, fathers renarrate their death as life. In doing so, they repair their burns and wounds by transforming new electronic and public modes of fathering and resisting to interrupt the settler-colonial structures of death and dispossession.

Making sense of a beloved one's death by framing and containing it within myths, beliefs, stories, moralities, and emotions is part of what human beings do as subjects conscious of mortality.[59] Accordingly, meaning-making of their sons' martyrdom by creating the concept of a "culture of life" and circulating it through FB is about e-fathering the dead, in the face of their martyred children's unchilding. Fathers deal with their sons' deaths by circulating them and getting others to engage with them. They refuse to allow the martyrs' message to fade, so they use FB to protect their sons' cause and message by memorializing it among the living. As noted earlier, Getty et al. suggest that bereaved individuals' memorialized posts seek collective support, as users will know where to look for the sort of support they need or wish to offer.[60]

Beyond protection and bonding, bereaved fathers' writings tell us that e-fathering also includes public fathering. As shown above, fathers use the FB platform to expand their fatherhood by educating martyrs' supporters and friends to pursue dignity and resist for the sake of freedom. This mode of e-fathering indicates that e-fathering can be expanded to public and to macrolevels, as Semley and Lawson extend the term "public motherhood" to include political influence in the mothers' communities.[61] Likewise, this study suggests that e-fathering by bereaved Palestinian fathers contains a pattern of "public fatherhood," as fathers try to guide their community politically. In doing so, fathers tell us that by creating public e-fathering, they push their fatherhood capacities far beyond the blood kinship of their dead sons and experience feelings of kinship toward the dispossessed and the unfathered. "Digital kinship" is a practice in which family ties (with both the original family and chosen family) are established and/or maintained through digital technologies.[62] Fathers' writings demonstrate that by enacting public e-fathering, they give support to the dispossessed fathers and unfathered freedom-seekers. Therefore, public e-fathering includes new psychosocial fathering modes that reject colonial loss and disposability, and further reclaim fatherhood, life, and dignity.

Conclusion

The study of fatherhood invoked under the constant, oppressive machinery of death and dispossession in the settler colony reveals the multiscaled complexity of fathering, loving, and resisting. Colonized fathers are aware that their colonized sons are unendingly unchilded, pictured as criminals, dangerous terrorists even in death. Palestinian bereaved fathers use cyberspace to overcome their loss and pain and connect the private with the public to renarrate their sons' deaths and transform old modes and meanings of fatherhood and fathering. In doing so, they create what I define as e-fathering, whereby fathers excavate their fatherhood from the barriers erected by the occupation, thus re-creating their own anticolonial psychosocial practices in cyberspaces. This study suggests that cyberspace provides fathers with a platform to e-father, to resist the unchilding of their martyred children and their own unfathering by cultivating hope and love against their dehumanization and criminalization, thus reviving the martyred sons' message and creating spaces of life for the dispossessed fathers despite ongoing elimination and surveillance.

Between "unfathering" and "e-fathering," this study reveals new understand-

ings of psychosocial loss and lived-resistance modes within settler-colonial structures.[63] While looking into fathers' writings about death and mourning on FB,
I discovered spaces of life, livability, and resistance. Indeed, Palestinian fathers'
writing and sharing posts about their martyred sons requires a different and
deeper analysis that takes the complexities of settler-colonial powers and psychosocial pain, agency, and resistance into account. This chapter explores the need
for new examinations of psychosocial and anticolonial dynamics in cyberspace,
to reveal new complexities of everyday survival against the dispossession of life.
Exposing the psychosocial cyberpractices of posting on FB as resistance can provide scholars with an additional lens by which to examine the dominant assumptions about the oppressed psychosocial dynamics and modes of coping with loss.

NOTES

1. Shalhoub-Kevorkian, *Incarcerated Childhood*.

2. Mbembe, "Necropolitics"; Shalhoub-Kevorkian, "Necropenology."

3. Viterbo, "Palestinian Men's Lives Matter."

4. Rod and Weidman, "Empowering Activists or Autocrats?"; Tufekci and Wilson,
"Social Media and the Decision"; Shalhoub-Kevorkian, "E-Resistance and Technological
In/Security."

5. Richter and Morell, *Baba*.

6. This research included bereaved fathers of sons and daughters who were killed by
the Israeli occupation forces. However, it is out of mere coincidence that the quotes presented in this chapter are taken from fathers of martyred sons.

7. Padilla, Ward, and Limb, "Urban American Indians"; Ball, "Indigenous Fathers'
Involvement"; Wolfe, "Settler Colonialism and the Elimination"; Brave Heart and De-
Bruyn, "The American Indian Holocaust."

8. Kral, "Postcolonial Suicide among Inuit"; Elias et al., "Trauma and Suicide Behavior Histories"; Erickson, "Constructed and Contested Truths"; Bohn, "Lifetime Physical
and Sexual Abuse"; Middlebrook et al., "Suicide Prevention"; Fischler, "Child Abuse and
Neglect."

9. Duran and Duran, *Native American Post-Colonial Psychology*; Hunter, "Fathers
Without Amandla"; Richter & Morrell, *Baba*; Manahan and Ball, "Aboriginal Fathers
Support Groups."

10. Peteet, "Male Gender and Rituals of Resistance"; Johnson and Kuttab, "Where
Have All the Women"; Shalhoub-Kevorkian, "Liberating Voices"; Giacaman and Johnson, "'Our Life is Prison'"; Barber, "Political Violence, Family Relations"; Qouta,
Punamäki and El Sarraj, "Child Development and Family"; Shalhoub-Kevorkian, *Incarcerated Childhood*; Gokani, Bogossian, and Akesson, "Occupying Masculinities"; Rabaia
et al., "Coping and Helping to Cope"; Otman, "Handcuffed Protectors."

11. Gokani, Bogossian and Akesson, "Occupying Masculinities," 212.

12. Ibid.

13. Shalhoub-Kevorkian, "Childhood: A Universalist Perspective."

14. Otman, "Handcuffed Protectors?"

15. Shalhoub-Kevorkian, *Incarcerated Childhood, 76.*

16. Otman, "Handcuffed Protectors?"

17. Khalili, *Heroes and Martyrs of Palestine.*

18. Allen, "Polyvalent Politics of Martyr Commemorations"; Khalili, *Heroes and Martyrs of Palestine.*

19. Puar, "The 'Right' to Maim"; Shalhoub-Kevorkian, "Childhood: A Universalist Perspective"; Steven, "Fatal Choices"; Rimon-Or, "From the Death of the Arab."

20. Segal, *No Place for Grief.*

21. Allen, "Polyvalent Politics of Martyr Commemorations."

22. Ibid.

23. Khalili, *Heroes and Martyrs of Palestine.*

24. Allen, "Polyvalent Politics of Martyr Commemorations."

25. Ibid.

26. Brubaker, Hayes, and Dourish, "Beyond the Grave."

27. Ibid.

28. Rothaupt and Becker, "Literature Review of Western Bereavement Theory"; Klass, Silverman, and Nickman, *Continuing Bonds.*

29. Carroll and Landry, "Logging On and Letting Out."

30. Gibson, "Death and Mourning."

31. Getty et al., "I Said Your Name."

32. Gibson, "Death and Mourning," 422.

33. De Choudhury et al., "Social Media Participation"; Bonilla and Rosa, "Digital Protest, Hashtag Ethnography"; Lawson, "Bereaved Black Mothers and Maternal Activism."

34. De Choudhury et al., "Social Media Participation."

35. Lawson, "Bereaved Black Mothers and Maternal Activism."

36. Zia, "Spectacle of a Good Half-Widow."

37. Martin-Baro, "Reparations: Attention Must Be Paid"; Martin-Baro, *Writings For a Liberation Psychology*; Brandon and Wilson, "Symbolic Closure through Memory"; Lykes and Mersky, "Reparations and Mental Health."

38. Lykes and Mersky, "Reparations and Mental Health."

39. Brandon and Wilson, "Symbolic Closure through Memory"; Moon, "Reconciliation as Therapy and Compensation."

40. Spears-Rico, "In a Time of War and Hashtags."

41. Tufekci and Wilson, "Social Media and the Decision."

42. Aouragh, "Everyday Resistance on the Internet"; Shalhoub-Kevorkian, "E-Resistance and Technological In/Security."

43. Aouragh, "Everyday Resistance on the Internet."

44. Shalhoub-Kevorkian, "E-Resistance and Technological In/Security."

45. Bonilla and Rosa, "Digital Protest, Hashtag Ethnography."

46. Ibid.

47. Mbembe, "Necropolitics"; Shalhoub-Kevorkian, "Human Suffering in Colonial Contexts"; Razack, *Dying From Improvement.*

48. Allen, "Polyvalent Politics of Martyr Commemorations"; Shalhoub-Kevorkian, "Human Suffering in Colonial Contexts"; Nashif, *Images of the Palestinian's Death*; Daher-Nashif, "Suspended Death."

49. Shalhoub-Kevorkian, "Trapped: The Violence of Exclusion"; Perera, *Survival Media*; Shalhoub- Kevorkian, "Criminality in Spaces of Death"; Puar, "The 'Right' to Maim"; Sayigh, "Silenced Suffering"; Allen, " Polyvalent Politics of Martyr Commemorations"; Khalili, *Heroes and Martyrs of Palestine*.

50. Kübler-Ross, *On Death and Dying*; Rothaupt and Becker, "Literature Review of Western Bereavement Theory"; Klass, Silverman, and Nickman, *Continuing Bonds*.

51. Shalhoub-Kevorkian, *Incarcerated Childhood*.

52. Qouta, Punamäki, and El Sarraj, "Child Development and Family"; Gokani, Bogossian, and Akesson, "Occupying Masculinities."

53. Otman, "Handcuffed Protectors?"

54. Shalhoub-Kevorkian, *Incarcerated Childhood*.

55. Otman, "Handcuffed Protectors?"

56. Zia, "Spectacle of a Good Half-Widow"; Lawson, "Bereaved Black Mothers and Maternal Activism."

57. Lykes and Mersky, "Reparations and Mental Health"; Spears-Rico, "In a Time of War and Hashtags."

58. Viaene, "Life Is Priceless."

59. Gibson, "Death and Mourning."

60. Getty et al., "I Said Your Name."

61. Semley, "Public Motherhood in West Africa"; Lawson, "Bereaved Black Mothers and Maternal Activism."

62. Wade, "When Social Media Yields More."

63. Shalhoub-Kevorkian, *Incarcerated Childhood*.

BIBLIOGRAPHY

Allen, L. A. "Mothers of Martyrs and Suicide Bombers: The Gender of Ethical Discourse in the Second Palestinian Intifada." *Arab Studies Journal* 17, no. 1 (2009): 32–61.

———. "The Polyvalent Politics of Martyr Commemorations in the Palestinian Intifada." *History and Memory* 18, no. 2 (2006): 107–38.

Aouragh, M. "Everyday Resistance on the Internet: The Palestinian Context." *Journal of Arab and Muslim Media Research* 1, no. 2 (2008): 109–30.

Ball, J. "Indigenous Fathers' Involvement in Reconstituting Circles of Care." *American Journal of Community Psychology* 45, nos. 1–2 (2010): 124–38.

Barber, B. K. "Political Violence, Family Relations, and Palestinian Youth Functioning." *Journal of Adolescent Research* 14, no. 2 (1999): 206–30.

Bohn, D. K. "Lifetime Physical and Sexual Abuse, Substance Abuse, Depression, and Suicide Attempts Among Native American Women." *Issues in Mental Health Nursing* 2, no. 4 (2003): 333–52.

Bonilla, Y., and J. Rosa. "Digital Protest, Hashtag Ethnography, and the Racial Politics of Social Media in the United States." *American Ethnologist* 42, no. 1 (2015): 4–17.

Brandon, H., and R. A. Wilson. "Symbolic Closure Through Memory, Reparation, and Revenge in Post-Conflict Societies." *Journal of Human Rights* 1, no. 1 (2002): 35–53.

Brave Heart, M. Y. H., and L. M. DeBruyn. "The American Indian Holocaust: Healing

Historical Unresolved Grief." *American Indian and Alaska Native Mental Health Research* 8, no. 2 (1998): 60–82.

Brubaker, J. R., G. R. Hayes, and P. Dourish. "Beyond the Grave: Facebook as a Site for the Expansion of Death and Mourning." *The Information Society* 29, no. 3 (2013): 152–63.

Burchianti, M. "Building Bridges of Memory: The Mothers of the Plaza de Mayo and the Cultural Politics of Maternal Memories." *History and Anthropology* 15, no. 2 (2004): 133–50.

Carroll, B., and K. Landry. "Logging On and Letting Out: Using Online Social Networks to Grieve and to Mourn." *Bulletin of Science, Technology, and Society* 30, no. 5 (2010): 341–49.

Daher-Nashif, S. "Suspended Death: On Freezing Corpses and Muting Death of Palestinian Women Martyrs." *Third World Thematics* 3, no. 2 (2018): 179–95.

De Choudhury, M., S. Jhaver, B. Sugar, and I. Weber. "Social Media Participation in an Activist Movement for Racial Equality." *Proceedings of the Tenth International AAAI Conference on Web and Social Media.* 2016. http://www.munmund.net/pubs/BLM_ICWSM16.pdf.

De Volo, L. B. "The Dynamics of Emotion and Activism: Grief, Gender, and Collective Identity in Revolutionary Nicaragua." *Mobilization: An International Journal* 11, no. 4 (2006): 461–74.

De Vries, M., A. Simry, and Y. Maoz. "Like a Bridge Over Troubled Water: Using Facebook to Mobilize Solidarity Among East Jerusalem Palestinians During the 2014 War in Gaza." *International Journal of Communication* 9 (2015): 2622–49.

Duran, E., and B. Duran. *Native American Post-Colonial Psychology.* Albany: State University of New York, 1995.

Elias, B., J. Mignone, M. Hall, S. P. Hong, L. Hart, and J. Sareen. "Trauma and Suicide Behavior Histories Among a Canadian Indigenous Population: An Empirical Exploration of The Potential Role of Canada's Residential School System." *Social Science and Medicine* 74, no. 10 (2012): 1560–69.

Erickson, L. "Constructed and Contested Truths: Aboriginal Suicide, Law, and Colonialism in the Canadian West(s) 1823–1927." *Canadian Historical Review* 86, no. 4 (2005): 595–618.

Fischler, R. S. "Child Abuse and Neglect in American Indian Communities." *Child Abuse and Neglect* 9, no. 1 (1985): 95–106.

Getty, E., J. Cobb, M. Gabeler, C. Nelson, E. Weng, and J. T. Hancock. "I Said Your Name in an Empty Room: Grieving and Continuing Bonds on Facebook." In *Conference on Human Factors in Computing Systems—Proceedings*, 997–1000. Vancouver: ACM: May 7–12, 2011

Giacaman, R., and P. Johnson. "'Our Life is Prison': The Triple Captivity of Wives and Mothers of Palestinian Political Prisoners." *Journal of Middle East Women's Studies* 9, no. 3 (2013): 54–80.

Gibson, M. "Death and Mourning in Technologically Mediated Culture." *Health Sociology Review* 16, no. 5 (2007): 415–24.

Gokani, R., A. Bogossian, and B. Akesson. "Occupying Masculinities: Fathering in the

Palestinian Territories." *International Journal for Masculinity Studies* 10, no. 3–4 (2015): 203–18.

Hunter, M. "Fathers Without Amandla: Zulu-Speaking Men and Fatherhood." In *Baba: Men and Fatherhood in South Africa*, edited by L. Richter and R. Morrell, 99–107. Cape Town: HSRC Press, 2006.

Johnson, P., and E. Kuttab. "Where Have All the Women (and Men) Gone? Reflection on Gender and the Second Intifada." *Feminist Review* 69, Winter 2001: 21–43.

Khalili, L. *Heroes and Martyrs of Palestine: The Politics of National Commemoration*. New York: Cambridge University Press, 2007.

Klass, D., P. Silverman, and S. Nickman, eds. *Continuing Bonds: New Understandings of Grief*. Washington, D.C.: Taylor & Francis, 1996.

Kral, M. J. "Postcolonial Suicide among Inuit in Arctic Canada." *Culture, Medicine, and Psychiatry* 36 (2012): 306–25.

Kubler-Ross, E. *On Death and Dying*. New York: Macmillan, 1969.

Lawson, E. S. "Bereaved Black Mothers and Maternal Activism in the Racial State." *Feminist Studies* 44, no. 3 (2018): 713–35.

Lykes, M. B., and M. Mersky. "Reparations and Mental Health: Psychosocial Interventions toward Healing, Human Agency, and Rethreading Social Realities." In *The Handbook of Reparations*, edited by Pablo de Greiff, 589–622. Oxford: Oxford University Press, 2006.

Lyon, D., ed. *Surveillance as Social Sorting: Privacy, Risk, and Digital Discrimination*. London: Routledge, 2002.

Manahan, C., and J. Ball. "Aboriginal Fathers' Support Groups: Bridging the Gap Between Displacement and Family Balance." *First Peoples Child and Family Review* 3, no. 4 (2007): 42–9.

Martin-Baro, I. "Reparations: Attention Must Be Paid—Healing the Body Politic in Latin America." *Commonweal* 117, no. 6 (1990): 184–186.

———. *Writings for a Liberation Psychology*. Cambridge, Mass.: Harvard University Press, 1994.

Mbembe, A. "Necropolitics." *Public Culture* 15, no. 1 (2003): 11–40.

McBath, L., and R. Davis. "Our Young Black Son, Jordan Davis, Was Murdered: How We're Turning Tragedy into Action." *Daily Beast*. November 23, 2015. https://www.the-dailybeast.com/our-young-black-son-jordan-davis-was-murdered-how-were-turning-tragedy-into-action.

McCubbin, H., B. Dahl, G. Lester, D. Benson, and M. Robertson. "Coping Repertoires of Families Adapting to Prolonged War-Induced Separation." *Journal of Marriage and Family* 38, no. 3 (1976): 461–71.

Middlebrook, D. L., P. L. LeMaster, J. Beals, D. K. Novins, and S. M. Manson. "Suicide Prevention in American Indian and Alaska Native Communities: A Critical Review of Programs." *Suicide and Life-Threatening Behavior* 31 (2001): 132–49.

Moon, C. "Reconciliation as Therapy and Compensation: A Critical Analysis." In *Law and the Politics of Reconciliation*, edited by S. Veitch, 163–84. Aldershot, England: Ashgate Publishing, 2007.

Nashif, E. *Images of the Palestinian's Death*. Doha: Arab Center for Research and Policy Studies, 2015. [In Arabic]

Otman, A. "Handcuffed Protectors? Palestinian Fatherhood Protection Unlocking Its Chains." *International Journal of Applied Psychoanalytic Studies* 17, no. 2 (2020): 1–19.

Padilla, J., P. Ward, and G. E. Limb, "Urban American Indians: A Comparison of Father Involvement Predictors across Race." *Social Work Research* 37, no. 3 (2013): 207–17.

Perera, S. *Survival Media: The Politics and Poetics of Mobility and the War in Sri Lanka.* New York: Palgrave Macmillan, 2016.

Peteet, J. "Male Gender and Rituals of Resistance in the Palestinian Intifada: A Cultural Politics of Violence." *American Ethnologist* 21, no. 1 (1994): 31–49.

Puar, J. K. "The 'Right' to Maim: Disablement and Inhumanist Biopolitics in Palestine." *Borderlands* 14, no. 1 (2015): 1–27

Qouta, S., R. L. Punamäki, and E. El Sarraj. "Child Development and Family Mental Health in War and Military Violence: The Palestinian Experience." *International Journal of Behavioral Development* 32, no. 4 (2008): 310–21.

Rabaia, Y., S. Kassis, Z. Amro, R. Giacaman, and R. Reis. "Coping and Helping to Cope: Perspectives of Children of Palestinian Political Detainees." *Children and Society* 32, no. 5 (2018): 345–56.

Razack, S. "Gendering Disposability." *Canadian Journal of Women and the Law* 28, no. 2 (2016): 285–307.

———. *Dying from Improvement: Inquests and Inquiries into Indigenous Deaths in Custody.* Toronto: University of Toronto Press, 2015.

Richter, L., and R. Morrell, eds. *Baba: Men and Fatherhood in South Africa.* Cape Town: HSRC Press, 2006.

Rimon-Or, A. "From the Death of the Arab to 'Death to Arabs': The Modern Jew versus the Arab Living Among Him." In *Coloniality and the Postcolonial Condition*, edited by Y. Shenhav, 285–318. Jerusalem: Van Leer Institute, 2004. [In Hebrew]

Rod, E. G., and N. B. Weidman. "Empowering Activists or Autocrats? The Internet in Authoritarian Regimes." *Journal of Peace Research* 52, no. 3 (2015): 338–51.

Rosenblatt, P. C. *Bitter, Bitter Tears: Nineteenth-Century Diarists and Twentieth-Century Grief Theories.* Minneapolis: University of Minnesota Press, 1983.

Rothaupt, J. W., and K. Becker. "A Literature Review of Western Bereavement Theory: From Decathecting to Continuing Bonds." *The Family Journal: Counseling and Therapy for Couples and Families* 15, no. 1 (2007): 6–15.

Sayigh, R. "Silenced Suffering." *Borderlands* 14, no. 1 (2015): 1–20.

Segal, L. B. *No Place for Grief: Martyrs, Prisoners, and Mourning in Contemporary Palestine.* Philadelphia: University of Pennsylvania Press, 2016.

Semley, L. "Public Motherhood in West Africa as Theory and Practice." *Gender and History* 24, no. 3 (2012): 600–616.

Shalhoub-Kevorkian, N. "Childhood: A Universalist Perspective for How Israel is using Child Arrest and Detention to further its Colonial Settler Project." *International Journal of Applied Psychoanalytic Studies* 12, no. 3 (2015): 223–44.

———. "Criminality in Spaces of Death." *The British Journal of Criminology* 54, no. 1 (2014): 38–52.

———. "E-Resistance among Palestinian Women: Coping in Conflict-Ridden Areas." *Social Service Review* 85, no. 2 (2011): 179–204.

———. "E-Resistance and Technological In/Security in Everyday Life." *The British Journal of Criminology* 52, no.2 (2012): 55–72.

———. "Human Suffering in Colonial Contexts: Reflections from Palestine." *Settler Colonial Studies* 4, no. 3 (2013): 277–90.

———. *Incarcerated Childhood and the Politics of Unchilding.* Cambridge, UK: Cambridge University Press, 2019.

———. "Liberating Voices: The Political Implications of Palestinian Mothers Narrating Their Loss." *Women's Studies International Forum* 26, no. 5 (2003): 391–407.

———. "Necropenology: Conquering New Bodies, Psychics, and Territories of Death in East Jerusalem." *Identities* 27, no. 3 (2020): 285–301.

———. *Security Theology, Surveillance, and the Politics of Fear.* Cambridge, UK: Cambridge University Press, 2015.

———. "Trapped: The Violence of Exclusion in Jerusalem." *Jerusalem Quarterly* 49, no. 7 (2012): 6–25.

Simpson, A. *Mohawk Interruptus: Political Life Across the Borders of Settler States.* Durham, N.C.: Duke University Press, 2014.

Spears-Rico, G. "In a Time of War and Hashtags: Rehumanizing Indigeneity in the Digital Landscape." In *Indigenous Interfaces: Spaces, Technology, and the Social Networks in Mexico and Central America*, edited by J. Gomez Menjivar and G. E. Chacon, 180–200. Tucson: The University of Arizona Press, 2019.

Steven, D. "Fatal Choices: Israel's Policy of Targeted Killing." *Mideast Security and Policy Studies* 51 (2002): 1–26.

Strier, R. "Fatherhood in the Context of Political Violence: Los Padres de la Plaza." *Men and Masculinities* 17, no. 4 (2014): 359–75.

Tufekci, Z., and C. Wilson. "Social Media and the Decision to Participate in Political Protest: Observations from Tahrir Square." *Journal of Communication* 62, no. 2 (2012): 363–79.

Veitch, S., ed. *Law and the Politics of Reconciliation.* Aldershot, England: Ashgate Publishing, 2007.

Viaene, L. "Life Is Priceless: Mayan Q'eqchi' Voices on the Guatemalan National Reparations Program." *The International Journal of Transitional Justice* 4, no. 1 (2010): 4–25.

Viterbo, H. "Palestinian Men's Lives Matter: The Problem with Singling Out Children and Women." *Jadaliyya*, May 20, 2021. https://www.jadaliyya.com/Details/42789.

Wade, A. "When Social Media Yields More Than 'Likes': Black Girls' Digital Kinship Formations." *Women, Gender, and Families of Color* 7, no. 1 (2019): 80–97.

Warren, T. C. "Explosive Connections? Mass Media, Social Media, and the Geography of Collective Violence in African States." *Journal of Peace Research* 52, no. 3 (2015): 297–311.

Wolfe, P. "Settler Colonialism and the Elimination of the Native." *Journal of Genocide Research* 8, no. 4 (2006): 387–409.

Zia, A. "The Spectacle of a Good Half-Widow: Women in Search of their Disappeared Men in the Kashmir Valley." *Political and Legal Anthropology Review* 39, no. 2 (2016): 164–75.

The Dialectics of Oppressions
Resisting the Negation of Childhood through Violence

RAMI SALAMEH

> With every event, there is indeed the present moment of its actualization, the moment in which the event is embodied in a state of affairs, which we designate as "*here*, the moment has come."
>
> —G. Deleuze, *The Logic of Sense*, 151

Walking in the narrow streets of the Al-Am'ari refugee camp heading to his family house, Ahmad, a fourteen-year-old third-generation Palestinian refugee of the camp, told me, "I do not feel like myself anywhere but in the camp." When I asked him if this is because of Israeli settler colonialism and the Israeli occupation, he answered, "Not only. I do not feel like myself when I go to Ramallah city center. I feel that I do not belong to this place, and the place does not belong to me." In this context, Ramallah represents for Ahmad a Palestinian space less defined by Israeli control than other parts of occupied Palestine. When I probed Ahmad on the reasons behind this feeling and perception, he answered, "Basically everything [there does not belong to me]: the cars, the buildings, the people, and especially the [Palestinian] security forces."

The tension in Ahmad's perception is revealing on many levels. Each of the reasons for his discomfort that he stated above represents a source of violence. Ahmad's perception of himself as someone out of place among certain Palestinians was a common sentiment among others that I met in the camp within the same age category. It is unlike the general sentiment of older generations from the camp. During the first intifada (1987–93) and the second intifada (2000–2005), refugee camps were the center of Palestinian social, political, and cultural life.[1]

However, over the last three decades, Palestinian society has been undergoing a massive transformation, particularly experienced by those living in the West Bank and Gaza Strip.[2] This transformation has been cultural, social, economic,

and institutional. It is a consequence of two main events. First, the signing of the
Oslo Accords in 1993 that marks the genesis of the neoliberal ideology. Second,
the post-Arafat intensifying of neoliberal policies, an era known as Fayyadism,
in which the logic of neoliberalism has been fully embraced in the Palestinian
Authority's Reform and Development Program.[3] Neoliberal transformations are
spatially visible in major Palestinian cities in area A, particularly Ramallah, yet
are less visible on an emotional level. What has been the impact on perceptions
of life and being, particularly among children such as Ahmad? How does he, and
others like him, experience being a refugee who is also part of the larger oppressive forces of settler colonialism and neoliberalism? What differentiates the experiences of children in Al-Am'ari refugee camp, located just outside Ramallah (i.e.,
the center of recent neoliberal transformation) from children in other West Bank
camp locations?

The Al-Am'ari camp was established in 1949, one year after the Nakba, in the
east of Ramallah in Al-Bireh municipality. Its first inhabitants were displaced Palestinians mainly from Jaffa, Ramleh, Lydd, and Jerusalem. Over the decades, half
of the approximately 12,000 original registered refugees living in Al-Am'ari have
moved outside the camp and into the nearby neighborhoods of Ramallah, Bitu-
nia, Al-Bireh, and Um Al-Sharayet. Currently, about 6,100 refugees live in Al-
Am'ari, an area size of 0.096 sq km, which makes the density roughly 72,916 people per sq km.[4]

This chapter argues that in addition to the well-documented direct/visible Israeli sources of violence that Palestinian children have to encounter and endure
on a daily basis, there are just as powerful indirect/invisible sources acting on
these young people today.[5] By indirect/invisible, I mean violence that is not physical but rather ontological, rendering deprivation in the everydayness of life for
the marginalized.[6] This chapter will begin with an overview of Palestine's changing neoliberal landscape, situating this transformation in a broader context of
what I call indirect/invisible violence. The bulk of this chapter unpacks what this
violence means, particularly for today's Al-Am'ari refugee camp children. I look
at three aspects of indirect violence, as manifest in spatial and socioeconomic
realms, and "state" violence. This chapter aims to understand the perception of
violence from the children's perspective, arriving in the end at a Palestinian refugee child's definition of the violence they are living.

From Social Solidarity to Social Beneficiaries
and the Doubling Status of Deprived Being

On January 2, 2013, both Nablus and Jenin municipalities announced that the
Palestinian Authority (PA) and the Popular Committees in refugee camps had

reached an agreement regarding the more than two decades' worth of accumu-
lated debts from refugee camp electricity bills. The PA would grant remission
to households that agreed to install a prepaid electric meter. The prepaid meters policy (that includes electricity and water), first introduced in 2010, aimed
to install over thirty thousand meters in households, including rural areas and
refugee camps.[7] Demonstrations and three days of strikes by Palestinians living
in the cities immediately ensued. For the first time in Palestinian modern history, Palestinians in the cities, sarcastically speaking, envied the camps' inhabitants and demanded to be treated similarly. Palestinians in the refugee camps,
however, largely rejected the prepaid meters policy, feeling upset that their debts
as refugees—symbolic pillars of Palestinian resistance to Israeli settler colonialism—were now viewed as burdens to Palestinian society. The prepaid electricity
meters controversy soon gave way to another controversial policy that sparked
a public protest. The PA required all "citizens" who request copies of civil documents to first issue a "certificate of payment" as proof that they had cleared their
utility bills. Palestinians in the refugee camp, who largely still had debts, saw this
as the neoliberal orientation of the PA to increase tax revenues while decreasing
public expenditure.[8] These two controversies reflect the tension that exists in Palestinian society due to the new socioeconomic reality.

The literature on the neoliberal shift in the Occupied Palestinian Territories (OPT) has focused extensively on the complex reality(ies) produced by
the amalgamation of neoliberal policies and Israeli settler colonialism. Tabar
and Salamanca reveal how settler-colonial policies and the neoliberal development orientation have fragmented Palestinians and their territories.[9] Khalidi and
Samour argue that neoliberalism, let alone under Israeli occupation, cannot ensure a pathway for sustainable growth in Palestine.[10] Dana demonstrates how the
interaction of neoliberal policies with Israel's "economic peace" approach creates
joint economic normalization projects that undermine the anticolonial struggle.[11]
He contends that the PA elites' involvement in the donor-backed neoliberal development, in the context of Israeli colonization, has resulted in the formation of
a crony capitalist system that relies on a corrupt patron-client regime to stabilize
the status quo, with far-reaching implications on redefining the social order according to the interests of the PA elite, Israel, and the donor liberal "peacebuilding" paradigm. Dana focusses particularly on how society's top-down transformation has been institutionalized through Palestinian civil society.[12] With a
predefined political, financial, and ideological conditionality, he reveals crucial
dimensions of the transformation of Palestinian civil society from mass-based
movements active in anticolonial resistance during the pre-Oslo era to elitist and
developmentist neoliberal-oriented NGOs that promote depoliticization and
values of individualism and consumerism. Clarno locates Palestine at the cen-

ter of global neoliberal racial capitalism, arguing that Israel's neoliberalism compounded with the PA's economic policies have resulted in "neoliberal enclosures,"
or enclaves that "contain a colonized population which has become increasingly
disposable with the restructuring of Israel's economy."[13]

In response to the grave consequences of neoliberalism on Palestinian society,
some scholars have proposed alternative strategies centered on the principle of
"resistance." Among these is the "resistance economy" paradigm, which seeks to
develop theoretical and practical models of resilient social and economic activities in order to deter the combined impact of Israel and the PA's neoliberal policies. According to Dana, resistance economy is a "strategic mode of economic
struggle that is based on a systemic reorientation of the economy and its institutions, and therefore the social structures at large, to operate as complementary
forces in service of the political aspirations and objectives of the Palestinian national struggle."[14] El-Zein suggests a different mode of strategies to develop the
notion of a resistance economy that views Palestinian labor, investment, and bu-
reaucracy as one interdependent nexus.[15] Tartir identifies the resistance economy
as a socially inclusive model that is cumulative, complementary, economical, social, and political, which fundamentally seeks to liberate human beings from de-
pendency and humiliation.[16] Seidel highlights the potential role that local actors
might take for liberation and developing Palestinian political economies of resistance against neoliberalism.[17]

The Oslo Accords in the 1990s and the intensifying of neoliberal policies in
the 2000s have collectively transformed the national liberation project to neoliberal state-building, undermining political emancipation and self-determination
by consolidating colonialism and normalizing life under oppression.[18] Furthermore, the consequences of neoliberalism are not solely political or economic but
also social. El Bashar Masri, one of the most influential Palestinian economists
and the founder of Palestine's first planned city, Rawabi, boasted in a TV interview that "happy Palestinians" drinking cocktails and smoking shisha and walking between clothing shops "are the real Palestinians." A few seconds later, in the
same report, another young Palestinian said, "This is a dream city for those who
can afford to live in it." Grandinetti highlights how neoliberalism shapes the formation of a new "middle class" in Palestinian society that defines its priorities according to market logic and capitalist reasoning. This class is mainly comprised
of "a young, upwardly mobile, business-minded—and importantly—moder-
ate middle class of Palestinians" whose neoliberal values are marketed as indispensable for promoting "peace" regardless of the active colonial dynamic on the
ground.[19] The author concludes that "despite attempts to reframe the Palestinian
resistance in capitalist terms, the occupier will not be ousted by individualistic
consumerism but by collective struggle and resistance."[20] A new social reality for

this "middle class" characterized by an increasing sense of alienation, the domi-nance of consumer culture, and the weakening social values of solidarity contrib-utes to the commodification of national discourse and practice.[21] Taraki, on the other hand, focuses on the new "social imaginary" of the Palestinian society, ar-guing that regardless of social positionality and material resources, there is a new social imagination dominated by "the middle-class idea" as a possibility and as an ambition for life, characterized by new social status, hierarchy, and privileges.[22] Furthermore, this increased awareness of social status and hierarchy is accompa-nied by a growing refusal of resistance and its culture for the sake of a more mod-ern and internationalized culture of life.[23]

With the new neoliberal policies that aim to depoliticize life, neutralize Pal-estinians' struggle for liberation, criminalize resistance, individualize surviving, transform civil society and solidarity into NGOs, and create a culture that op-poses resistance, the very foundation of the refugee camp as a political and prac-tical symbol of Palestinian resistance to longstanding settler-colonial injustice is being shattered.[24] A new invisible wall has been built around refugee camps.

Defining Violence in a Neoliberal Colonial Context

Marxist theory indicates that violence, as an entangled dialectical phenomenon, is an embedded peculiarity of capitalist class societies, in the sense that it is struc-tural and institutional. The Weberian understanding of violence considers the political domain, particularly state violence, as a legalized means and ends to claim and to assert legitimacy. Hannah Arendt introduces a different reading of violence, associated in a nondialectical manner with individual illegitimate or legitimate pursuits. Thus, for Arendt, violence is mere subjective instrumental means, while in Marxian and Weberian understanding, it is also structuralized by the state, the economy, and the law.[25] Walter Benjamin's account on violence as a dialectical relation indicates that subjective and objective violence is inher-ent in the law (colonial law, state law, economic law), where systems of violence (whether by or against the state) are always justified. He calls violence grounded in the law "mythical violence" and the destruction of that law "divine violence." According to Sami Khatib, scholar of violence, all these above-stated definitions of violence (as law-making and/or law-preserving) are blurred in colonial spaces, where "the distinction of subjective and objective, individual and structural vio-lence seems to lose its significance." For example, counterviolence (for the sake of decolonization) may reproduce the colonizer's violence or may also transfer the violence of law-making and law-preserving from the colonizer to the colonized.[26]

From an ontological perspective, we learn that humans are never fixed beings. Instead, what denotes being is the process of becoming, or always transcending what is deemed determined or fated. In the context of this chapter, resistance represents the process of becoming, regenerating life and reshaping the world as a refugee living amid an ongoing oppression that marks the colonized bodies as nonexistent and as the perfect place of death. Neoliberal policies double the state of deprivation. Refugees challenge their reality by posing the question (in Fanonian terms): In reality, who am I?[27] This question foregrounds the dialectical complexity of being-in-itself as mere life "deprived of ethical categories: freedom, truth, and justice" versus the more conscious being-for-itself, which objects to one's conditions.[28] This dialectical relationship is incarnated at the bodily level, such that Fanon concluded that the colonized can only be neurotic: he is penned in. "The first thing the colonial subject learns is to remain in his place and not overstep its limits. Hence the dreams of the colonial subject are muscular dreams, dreams of action, dreams of aggressive vitality. I dream I am jumping, swimming, running, and climbing. I dream I burst out laughing, I am leaping across a river and chased by a pack of cars that never catches up with me," explains Fanon.[29] The need for and dream of a free body that reclaims one's belonging starts the decolonization process, regenerating the colonized body and creating the new humanity that Fanon envisioned. Thus, the act of resistance against an unlawful power through violence can be an act of becoming. Becoming, Deleuze argues, is man's only revolutionary hope and "the only way of casting off their shame or responding to what is intolerable."[30]

For many of the children I discuss in this chapter, violence for the sake of becoming is the subversion of colonial and neoliberal powers that mark and encage their bodies as stagnant. Anger emerges from the overwhelming grief that results from the loss of being-in-itself, the loss of body in the first place. And in our case, the loss of childhood, or as Shalhoub-Kevorkian calls it "unchilding."[31] Violence has an emancipatory intent because revenge accomplishes justice beyond the political goal.[32] Whether it succeeds or not, the act of violence liberates and reclaims, denoting that justice is possible.

To conclude, unlike the systematic/institutionalized (objective or subjective) colonial or state violence, the colonized subject's violence is law-destroying. It is immediate and temporal rather than structural. The colonized violence is a radical break with the lived experience of being colonized, one that upsets, refutes, and rejects the fabric of the colonial and neoliberal power and its modalities of control and exclusion. Desire, as Deleuze argues, is productive, and its products are tangible, or in other words, desire produces desired realities. Freedom is a practical and immediate becoming, and the immanent source and goal of the act of violence against the colonizer. Violence negates being colonized to accomplish justice when justice cannot be obtained deliberately through colonial law or reason. Justice and violence both belong to the realm of the productive desire to become free. Let us now turn to how exactly these ideas about violence are expressed by the children under consideration in this chapter.

Spatial and Socio-economic Violence

Walking alongside Adam, a fourteen-year-old in the Al-Am'ari refugee camp, he gestured to me to look at the surrounding view. He said, "Look from there [east] you see the [Israeli] settlement, and from there [west] you see the five-star [Palestinian] hotel." The five-star luxury hotel opened in 2010 in Ramallah, initially under the umbrella of Mövenpick and then Millennium. It is a manifestation of the PA's neoliberal policies to turn Ramallah into a consumption hub of middle-class lifestyle, which has gone hand in hand with financial and real-estate capital being poured into commercial buildings and apartments, creating new hierarchical relations, whether spatial or social.[33] The hotel's website says it offers a "truly memorable" experience, being as it is "2 km from the Dar Zahran Heritage Building and 17 km from the ancient Tomb of Samuel." This geographical description omits the fact that within 1 km from the hotel façade is P'sagot, the Israeli colonial settlement (built in 1981 on the hilltop Jabel Tawil) next to Al-Am'ari, a historic symbol of injustice, colonialism, and forced displacement. For Adam and other children in the camp, the settlement represents a place of physical enclosure and threat: a constant reminder of living as a colonized subject. Al-Am'ari resident Muna (fifteen years old) says the settlement represents death, or in her words: "Every time I look at the settlement, I only remember martyrs." For Muhannad, sixteen years old, the settlement is a confusing place because looking at it from the western side, one only sees barbed wire, with no signs of life. He says, "You look at the settlement, you see nothing as it is a dead zone, while in fact, it is the zone that produces our death." For the camp children, the settlement stands as the symbol of colonial violence and ongoing physical erasure. The five-star hotel represents a symbol of a different source of violence, which is materialized by spatial violence and exclusion.

The sense of spatial violence and exclusion also materializes at the very entrance to the camp itself. Al-Am'ari refugee camp is located on the very busy Jerusalem Road, which connects Ramallah with Jerusalem. In the late 1990s, the municipality of Al-Bireh installed traffic lights on the section of Jerusalem Road that passes by the camp, noticeably omitting the installation of lights for traffic turning off Jerusalem Road and into the camp entrance (and likewise for cars leaving the camp and turning onto Jerusalem Road). This lack of regulation from both sides of the road sends the message that the camp is nonexistent and that any traffic seeking to come into or out of the camp does so at its own risk of death. (This is eerily similar to the way Israel blocked the camp entrance with barrels during the first intifada.) Fanon captures colonialism's spatial implications when he writes: "The world cut in two. The dividing line, the frontiers are shown by barracks and police stations."[34] In 2010, the municipality added a roundabout to the intersection, but it only allowed the camp's right-side entrance to be regulated. Children of Al-Am'ari camp often use this intersection as a site to wage clashes with PA security forces, as if reappropriating this space as something more than a death zone.

Over the last three decades, the surrounding area of the camp has been changing in a rapidly antagonistic way. In addition to the construction of the five-star luxury hotel and the changes made to the entrance of the camp, a new, eleven-story Palestine Red Crescent Society building emerged outside the camp in 2005, despite camp residents' protests. The new building looms over the nearby camp houses, with a mere one-meter distance between them. The building contains a hotel, a restaurant, meeting rooms, and offices, representing and materializing the neoliberal growth in the post-Oslo era. Camp residents resent the building, which reinforces feelings of spatial exclusion among the camp residents.[35] Fifteen-year-old Al-Am'ari resident Sara points out the irony: "I feel that not only the Israelis want us to vanish, but also the municipality of Ramallah and Al-Bireh will be happy if we just disappear." Palestinian sociologist Lisa Taraki indicates that Ramallah's transformation into a hub of living and working, with an active nightlife, expensive villas, and luxury cars, has dissipated the harmony between the camp and its surroundings.[36] The city's foundations have shifted away from solidarity with the camp to individual consumerism, and in doing so "it fractures notions of national resistance and shared struggle and erodes the foundation of solidarity between Palestinians."[37]

The modernization of Ramallah through spatial restructuring has been perceived by the Al-Am'ari children as a source of violence. The architectural real-estate boom has created "a new globalized urban middle-class ethos and lifestyle," and on the other hand, poor residents, including refugees, have been pushed away to the outskirts of the city.[38] Noor, fifteen years old, told me that when he is outside the camp, he tries to hide his identity: "This new lifestyle makes me feel bad for being a refugee." On a political level, children of Al-Am'ari generally express that they are proud of their refugee status, as it represents resistance and *sumud* (steadfastness). However, at a socioeconomic level, they say they feel as though they do not belong to the rest of Palestinian society. Children in the Al-Am'ari refugee camp are caught between colonized space and colonizer space, creating an exceptional triple degree of deprivation.

"State" Violence

Sixteen-year-old Al-Am'ari camp resident Nader described what happened to him after the PA's police took him to the police station for engaging in a street fight in downtown Ramallah: "As soon as the police officer discovered that I am from a refugee camp, his tone started to change . . . you know they think we are the troublemakers, and we are the violent kids." Refugee camps have been portrayed and presented by PA official statements as lawless places, where warlords, drug trafficking, and other criminal activities occur. Between 2007 and 2013, the PA, under the supervision of international donors, launched Security Sector Reform (SSR) to restore "law and order" in refugee camps.[39] Tartir writes: "The idea was to cleanse the camps of non-PA weapons, to conduct a disarmament process, to arrest those that challenged the PA's authority. . . . Achieving a monopoly of violence and consolidating power in the security sector were key objectives as the PA's security apparatus had not been allowed into the camps throughout the period of the second intifada . . . the PA targeted the camps and systematically criminalized resistance."[40] The new campaign resulted in the criminalization of the children of the camps. Nader continues, "He [the police officer] did not even ask what really happened. He started to check our background, and immediately if you are from a refugee camp you are the one who will be blamed and judged . . . but regarding that particular fight, I really was not the one who caused and started it." During my fieldwork in the Al-Am'ari refugee camp, almost all the children I met expressed and shared Nader's perception of the PA's security forces as hostile to them.

The police held Nader in custody overnight. In the morning of the following day, I went to the police station to meet with the police officer to try to uncover his perspective on the fights and disputes that take place among children in Ramallah's city center. In discussing different issues related to the topic, the police officer explained that the educational background of children plays a crucial role in determining whether or not they are troublemakers. He told me that a child's lack of good social and cultural education is the reason they may be hostile in public spaces. Suddenly he said, "You know, they keep harassing and attacking *wlad el nas* [the respectable children]." When I inquired who he meant by "they," he said, "You know." I replied that I did not know. He was reluctant to elaborate, but, ultimately, after much insistence from me, he said: "They. Boys from the camps." Nader's story and experience clearly reflects the ways children from the camp are stereotyped by fellow Palestinians as troubled social and cultural misfits, and in need of special care to render them acceptable in mainstream Palestinian society. This consequently alienates the refugee children even further within Palestinian society. Mahmoud, a sixteen-year-old friend of Nader, told me, "If the fight had been between boys who are not from the camp, it would have been fine. This is [considered] normal. But if we [refugee camp children] are involved in any fight, it is always not fine, and it is not normal . . . you always hear this phrase 'boys from the refugee camps.'"

In an environment that (V)iolently criminalizes and stereotypes them, the refugee camp children view their sabotage of the surrounding areas of the camp and fights in the city center as (v)iolent events of "becoming" and reclaiming space, not merely reactions to living conditions. Alienated by the (V)iolence of colonialism and neoliberalism, Mahmoud and his fellow refugee camp children use (v)iolence to seek to redeem their sense of belonging and existence. In other words, the children confront (V)iolence with (v)iolence. Stone throwing is another manifestation of this phenomenon. For example, when the Israeli army invades Ramallah, city life abruptly turns upside down; shops, restaurants, and coffee shops shut down, streets are emptied of people, cars, and Palestinian security forces. There is no sign of life except for heavily armored Israeli military vehicles and soldiers, at whom some Palestinian refugee camp children may throw stones. For such children, stone throwing represents momentary liberation and becoming. Mahmoud told me, "We never hesitate to go where the Israeli army is to throw stones at them. In fact, when my friends and I arrive at the clashing spot, I see many other boys from the camp." Nader sarcastically jumped into the conversation and added, "The refugees start pilgrimages to the city!" Apart from seeing these "pilgrimages" as a leading form of colonial resistance, the camp children also see them as an explicit way to declare that the camp is part of the city and vice versa. The invasion of Ramallah and Al-Bireh city by the Israeli army, which happens continuously and regularly since the end of the second intifada in 2005, is seen by the refugee children as an opportunity to reclaim their sense of belonging to the broader place outside the refugee camp, a chance of refuting the spatial (V)iolence and exclusion.

Conclusion

Neoliberal policies and the deeply entrenched Israeli colonial order redouble the life of uncertainty and deprivation for the children of the Al-Am'ari refugee camp. The ramifications on their self-perceptions and life experiences have a tremendous twofold effect. First, the (V)iolent conditions have created a sense of social and political uprootedness and alienation. Refugee camps, as the foundation of Palestinian political identity since the Nakba, are detached from the new reality of neoliberal lifestyles that dominate the larger society. Second, neoliberalism has created for the camp children an additional layer of Othering. The children of the camp perceive themselves as the anomalous Others of the already-Othered bodies by Israeli colonialism. Living amid these multiple and intertwined layers of structural (V)iolence has created a complex way of being and living, represented and articulated by how the children of the camp redefine violence in this setting.

Without even ever hearing or reading about Walter Benjamin's treatise on mythical violence vs. divine violence, children of Al-Am'ari clearly distinguish between the two on their own. Although Palestinian camp-children's resistance can include "violent" acts, they do not perceive them as Violence (capital v). Resistance is pure, random, and spontaneous. It is also a form of self-realization, or the assertion and reclamation of their sense of belonging and being from the colonial power and from the new socio-economic neoliberal reality. violence (lowercase v) aims not to accomplish any sort of order but rather to refute being alienated from space, from history. Thus, in Walter Benjamin's words, violence is a way for justice-making, law-destroying, and not law-making or law-preserving. Justice, thus, is accomplished temporarily in the very event of violently sabotaging "public spaces" and in confronting the Israeli colonial forces. Ahmad told me once, "You know what our happy days are . . . it is when the Israeli army storms the camp or when the Palestinian security forces surround it . . . it is the only way that we feel that we are alive." In this sense, children's (v)iolence, whether against colonial Israel or Palestinian security forces or "public spaces," should be understood as an intentional dialectical desire, either to reclaim children's sense of belonging or to reassert that sense of belonging and existence. (v)iolence in this context represents the dialectical relation between being excluded, marginalized, and oppressed and the desire for the children to become, to exist as children and to belong. Children's understanding of (v)iolence is the ultimate response to the politics of unchilding and reflects a process in which violent practices are used to neutralize unchilding and reaffirm childhood. These children's ideas about resistance are complex and embody the concept of lived resistance. Their ideas line up with Franz Fanon's theory of revolutionary violence and his notion of violence and reconstituting the subjectivity of the colonized; with Walter Benjamin's theory of distinguishing between mythical violence and divine violence; and finally, with Gilles Deleuze's theoretical engagement with the notions of desire and of becoming. Finally, if children are the embodiment of hope and promise, it is urgent that we understand their world, especially those living on the margins.

NOTES

1. Rosenfeld, *Confronting the Occupation.* Taraki, "Ramallah—Al-Bireh: Communities and Identities."

2. Dana, "Structural Transformation of Palestinian Civil Society."

3. Khalidi and Samour, "Neoliberalism as Liberation"; Hanieh, "Development as Struggle," 40.

4. UNRWA, "Profile: Am'ari Camp."

5. Shalhoub-Kevorkian, *Incarcerated Childhood*; Shalhoub-Kevorkian, "Gun to Body."

6. Mahdi Fleifel revisited his childhood memories in the Ain El-Helweh Palestinian refugee camp in Lebanon in his dazzling biography film, "A World Not Ours," produced in 2012. The unique aspect of the film is in introducing refugees' life experiences from an ontological lens, meaning exploring what it means to live and to have a body as a Palestinian refugee in this world.

7. Khalidi and Samour, "Neoliberalism and the Contradictions."

8. Ibid.

9. Tabar and Salamanca, "After Oslo."

10. Khalidi and Samour, "Neoliberalism as Liberation."

11. Dana, "Symbiosis between Palestinian 'Fayyadism'"; Dana, "Localising the Economy."

12. Dana, "Structural Transformation of Palestinian Civil Society."

13. Clarno, *Neoliberal Apartheid*, 90.

14. Dana, "Localising the Economy."

15. El-Zein, "Developing a Palestinian Resistance Economy," 22.

16. Tartir, "Contentious Economics in Occupied Palestine."

17. Seidel, "Neoliberal Developments, National Consciousness."

18. Khalidi, "Structural Transformation of the Palestinian Economy."

19. Grandinetti, "Palestinian Middle Class in Rawabi," 7.

20. Ibid., 13.

21. Hilal, *The Palestinian Middle Class.*

22. Taraki, "After Oslo."

23. Ibid., 53.

24. Khalidi and Samour, "Neoliberalism and the Contradictions"; Tabar and Salamanca, "After Oslo," 12; Tartir, "Criminalizing Resistance"; Hanieh, "Development as Struggle," 41-42; Dana, "Structural Transformation of Palestinian Civil Society"; Taraki, "After Oslo."

25. Khatib, "Society and Violence," 612.

26. Ibid., 616–17.

27. Fanon, *The Wretched of the Earth*, 182.

28. Khatib, "Society and Violence," 618.

29. Fanon, *The Wretched of the Earth*, 15.

30. Deleuze, *The Logic of Sense,* 171.

31. Shalhoub-Kevorkian, *Incarcerated Childhood.*

32. Benjamin, "Critique of Violence."

33. Hilal, "Ramallah," 10.

34. Fanon, *The Wretched of the Earth*, 182.

35. Johnson and Abu-Nahleh, "Community and its Contradictions," 55.

36. Taraki, "Ramallah—Al-Bireh: Communities and Identities," 38.

37. Grandinetti, "Palestinian Middle Class in Rawabi," 5.

38. Taraki, "Urban Modernity on the Periphery," 4; Grandinetti, "Palestinian Middle Class in Rawabi," 5.

39. Tartir, "Criminalizing Resistance."
40. Ibid., 10.

BIBLIOGRAPHY

Benjamin, W. "Critique of Violence." In *1913–1926*, Vol. 1 of *Walter Benjamin: Selected Writings*, edited by M. Bullock and M. W. Jennings, 236–52. Cambridge, Mass.: Harvard University Press, 2004.

Clarno, A. *Neoliberal Apartheid: Palestine/Israel and South Africa after 1994*. Chicago: University of Chicago Press, 2017.

Dana, T. "Crony Capitalism in the Palestinian Authority: A Deal among Friends." *Third World Quarterly* 41, no. 2 (2019): 247–63.

———. "Localising the Economy as a Resistance Response: A Contribution to the 'Resistance Economy' Debate in the Occupied Palestinian Territories." *Journal of Peacebuilding and Development* 15 no. 2 (2020): 192–204.

———. "The Structural Transformation of Palestinian Civil Society: Key Paradigm Shifts." *Middle East Critique* 24, no. 2 (2015): 191–210.

———. "The Symbiosis between Palestinian 'Fayyadism' and Israeli 'Economic Peace': The Political Economy of Capitalist Peace in the Context of Colonisation." *Conflict, Security & Development* 15, no. 5 (2015): 455–77.

Deleuze, G. *The Logic of Sense*. Edited by C. V. Boundas. Translated by M. Lester and C. Stivale. New York: Columbia University Press, 1990.

———. *Negotiations*. New York: Columbia University Press, 1990.

El-Zein, R. "Developing a Palestinian Resistance Economy through Agricultural Labor." *Journal of Palestine Studies* 46, no. 3 (2017): 7–26.

Fanon, F. *The Wretched of the Earth*. Translated by Richard Philcox. New York: Grove Press. 2004.

Grandinetti, T. "The Palestinian Middle Class in Rawabi: Depoliticizing the Occupation." *Alternatives* 40, no. 1 (2015): 63–78.

Hanieh, A. "Development as Struggle: Confronting the Reality of Power in Palestine." *Journal of Palestine Studies* 45, no. 4 (2016): 32–47.

Hilal, J. "The Palestinian Middle Class: A Research into the Confusion of Identity, Authority, and Culture." Beirut: Institute of Palestine Studies, 2006. [In Arabic]

———. "Ramallah: The City and the Story." In *Ramallah and Kafr Aqab: A Reading of Socio-urban Changes*, edited by J. Hilal and A. Sakka, 8–39. Ramallah: Center of Development Studies at Birzeit University, 2015. [In Arabic]

Johnson, P., and L. Abu Nahleh. "Community and its Contradictions: An Overview of Am'ari Camp." In *Three Palestinian Neighborhoods Under Occupation*, edited by R. Abu Duhou, L. Abu Nahleh, L. Taraki, P. Johnson, A. Selmi, and J. Hilal, 49–95. Beirut: Institute for Palestine Studies, 2010. [In Arabic]

Khalidi, R. "The Structural Transformation of the Palestinian Economy after Oslo." In *From the River to the Sea: Palestine and Israel in the Shadow of "Peace,"* edited by Turner, M. Pennsylvania: Lexington Books, 2019.

Khalidi R., and S. Samour. "Neoliberalism and the Contradictions of the Palestinian Authority's State-building Programme." In *Decolonizing Palestinian Political Economy: De-development and Beyond*, edited by M. Turner and O. Shweiki, 179–199. London: Palgrave Macmillan, 2014.

———. "Neoliberalism as Liberation: The Statehood Program and the Remaking of the Palestinian National Movement." *Journal of Palestine Studies* 40, no. 2 (2011): 6–25.

Khatib, S. "Society and Violence." In *The Sage Handbook of Frankfurt School Critical Theory*, edited by B. Best, W. Bonefeld, and C. O'Kane, 607–24. London: SAGE Publications, 2018.

Rosenfeld, M. *Confronting the Occupation: Work, Education, and Political Activism of Palestinian Families in a Refugee Camp*. Stanford, Calif.: Stanford University Press, 2004.

Seidel, T. "Neoliberal Developments, National Consciousness, and Political Economies of Resistance in Palestine." *Interventions* 21, no. 5 (2019): 727–46.

Shalhoub-Kevorkian, N. "Gun to Body: Mental Health against Unchilding." *International Journal of Applied Psychoanalytic Studies* 17, no. 2 (2020): 126–45.

———. *Incarcerated Childhood and the Politics of Unchilding*. Cambridge, UK: Cambridge University Press, 2019.

Tabar, L., and O. J. Salamanca. "After Oslo: Settler Colonialism, Neoliberal Development, and Liberation." In *Critical Readings of Development Under Colonialism*, 9–27. Ramallah: Center of Development Studies at Birzeit University, 2015.

Taraki, L. "After Oslo: The New Palestinian Social Imaginary." *Idafat: The Arab Journal of Sociology,* nos. 26/27 (2014):48–58.

———. "Ramallah—Al-Bireh: Communities and Identities." In *Three Palestinian Neighborhoods Under Occupation*, edited by R. Abu Duhou, L. Abu Nahleh, L. Taraki, P. Johnson, A. Selmi, and J. Hilal, 15–48. Beirut: Institute for Palestine Studies, 2010. [In Arabic]

———. "Urban Modernity on the Periphery: A New Middle Class Reinvents the Palestinian City." *Social Text* 26, no. 2 (2008): 61–81.

Tartir, A. "Contentious Economics in Occupied Palestine." In *Contentious Politics in the Middle East*, edited by F. A. Gerges, 469–99 . London: Palgrave Macmillan, 2015.

———. "Criminalizing Resistance: The Cases of Balata and Jenin Refugee Camps." *Journal of Palestine Studies* 46, no. 2 (2017): 7–22.

United Nations Relief and Works Agency (UNRWA) for Palestine Refugees in the Near East. "Profile: Am'ari Camp—Ramallah and al-Bireh Governorate. "March 2015. http://www.unrwa.org/sites/default/files/amari_refugee_camp.pdf.

"They Don't See Anything but This Kind of Treatment"

Loss and Reclamation of Palestinian Childhood through the Eyes of Mothers

CINDY SOUSA AND SARA BRESSI

Palestine is one of the most dangerous places in the world to be a child.[1] Of course, the ongoing political violence in Palestine must be understood as a part of Israel's settler-colonial project, which rests on an ongoing Israeli civilian and military occupation aimed at undermining individual and collective sovereignty through violence, humiliation, and control.[2] Both direct violence and ongoing oppression within the Israeli settler-colonial project pose threats for the individual and collective selves of Palestinian children. In this context, children are used as political capital, as Shalhoub-Kevorkian so eloquently argues.[3] Hostility and violence from the Israeli army and Israeli settlers; arrest and detainments; economic de-development; interrupted access to education, health care, and sacred sites; and home invasions and demolitions all represent significant challenges to Palestinian childhood, resulting in what Shalhoub-Kevorkian terms "unchilding": a strategic, purposeful project of diminishing childhood as part of systematic control and attempts at erasure of an entire people.[4]

The unrelenting and intrusive nature of the occupation of Palestine results in children and families being exposed to acute forms of violence (i.e., shootings, arrests, home demolitions). Just as importantly, children also are exposed to more pernicious, quotidian threats within political violence. In Palestine, military operations take place within civilian areas. Locations previously assumed to be safe sites for maintaining daily activities of family life are radically transformed into contested terrain for years or even decades, including marketplaces, restaurants, schools, hospitals, sites of worship, and homes.[5]

Another dynamic that fundamentally threatens the experience of childhood within political violence—particularly within protracted conflicts that include foreign occupation, as in Palestine—is the constant surveillance and increasing militarization of everyday life.[6] One example of this is the growing use of puni-

tive measures against children deemed "security threats," which has led to the detention and incarceration of an expanding number of children around the world,
including in Palestine.[7] In fact, we write this in the shadow of the decision to
hold Ahed Tamimi, a sixteen-year-old Palestinian child and activist, for allegedly
slapping an Israeli soldier as he tried to enter the family home, after he had already shot her cousin in his face with a rubber bullet. Ahed, and her family, are
not strangers to struggle. In a video of her, she famously says, "If there was no occupation, I would be a soccer player."[8] This is the cost of childhood under military rule: the childhood condition of imagining one's future and one's dreams
becomes eclipsed by the looming threat of both violence and occupation, and
the formidable task of resistance—a living, dynamic, and highly embodied project through which children's agency both grows and becomes acutely visible, as
Morrison points out in the introduction to this volume.

In this chapter, we consider, from the vantage point of mothers, several fundamental questions related to childhood in Palestine, based on data gathered
through participant observation and a series of focus groups with Palestinian
women in the West Bank. Our two essential areas of exploration are: What does
childhood look like within contexts of unrelenting terror and threat, where children cannot be assured of their basic needs for safety, sustenance, and security
of place, much less their emotional or physical survival?[9] How do mothers and
children establish the durability of their place in the world, when the political
context surrounding them demonstrates sustained animosity to both individual
children and their collective culture?[10] What is the role of agency, and of, as Morrison (this volume) describes, "lived resistance" within the profound unchilding
within settler-colonial projects?[11] Using these analytic questions as a guide, we
explore the need to reenvision the canonized views of motherhood and childhood held by scholars concerned with child development in contexts of political
violence and occupation.

In the sections that follow, we begin by presenting an overview of "classical"
(Western) views on motherhood and childhood, as well as an examination of
what these concepts entail within a feminist, postcolonial framework. We then
analyze our findings in light of these theoretical frameworks. We conclude by
discussing how a more nuanced understanding of mother-child relations in settings of oppression will deepen our conceptualization of child development.

Western Theoretical Conceptions of
Childhood and the Maternal-Child Dyad

In considering the impact of political violence and oppression on the experience
of the maternal-child dyad, it is valuable to take a closer look at several predomi-

nant conceptualizations of the child's relational world, as suggested by a Western point of view. Beginning here is important, as Western theoretical constructions of childhood set a frame of normativity. In so doing, they often denote sequelae of developmental disruptions to this frame—problematizing development for children around the world rather than understanding the varied and various ways it occurs around the world.[12] Indeed, purporting a frame of normativity, marginalized groups are subject to being pathologized rather than being understood and celebrated for their abilities to negotiate worlds steeped in oppression and violence.

Western psychological and sociological constructions of childhood emphasize a few core assumptions, including that children think, act, and regulate *differently from*, albeit *in interaction with*, adult minds over the course of development. For example, Piaget argues that prior to adolescence, children cognate more concretely and are less able to make sense of complex problems in contrast to older children and adults.[13] Children tend to negotiate and learn about the world through play, become more reliant on peers than caregivers for identity formation over time, and in adolescence tend toward creativity, exploration, and risk taking.[14]

Relationally, children are motivated to attain and maintain relationships with primary caregivers throughout childhood.[15] Only as their cognitive capacity changes does the mind of the child shift in its ability to hold other perspectives in mind and to venture forward and away from their family of origin.[16]

Object relations theory emerged midcentury largely in reaction to classical Freudian explanations of the primary motivators of the human psyche. Freud and his followers postulated that the central psychic task of childhood is to repress, relinquish, and develop the capacity to control animalistic sexual and aggressive drives, which were considered to be innate and universal.[17] Through his explication of the Oedipal complex, Freud postulated these processes turn on the child's ability to repress sexual and aggressive wishes toward a heterosexual mother and father. Repression works in the service of an adult mind that can forgo gratification of these base desires in alignment with social mores. In this model, the other (i.e., the object) is viewed in the mind of the child to be only thwarting or gratifying of the child's drives—which are defined as internal pressures needing fulfillment from the other. This is a highly individualized, one-person psychology that views the caregiver as an object, wholly independent of the child and with their own innate drives.

Object relations and attachment theory create a frame for child development in outlining optimal caregiving conditions to facilitate a child's relational growth, sense of self, agency, and safety. In laying a normative path of development, these theories also inform our understanding of the impact of trauma and oppression on the experience of caregivers and children. Their emphasis on the important influence of the caregiver has been pivotal for examining the impact of relational trauma on the developing child, the impact of a lack of safety or security in the mother that would impinge on the experience of the child, and the intergenerational transmission of traumatic experience and oppression.[18]

In reaction to the objectification of caregivers, object relations theorists shifted the frame of relating in childhood from a one-person to a two-person psychology. The relational baby is no longer just love seeking, social from birth, and acting on others but is also responsive to and thus acted upon by the caregiver. These theorists in Britain and the United States (e.g., Winnicott, Fairbairn, Mahler) disputed Freud's Oedipal conflict and identified the core motivation of children to be a drive toward relationship—toward maintaining love and nurturance from caregivers, and in particular, early in life, from the mother.[19] These theorists, for the first time, addressed the experience of the infant in interaction with the mother, and as such, the maternal-infant dyad became the centerpiece of all later developmental gains and losses.

Attachment theory—perhaps the most influential Western explanatory frames for understanding the impact of the relational world of childhood—was developed by John Bowlby, a psychoanalyst trained in the tradition of object relations. However, Bowlby, in witnessing the outcomes of deprivation and abuse firsthand in his patients, built his theory to hold the importance of actual behavioral patterns of relating that emerged between mother and child.[20] Attachment theory considers attachment behaviors in the infant as innate, biologically based observable behaviors that seek to attain and maintain physical proximity to an attachment figure, most often identified as the mother, who is perceived to be competent to provide care.[21] Bowlby was influenced by animal models from ethology and he noted the universality of behavioral patterns in the animal kingdom toward seeking actual physical nearness to the mother for safety and survival. Once again, Bowlby's original construction placed the maternal-child dyad at the center of all future relating. He posited that attachment behaviors and patterns that emerged in infancy and early childhood would become internal working models for maintaining safety through relationship throughout the life course.

Much of the expansion of attachment theory following the work of Bowlby, including the work of Mary Ainsworth and others, has centered on identifying attachment-based behavioral patterns between mothers, infants, and young children, and linking these to behavioral patterns later in the life course.[22] Mary Ainsworth used laboratory-based situations to examine the behaviors used by infants and toddlers upon parental separation. Based on these laboratory studies, she identified two primary types of attachment: secure attachment and insecure attachment. Babies and toddlers who are securely attached, while dysregulated by separation from the parent, are easily soothed and returned to an optimal state of arousal (i.e., safety) upon the parent's return and with the parent's holding and encouragement. In contrast, insecurely attached children, upon return of the parent, are difficult to soothe, hostile or avoidant of the mother all together.

These attachment styles were also examined in much younger babies.[23] Using extensive inspection of frame-by-frame videotapes, these researchers studied the relational dance between mothers and infants at four months of age by examining key mechanisms for infant and mother bonding, including use of the face, gaze, touch, and prosody of speech. Other theorists in the realm of infant mental health, including Tronick and Beeghly, have outlined the importance of these repeated patterns of relating over many interactions between mother and baby in the earliest years of life.[24] Again, recognizing the inevitable gaps and misattunements that may occur between baby and mother, Tronick suggests relating in infancy is a series of opportunities for relational repair after these brief ruptures between mother and child.

As such, the nature of the mother's responsiveness to their baby in everyday life, over time, and in the context of separation and reuniting, both figuratively and literally, is considered the key facilitative ingredient for secure attachment. Securely attached infants attain and maintain connection to caregivers that are available and soothing but also feel a freedom to emerge and explore the environment. The caregiver of a securely attached child creates a secure base from which the child can move away to explore but also return to for safety, connection, and understanding. A secure base provides safety and comfort, but also allows for the child to find ever-increasing distance for exploration of the world.

In enlivening the impact of the mother on the baby, and the impact of the baby on the mother, object relations reframed the construction of child development and motherhood all together. Winnicott emphasized the concept of the "good enough mother," who is attuned to her child's needs and available for providing care and safety, but also a human figure subject to disruptions in attentiveness and having a varying capacity to uphold the illusion of safety at all times.[25] The mother, her experience in the world, and her own developmental experience and capacities became crucial for understanding the life trajectory of the baby. Furthermore, this body of work postulates the availability and attunement of a loving mother is central for experiencing the world as a safe place, and for the psychic process of taking into one's own developing mind the capacity for feeling positive about oneself, for developing the ability for self-comfort in times of distress, and for the capacity to feel separate and intact in the absence of the caregiver. Likewise, the child was no longer just dependent on the mother for survival but rather the survival of the dyad was cast as a process of interdependency.

Interestingly enough, much of the Western theoretical framework about parenting emerged from psychologists studying children within the context of war; Freud and Burlingham, Winnicott, and Bowlby all based much of their work on their early studies of children who were traumatized by World War II.[26] Despite this context, most of the subsequent literature on child development fails to take deliberate account of the social and political context of children and those who care for them. Luckily, there is evidence of a change in approach.[27] This evolving body of work points to several important dimensions around childhood, including that we must account for variations in the geographical and political realities of children and those who care for them. Moving away from an overreliance on Western frameworks of health and development enables a more specific and accurate view of well-being.[28]

Conceptualizing child development within oppression, including the wars, occupation, and sieges people experience in Palestine, requires us to reenvision both childhood and caretaking in these contexts.[29] To uncover processes related to individual-collective survival and reclamation of dignity requires attention to the everyday strategies of mothers and children within their social and political context—what has been described as the "pragmatics" of mothering and distinctive, intensive, and often communal patterns of "maternal thinking."[30] This requires a turn from seeing the mother as an object and a relatively stoic being devoid of context or agency, to a subject—a person that operates within complex political realities, and within dynamic communities.

With this commitment in mind, in the work presented here, we explore how, within the mother-child dyad, childhood is experienced, redefined, and defended in Palestine. Our data is drawn from several months of participant observation from three trips over three years (2007, 2008, 2009), with field notes via text and photographs. We also collected data from focus groups in five sectors of the West Bank with thirty-two Palestinian women in 2008; their narratives are included here. All procedures were approved by the University of Washington's Human Subjects Division. Focus groups lasted about an hour and were conducted in Arabic by two Palestinian women. They were later translated into English for analysis and interpretation. Content analysis was used for coding and analysis, which enabled a balance of inductive and deductive approaches.[31] We used in vivo coding and coding for processes, emotions, and consequences.[32]

Through our interpretation of this data alongside critical theories related to childhood and motherhood in violence and settler colonialism, we argue that, for understanding childhood within ongoing situations of political violence and oppression, understandings of children and their development needs to tend more to two important dimensions: (1) the imbrication of place and power within the experience of mothers and children, and (2) the cross-generational experience of and resistance within trauma, which is experienced simultaneously—though distinctly—by children and mothers.

Emplaced Experiences of Childhood in Palestine:
Geographies of Power and Crisis

The settler-colonial system of control and constriction of place has profound implications for the experience of both parents and children.[33] In Collins's work on motherhood, she brought forward an essential proposal that ought to form the basis for conceptualizing the experience of childhood within political violence: motherhood (and therefore childhood) cannot be separated from deep understandings of power.[34]

Power is spatially deployed.[35] Place is central to how power "divides, then keeps what it has divided in a state of separation."[36] In so doing, the ability of children to experience place with the necessary sense of freedom and safety becomes compromised. This is no accident. Rather, as we see in Palestine, the harnessing and control of indigenous place is central to the project of settler colonialism.[37] Fanon described the colonial world as one severed into parts.[38] These disruptions to place have implications, as he writes: "It is probably unnecessary to recall the existence of native quarters and European quarters, of schools for natives and schools for Europeans; in the same way we need not recall apartheid in South Africa. Yet if we examine closely this system of compartments, we will at least be able to reveal the lines of force it implies."[39]

The ability to have power over place—that is, to feel rooted, and also free to be mobile, in a piece of place—is an essential affirmation of a safe and stable self, a crucial component of attachment, and central for child development.[40] Indeed, the possibility to take for granted, and count on, land in many ways represents an ability to count on not only your individual place in the world, but also that of your community. But safety in place is only one part of the child's experience of self in place: movement is also fundamental to the development of our selves. In fact, Bourdieu reminds us that "the relation to what is possible is a relation to power," and this relation is transcribed into our bodies through our movement (or lack thereof) through places.[41] With regard to childhood, then, the severing and control of place has particular implications for the two spheres that typically encompass our understandings of children's geographies—play and mobility.[42]

Childhood as a time and metaphorical place for innocence—a symbolic site to safeguard life, normalcy, the right to have rights and expectations for both play and agency—depends, though, on the existence of an *actual* physical place for individual and collective safety, agency, and freedom.[43] Play—and the freedom and

Author in front of the wall in Qalquilya, under surveillance device, shortly before being warned by children to not stand so close to it. Photograph by R. Smith.

Children being hit by Israeli soldiers as they attempt to pass through border that separates Palestinian land from Palestinian people so that they may farm their land. The Israeli soldier ended by spitting in the children's face, and the children eventually turned back. Photograph by C. Sousa.

security of place to do so—is therefore a cornerstone of childhood.[44] In the case of Palestinian children's lives, safety and freedom of place to play and explore is fundamentally constrained, as our data demonstrated.[45]

For example, on a visit to the city of Qalqilya, we could not avoid seeing the looming monstrous wall. Almost instantly, a group of children, around ages seven to about twelve, interrupted their nearby playing to run up and warn us to not stand so close to the wall. They explained that the Israeli snipers who stand guard at the wall may shoot. This experience drew into sharp relief the kind of environment that exists for Palestinian children's play and exploration. Children undertake their tasks of cognitive, emotional, and social growth and development under the looming presence of occupation. Afterward, another group of children found us wandering and interrupted their playing because they wanted to give us a tour. They showed us pictures and places that are monuments to murdered Palestinians, some of whom are children. Again, places of play and freedom for this group of children exist under the constant reminders of occupation and its associated systems of violence, control, and surveillance.

Place represents possibilities.[46] The visual experience of place is closely tied to our visceral experience of it, as our daily experiences become ingrained in our bodies through our movement within place.[47] Thus, the limitations we face within place become embodied, mapping on to our mental conceptions of what may be possible within our individual and collective lives. Unrelenting Israeli attempts to control and constrict place transfers to people's experience of freedom or mobility.[48] Israeli checkpoints, walls, and settlements bisect Palestine, turning a contiguous place into a series of closely monitored and controlled enclaves. In this context, maternal care is upended. The disruption to place makes it very difficult for mothers to mother. In our focus groups, Palestinian mothers expressed an inability to obtain education or medical care for their children. They also lamented not being able to take their children on enriching visits to important cultural and historic sites, such as the Dome of the Rock or the Dead Sea.

Speaking of the constraints on freedom in place and how it has impacts on childhood that are at once practical and imaginative, Palestinian mothers shared simple yet profoundly important statements, such as: "kids cannot play"; "they [Israeli military] don't give any permission for kids to go anyplace"; and "kids don't see anything but this kind of treatment and occupation." As one mother expressed, "You know—the kid wants to go play in the street and he can't have his freedom to play in the street because they will shoot sometimes." Again and again, mothers describe a profound loss of childhood—that is deeply linked to the constraints on place and freedom. As Shalhoub-Kevorkian points out, this loss of childhood is not accidental, but is a purposeful dynamic wherein children are used as political capital within the violence and oppression of the occupation.[49]

One woman said: "Children are born and live under the circumstances of the occupation, full of fears." Women in our groups shared about children: "Their lives are miserable and there is no life for them"; this woman went on to say, "They don't have a normal life; no one is living a normal life." This sentiment reflects a deeply felt desire to have children experience a sacred childhood—and to have the place, literally and figuratively, to claim this as a right. Indeed, another woman simply said, "No one is taking into consideration those kids and that they have the right to live."

Perhaps no place is as fundamental to a child's inner and outer life as the family home. Home holds profound import as it upholds our needs for privacy and control; safety, security, refuge, and protection; and the formation and fostering of relationships, which inform and undergird belonging and identity.[50] Yet, as the Israeli occupation in Palestine intrudes into even the most intimate domains of the lives of Palestinians, even home is not safe. Women talked about Israeli home invasions and demolitions, about children being afraid and hiding in corners or under buildings from Israeli authorities.[51] Mothers also described quite often the experience of enduring terrible circumstances with their children, like this mother who recounted the experience of hiding in her home with her daughter:

> My daughter and I one time were going up the stairs and she sat on the stairs because she heard shooting. We were sitting and hiding—we were so afraid— we had a feeling they were watching us. The only way we can move sometimes is by crawling on our stomach instead of standing so they don't see us. We [still] cry and are afraid.

Here, several themes are revealed: the tendency (and need) for mothers and children to suffer—and resist—together; the location of the home as a site of violation, and also protection; and the lasting effects of not only acute violence but the violation of the privacy of the home via ubiquitous Israeli surveillance in Palestine.

Suffering and Resilience as a Dyadic Experience:
Trauma and Resistance across Generations

Some contemporary psychoanalytic scholars have problematized, from a feminist perspective, the implicit demand by early object relations theorists for a serene, unflappable mother, whose mind and subjectivity must be subjugated to advance the well-being of a passive child. In contrast, the relational baby is "more active-reactive to, and a participant in, mother's own pulls and pushes."[52]

In enlivening the existence, importance, and developmental experience of the mother, family system theories (such as object relations and attachment) open up explanations for understanding the intergenerational impact of trauma and oppression.[53]

Indeed, contexts of long-standing political violence in settler-colonial projects compound the relational risk for children, as settler colonialism is marked by assaults on individual and collective dignity and freedom across generations.[54] In these settings, children must contend with traumatogenic material they *directly* experience through ongoing conflict, as well as *indirectly* in being parented by persons with enduring wounds. These wounds arise from individual and collective trauma of war, and also from the structural violence associated with the horrors and the humiliating and dehumanizing nature of political violence and colonialism.[55] Research postulates maternal trauma may influence the experience of the developing child through impairing attachment and destabilizing the role of the parent.[56] Disruptions to maternal responsiveness are credited to the mother's own history of trauma and its impact on her developmental course, sense of self, and also her internal ability to locate a sense of safety. These "ghosts in the nursery" leave a lasting impact on the experience of the children of future generations.[57] There is even increasing evidence that trauma is passed on in the genes.[58]

The trauma of the mother, however, is not stagnant, but exists within the complex, ongoing dynamics of parenting. Speaking to this highly relational work, authors such as Benjamin and Chodorow argue for greater emphasis on the mother's subjectivity and her interaction and collaboration with her child's subjectivity. In Benjamin's view, this is necessary for the creation of what she labels the emergence of "the third," an intersubjective space where mother and child are separate but are both mutually recognized and seen by the other. In this space resides the grief evident in mothers' narratives about witnessing their children's suffering and feeling unable to heal it. In our focus groups, women talked about children having such deep fear that the color in their faces would change or that they would regularly shake. Mothers expressed grief at their lack of power to shield their children from violence and atrocities. One woman expressed, "Especially when you have little kids and they are suffering, it affects you."

The experience of being seen and finding mutual recognition with caregivers and with others is the most longed for experience in the human condition.[59] Relatedness and the intersubjective space is also, as Stern writes, the "nexus from which experience emerges ... meaning is potentiated and prohibited by what transpires between us."[60] Together, mothers and children face a life that is unpredictable, for, as women said in our focus groups, "We don't know what our future is." The work of interpersonal construction of meaning allows for growth and resilience, and provides multiplicity in making sense of the past and the future.

The maternal-child relationship is a crucial site for the dynamic, ongoing, and highly collaborative processes of survival and meaning-making. Indeed, our results demonstrate how mothers and children very much encounter violence and oppression together, and negotiate a response in concert. For example, a mother who described going through a checkpoint with her daughter, and having the Israelis flirt with them, illustrated how her responses depend, in part, on what she wants to show to her daughter regarding resistance and resilience in that situation. Research (and our data) demonstrates that, even within ongoing violence and oppression, mothers tend to mobilize considerable strength and ingenuity to comfort and safeguard their children—physically, emotionally, and spiritually.[61] Mothers who described the fear of shooting and attacks on their house demonstrate that their patterns of survival, both physical and emotional, are established not in some sterile environment but within the moment with their children, within the relationship. Faced with these profound and ongoing threats, mothers and children together grapple with significant and harmful negotiations of power, in their quest for survival and promotion of individual and collective identity.[62]

Living in a setting of incomprehensibility, and the trauma it creates, makes difficult their work to transmit articulations of the world as coherent and just. In such contexts, collaborative meaning-making between mothers and children fully brings minds into interaction and—as families and communities struggle together—their emotional and physical survival exists *between* as opposed to *within*. Our data showed how, in multiple moments, mothers do important, highly political work to make sense of the struggle for individual and collective survival and dignity not only *for* but also *with* their children through actions that nurture both comfort and also resistance.[63]

Related to comforting, mothers described their attempts at comforting and protecting in our focus groups. In describing attacks they endured with their children, mothers talked about holding their children, reassuring them, and trying to take away their anxiety. Women also talked about trying to provide a sort of intellectual comfort, as they tried to help create sense within the unrelenting assaults. For example, there were heated discussions about what kinds of messages to convey to their children when faced with atrocities. A mother in one of our focus groups said, "When my daughter sees somebody wounded, with an eye or hand missing, and she comes and asks me and complains to me, I don't know what to explain to her sometimes. Sometimes, if I see somebody like this wounded, I don't have the heart to even look at this person. This is my feeling, so what do you expect from a child seeing these things?" This was met with affirmations from mothers in the group, who expressed affinity with this statement.

Moving away from comfort as ease, women also talked about fostering a sense of resistance tied to dignity; one mother was very clear about wanting her daughter to maintain a sense of self-righteousness that spanned from the individual to the collective: "I tell my daughter and my son—be courageous and you should not be afraid of the Israelis; we give them courage." Much of what mothers and children did to fortify their sense of courage and endurance was rooted in place; previously, we wrote about how mothers enact practices of spatial defense and their attempts to teach this to their children.[64] One woman said, for example: "My daughter is now afraid to stay outside alone; my daughter comes sometimes and says 'oh mother, I am afraid, the Israelis are here,' and I tell her don't be afraid of them, don't worry. Every time she hears shooting, my daughter comes and screams and says, 'Mother, I'm afraid,' and I tell her don't worry." This mother went on to express how she tries to endow her daughter with pride, rooted in the land of Palestine and her identity as a Palestinian.

Critical scholarship on the psychological effects of colonialism maintains how the struggle for the mind of the oppressed is one of the grandest struggles within colonialism.[65] We argue here that, within the context of Palestine, as in so many others, the greatest task of childhood (and, therefore, of motherhood) is to maintain children's minds apart from their oppressor, as Collins suggested so many decades ago.[66] For example, one mother articulated that she believes it's important for children to understand the situation, and to not hide the reality from them, because the mothers don't want the children to absorb the rhetoric that they are terrorists, but rather to understand the nature of the conflict as one that is about violations to their homeland and dignity. Political meaning-making and action is central to life in Palestine, and to the experience of childhood, and of parenting in Palestine—and has been shown in fact to be protective in this context.[67] Another mother asserted that mothers try hard to teach children to be good to everyone, to "not take advantage of others and to be fair with them," although the life they are living is full of injustice for them.

It is also important to consider that the reciprocal maternal-child bond exists within, and typically depends upon, a community. As one woman in our focus group said, "I personally think the Palestinians still stand together. Let's say if the Israelis come to a certain area—don't you think we still come together to defend it? And if someone becomes a martyr in that area, everyone goes and stands with his family." The implicit bias toward separation and individualism as the chief goal of development undermines the influence of collective strategies for safety and ongoing well-being.[68] Conceptualizations of a sole mother devoid of a social-political context must give way to understandings of childhood and motherhood within a collaborative trajectory, where interdependence might well be the goal. This sense of a collective is an important source for coping and caretaking, as it provides practical and emotional support and a sense of shared meaning and resilience.[69] As Collins has suggested, we must do better at uncovering and understanding the potential for "othermothering," wherein childhood is not solely (or even primarily) an experience between two (a mother and a child), but a communal process of caretaking that involves extended family, neighbors, friends, coworkers, and others. Mothers draw strength from their social-political worlds. In turn, their identity as mothers might provide an amplified sense of meaning for survival and for political struggle, with empowerment that inspires engagement with the collective.[70]

Politics, struggle, and resilience are knitted together in dynamics where mothers and children move seamlessly from suffering and surviving as individuals to doing this as a collective. In narratives that spanned from talking about children to talking about all Palestinians, mothers explained individual and collective perseverance as dependent on strong wills and histories of endurance and resistance.

Discussion

Here, we have urged a shift in how we talk about mothers and children. Our findings point to the importance of children's rights—particularly to those geographical elements that are so essential for childhood—play and mobility.[71] In the appropriation of place, the occupation of Palestine violates principles of not only safety, but also of a claim to being represented and enacted in place. The shrinkage of safe geographies and spaces for children to appropriately interact with meaningful people, places, and experiences undermines children's freedom and rights to play, education, and ease. As others have enumerated, restrictions on place and movement therefore have profound implications for children in Palestine, and for the parent-child relationship.[72] Our study thus joins many others in this growing field of children's geographies, adding to the evidence for the urgent need to examine and expand the rights of children within armed conflict to include loss of place and home in considering the ways political violence harms children.[73]

We have also argued for greater focus on intersubjectivity in conceptualizing the experiences of children and mothers within political violence. A pivotal shift required of this view is understanding that children living within political violence are not solitary, passive victims. Rather, in these contexts, mothers and children are socially and politically engaged actors, continually seeking meaning and ensuring emotional and physical survival for themselves, their families, and their communities.[74]

NOTES

1. United Nations General Assembly Security Council, "Children and Armed Conflict."

2. Giacaman, "Reframing Public Health in Wartime"; Peteet, *Space and Mobility in Palestine*; Salamanca et al., "Past Is Present"; Sousa, Kemp, and El-Zuhairi, "Place as a Social Determinant."

3. Shalhoub-Kevorkian, *Incarcerated Childhood*.

4. Barber et al., "Politics Drives Human Functioning"; Giacaman and Johnson, "'Our Life Is Prison'"; Hammami, "On (Not) Suffering"; McNeely et al., "Political Imprisonment and Adult Functioning"; Roy, *Gaza Strip*; UN OCHA, "Humanitarian Impact on Palestinians"; Weizman, *Hollow Land*; Shalhoub-Kevorkian, *Incarcerated Childhood*.

5. Coward, "Urbicide in Bosnia"; Sousa, Kemp, and El-Zuhairi, "Dwelling Within Political Violence"; UNRISD, "Impacts of Conflict on Women"; Violich, *The Bridge to Dalmatia*.

6. Shalhoub-Kevorkian, *Incarcerated Childhood*.

7. ICRC, *Children and Detention*; Addameer, "Imprisonment of Children."

8. Tamimi, *Profile: Palestinian Youth Activist*.

9. Davis, "'Bone Collectors' Comments for Sorrow"; Robertson and Duckett, "Mothering during War and Postwar"; Shalhoub-Kevorkian, "Infiltrated Intimacies"; Smith, "Facing the Dragon."

10. Collins, "Shifting the Center"; Davis, "'Bone Collectors' Comments for Sorrow"; Scheper-Hughes, *Death Without Weeping*.

11. Shalhoub-Kevorkian, *Incarcerated Childhood*.

12. Morrison, *Global History of Childhood Reader*; Skelton, "Children's Geographies/ Geographies of Children"; Smidt, *The Developing Child*.

13. Piaget, "Cognitive Development in Children."

14. Siegel, *Brainstorm*.

15. Bowlby, *Attachment and Loss*, Vol. 1.

16. Gopnik and Wellman, "Child's Theory of Mind."

17. Berzoff, Flanagan, and Hertz, *Inside Out and Outside In*; Mitchell and Black, *Freud and Beyond*.

18. Slade, "Attachment Theory and Research."

19. Mitchell and Black, *Freud and Beyond*.

20. Slade, "Attachment Theory and Research."

21. Bowlby, *Attachment and Loss*, Vol. 1; Bretherton, "The Origins of Attachment Theory."

22. Ainsworth, Blehar, Waters, and Wall, *Patterns of Attachment*; Beebe and Lachmann, *The Origins of Attachment*; Bretherton, "The Origins of Attachment Theory."

23. Beebe et al., "The Origins of 12-Month Attachment"; Beebe and Lachmann, *The Origins of Attachment*; Beebe et al., "Systems View of Mother-Infant."

24. Tronick and Beeghly, "Infants' Meaning-Making."

25. Winnicott, *The Child, the Family*.

26. Freud and Burlingham, *War and Children*; Winnicott, *The Child, the Family*; and Bowlby, *Attachment and Loss*, Vol. 1.

27. Morrison, *The Global History of Childhood Reader*; Skelton, "Children's Geographies/Geographies of children"; Smidt, *The Developing Child*.

28. Giacaman et al., "Mental Health, Social Distress"; Marshall and Sousa, "Decolonizing Trauma."

29. Akesson, "Holding Everything Together"; Robertson and Duckett, "Mothering during War and Postwar"; Sousa, El-Zuhairi, and Siddiqi, "'Utmost Strength I Can Bear'"; Takševa and Sgoutas, *Mothers Under Fire*.

30. Scheper-Hughes, *Death Without Weeping*; Ruddick, *Maternal Thinking*.

31. Hsieh and Shannon, "Three Approaches to Qualitative Content Analysis."

32. Corbin and Strauss, "Grounded Theory Research"; Saldaña, *Coding Manual for Qualitative Researchers*.

33. Hanafi, "Spacio-cide"; Salamanca et al., "Past Is Present."

34. Collins, "Shifting the Center."

35. Collins, "Shifting the Center"; Graham, "Introduction"; Gregory, "The Biopolitics of Baghdad"; Wolfe, "Settler Colonialism and the Elimination."

36. Lefebvre, *The Production of Space*, 358.

37. Peteet, *Space and Mobility in Palestine*; Salamanca et al., "Past Is Present."

38. Fanon, *The Wretched of the Earth*.

39. *Ibid.*

40. Chawla, "Childhood Place Attachments."

41. Bourdieu, "Structures, *Habitus*, Practices."

42. Skelton, "Children's Geographies/Geographies of Children."

43. Cavazzoni et al., "Agency Operating within Structures."

44. Jack, "Place Matters."

45. Marshall, "Existence as Resistance."

46. Norberg-Schulz, *The Concept of Dwelling*.

47. Bourdieu, "Structures, *Habitus*, Practices."

48. Hochberg, *Visual Occupations*.

49. Shalhoub-Kevorkian, *Incarcerated Childhood*.

50. Bachelard and Jolas, *The Poetics of Space*; Tuan, *Space and Place*; Young, "House and Home."

51. Sousa, Kemp, and El-Zuhairi, "Dwelling within Political Violence."

52. Slochower, "Going Too Far," 17.

53. Felsen, "Adult-Onset Trauma"; Fonagy et al., *Affect Regulation, Mentalization*; Slade et al., "Maternal Reflective Functioning, Attachment."

54. Evans-Campbell, "Historical Trauma in American Indian."

55. Dickson-Gomez, "The Sound of Barking Dogs"; Simpson, "Bitter Waters."

56. Afifi et al., "'Fractured Communities'"; Afifi et al., "Relative Impacts of Uncertainty"; Belsky, "War, Trauma, and Children's Development"; Field, Muong, and Sochanvimean, "Parental Styles in the Intergenerational Transmission"; Silber, "Ghostbusting Transgenerational Processes."

57. Fraiberg, Adelson, and Shapiro, "Ghosts in the Nursery," 387.

58. Walters et al., "Bodies Don't Just Tell Stories."

59. Aron, *Meeting of Minds*.

60. Stern, *Partners in Thought*, 4.

61. Atallah, "Community-Based Qualitative Study"; Pavlish, "Action Responses of Congolese Refugee Women."

62. Chodorow, "Reflections on the Reproduction of Mothering."

63. Collins, "Shifting the Center"; Sugiman, "'A Million Hearts from Here.'"

64. Sousa, Kemp, and El-Zuhairi, "Dwelling within Political Violence."

65. Fanon, *The Wretched of the Earth*; Freire, *Pedagogy of the Oppressed*.

66. Collins, "Shifting the Center."

67. Barber, "Contrasting Portraits of War"; Barber et al., "Politics Drives Human Functioning"; Otman, "Handcuffed protectors?"; Punamäki and Suleiman, "Predictors and Effectiveness of Coping."

68. Causadias, "A Roadmap For the Integration"; Jeffrey, "Geographies of Children and Youth I."

69. Baines, "Motherhood and Social Repair"; Eggerman and Panter-Brick, "Suffering, Hope, and Entrapment"; Shalhoub-Kevorkian, "Liberating Voices."

70. Hernández and Torres, "Dilemmas on Motherhood and Social Activism"; Martín-Baró, *Writings For a Liberation Psychology*; Pavlish, "Action Responses of Congolese Refugee Women."

71. Skelton, "Children's Geographies/Geographies of Children."

72. Akesson, "The Concept and Meaning of Place"; Harker, "On (Not) Forgetting Families"; Marshall, "'We Have a Place to Play.'"

73. UNICEF, "Machel Study 10-Year Strategic Review"; Akesson, Basso, and Denov, "The Right to Home."

74. Gilligan, "'Highly vulnerable'?"; Marshall and Sousa, "Decolonizing Trauma"; Sousa, El-Zuhairi, and Siddiqi, "'The Utmost Strength I Can Bear'"; Veronese and Castiglioni, "'When the Doors of Hell Close.'"

BIBLIOGRAPHY

Addameer. "Imprisonment of Children." December 2017. https://www.addameer.org /the_prisoners/children.

Afifi, T. D., W. A. Afifi, A. F. Merrill, and N. Nimah. "'Fractured Communities': Uncertainty, Stress, and (a Lack of) Communal Coping in Palestinian Refugee Camps." *Journal of Applied Communication Research* 44, no. 4 (2016): 343–61.

Afifi, W. A., T. D. Afifi, S. Robbins, and N. Nimah. "The Relative Impacts of Uncertainty and Mothers' Communication on Hopelessness among Palestinian Refugee Youth." *American Journal of Orthopsychiatry* 83, no. 4 (2013): 495–504.

Ainsworth, M. S., M. C. Blehar, E. Waters, and S. Wall. *Patterns of Attachment: A Psychological Study of the Strange Situation*. Oxford, England: Lawrence Erlbaum, 1978.

Akesson, B. "The Concept and Meaning of Place for Young Children Affected by Political Violence in the Occupied Palestinian Territories." *Spaces and Flows: An International Journal of Urban and Extra Urban Studies* 2, no. 2 (2011): 245–56.

———. "Holding Everything Together: Palestinian Mothers under Occupation." In *Mothers Under Fire: Mothering in Conflict Areas*, edited by T. Takševa and A. Sgoutas, 40–56. Bradford, Ont.: Demeter Press, 2015.

Akesson, B., A. R. Basso, and M. Denov. "The Right to Home: Domicile as a Violation of

Child and Family Rights in the Context of Political Violence." *Children and Society* 30, no. 5 (2016): 369–83.

Aron, L. *Meeting of Minds: Mutuality in Psychoanalysis.* New York: Analytic Press, 2001.

Atallah, D. G. "A Community-Based Qualitative Study of Intergenerational Resilience with Palestinian Refugee Families Facing Structural Violence and Historical Trauma." *Transcultural Psychiatry* 54, no. 3 (2017): 357–83.

Bachelard, G., and M. Jolas. *The Poetics of Space.* Boston: Beacon Press, 1994.

Baines, E., and L. R. Gauvin. "Motherhood and Social Repair after War and Displacement in Northern Uganda." *Journal of Refugee Studies* 27, no. 2 (2014): 282–300.

Barber, B. "Contrasting Portraits of War: Youths' Varied Experiences with Political Violence in Bosnia and Palestine." *International Journal of Behavioral Development* 32, no. 4 (2008): 298.

Barber, B., C. Spellings, C. McNeely, P. Page, R. Giacaman, C. Arafat, M. Daher, E. El Sarraj, M. Abu Mallouh. "Politics Drives Human Functioning, Dignity, and Quality of Life." *Social Science and Medicine*, no. 122 (2014): 90–102.

Beebe, B., J. Jaffe, S. Markese, K. Buck, H. Chen, P. Cohen, , L. Bahrick, H. Andrews, S. Feldstein. "The Origins of 12-Month Attachment: A Microanalysis of 4-Month Mother-Infant Interaction." *Attachment & Human Development* 12, no. 1–2 (2010): 3–141.

Beebe, B., and F. Lachmann. *The Origins of Attachment: Infant Research and Adult Treatment.* New York: Routledge, 2014.

Beebe, B., D. Messinger, L. E. Bahrick, A. Margolis, K. A. Buck, and H. Chen. "A Systems View of Mother-Infant Face-to-Face Communication." *Developmental Psychology* 52, no. 4 (2016): 556–71.

Belsky, J. "War, Trauma and Children's Development: Observations from a Modern Evolutionary Perspective." *International Journal of Behavioral development* 32, no. 4 (2008): 260–71.

Benjamin, J. "Beyond Doer and Done To: An Intersubjective View of Thirdness." *The Psychoanalytic Quarterly* 73, no. 1 (2004): 5–46.

———. *Shadow of the Other: Intersubjectivity and Gender in Psychoanalysis.* New York: Routledge, 1998.

Berzoff, J., M. Flanagan, and P. Hertz. *Inside Out and Outside In: Psychodynamic Clinical Theory and Psychopathology in Contemporary Multicultural Contexts*, 4th ed. New York: Rowman and Littlefield, 2018.

Bourdieu, P. "Structures, *Habitus*, Practices." In *Contemporary Sociological Theory*, edited by C. J. Calhoun, 257–70. New Jersey: Wiley, 2022.

Bowlby, J. *Attachment and Loss.* Vol. 1, *Attachment*. 1969. Reprint, London: Hogarth Press, 1982.

Bretherton, I. "The Origins of Attachment Theory: John Bowlby and Mary Ainsworth." *Developmental Psychology* 28, no. 5 (1992): 759–75.

Causadias, J. M. "A Roadmap for the Integration of Culture into Developmental Psychopathology." *Development and Psychopathology* 25, no. 4, pt. 2 (2013): 1375–98.

Cavazzoni, F., A. Fiorini, C. Sousa, and G. Veronese. "Agency Operating within Structures: A Qualitative Exploration of Agency amongst Children Living in Palestine." *Childhood* 28, no. 3 (2020): 363–79.

Chawla, L. "Childhood Place Attachments." In *Place Attachment: A Conceptual Inquiry.*

Human Behavior and Environment 12, edited by I. Altman and S. M. Low, 63–86. New York: Plenum Press, 1992.

Chodorow, N. *Femininities, Masculinities, Sexualities: Freud and Beyond.* Lexington: University Press of Kentucky, 1994.

———. "Reflections on the Reproduction of Mothering—Twenty Years Later." *Studies in Gender and Sexuality* 1, no. 4 (2000): 337–48.

Collins, P. H. *Black Feminist Thought: Knowledge, Consciousness, and the Politics of Empowerment.* 2nd ed. New York: Routledge, 2000.

———. "Shifting the Center: Race, Class, and Feminist Theorizing about Motherhood." In *Mothering: Ideology, Experience, and Agency*, edited by E. N. Glenn, G. Chang, and L. R. Forcey, 45–67. New York: Routledge, 1994.

Corbin, J. M., and A. Strauss. "Grounded Theory Research: Procedures, Canons, and Evaluative Criteria." *Qualitative Sociology* 13, no. 1 (1990): 3–21.

Coward, M. "Urbicide in Bosnia." In *Cities, War, and Terrorism: Towards an Urban Geopolitics*, edited by S. Graham, 154–171. London: Verso, 2004.

Davis, D.-A. "'The Bone Collectors' Comments for Sorrow as Artifact: Black Radical Mothering in Times of Terror." *Transforming Anthropology* 24, no. 1 (2016): 8–16.

Dickson-Gomez, J. "The Sound of Barking Dogs: Violence and Terror among Salvadoran Families in the Postwar." *Medical Anthropology Quarterly* 16, no. 4 (2002): 415–38.

Eggerman, M., and C. Panter-Brick. "Suffering, Hope, and Entrapment: Resilience and Cultural Values in Afghanistan." *Social Science and Medicine* 71, no. 1 (2010): 71–83.

Evans-Campbell, T. "Historical Trauma in American Indian/Native American Communities: A Multilevel Framework for Exploring Impacts on Individuals, Families, and Communities." *Journal of Interpersonal Violence* 23, no. 3 (2008): 316–38.

Fanon, F. *The Wretched of the Earth.* New York: Grove Press, 1965.

Felsen, I. "Adult-Onset Trauma and Intergenerational Transmission: Integrating Empirical Data and Psychoanalytic Theory." *Psychoanalysis, Self and Context* 12, no. 1 (2017): 60–77.

Field, N. P., S. Muong, and V. Sochanvimean. "Parental Styles in the Intergenerational Transmission of Trauma Stemming From the Khmer Rouge Regime in Cambodia." *American Journal of Orthopsychiatry* 83, no. 4 (2013): 483–94.

Fonagy, P., G. Gergely, E. Jurist, and M. Target. *Affect Regulation, Mentalization, and the Development of the Self.* New York: Other Books, 2002.

Fraiberg, S., E. Adelson, and V. Shapiro. "Ghosts in the Nursery: A Psychoanalytic Approach to the Problems of Impaired Infant-Mother Relationships." *Journal of American Academy of Child Psychiatry* 14, no. 3 (1975): 387–421.

Freire, P. *Pedagogy of the Oppressed.* New York: The Seabury Press, 1968.

Freud, A., and D. T. Burlingham. *War and Children.* New York: Medical War Books, 1943.

Giacaman, R. "Reframing Public Health in Wartime: From the Biomedical Model to the 'Wounds Inside.'" *Journal of Palestine Studies* 47, no. 2 (2018): 9–27.

Giacaman, R., and P. Johnson. "'Our Life is Prison': The Triple Captivity of Wives and Mothers of Palestinian Political Prisoners." *Journal of Middle East Women's Studies* 9, no. 3 (2013): 54–80.

Giacaman, R., Y. Rabaia, V. Nguyen-Gillham, R. Batniji, R. L. Punamäki, and D. Summerfield. "Mental Health, Social Distress and Political Oppression: The Case of the Occupied Palestinian Territory." *Glob Public Health* 6, no. 5 (2010): 1–13.

Gilligan, C. "'Highly Vulnerable'? Political Violence and the Social Construction of Traumatized Children." *Journal of Peace Research* 46, no. 1 (2009): 119–34.

Gopnik, A., and H. M. Wellman. "Why the Child's Theory of Mind Really Is a Theory." *Mind & Language* 7, nos. 1–2 (1992): 145–71.

Graham, S. "Introduction." In *Cities under Siege: The New Military Urbanism*, edited by S. Graham, xi–xxx. London; New York: Verso, 2004.

Gregory, D. "The Biopolitics of Baghdad: Counterinsurgency and the Counter-City." *Human Geography* 1, no. 1 (2008): 1–21.

Hammami, R. "On (Not) Suffering at the Checkpoint; Palestinian Narrative Strategies of Surviving Israel's Carceral Geography." *Borderlands* 14, no. 1 (2015): 1–17.

Hanafi, S. "Spacio-cide: Colonial Politics, Invisibility and Rezoning in Palestinian Territory." *Contemporary Arab Affairs* 2, no. 1 (2009): 106–21.

Harker, C. "On (Not) Forgetting Families: Family Spaces and Spacings in Birzeit, Palestine." *Environment and Planning* 42, no. 11 (2010): 2624–39.

Hernández, P., and A. Torres. "Dilemmas on Motherhood and Social Activism in Times of War: A Clinical Consultation." *Journal of Family Psychotherapy* 16, no. 4 (2005): 65–82.

Hochberg, G. Z. *Visual Occupations: Violence and Visibility in a Conflict Zone*. Durham, N.C.: Duke University Press, 2015.

Hsieh, H. F., and S. E. Shannon. "Three Approaches to Qualitative Content Analysis." *Qualitative Health Research* 15, no. 9 (2005): 1277–88.

International Committee of the Red Cross (ICRC). "Children and Detention." 2014. https://www.icrc.org/eng/assets/files/publications/icrc-002-4201.pdf.

Jack, G. "Place Matters: The Significance of Place Attachments for Children's Well-Being." *British Journal of Social Work* 40, no. 3 (2008): 755–71.

Jeffrey, C. "Geographies of Children and Youth I: Eroding Maps of Life." *Progress in Human Geography* 34, no. 4 (2010): 496–505.

Lefebvre, H. *The Production of Space*. Oxford, UK: Blackwell, 1991.

Marshall, D. J. "Existence as Resistance: Children and Politics of Play in Palestine." In *Geographies of Children and Young People: Politics, Citizenship, and Rights*, edited by K. P. Kallio, S. Mills, and T. Skelton, 245–262. Singapore: Springer, 2016.

———. "'We Have a Place to Play, but Someone Else Controls It': Girls' Mobility and Access to Space in a Palestinian Refugee Camp." *Global Studies of Childhood* 5, no. 2 (2015): 191–205.

Marshall, D. J., and C. Sousa. "Decolonizing Trauma: Liberation Psychology, Postcolonial Theory, and Childhood Trauma in Palestine." In *Conflict, Violence, and Peace*, edited by C. Harker and K. Horschelmann, 287–306. Singapore: Springer, 2016.

Martín-Baró, I. *Writings for a Liberation Psychology*. Edited by A. Aron and S. Corne. Cambridge, Mass.: Harvard University Press, 1994.

McNeely, C., B. Barber, C. Spellings, R. Belli, R. Giacaman, C. Arafat, M. Daher, E. El Sarraj, and M. Abu Mallouh. "Political Imprisonment and Adult Functioning: A Life

Event History Analysis of Palestinians." *Journal of Traumatic Stress* 28, no. 3 (2015): 223–31.

Mitchell, S., and M. J. Black. *Freud and Beyond.* New York: Basic Books, 1995.

Morrison, H. *The Global History of Childhood Reader.* London and New York: Routledge, 2013.

Norberg-Schulz, C. *The Concept of Dwelling: On the Way to Figurative Architecture.* New York: Rizzoli, 1985.

Otman, A. "Handcuffed Protectors? Palestinian Fatherhood-Protection Unlocking Its Chains." *International Journal of Applied Psychoanalytic Studies* 17, no. 2 (2020): 146–64.

Pavlish, C. "Action Responses of Congolese Refugee Women." *Journal of Nursing Scholarship* 37, no. 1 (2005): 10–17.

Peteet, J. *Space and Mobility in Palestine.* Bloomington: Indiana University Press, 2017.

Piaget, J. "Part I: Cognitive Development in Children: Piaget Development and Learning." *Journal of Research in Science Teaching* 2, no. 3 (1964): 176–86.

Punamäki, R. L., and R. Suleiman. "Predictors and Effectiveness of Coping with Political Violence among Palestinian Children." *British Journal of Social Psychology* 29, no. 1 (1990): 67–77.

Robertson, C. L., and L. Duckett. "Mothering during War and Postwar in Bosnia." *Journal of Family Nursing* 13, no. 4 (2007): 461–83.

Roy, S. *Gaza Strip: The Political Economy of De-Development.* 3rd ed. Washington, D.C.: The Institute for Palestine Studies, 2016.

Ruddick, S. *Maternal Thinking: Toward a Politics of Peace.* Boston: Beacon Press, 1995.

Salamanca, O. J., M. Qato, K. Rabie, and S. Samour. "Past Is Present: Settler Colonialism in Palestine." *Settler Colonial Studies* 2, no. 1 (2012): 1–8.

Saldaña, J. *The Coding Manual for Qualitative Researchers.* Thousand Oaks, Calif.: Sage, 2016.

Scheper-Hughes, N. *Death without Weeping: The Violence of Everyday Life in Brazil.* Berkeley: University of California Press, 1993.

Shalhoub-Kevorkian, N. *Incarcerated Childhood and the Politics of Unchilding.* Cambridge, UK: Cambridge University Press, 2019.

———. "Infiltrated Intimacies: The Case of Palestinian Returnees." *Feminist Studies* 42, no. 1 (2016): 166–93.

———. "Liberating Voices: The Political Implications of Palestinian Mothers Narrating Their Loss." *Women's Studies International Forum* 26, no. 5 (2003): 391–407.

Siegel, D. *Brainstorm: The Power and Purpose of the Teenage Brain.* New York: Penguin Books, 2015.

Silber, L. M. "Ghostbusting Transgenerational Processes." *Psychoanalytic Dialogues* 22, no. 1 (2012): 106–22.

Simpson, M. A. "Bitter Waters: Effects on Children of the Stresses of Unrest and Oppression." In *International Handbook of Traumatic Stress Syndromes,* edited by J. P. Wilson and B. Raphael, 601–24. New York: Plenum Press, 1993.

Skelton, T. "Children's Geographies/Geographies of Children: Play, Work, Mobilities, and Migration." *Geography Compass* 3, no. 4 (2009): 1430–48.

Slade, A. "Attachment Theory and Research: Implications for the Theory and Practice of Individual Psychotherapy with Adults." In *The Handbook of Attachment: Theory, Research, and Clinical Applications*, edited by J. Cassidy and P. R. Shaver, 575–94. 3rd ed. New York: Guilford Press, 2016.

Slade, A., J. Grienenberger, E. Bernbach, D. Levy, and A. Locker. "Maternal Reflective Functioning, Attachment, and the Transmission Gap: A Preliminary Study." *Attachment and Human Development* 7, no. 3 (2005): 283–98.

Slochower, J. "Going Too Far: Relational Heroines and Relational Excess." In *De-idealizing Relational Theory*, edited by L. Aron, C. Grand, and J. Slochower, 8–34. New York: Routledge, 2018.

Smidt, S. *The Developing Child in the 21st Century: A Global Perspective on Child Development*: London: Routledge, 2013.

Smith, C. A. "Facing the Dragon: Black Mothering, Sequelae, and Gendered Necropolitics in the Americas." *Transforming Anthropology* 24, no. 1 (2016): 31–48.

Sousa, C., S. Kemp, and M. El-Zuhairi. "Dwelling within Political Violence: Palestinian Women's Narratives of Home, Mental Health, and Resilience." *Health and Place* 30 (2014): 205–14.

———. "Place as a Social Determinant of Health: Narratives of Trauma and Homeland among Palestinian Women." *The British Journal of Social Work* 49, no. 4 (2019): 963–82.

Sousa, C., M. El-Zuhairi, and M. Siddiqi. "'The Utmost Strength I Can Bear': Strategies and Psychological Costs of Mothering within Political Violence." *Feminism and Psychology* 30, no. 2 (2020): 227–47.

Stern, D. B. *Partners in Thought: Working With Unformulated Experience, Dissociation, and Enactment*. New York: Routledge, 2010.

Sugiman, P. "'A Million Hearts from Here': Japanese Canadian Mothers and Daughters and the Lessons of War." *Journal of American Ethnic History* 26, no. 4 (2007): 50–68.

Takševa, T., and A. Sgoutas. *Mothers under Fire: Mothering in Conflict Areas*. Bradford, Ont.: Demeter Press, 2015.

Tamimi, A. *Profile: Palestinian Youth Activist Ahed Tamimi*. Uploaded by FOSNA Friends of Sabeel—North America. February 24, 2017, https://www.youtube.com/watch?v=cMWuk_mi5kw&t=19s.

Tronick, E., and M. Beeghly. "Infants' Meaning-Making and the Development of Mental Health Problems." *The American Psychologist* 66, no. 2 (2011): 107–19. https://doi.org/10.1037/a0021631.

Tuan, Y.-F. *Space and Place: the Perspective of Experience*. Minneapolis: University of Minnesota Press, 1977.

United Nations Children's Fund [UNICEF]. "Machel Study 10-Year Strategic Review: Children and Conflict in a Changing World." New York: UN Children's Fund, April 2009. https://childrenandarmedconflict.un.org/publications/MachelStudy-10YearStrategicReview_en.pdf.

United Nations General Assembly Security Council. "Children and Armed Conflict: Report of the Secretary-General." Geneva: United Nations, 2015.

United Nations Office for the Coordination of Humanitarian Affairs UN OCHA. "The Humanitarian Impact on Palestinians of Israeli Settlements and Other Infrastructure

in the West Bank." July 2007. https://www.ochaopt.org/sites/default/files/ocharpt
_update30july2007.pdf.

United Nations Research Institute for Social Development (UNRISD). "The Impacts of
Conflict on Women." In *Gender Equality: Striving for Justice in an Unequal World*,
207–31. Geneva: UNRISD, 2005.

Veronese, G., and M. Castiglioni. "'When the Doors of Hell Close': Dimensions of Well-
Being and Positive Adjustment in a Group of Palestinian Children Living amidst Military and Political Violence." *Childhood* 22, no. 1 (2015): 6–22.

Violich, F. *The Bridge to Dalmatia: A Search for the Meaning of Place*. Baltimore: Johns
Hopkins University Press, 1998.

Walters, K. L., S. A. Mohammed, T. Evans-Campbell, R. E. Beltrán, D. H. Chae, and B.
Duran. "Bodies Don't Just Tell Stories, They Tell Histories: Embodiment of Historical
Trauma among American Indians and Alaska Natives." *Du Bois Review: Social Science
Research on Race* 8, no. 1 (2011): 179–89.

Weizman, E. *Hollow Land: Israel's Architecture of Occupation*. New York: Verso, 2007.

Winnicott, D. W. *The Child, the Family, and the Outside World*. Cambridge, Mass.: Per-
seus Publishing, 1992.

Wolfe, P. "Settler Colonialism and the Elimination of the Native." *Journal of Genocide Research* 8, no. 4 (2006): 387–409.

Young, I. M. "House and Home: Feminist Variations on a Theme." In *On Female Body
Experience: "Throwing Like a Girl" and Other Essays*, edited by I. M. Young, 123–45.
New York: Oxford University Press, 2005.

Closing
"I Wish You ... Happy"

NATALIA MOLEBATSI

In late 2014 I was asked by the United Nations SRC Society of Writers to submit a poem to a book it was publishing honoring the "International Day of Happiness." Until then I had no idea such a day existed, especially with all the sadness and suffering around the world. Around the same time the state of Israel was launching heavy attacks on the people of Gaza yet again. So I wrote this poem with the children of Gaza heavy in my heart. The poem is dedicated to the children of Gaza specifically—and to the people of Palestine as a whole. It is to remind the world that Palestinian people deserve to be alive and happy.

Since 1948, we have been keeping the hope and the activism alive, to create more awareness about the occupation of Palestinian land. As South Africans, we also relate to the struggles of the people of Palestine, because Apartheid South Africa was also officially put in place in 1948. Most of the land was seized by the minority white population. Black people were forcefully removed from their homes and massacred or jailed for demanding equality. South Africa finally found a solution, albeit flawed, so we believe that the people of Palestine will also finally be afforded their well-deserved freedom. We continue to stand with the people of Palestine. It is my hope that the international community will put sanctions upon the state of Israel, the same way that they put sanctions against the South African government. It is our hope that the sanctions will also force the state of Israel to release political prisoners. In the words of Nelson Mandela, "We know too well that our freedom is incomplete without the freedom of the Palestinians."

i wish you . . . happy

i wish you whole
as words water a flower
beneath the yellow rays of yearning
beyond the reach of growling pain
i wish you inviolable dreams
flourishing under the
silent and attentive gaze of the moon
i wish you a sky,
open enough and ready
for thoughts of light
simple earthly delights
pouring in and out of this moment
i wish you alive
child in Jenin, child of Gaza
playing a game of cards
in the blossoming
pathway of unfolded wings
here, a wish for you,
of brave dreamlings
touching your eyes at dawn
picking shells along the beach with your brother
on the roof of your home, feeding doves
marvelling at the beat of your sister's heart
laughing at your grandmother's funny stories
happy . . .
harvesting olives and memories
© natalia molebatsi

CONTRIBUTORS

Yousef M. Aljamal holds a PhD in Middle Eastern studies from the Middle East Institute, Sakarya University, Türkiye. Aljamal obtained his MA in international relations from the University of Malaya, Malaysia, where he is now a nonresident scholar at the Hashim Sani Centre for Palestine Studies. He has published a number of journal articles on Palestine. He has coauthored/translated three books on Palestinian prisoners in Israeli jails, *The Prisoners' Diaries: Palestinian Voices from the Israeli Gulag*, *Dreaming of Freedom: Palestinian Child Prisoners Speak*, and *A Shared Struggle: Stories of Palestinian and Irish Hunger Strikers*.

Mohammed Alruzzi is a lecturer in childhood studies at the University of Bristol. He completed his PhD in social anthropology at the University of Fribourg and his master's in childhood studies at the University of Edinburgh. Alruzzi worked as a postdoctoral research associate at the University of Bath and has worked as a consultant with international organizations such as World Vision, Terre des Hommes, and UNICEF. His work experience involves childhood and international development issues in policy and practice, with a particular focus on child incarceration and children's work.

Jana Jihad Ayad is an activist and an amateur journalist. Jana was known for being the youngest Palestinian journalist after she started filming with her mother's iPhone to document the human rights violations in Nabi Saleh at the age of six years old. Jana was frustrated by the lack of documentation of the violations of human rights in Nabi Saleh and took matters into her own hands. Jana's father is from the village of Silwan and her mom is from Nabi Saleh. She hopes to go to university in the United States.

Amneh Badran is an assistant dean at AQB College, AlQuds University. She has a PhD in political science and is a graduate of Exeter University in the UK. Her publications include *Zionist Israel and Apartheid South Africa: Civil Society and Peace Building in Ethnic-National States*. Her chapters in edited books include "The Many

Faces of Protest: A Comparative Analysis of Protest Groups in Israel and South Africa," in *Israel and South Africa: The Many Faces of Apartheid*, and "The Future of Jerusalem as Envisioned by Israeli (Jewish) Protest Groups," in *Locating Urban Conflicts: Ethnicity, Nationalism, and the Everyday*. Her research interests include: the Palestinian-Israeli conflict, social movements and political change, and comparative political systems.

Amahl Bishara is associate professor in the Anthropology Department at Tufts University. She is the author of *Crossing a Line: Laws, Violence, & Roadblocks to Palestinian Political Expression*, about different conditions of expression for Palestinian citizens of Israel and Palestinians in the West Bank. She also writes about popular refugee politics in the West Bank. Her first book, *Back Stories: U.S. News and Palestinian Politics*, is an ethnography of the production of U.S. news during the second Palestinian intifada.

Sara Bressi is an associate professor at Bryn Mawr College's Graduate School of Social Work and Social Research. She is a licensed social worker and a psychoanalyst, practicing with children and adults. Her scholarship addresses the needs of persons with behavioral health challenges across clinical landscapes. Her research in the areas of mental health and health services with adults with serious mental illnesses has been funded by the National Institute of Mental Health. Her current scholarship emphasizes the translation of psychoanalytic theory to inpatients, community mental health, and substance use treatment settings.

Janette Habashi is a full professor in the Department of Human Relations at the University of Oklahoma. Her research examines children's sociopolitical development, the formation of children's agency, and how both formal and informal educational systems affect their personal and community discourse. One derivative of her scholarly research includes the founding of a nonprofit, Child's Cup Full, in 2009. The mission is to create sustainable economic opportunities for refugee and low-income communities in the West Bank by training and employing women.

Valentina Marconi is a postdoctoral researcher in sociology at the University of Trento in Italy. She completed her PhD in global studies at the University of Urbino, where she focused on border violence within the European migration regime, with the focus on the lived experiences of irregular migrants. She holds a master's degree in Arab world studies from the University of Durham in the UK. Her research interests include irregular migrations, borders, political violence, and remittances.

Natalia Molebatsi is a Pan-African feminist and queer poet, writer, and cultural worker from South Africa. She is the editor of two poetry anthologies, *We Are: A Poetry Anthology* and *Wild Imperfections: An Anthology of Womanist Poems*. She is the author of two poetry collections, *Sardo Dance* and *Elephant Woman Song*. Her collaborative music and poetry albums include *Natalia Molebatsi and the Soul Making* and *Come as You Are: Poems for Four Strings*. Her scholarly writing is included in, among other journals, *Rhodes Journalism Review*, *Agenda*, *Muziki*, the *National Po-*

litical Science Review, and *Third World Thematics*. Natalia is a PhD candidate in performance studies at Northwestern University, Illinois, U.S.A.

Heidi Morrison is associate professor of history at the University of Wisconsin in La Crosse. She specializes in the modern Middle East, the global history of childhood, and oral history. Morrison is the author of *Childhood and Colonial Modernity in Egypt*, the editor of *The Global History of Childhood Reader*, and co–general editor of the six-volume *A Cultural History of Youth*. Her forthcoming books are *Inner Wounds: Listening to How Young Palestinians Remember, Narrate, and Experience the Effects of War* and *What is the History of Childhood?*. Between 2020 and 2022 she was a senior research fellow at the Center of Excellence in the History of Experiences (HEX) at Tampere University, Finland. She holds degrees from the University of California at Santa Barbara, Harvard University, and the University of California at Berkeley.

Shahrazad Odeh is a human rights lawyer and researcher. She is involved with various women's rights organizations and research initiatives focusing on the eradication of gun violence among Palestinian citizens of Israel. She is currently a PhD student at Queen Mary University of London.

Abeer Otman is a postdoctoral fellow at the Centre for Researching and Embedding Human Rights (CREHR), Department of Psychosocial Studies, Birkbeck, University of London, and a postdoctoral fellow at the Faculty of Law at the Hebrew University of Jerusalem. Abeer has a doctorate in social work from the Hebrew University of Jerusalem. Her doctoral research focused on fathers and fatherhood in a settler-colonial context: the case of Occupied East Jerusalem (OEJ). Her research interests include fatherhood, father-child connectivities, psychosocial trauma, secrecy and surveillance, social media, livability, hope, and futurity.

Rami Salameh is an assistant professor at the Department of Philosophy and Cultural Studies at Birzeit University. He is currently the department's chairperson and the director of the MA Program in Contemporary Arab Studies. He completed his PhD in anthropology and sociology from the Geneva Graduate Institute in 2018. His research interests cover issues related to bodily lived experiences, perceptions, pain, death, colonialism, and settler colonialism.

Nitin Sawhney is a professor of practice in the Department of Computer Science at Aalto University and leads the CRAI-CIS (CRitical AI and Crisis Interrogatives) research group. Working at the intersection of human computer interaction (HCI), responsible AI, and participatory design research, he examines the critical role of technology, civic agency, and societal interaction. He is leading several transdisciplinary research projects, supported by the Research Council of Finland, examining crisis narratives and sensemaking, responsible AI practices in the public sector, and the design of trustworthy and inclusive digital public services for migrants. He has previously conducted participatory media programs and psychosocial research with marginalized youth, and codirected two feature-length documentary films in Gaza and

Guatemala. His work has been published in several academic journals and he is an associate editor for the *International Journal of Child Computer Interaction*.

Nadera Shalhoub-Kevorkian, a Palestinian feminist, is the Lawrence D. Biele Chair in Law at the Faculty of Law-Institute of Criminology and the School of Social Work and Public Welfare at the Hebrew University of Jerusalem, and the Global Chair in Law at Queen Mary University of London. She is the author of various books, among them: *Militarization and Violence Against Women in Conflict Zones in the Middle East: The Palestinian Case Study*; *Security Theology, Surveillance, and the Politics of Fear*; and *Incarcerated Childhood and the Politics of Unchilding*. She has also coedited *Engaged Students in Conflict Zones: Community-Engaged Courses in Israel as a Vehicle for Change*; *When Politics are Sacralized: Comparative Perspectives on Religious Claims and Nationalism*, and *The Cunning of Gender Violence*.

Cindy Sousa, PhD, MSW, MPH, is an associate professor of social work at Bryn Mawr College. In her work, Cindy examines conditions underlying health, informed by feminist, indigenous, and critical race theories that prioritize the social-environmental-political contexts of well-being. Cindy's scholarship highlights the health implications of violations to the lived environment; the impacts of violence and oppression on parenting (particularly mothering); the importance of culture, place, and social/organizational supports within adversity; and professional responsibility in the face of collective suffering. Current projects focus on the challenges, strengths, and strategies of families within war, the refugee experience, and climate disasters.

Ahed Tamimi from Nabi Saleh was born in 2001. Ahed became an icon in Palestine and abroad after she was arrested on December 19, 2017, and she was detained until July 30, 2018. Ahed was a minor when she was arrested. She was arrested by the Israeli army on the charge of having slapped an Israeli soldier after the army shot her cousin in the face in front of her, and then invaded their house. Ahed is studying law at the University of Birzeit and hopes to go to Qatar to continue her education.

Lama Yahya is an MA student in Israeli studies at Birzeit University. She is the director of the Palestinian Association of Cultural Exchange (PACE), which seeks to protect and promote Palestinian cultural heritage through education, preservation work, research, and exchange programs.

CHILDREN YOUTH + WAR

The Vietnam War in American Childhood, by Joel P. Rhodes

Breaking the War Habit: The Debate over Militarism in American Education,
by Seth Kershner, Scott Harding, and Charles Howlett

Lived Resistance against the War on Palestinian Children,
edited by Heidi Morrison

www.ingramcontent.com/pod-product-compliance
Lightning Source LLC
Chambersburg PA
CBHW022301280326
41932CB00010B/945